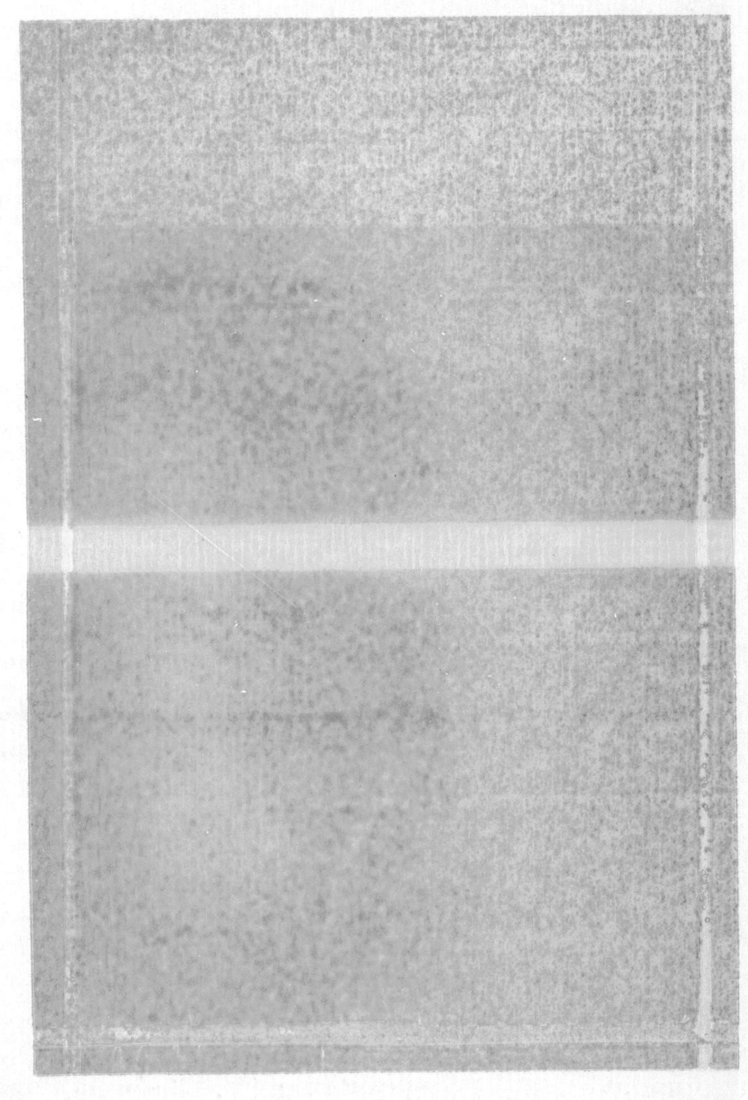

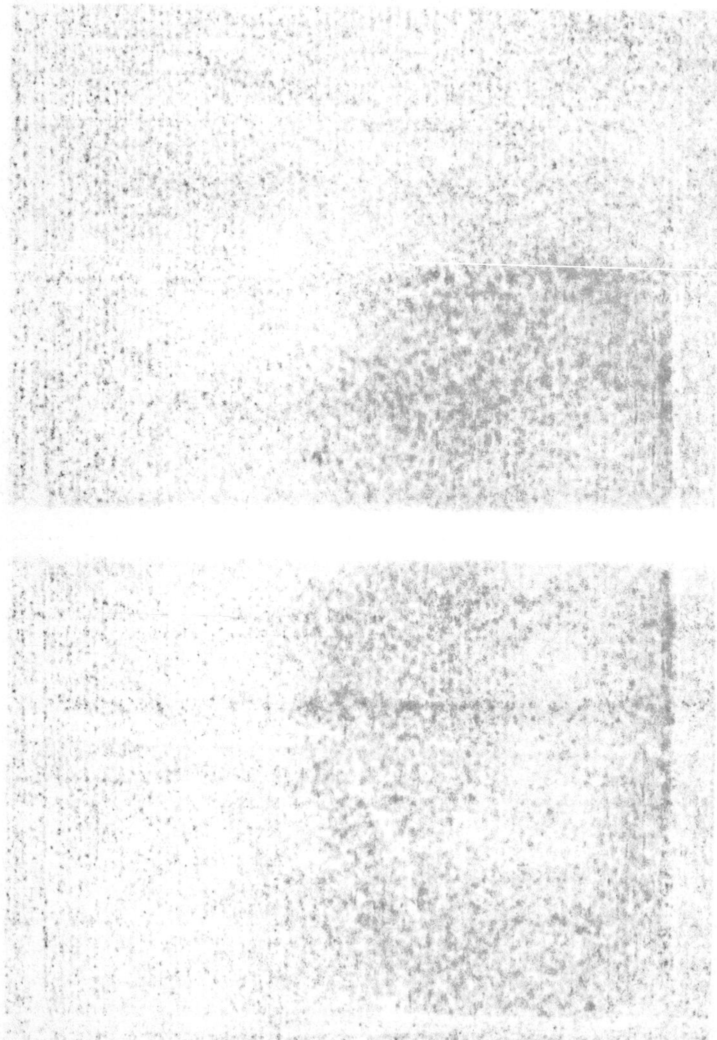

# ENGLISH RECUSANT LITERATURE
1558—1640

*Selected and Edited by*
D. M. ROGERS

Volume 191

## JOHN COPINGER
*The Theatre of Catholique and Protestant Religion*
*1620*

# JOHN COPINGER

## *The Theatre of Catholique and Protestant Religion*

*1620*

The Scolar Press
1974

ISBN 0 85967 167 4

*Published and printed in Great Britain by*
*The Scolar Press Limited, 59-61 East Parade,*
*Ilkley, Yorkshire and*
*39 Great Russell Street,*
*London WC1*

*NOTE*

Reproduced (original size) from a copy in the library of Ushaw College, by permission of the President.

*References:* Allison and Rogers 256; STC 5558/4284.

# THE THEATRE OF CATHOLIQVE AND PROTESTANT RELIGION, DIVIDED into Twelue Bookes.

Wherein

The zealous Catholike may plainelie ſee, the manifeſt truth, perſpicuitie, euident foundations and demonſtrations of the Catholique Religion; Together with the motiues and cauſes, why he ſhould perſeuer therin.

*The Proteſtant alſo may eaſilie ſee, the falſitie and abſurditie, of his irreligious, and negatiue Religion; Together with many ſtrong and conuincing reaſons, why he is bound to embrace the Catholique faith, and to returne againe to the true Church from whence he departed.*

WRITTEN

By I. C. Student in diuinitie,

*With permiſſion*, Anno 1620.

M*Agni periculi res est, &c.* It is a thinge of great danger, if after the oracles of the Prophets, after the testimonies of the Apostles, after the woundes of the Martyrs, thou presume to discusse our ould faith, as if it were new; if after such expert guides, thou neuertheles wilt remaine in error: if after the combatts of such as did strugle vnto death for the defence thereof, thou wilt yet oppugne it with idle disputation: let vs therfore reuernēce our faith, in the glory of the Saintes. S. *Ambrosius in sermone de SS. Nazario & Celso.*

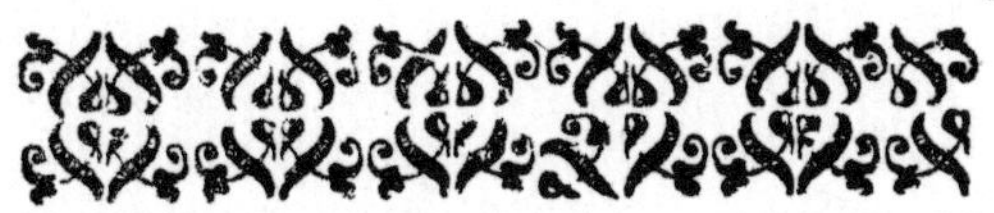

# TO THE BLESSED *and vnspotted Virgin Marie, Mother of God, and Queene of heauen, by whom saluation and redemption, came to the worlde.*

1. BOOKES of greatest estimation and noblest subiect (most gratious Virgin) ought to be dedicated and offred to the noblest and eminentste personages, and that for two causes; th'one to be protected and patronized by them against malignant and malitious people, to whome the obiect or matter might be offensiue: the other to gratifie them for the benefites receaued of thẽ. the obiecte of this booke which is the theater and true representation both of the Catholique, and protestant religion, being so eminent that it excelleth and exceedeth all obiects whatsoeuer; ought to be dedicated and consecrated vnto thee most sacred Virgin, being the worthiest creature amongest all meere Creatures that euer were.

2. The

*Contraria se posita magis illucescsit.*

2. The opposition of two extremities can neuer be better declared or knowen, thẽ to oppose the one to the other, as things positiue, and thinges priuatiue, light and darknesse, thinges contrarie, as heate and cold, thinges contradictory, or thinges affirmatiue and negatiue, as a man, and noe man: nothinge is soe repugnant or hurtfull to the Catholique religion, as heresie, and especially that of the sectaires of our vnfortunate daies: nothinge soe contrary to Christe as Antechriste: nothinge soe offensiue to the Catholique Church, as the malignant Congregation of Caluinistes & Anabaptistes. So as the trueth of the one, cãnot be made more apparant, more euident, and more cleere, then by the falshoode of the other: nor the goodnesse of the one, be better made knowẽ, then by the mischeefe & euill of the other.

3. Vouchsafe therfore (ô gratious virgin and mother of the Sauiour of the worlde) that the trueth and goodnesse of the one, beinge made knowen, and the falshoode and wickednesse of the other, being detected: with thy most precious intercession to thy Sonne Iesus, to lighten and illuminate the hartes & vnderstãdings of such as are ouerwhelmed, and ingulfed in the dangerous abisme of darcknesse, and are gone astraye in the intricat labernith of heresies. Deliuer thẽ (ô blessed mediatrixe) that doe walke awry in the darcknes and shadowe of death. Pro-

tecte

tecte and defend the Catholique Church (for the saftie of which, Christe Iesus tooke flesh of thee, and for the establishing whereof, he suffered his bitter passion, yealded himselfe to death, and triumphed ouer the powers of darcknesse) from the malice and dangerous purposes, of all such as bend all their plotts and pollices to destroy her.

4. By whom should the religion of virgins, vowes, and votaries be protected and vpholden, but by her that made the first solemne vowe and profession thereof? To whō should the religion of Christ be dedicated, but to the mother of Christ? Or the law of grace be addressed, but vnto her that is ful of grace? What better aduocate can the Church haue, then shee who is placed betwixt the sunne and the moone, as S. Bernard saieth, which is mary betwixt Christ & his Church? What better defense can there be against heretiques, then shee (as S. Bonauenture saith) that destroyeth all heresies? and according to S. Bernard, *omnis hæresum interemptrix*, that killeth all heresies. Therfore, ô blessed Virgin, *Dignare me laudare te Virgo &c.* Vouchsafe me to praise thee, ô sacred virgin: fortifie me against thine enemies, and the enemies of the Church of Iesus Christ; which being his only comō wealth, kingdom, patrimony, vineyarde and mystical body, euery member thereof, ought to defend, yea is more bound thervnto, then to

to the defense of any earthly comon wealth.

5. As for thyne incpmparable, and vnspeakeable merittes and benefites towardes me, and towards the whole world, all true Christian hartes doe acknowledge them; & with Aristotle I confesse, *Qui beneficium accipit, libertatē perdidit*, He that receueth a benefit loseth his liberty & becometh a slaue to his benefactors. How then should not I & the whole world, confesse our selues to be obliged vnto thee for soe generall and soe worthy a benefit as we haue receaued at thy handes, Iesus Christ taking that flesh of thee, in which he would dye for our offēces? Therfor (ô blessed virgin) I offer my self with this my labour as a poore slaue vnto thee, I prostrate my selfe like a poore wretched & sinfull creature before thee, confounded and oppressed with many imperfections and defects, voide of merits, destitut of grace, ouercharged with the dreadfull assaultes & machinations of powerfull enemies, they to stronge to offend, and I to weake (without thy helpe) to defend my selfe against them. We therfore, *Sub tuum præsidium confugimus sancta Dei genitrix, &c.* flie vnder thy sauegard, ô mother of God, for none that euer relyed vpon thee, was frustrated of his expectation, none was euer deceaued of his hope, none was euer cōfounded or discomforted, who hath at any time fled to thy intercession, as holy Church in all ages by experience hath

*De cōgruo non de cōdigno.*

hath proued, and all holy sainctes, that euer were, haue solemnly auouched.

6. Thou therfore, ô only [a] hope of sinners. Thou, ô [b] ioy, saluation, and peace of the worlde. Thou, ô [c] ocean & gulfe of grace. Thou ô [d] liuing arke of the liuing God. Thou, [e] the mother of all liuing, and the cause of life, who broughtest forth life vnto the world. Thou [f] the pretious marguerit of the worlde, the inextinguible light thereof, the crowne of virginitie, the scepter of the Catholique faith, and the indissoluble temple containing him, who can be no where contained. Thou, ô [g] East gate, euer shut, and euer shining, bringing forth the holy of holies. Thou ô [h] mountaine which far surpassest in height, all height of creatures. Thou, [i] in heauen the queene of Sainctes, in earth the queene of Kingdomes. Finallie thou art she, then which [k] nothing was euer seene more noble or more excellent, thou art she who only surpassest heauen and earth: what can be more holie then thou? Not Prophets, not Apostles, not Martyrs, not Patriarkes, not Angels, not Dominations, not Seraphins, not Cherubins, nor any thing amongst the visible or inuisible creatures, can be found more excellent then thou, ô Marie, for thou art his mother, who was begotten of his father before all beginninges. Will we know therfore how far thou excellest all celestiall powers?

a *Aug. ser. 2. de Annunc.*
b *S. Ephrē de laud. B. Mariæ.*
c *Damasc. orat. 2. de Assump.*
d *Damasc. orat 2. dormit. Virg.*
e *Epiph. l. 3. Hier. 78*
f *Cyril. Alex. hom. 10.*
g *Ierem. adu. Iouin.*
h *S. Greg. in 1. Reg.*
i *Rup. lib. 3. in cant.*
k *S. Chry. ser. de Natiuit.*

powers? These with feare and trembling stand hiding their face, but thou doost offer vp mankind vnto him whome thou hast begotten, by whom we obtaine the pardon of our offences.

I therfore thy humble and most vnworthy supplіant, doe here present and offer vnto thy protection, this worke and labor (though far vnworthy of thy patronage) beseeching thee, that through thy fauorable assistance (O most glorious virgin) it may serue for the reclayming of deceaued soules into the sheepfould of Iesus Christ; for the confusion of Heretiques, and consolation of Catholiques; for the detection of falsitie, and aduancement of verity; and lastlie, for the greater honor and glory, both of thee, and of thy B. Sonne, our Lord and Sauiour Iesus, to whom with the Father, & the Holy Ghost, be honor and glory, world without end, Amen.

THE

# THE PREFACE TO THE READER.

1. *A Certaine Protestant (gentle Reader) quaffinge, and caurrousſinge in a place, cried out againſt the Pope, which is a custome nowe a dayes, aſwell with the meanſeſt, as with the greateſt, & cheefest perſonages, hauing their ministers at their elbowe when they are at meate, to ſclander the Pope, Prieſtes and Catholikes. I woulde they had read and obſerued the verſe of S. Auguſtine.*

*Quiſquis amat dictis abſentum rodere vitam,*
*Hanc menſam vetitam nouerit eſſe ſibi.*

Who ſoe ſpeakes ill of thoſe that abſent be,
Forbidden is this tables companie.

*But theſe men when they are in their greateſt diſſolution, then they raile againſt religion, which should bridle, and reſtraine them from their riotous, and wanton exceſſe. This partie being reproued by a certaine Catholike gentleman, that was at the boorde, began preſently to defend his liberty, and licentiouſnes by holy ſcripture, and by the wordes of our Sauiour miſtaken & ill applied, anſwered, that whatſoeuer entereth into the belly, doth no harme to the ſoule, but that which cometh from the harte. This is noe newe practiſe in the*

*the malignant Church, as Eusebius saith of the Heretike Cerinthus, who because he was giuen to the bellye and beastly pleasures, framed holy scripture accordinge to his sensualitie, as this protestant alleadged Scripture against fastinge, and began to prouoke the Gentleman to dispute with him; who answered him, that it was not his part to reason or iudge of holy Scripture, being soe mysticall, and so far exceedinge his capacity, especially in such disordered places amoungest the cuppes; the fruite whereof would rather tende to confusiõ, then to edificatiõ or deuotiõ. The Protestante replyed, that if any man could answeare to his demaundes or questions at the full, and satisfie him truly and effectually, he would become Catholike: the Gentleman said he would doe his endeuour to propounde such demaundes to others; and soe he went vnto the cheefest protestants of that place, who haue sett downe these challenges & deliuered thẽ vnto the said gent. who deliuered them vnto me; beinge in one house with him.*

*2 These propositions were nothinge else, but the old heresies of auncient hereticks, and were long since condemned, and anathematized by the auctority of the Catholike Churche in all ages, wherein those heretikes did springe vp. As by S. Peter against Simon Magus. By Liberius the Pope, S. Athanasius and S. Hillary, against Arrius. By S. Damasus, S. Gregory Nazianzen & S. Basil against Macedonius. By S. Celestinus Pope and S. Cyrill of Alexandria, against Nestorius. By S. Leo against Eutiches. By Irenus against*

*gainst Valentine. By Tertulian against Marcion. By Origine against Celsus. By S. Cyprian against Nouatus. By S. Hierom against Heluidius; Iouinian, Vigilantius, Luciferans. By S. Augustine against Donatists & Pelagians. By Agath against Montolistes. By Tarasius against Imadge breakers. By Lanfrancus, Guitmundus and Algerius, against Beringarius. By Petrus Cluniacensis against Henricians and Petrobrusians, and against Adelhard. By S. Bernard against Thomas Waldensis, and Witcleefe. By the Bushoppe of Rochester, as well by his bookes as by his blood, against Luther and Zuinglius. By Kinge Henry the 8. himselfe, against the said Luther, whose booke I haue. Finally by soe many generall Councells of the world in all ages, and by the most famous & generall Councell of Trente, which sate vpon this matter the space of 16. yeares.*

3. *Touching the aforesaid propositions, truly I was loath (though earneastly entreated by the Gentleman) to trouble my selfe to answere them. and that for many causes. First for that Protestantes are voide of all humility, whose religion is nothing elce thē a peruerse and self-wild denial of religiō, neuer learning the trueth simply but oppugning it wilfully. The second, because whatsoeuer Protestants write, they doe it not nether for gods sake, or for their owne edification, but for the destruction and confusion of others, as Luther himselfe their Author did confesse disputinge with Eckius, who said, that it was not for godes sake, he tooke that matter in hande: and therfore none*

*more*

more maleparte or saWcie then they be, for they denie all groundes of disputation; all traditions of the Apostles, Doctors, Councells, and testimonie of holy Martyres. For as When S. Augustine, and the holy Doctors of the Church, reasoned With the Donatists, Arrians, Maniches, and others, and vrged them With the aucthoritie of godes Church, With the iudgmente of the sea Apostolique, With the succession of Bishoppes in the same, With the Councells, and finallie With the name Catholike, those heretikes quite reiected all those groundes and meanes of tryall: euen so Luther the captaine and ringleader of these late heretiques said. I set not by a thousande Augustines, and a thousand Cyprians alleadged against me alone: calling S. Augustine, S. Hierom and S. Gregorie, the Iustices af the Papisticall kingdome. Thus also did that proud Beza, charge Origines With blasphemie, adding that neither S. Chrysostome, nor any of the Greeke fathers, did euer declare the trueth simply: & charged Saint Hierom With shamles errors, as inuocation of Saincts, and the practise of chastitie or virginitie in the Church. Musculus also said, that S. Hierom did deserue rather hell then heauen. Brentius did charge the first Councell of Nice With foule errors. Caluine called the fathers thereof Lunatick and franticke people. Musculus saith, they Were instigated and led by the diuill, and that all Councells Were pernitiouslie fallen into errors. Vrbanus Regius said, that in the best tymes of the Church, Sathan ouerruled all Bushoppes. Peter Mar-

Osuis. lib. 2. de here. Sur. hist. Anne. 1519. Beza in pref. noui testam. An 1565. Tom 2. Lib. 3. Regem Angliæ to. 5 ad Galat. c. 3. Beza act. c. 10. in pref. noui test. Mus. in locis cõmunib. c. 10. Bren. in Apolo. conf. witenb. c. de cõcil. Calu. de vera eccl. reformat. Musc. de comm. loc. c. de ministrat. inter. prep. locor. commu. Martyr de votis. Illir. pref.

*Martyr called the aunciente Fathers, pratlers, but no diuines. Illiricus reiected the ſaid Fathers. Peter Martyr alſo ſaid, that as longe as men relie vpon the Fathers, they muſt be deluded with errors. Doctour Humfrie at Oxford ſaid, that Iuell gaue a great ſcope vnto the Papiſts, and did himſelfe greate wronge, in alleadginge the Fathers for himſelfe: for what haue we to doe with fleash & and bloud? The ſame alſo Caluine and Peter Martyr wrote. Whitakers alſo vnto Doctour Sanders anſwered ſayinge. We care not for your hiſtories. Doctour Toby Mathewe ſaid to Father Campion. If he should beleue the Fathers, he could not be a proteſtante. Beza cried out againſt Athanaſius, and the Fathers of the Councell of Nice, for that (ſaith the) Athanaſius found out this Tripartite god (he meant the bleſſed Trinte.) He ſaid alſo that he Fathers of that Councell were blinde ſophists, the miniſters of the the beaſt, & the bondſlaues of Antechriſt.*

*noui teſta. Pet. in pref. 1. cor. Humfred. in vit. Iuelli par. 212. Calu. in pref. inſtit. ad Regem Galli. Martyr de votis pag. 566. 10. reſ. Camp. 5. ratio. Beza exempla Theologica.*

4. *The third cauſe of this mine auerſion was, becauſe proteſtantes are hard to be reclaimed: for that amougeſt all the ſects that euer were none were more inconſtant, or variable in their Doctrine then the Proteſtants. For neither birdes, or beaſtes (as Plinie ſaith) doe watche to breake other birdes egges, or deſtroie others of-ſpringe, as theſe Proteſtantes watche to deſtroye and abrogat the Doctrine which was hatched before them: ſo as whatſoeuer the firſt goſpeller doth ſettle, the whelpe that comes from him doth deſtroye it: as in ſteede of many examples the confeſsion of Au-*

*Plin. natural. hiſt. lib. 10. c. 74*

*gusta may serue for one, so called for that in that* Colloq. al-
*citty, the Lutheranes did exhibit to Charles the* tenbar. f 4
*5. a booke Which Were Written all the articles* 39.
*of their Doctrine, Which Was 50. times chaunged* Colloq. al-
*and mangled, as they themselues affirme, in all* tenb. fol.
*Which, the last is nothinge like the first, and soe,* 464.
*they call it.* Cothurnum &c. *A dislikinge vnto all the rest, notWithstandinge Luther said it to be.* Fundamentum quod hactenus papistis opposuimus. *The fundation Which hitherto We opposed against the Papists, the grounde of our religion according to the Word of god, and the onlie rule of the peace and establishinge of träquillitie in Germany (saith he) but in very trueth Was the cause of all the Warres, and troubles thereof: and Which Was abolished out of Germany, yea out of Augusta it selfe, and Within feWe yeares became zuinglians & Zuingfeldians, and is in noe place accepte in Saxonie: For other sectes (With Which that miserable Country doe abounde, being in nüber 20. as Stanislaus Rescius describeth) carrienge With thē all the sWay, did steppe in amoungest them, and so at the last Luthers Doctrine Was vtterly reiected. Count Palatines Country can beare Witnes of this mutabilitie, Which from Zuinglianisme, turned to Lutheranisme, & againe from Lutheranisme to zuinglianisme. As also vpper Germany When one Prince, or great superintendent dies, the people after their death doe change their religion.*

Smidlerus in vita Bullen. f. 35.

*5. England alsoe cannot denye this to be true, Which a certaine Pope many hundred yeares pro-*

*prophesied of them, saying. English men, of all nations are most inconstant and waueringe in their faith, the time shall come (saith he) that when Christendom shall haue most neede of them, they shall suarwe from their faith, and fall into sectes, and heresies. For in our daies it changed her religion 4. times within 30. yeares: vnder kinge Henry the 8. kinge Edward his sonne: Queene Marie; and Elizabeth; And as Fox saith, kinge Edward beinge a childe after his fathers funerall, by the instigation and settinge on of his Vncle the Duke of Somersett, did abolish the religion, which his Father had by lawe ordained viz. The six articles, containing. 1. The trueth of the Reale presence. 2. That both kindes for all persons, are not necessarie. 3. That marriage of Priests is prohibited by the lawe of God. 4. That Vowes and votaries are confirmed by the lawe of God. 5. That the Masse is agreable to Christes institution. 6. That Auricular confession, is warranted by the word of God. This kinge sett foorth two bookes of reformation & afterwards a third. These articles of our faith were made at one parlamente by the said kinge Henry the 8. and were abrogated as superstitious inuentions by another Parleamēt.* Anunas & menstruas fides, *as Hillarie and S. Basil say of the Arrians, euery newe yeare and moneth a newe faith. And what I pray you can be amoungst Christians, more disgracefull then this? For ought not our Religiō, & euery article thereof, to be as the same S. Basil saith;* eadem heri, hodie & in sæcula? *to admits mitt noe change, but to continewe his vigor, aswell yesterdaye, to daye, as alsoe for euer? According whereunto our Sauiour alsoe saith, that heauen and earthe shal passe, but my wordes shal not passe, nor any iott, nor sillable thereof till al be fulfilled. Is there any Christian to be found, who dares be so bould to say that our Parlament exceedeth the power of God? But god by his absolute power (as Aristotle and all diuines, and Philosophers affirme) cannot make two contradictories or contraries to be trewe, because of the implication therein (for if the one be trewe, the other must be false) and truly noe more can these opposite and contradictorie Parleaments, be possible true.*

*6. The 4. cause was, that Protestantes make but a mockery of all religion, for that they follow Nicholas Machauailes precepts, holding that the Catholike religion is a hinderance to state, and that Princes shoulde followe that religion (though the groundes thereof be neuer soe false) which doth aduance their present estate: but contrarie to this S. Thomas saith, that wisdome and power are companions of trewe religion, which when it faileth, the power of state alsoe faileth:* non veniat anima mea, *saith S. Bernard,* in Concilium eorum qui dicunt &c. *my soule shall not follow their Coucells who say, that the exaltation and and peace of the Empire, will hunder the peace of the Church. If Iustice be a vertue to giue euerie man his owne, to giue to Cesar his owne, and to God his owne, how doth the Prince keepe Iustice*

*with*

with god, that takes from God his righte, which is religion, & depriues his diuine maiestie of that worshipp & reuerēce which is due vnto him? This is proued, for that Princes followinge this false reason of state, haue beene put by God frō their state, as Ieroboam the seruant of Salamon, to cōtinewe himselfe in the kingdome which he had taken from Roboam, did alter the Religion & made a false religion. For he made two golden calues, one at Dan, and the other at Bethell: and also altered the order of priestoode, by ordaininge others that were not of the order of Leuie. For which both he and his yssue were depriued of their kingdome, and destroied of their liues. The Princes of the Iewes, by reason of their state, put Christ to death, least the Romaines shoulde come vpon thē, neuerthelesse the Romaines came vpon them, and destroyed them.

7. Vetiza a kinge of Spaine and his successor Rodorigus, fearinge the rebellion of their subiectes, for their owne wicked actes, destroied and rased downe all the stronge holdes of Spaine: which was the cause that, that Country was broughte in one quarter of a yeare in subiection by the Moores, which were not expelled Spaine in 700. yeares after. The kinges of Fraunce, Francis the first, and his sonne Henry the second, the one brought in the Turcke, thinckinge to bringe him in to Spaine against Charles the fift Emperour & kinge of Spaine, to destroy Spaine. But whether did the tempest driue the Turcke, but to Tolouse within France, which afterwards with great a

doe, makinge many spoiles of that Countrie; were driuen out, after burninge the Cittie of Nicea & other citties out of which they brought with them 5200. Christians as slaues, amongest which number were 200. consecrated virgins; the other did ioyne with the rebellious protestāt Princes against the said Charles, by whom they were ouerthrowen and brought to subiection. Kinge Henry the third of Fraunce, beinge perswaded, that he should neuer be obeyed of his subiectes, vnles he should make away the Catholique Princes, as Henry of Loren Duke of Guise and Luyes of lorē, the Cardinall his brother: murthered them in the assembly of Bloys 1588. but for that he was led rather by the wicked Councell of Macheuillians, and not by the lawe of God, he was punished himselfe by a poore sillye friar without the procurment of any, but of his owne head, who thrust him thorough with a knife beinge in the middest of his army, purposing to besidge Paris. Iohn Fredericke Duke of Saxonie, intendinge to take the Empire from the house of Austria, followed Martine Luthers Councell, that he should change his religion, soe that by the procurment of Luther he rebelled against his soueraigne. But the frute that he reaped by this false reason, was to be apprehended, put in to prison, depriued of his estate, Dukedome and dignity of elector shipp: was not Absolon destroyed by the false Councell of Architofell? And Aman by his wicked plottes, by which he tought to destroie Mardocheus and the chilren of Israell? For there is noe wisdome or Councell

*cell of Macheuillians against God & his Church. Thomas Cromwel was put to death (as Fox saith) by the cruell lawe he made himselfe, as by a certaine fatall destinie (these be Foxes wordes) that whosoeuer should be cast into the Tower, he should be put to death without examination; the said Fox calleth this Cromwell the wall and defense of protestant religion. But,* qui hominibus placent confusi sunt, quoniam Deus spreuit eos, *those which doe please men are confounded, for God despiseth them.*

*8. The principal and last reason or cause is, for that these articles are already condemned by the generall Iudgement and verdit in soe many generall Councells as haue beene in the world, & specially by the last generall Councell of Trent, therfore nowe they ought not to be called in question. Whereupon Gelasius the Pope saith.* Maiores nostri diuina inspiratione cernentes, &c. *Our Ancestours foreseinge by diuine inspiration, did most earnestly pray the faithfull, that whatsoeuer was decreed by any Councell against anny heresie, for the faith of the Catholiks and the Catholike trueth, it should neuer be broughte in question againe. Also Leo the Pope did desire the Emperour Marcianus, that there should be noe retractation in any thinge defined by the holy Councell, and soe the said Marcianus established by lawe accordinge to his request, that none should dispute of the definition of the Councell. The said Leo also taught the same in his Epistle to the Councel of Chalcedon, & to Maximus the Bus-*

bopp of Antioch. The same is also decreede in the Councell of Ephesus, and in the Councell of Chalcedon, S. Augustine also said, that it is an insolent madnes to disputed against any thinge, that the Catholike church had defined. For our Sauior saith, Whosoeuer heareth your, heareth me, and whatsoeuer they will you to doe, that doe yee.

5. For as much therfore, as these heresies were condemned (as I haue said) by the generall Councell of Trent, vnto whom protestantes refused to come to trye their doctrine (for none euer refuseth the triall of generall Councells, but heretikes) therfore we ought not to dispute with them any more. Which also rightly agreeth with the coũcell of S. Paul vnto Titus saying. A man that is an hereticke after the first and second admonitiõ, shunne, knowinge that such a one is peruerted. And to Tomothy he saith, these be they that craftilie enter into houses, and leade captiue silly women, alwaies learninge and neuer attaininge vnto the knowledge of the trueth, but as Iames and Mambris resisted Moyses, soe these also resist the trueth, men corrupted in minde, reprobate cõcerninge the faith. All the while that S. Augustine was an Heretick S. Ambrose would neuer dispute with him; And the Empresse Placilla, wife vnto the great Theodosius, vnderstanding that Eunomius the Hereticke would faine reason with her husband, for eschewinge danger of being corrupted by him, did with great wisdome hinder the conference. And Nazianzenus saith, we ought to abhor Heretikes as the destructiõ of the church, and the poyson of trueth, not cariенge any hatred

*vnto their persons, but hauing pitty of their errors. Ignatius likewise saith,* vt filij lucis fugite diuisionem vnitatis,& malam hæreticorum doctrinam. *As the children of light, shunne diuision of vnitie, and the wicked doctrine of Hereticks, by whom the whole world is defiled, refraine from those euill hearbes, which Christ did neuer plant, for they be not the seede of God, but of the deuill. Be not deceaued brethren, saith he, whosoeuer shall followe a seducer, shall neuer possesse the kingdome of heauen: and whosoeuer departes not from a false preacher, shall purchase euerlastinge damnation.*

10. *Thus he admonished, that we should beware of wicked Heresies, the reason of his caueat is, for that Heresie (as the holy Doctors saye) is a certaine mischeefe of the diuill and a firebrande, that cometh from hell, a pestilente, corrupt, and poysoned aier, a cancker that consumeth the body in which it is norished, a certaine disease, that doth penetrate the intralles, and doth corrupt and infest the soules of Christians: and not only doth kill with her touche as the Viper doth, or with her sighte as the Basilike, or with her belching as the dragon, but after all these fashions and many more, doth destroy, confounde, and cast away all that approache it, neither is there any other remedie but to flie, nor any other refuge then to departe from such a one, as is intangled with it; no other security, then to be far from such an infernall and contagious mischeefe, which with the name of Christe, destroieth Christ in our hartes,*

*and*

*and vnder the pretence of faith, destroyeth faith. And S. Augustine saith; let euery Catholike flie and abhor them, with whom the Church communicateth not: for we ought not, saieth he, to haue parte with them, that haue no participation with themselues, and which are not vnited to the body of the whole Church; and to conclude with our Sauiour, one should neuer otherwise accompte of them, then as of heathens and publicans, and his holy Euangelist S. Iohn forbiddeth vs to salute them.*

*11. Therfore (gentle Reader) these be sufficiēt reasons wherfore we should be loath to dispute with Protestantes, which through their fall from godes Church are voide of all humility, intoxicated with pride, and are so blinded with malice, that they cannot learne or imbrace the trueth, or haue any trewe wisdome. For as the holly scripture saith, into a malicious soule, wisdome shall not enter: For in all ciuill conuersation or disputation, especially in matters of religion, we should intend nothinge els but the consolation of our soules, and the edification of our neighbours, and as the Apostle saith,* Non nosmetipsos, sed Iesum Christum prædicamus, *not our selues or our owne glory should we ayme at, but that of Christ Iesu, whose cote without seame is rente in peeces by so many wilfull inuēted opinions of protestāts: whose mysticall body (I meane his Church) is despised, forsaken, & persecuted: the fruite of whose doctrine, and the proiect of their strange deuises, tendes to nothinge els, then to shake the very pil-*

lars

*lars, stroungest foundations, and fortresses of all Christianity: and at lenght to bringe in all coldnes, and doubtfulneße in our beleefe, and misbeleefe in the principaleste misteries in our Catholike religion, plaine Athesime and confusion of all Christian piety, a gate for all disorders, and dissolution of life and manners , a shipwreacke of Conscience, and other marckable and sutable effectes to their doctrine and behauiour, which are practised by them daily in all places where they beare sway. And although euery man (as S. Naz. saith) may thinke of God, but not euery man dispute of him, so euery man ought not to dispute or doubte of the cheefest misteries of Catholike religion, but beleeue them simply with the vniuersall Church, which is (accordinge the Apostle) the firmamente and foundation of trueth: and therfore can not in any sorte deceaue vs.*

Chap.

Chap-

uen

Chap-

## APPROBATIO.

Hic Liber cui Titulus (*The Theater of Catholicke and Proteſtant Religion*) nihil continet quod fidei vel moribus aduerſatur, quin potius multa, quæ tam ad fidem Catholicam ſtabiliendam, quam ad hæreſes huius temporis impugnandas optimè inſeruiunt.

*Matthæus Kelliſonus*
*S. Theol. Doct.*

# WHETHER THE RELIGION WHICH

## *Proteſtants profeſſe be a new Religion: or whether the Romish Religion be new, and that of the Proteſtant be ancient and ould.*

## CHAPTER I.

1. IF Proteſtants were of ſound iudgment, or nott diſtracted of their wittes, they would neuer ſuppoſe, much leſſe auerre ſo manifeſt an vntruth, as that the religion of the church of Rome is a new religion: or defend an abſurditie ſo egregious, as Proteſtant religion, to be the more auncient; Wherfore this firſt aſſertion being ſo euident, and knowen an vntruth, ſuch as doe follow, are the leſſe to be beleeued.

2. It is well knowen, that before theſe 80. or 100. yeares, all Chriſtendome did imbrace the catholike Roman religion, ſo that it was, *terræ vnius labii*, as it is written in Geneſis, a countrie of one language, and one ſpeeche; and as we reade of the chriſtians in the Actes of the Apoſtles, that firſt be- *Gen.* 11. *Act.* 4.

leeued in Christ, that they were of one hart, and of one accord: and as one God was honored, and worshipped of all, soe one faith was embraced of all, they obserued one order of administration of the Sacraments, they vsed, and kepte one obseruation of ceremonies: all were called Christians, (which blessed name none disdayned) none were called Gospellers, Lutherans, Caluinists, Zuinglians, Protestantes, or Puritans, Anabaptistes, Trinitarians or any other sect, with innumerable others which the Protestant religion hath sett abroach and inuented: men were simple, and honest in their dealinges, faithfull of their promisses, charitable in their workes, zealous in their beleefe, obediente vnto their Prelates, and Pastors. This is soe euident a trueth, as that all bookes, recordes, generall and prouinciall councells, all parleamentes of kingdomes, all vnctions, and inuestinge of Emperours and Kinges, all consecration of Bishoppes, all holy orders of Priestes, all churches, monasteries, and chappels, in the worlde, all the gates of townes, and cyttyes, all monuments, and recordes both spirituall and temporall, all vniuersities and doctours of Christendome, both comon and ciuill lawes of all countries, yea Protestantes themselues doe plainly witnesse.

3. But that Protestant religion is new, is a thing most certeine, for there are men yet liuinge

liuinge at this day more auncient then it, and can remember, when it first came into England, and Irelande. Wee can shewe you the first inuentours, and authors therof. The place, the time, and the occasion by which it crepte in, and infected these miserable northen countries. Who haue opposed themselues against it. What garboyles, & callamities came into those conntryes, that nourished the same. What rebellion and insurrectiō of subiects against their princes, for defending the same. What were the motiues of such as inuented yt, and occasions of others, that imbraced it. The successe of the one and the other, and by whome, and how the same was condemned. I pray you what can be more euident signes and tokens of noueltie? for noueltie in all common wealthes (but especially in matters of religion as S. Nazianzenus saith) is to be auoided, yea the Emperour of the Turckes did aduise the Queene of Transiluania, to beware of the noueltie of hereticall sectes, and that shee should neuer suffer the same to creepe into her countrie. It is well knowen also, that the name of protestāt religion was neuer heard of, before the yeare of our Lord 1529. in the towne of Spira in Germany, where the Lutheranes beinge as it were combined against the Emperour Charles the 5. did vse a kinde of protestation, wherupon afterwardes they were called Protestantes.

4. If thou say, that it lay lurkinge and hidden in the worlde, I aske where, or in what place of the world, in what kingdomes and townes, or who were the defenders therof? Truly no writer or historiographer, did, or could euer make mētion of any such, nor euer before that time any mention was made of them, nor was it euer heard, that any hereticall secte was so closelie hidden in the worlde, but it might be knowen: at least, when Luther himselfe taught the same, they should then haue manifested themselues, and yet we can finde none such: for such as followed Luther, they were before Catholickes. *Ex nobis prodierunt* (saith Saint

Ioan. 2. John) *sed non erant ex nobis*. They went foorth frō vs, but they were not of vs, for if they had bin of vs, they had remayned with vs: it is cleare therfore they were not good Christians, who forsakinge the narrowe way of saluation, runne headlonge into the broade way of perdition, and licentious doctrine of newe sectaries; Whereas the religion of Christ, is a religion moste auncient, sacred, immutable, impregnable, inuiolable, alwaies the selfe same, holdinge and continuinge his vigor and force, vnto the worldes ende, it is the soule, and life of the Church. For euen as by the soule, fleash is vnited vnto the liuinge man: soe by religion mākinde is ioyned vnto the church of Christe, beinge his spirituall kingdome,

and

and all that euer were saued either before, or after Christe, oughte to be called Christians, as Iustinus martyr, and other holy Doctors doe say, for that they embraced Christian religion, and as saint Augustine saith. *Ipse vnigenitus Dei filius homo propter nos factus est, &c.* The only begotten Sonne of God became man for vs, that he should become the head of his whole Church, against which the gates of hell shall not preuaile, vnto whome Christe promised to remaine withall, vnto the consumation of the worlde. So that the religion by which this church is vpheld and Christe professed, did and shall allwaies continue.

*Iustinus mart. orat. ad Anto. Aug. l. 10 confess. ca. 43.*

*Matt. 16.*

*Matt. vlt.*

5. It is well knowen that the name of hugonots began in France an. 1562. (as themselues, of their asseblies made in the nighte at a gate in Tours in France called Hugon confesse to haue taken their denomination) went out of the Catholique churche, and did embrace the impiety of Caluine. In Scotland they fell alsoe from the Catholique Church into Caluinisme, anno Domini 1560. In Flanders the Geuses reuolted from the said church ouerwhelmed in the pit of soe manny heresies, anno 1566. In England they chaunged religion anno 1535. and first fell vnto Lutheranisme, afterwardes to Zuinglianisme, afterwardes the bodye of the realme fell from Zuinglianisme, to puri-

tanisme, the next degree vnto Anabaptisme: and since what numbers are fallen to the familie of loue? And what swarmes of Athistes are sprunge vpp in euerie shire, as Whittguifte noteth against Cartwrith?

6. Are not the first Authours of the protestancy also knowen, as Luther, Carolastadius, Oecolampadius in Germanie, Pharell in France, Thomas Crammer in England, Iohn knox, and Paule Methen a baker in Scotland, George Browne in Irlād? In the Apologie of the church of England pag. 142 it is said, that Luther and Zuinglius came first to the knowledge of the truth, and preaching of the ghospell. Luther said that God reuealed vnto him the knowledge of his Sōne, that he at lenghte might euangelize it to others, and that the Gospell was first preached by him. (D Kellyson reply to Surcliffe fol. 149.) But we knowe that they cannot alleadge the author of our religion, neither can they nominate vs from any particuler man, nor can they chardge the Catholique church with any priuate opinion, or faith, that is not vniuersally allowed & embraced of all Catholiques: neither can they nominate the time that shee fayled of her faith. Neither can they obiect that our church hath separated herselfe from the greater church: or that such as did adhere to the Pope, were in number lesse then any Church. For it is written in S. Gregories

Luth. tom. 7. f. 307.

ries Epistles to the Bishoppes of the Easte, that Affrique, Spaine, France, Italie, and all the worlde, did communicat with him. This verie argument other Doctours did vse against other heretiques, as Tertullian. *Qui estis vos inquit, &c.* What are yee (saith he) from whence, and when came you? where did you lie hidden all this while? alsoe. *Optatus mileuita. lib. 2. contra Parmenand. Vestræ, inquit, Cathedræ originem ostendite &c.* Shew the beginninge of your Chaire, you who challenge vnto your selues the churche, & so other doctors doe speake to this effect. *Tertull. lib. de præscrip.*

7. Caluine your cheefe prophet, when he oppugneth our religiō, he saith plainly, *se toti antiquitati repugnaturum.* That he opposeth himselfe against all antiquitie, & saith, that he will admitt no auncient Father, but S. Augustine. And in another place he reprehendes S. Augustine himselfe for sainge that our willes doe cooperate with the grace of God. For God made all thinges perfecte, & in cōplete order, but innouatiō came by the diuell: Wee read in the ghospell, that after the good seede was sowen by God, the diuell did sowe darnell & cockle: euen so after the trewe christian religion was sowen by the Apostolicall, and catholicke Pastors in euery place of the worlde, the enemy of mankinde by Martyn Luther an Augustine Frier, did sowe and teach the darnell of absurde, daungerous and damnable here- *Calu. l. 2. instit. 2. parag. 2.* *Lib. 2 c. 3.* *Matt. 13.*

heresies anno 1517. beinge the first author of the protestant religion. So wee knowe the author of the Arrian heresie, to be one Arrius a Priest of Alexādria in Egypte anno 324. Of the Nestorian heresie, to be Nestorius Archbishop of Constantinople, who taught his heresie in Thrasia anno 431. as the other also haue taughte, the one in Egypte first, and the other in Saxonie afterwardes. Wee knowe the author of the catholicke religion to be Christe, from whence wee are called christians in all ages, before Luther first inuented the name of Papistes, for that wee obey and embrace Christs vicar generall, our holy Father the Pope, the successor of S. Peter vnto whom Christ committed the regimente of his church, feedinge of our soules, and the charge of his
*Matt. 16.* flocke. This christian religion was first preached in Iurie the 15. yeare of Tyberius Cesar:
*Ioan. vlt.* as alsoe wee knowe that the same was oppugned and gainsaid first by the Scribes and Pharises, afterwardes by the Gentyles, and with all penall statutes of forcible lawes made by the Romaine Emperours, & other potentates of the worlde, which were practised and put in execution for the space of 300. yeares, to supplant and deface the same. This christian religion was vpholden and defended by all the Popes, and confirmed by all the generall approued councells that euer were: But the protestant religion was dis-

disproued and condemned for heresie by Leo the tenth, and by the generall Councell of Trent, and by all Catholick vniuersities of the worlde; as the Arrian heresie was contradicted and condemned by Syluester then Pope, and by the generall Councell of Nice, by S. Athanasius and Hillarius, and other holye Doctors: as the Nestorian heresie alsoe, was reiected by Pope Celestinus and the Councell of Ephesus, S. Cyrill & others. So that though wee haue shewed your authors or ofspringe, the time & place, when it began, and where it began, yet the like you cannot once nominate of vs since Christe, and his Apostles, who are the only authors of our beleefe, and religion.

6. You affirme, that the protestant religion was since Christe, and his Apostles in the world, but it was hidden. I answere that seeinge the Church and religion of Christe ought to be a cittie placed vppon a mountaine, or hill, to be seene of euerie one, (as in many places the holye scripture doth proue) it ought not to be hidden, but manifest to the whole worlde, otherwyse it shoulde not be the religion of Christ, soe *Matt. 5.* that I must cōclude with S. Hierom saying. *Isa. 2.* *Breuem tibi apertamque animi mei sententiam* *Psal. 71.* *proferam, in illa Ecclesia esse permanendum, quæ* *Daniel. 2.* *ab Apostolis fundata vsque ad diem hunc durat:* *Dial. lucifer in fine.* I must be plaine and declare my mynde sincerely, that wee must abide in that Church, which

which was founded by the Apostles and continewed vnto this verie daye. If you shall heare such as be christians to be nominated rather of some other head then of Christe, Marcianistes, Valentinians, Montanistes, know then they oughte not to be called the church of Christe, but the synagoge of Antechriste: euen so such as are nominated Gospellers, Caluinistes, and Lutherans &c. which are the founders of your religion and the inuentors of strange newe and deuised opinions, contrarie to the vniuersall catholicke church, and to the auncient Doctours thereof: ar rather as S. Hierom saith, members of that synagoge, then of the church of Christe, and as they were most peruerse & obstinate in their doctrine: soe they were most shameles and licentious in their liues: and as the tree beareth in his braunches the corrupte humours, that they drawe from the roote: as the vertue of the cause is knowen by the effecte, and the nature of the springe doth shewe it selfe in the brooke, and as the springe beinge vncleane, the brooke cannot be cleere, and the roote beinge withered, the braunches can beare noe fruite: so Luther & Caluine beinge your roote and of-springe, and beinge vncleane, filthie, leacherous, and altogether wedded to carnalitie and licentiousnes, beinge rebellious apostates, noe doubte of such as shall followe or embrace them,

them, no better fruite can be expected of them: hence Zuinglius himselfe did cōfesse, that as soone as he did embrace this ghospell of Luther, he was attached with the raginge flames of fleshly concupiscence and sensualitie. *Zuing. t. 2. Resp. ad Luth.*

*The occasion of Luthers fall, and of other hertikes from the Catholike Churche.*

## CHAPTER II.

1. WEE may applie S. Augustine his sentēce vnto this subiect, that there are two rootes plāted in two fieldes, by two tillers, or husbadmen: the one Christ doth plant in the hartes of the good, the other the diuill planteth in the hartes of the wicked And as this is Couetousnes, which is the roote of euill: soe the other is charitie, beinge the roote, and of-springe of all goodnes: accordinge to the saying of the Apostle, that wee should be planted and rooted in charitie, for as no euill can springe from charitie, so no goodnes can come from couetousnes, soe that you may perceaue from which of these rootes Luthers cause proceeded, and which of these husbandmen did plante the same. For, not obtayninge the promulgating of certaine indulgences, whereby he hoped to gett money; first he rayled against them who denied him the same; then he was infected with

*Aug. serm. de tempo. 44.*

*1. Tim. 6. Ephes. 3.*

with a deſire of vaine-glory; thirdly with a deſire of reuenge, for that he had a repulſe from the Pope called Leo the tenth; afterwardes pricked forward with a moſt filthie appetite of fleaſhlye concupiſcence, beinge a profeſſed frier fifteene yeares, he came out of his monaſterie, and tooke with him a profeſſed Nunne wherby he might ſatisfye his filthie luſte withall, ſo that he committed ſuch ſinne, & ſacriledge by breakinge and violatinge his vowes, that all the world were ſcandalized therat. And ſo far did he defend his riotouſnes and beaſtlie debauchedneſſe therin, as to teach that a woman was as neceſſarie for a man, as meate, drinke, or ſleepe: and ſaid moreouer, that if a married woman would not render the con- *Lib. de vita coniug. ſerm. de matrimonio.* iugall debpte of matrimonie, that the husband ſhould not ſpare his maide. The like filthie luſt (but farre more deteſtable) was the occeſion of Caluine his hereſie. For it is well knowē as may appeare by the iudiciall *Bolſecus in vita Calu. cap. 5. Iul. Brig. pag. 59.* actes and recordes of Nouodiū; that he was condemned of the filthie ſinne of the fleſh againſt nature, & had it not beene for the intreatie of the biſhop there (which obtayned that his puniſhmente, ſhould be turned, vnto a hoate burninge iron on his backe) he ſhould haue bene altogether burnt. Iohn Witcliffe, for that he was depriued of his perſonnage in Oxforde, for his vitious miſdemenor, began his hereſie. Arrius, becauſe Ale-

Alexander was preferred to the Archbisho-pricke of Alexandria before him, gaue occasion of the Arrian heresie against the deitie of Christe. Mõtanus for that he was denyed the primacy of Asia, which he soughte verie earnestlie, troubled the Church with newe heresies, as Nicephorus wyttnesseth, *de penitentia lib. 5. cap. 15.* Aerius alsoe, for beinge denyed of a Bishopricke fell into Arianisme, and afterwardes inuented himselfe a newe heresie, which was, that wee ought not pray for the dead.

*Nicep. de pen. l. 5. c.*

2. Henry the eighte (as Iohn Foxe a greate puritan in England doth wyttnes, & all the world knoweth to be true) for his diuorce made from Queene Catherine his wyfe, was by the Bishoppe of Rome excommunicated: who beinge sore exasperated therby, assembled a parlamente, by which he brought to passe, that he banished the Popes authoritie out of England, & made himselfe head of the Church: thus far Iohn Foxes owne wordes. For it is certainly knowen, that from the conuersion of England by S. Augustine duringe soe many hundred yeares, vnto Kinge Henry the 8. as all English historiographers and ministers themselues doe acknowledge, the Catholicke or papisticall religion (as it pleaseth them to tearme it) did florish in England, & that the cheefe pointe thereof was, that the Pope was iudge, moderatour and cheefe

*Fox. in historia pa. 512. edit. 1*

*Hollin. in descrip. Brita. l. 1. cap. 7.*

Pastor

Pastor aswell of the English Church, as of all other Churches of the Christians in Ecclesiasticall matters: which Catholicke faith the said Kinge Henry defended the space of xx. yeares, as longe as he liued with his lawfull married wife, aswell against domesticall heretickes, that were his subiects, by all penall statutes and exquisit torments, as alsoe against forraine hereticks by a most learned booke in the defense of the 7. Sacraments (which booke I haue in myne owne custodie) for which he was ennobled and honored by Pope Leo the tenth, with the title of defēder of the Catholicke faith, which was neuer giuen to any kinge in the worlde before, which he receaued as Foxe saies, with great ioy: for when it came to the kinge, beinge then at Greene wich, he went to his chapel, accompanied with manny nobles & Ambassadors, Cardinall Wolsey said Masse, the Earle of Essex brought the basen of water, the duke of Suffolke gaue the assay, the duke of Norfolke held the towell, the Heraldes with their company began their accustomed cryes, prononcinge. *Henricus Dei gratia Angliæ, Franciæ defensor Fidei, Dominus Hiberniæ*. And amongest his other magnificent titles, he lefte to this day this title to his posterity, as is well knowen to the world. Neyther only with bookes, but alsoe with his victorious and inuincible armes did he defende the Catholicke

Fox anno 1528. fol. 441.

ſike Romane faith, and the dignitie thereof, for the which he foughte againſte ſundrie princes, and their confederates; as againſte Lodowicke the 12. kinge of France, and Iames the 4. kinge of Scottes, though married to his ſiſter. Who beinge vanquiſhed, and his great armie ouerthrowen by the Earle of Surrie in England, and the ſaid kinge himſelfe being *ſlaine in the battle, for that he was excommunicated*, was not ſuffred to be buried in any Chriſtian graue. Alſo he ſent his Armie by ſea to ioyne with the Spaniardes againſte the kinge of France, to aſſaulte France in the frontiers of Spaine by the powerfull force of the Engliſh. Iohn Albertus the kinge of Nauare was driuen altogether out of the kingdome beinge, excomunicated by the Pope, which Spaine doth poſſeſſe at this daye. Did not the ſaid kinge within fewe yeares after ſend an Armie into Italie againſt the Emperor Charles the firſt, in the defence of Clement the 7. then Pope? And notwithſtanding he was his great frinde and his Nephewe, for that Queene Cathrine was his Aunte, yet through the filthie concupiſcence by which he was beſotted and blinded to marrye Anna Bullene, and ſoe to be diuorced from his lawfull marryed wife, he turned all thinges topſie turuie, reiected the Popes authoritie (which he before aſwell by Gods

B lawes,

lawes, the holy scriptures, as by the fathers and Councells of the Church defended) and soe by a parlament of one Realme or kingdome, he disanulled and abrogated that which was established by soe manny generall parleaments and generall Councells of all Christendome, yea by Christe himselfe and by all such as trulye beleeued in him. And for not yealding vnto his desire herein. manny religious and constant Martyrs offred their liues, and their bloode, amoungest whome was the lighte of England that most sacred Martyr and learned diuine Iohn Fisher Bishopp of Rochester, & Sr. Thomas More Lord Chancelor of England: of these
*Act.* 20 sorte of people our Sauiour wished vs to beware: the Apostle alsoe saith, woulues shall enter after my departure and shall not spare
*Rom.* 16. the flocke. Therfore in another place he requested vs to marke and knowe what people they be, that raise dissentions and scandalls in the Churche, and doe teach otherwise then wee haue alreadye receaued, and to fly from them. He alsoe exhorted vs,
*Heb.* 4. that wee should not be lead away with
*Iohn.* 4. mutable and strange doctrine. S. Iohn alsoe wished vs not to beleeue euerie spiritt, but that wee should trye whether they be of God.

3. But the doctrine of Luther cannot by any triall be founde true, so that as Christ saith,

saith, my doctrine is not myne but my fathers which did send me : soe Luther may say his doctrine is not his, but his fathers the diuell that did send him, whom he boasted to haue suggested vnto him arguments to ouerthrowe priest-hoode and sacrifice, that by that meanes he should ouerthrowe and confounde the true worshipp of the true God, for God as the Apostle saith is the God of peace and charitie, not of dissention. For whosoeuer procures sectes and diuision betwixt brethren ( saith the prophett) is a diuell. When therfore by Luthers meanes, wee see so manny sectes against Godds Churche, wee must not thincke that euer his doctrine was of God, for in his disputation against Eckius, he fell into such rage and furie, that being admonished, forasmuch as the cause of God was handled, he should not transgresse the boundes of modestie, he answered, that this matter, as it was not begunne for godes sake, soe it should not be ended for his sake, for that truly not charitie, but enuye and malice, was the motiue and cause of Luthers doctrine, against the Pope and Churche of Christ. For when he euen departed from his disciples he was wont to saye; *Benedicat vos pater cælestis omni benedictione & odio Papæ.* The celestiall Father, blesse you with all benediction, and with the hatred of the Pope, soe as you may perceaue of what spirit he

*Iohn. 7.*

*Luth. lib. de Missa. Ang. to 6 Ienens. Ger & to. 7. witteb.*

*1. Cor. 13. 1. Cor. 14.*

*Hosius lib. 1. de heresi. Zurius hist. Anno 1519.*

*The malediction of Luther. Theod. to. 4. operum Lutheri in Ioel.*

he was. For I am ſure you would not thinke that ſpiritt to be of God, which diſſolueth the vnion of the bodie of IESVS Chriſt, but of Antechriſte: for whoſoeuer endeuors to diſioyne the Church from Chriſte, or to diſmember himſelfe from the ſaid Churche, or goeth aboute to deuide and ſeperate the Church in herſelfe (as S. Aug. ſaith) he diſſolueth & diuides IESVS, and his Church which Chriſte boughte with his pretious bloode, who declared in his death how diſpleaſant diuiſion and diſſention ſhould be vnto him, ſoe as without any other ſcripture, as Theodoretus ſaith. *Impia & execranda dogmata per ſe ſufficiunt ad ſuum patrem oſtendendum:* wicked and execrable opinions are ſufficient of themſelues, to declare vnto the world their father and patrone.

*Aug. trac. in epiſt. Iohn.*
*Epheſ. 5.*

4. In the laſt of theſe lamẽtable examples, I ought not to lett ſlippe that of Conſtance the vncle of Michaell Paleologus Emperor of Conſtantinople, who puttinge away his married wife, married his daughter in in lawe, for which he was excomunicated by Ignatius the Patriarch of that Cittie of Conſtantinople: and the Emperor and his vncle beinge offended therwith, Photius was inueſted in that Sea, and ſoe to maintayne himſelfe in that dignitie, he ſaid that the Pope was an hereticke, and that the whole latine Church erred; ſoe as you ſee, luſt and enuie brought in hereſie, hereſie

other

other mischeefes and wickednes into the world.

*By what deceite, hypocrisie, and dissimulation this heresie crept into other Countries, by what periurie and forgerie they were deluded by it, and what destruction, and desolation it brought with it.*

## CHAPTER III.

1. AS in the tyme of the Romaine Emperor Heraclius, one Mahomett a souldior did combine with others against the said Emperor, by the craftie deuises of which companion, many Prouinces banded themselues againste him, where vpon ensued a suddaine decaye, both in the ecclesiasticall & ciuill gouernment of the Easte: euen so Luther no sooner had hatched his heresie, but that he procured by his deceite and hipocrisie, the Princes of Germanie to enter into the like combination or conspiracye againste Charles the fift at Smacalde, notwithstandinge they swoare allegeance vnto the said Emperor, which Luther said was not lawfull to be obserued or performed. So Sleydan a protestant writer saies, that because Cesar went aboute to hinder the religion which they lately brought in, he gaue them cause in conscience to op-

*Gusp. in mahometo.*

*That league was renewed, first betwixt the lantgraue and other princes 22 of Decẽb. 1530. and afterwardes the 29 of March 1531. against Charles the 5. Sleyd. l. 18*

pugne him, where vppon there followed a cruell and bloody warre betwixt Cesar and the Protestants, which brought many prouinces to ruyne and destruction, besides the miserable thraldome and slauerie of the Turcks, vnder whose dreadfull yoke, Hungarie and other Prouinces adioininge therunto, doe lye groueling at this daye.

*Surius. An.* 1525. *Michell ab Iselt in sua hist.* 1525.

2. At that tyme allso Thomas Monzer priest, by Luthers instigation did stirr vpp a weake and slender rable of Peasantes, against the nobilitie and Cleargie, soe as there were slaine of them more then an hundreth thowsand in Germanie that yeare. He burned 200. Castells and monasteries, murthered the Earle Heluesten, with manny other nobles, soe as Germanie suffred more calamities that present yeare of the Lutheranes, then they receaued of the Spaniardes and French men the space of 10. yeares before. Allsoe the Duke of Lorrayne slewe in one Daye 27. thowsand Peasantes that made insurrection against him, by the said Luthers procurement: in Franconia 200. Castles and and Monasteries were burned by those rebells. The like hauoke they made at Francfort, Mongontia, and Collen. The like garboiles combustion and bloody tragedies, surpassinge the other in horrour and detestation, in all other Countries where this Hydria and infernall heresie once got footinge, was stirred vpp and enkendled:

*Surius. An.* 1525

as in

as in Sauoy, Scotland, France, Flanders, and in other borderinge Countries: and by what falſhoode, periurie and diſsimulation yt infected Flanders, you ſhall imediatly ſee.

3. Firſt this hereſie was neuer knowen in Flanders before Anna Saxonia, a woman of Saxonie, who was infected with Luthers hereſie, was married to the Prince of Aurenge, as other noblemen in Flanders vnhappily were married to other weomen heretikes, as Herman was married with Count Hermans ſiſter, Florentius Pallentius, the Counte of Cullenburge, and William Counte of Herenberge, all which were married to women of Germanie. By theſe women the wicked people called the Geuſes of Flanders, made their inſurrection againſte Margarett de Auſtria, Duches of Parma, and gouerneſſe of Flanders, who was faine to flye from them as being ouer ſtronge for hir. But yet to putt her in ſome comfort, one of her nobilitie ſaid vnto her. *Non, non Madame, ne craigne pas les Geux*, that is to ſay, do not feare theſe wicked people: from which tyme the hereticks of Flanders were called Geuſes, that is to ſay, a ſorte of ragamuffines or miſcreantes, whom the ſaid Prince of Aurenge made his inſtruments to make a ſtronge rebellion in Flanders againſt Philipp the 2. king of Spaine by whome he was made Gouernor and deputie of Hollande, & by whoſe father the Em-

*Michell ab Iſelt in hiſt Surius hiſtoria. Florentius vander Haer de initijs tumultuum Belgiorũ.*

*Idem in ſua hiſtoria.*

*The prince of Aurenge the enginer of all the troubles of Flãders*

peror Charles the fifte, he was made soe great, as he was.

4. This rebellious prince of Aurenge, vnder pretence of deliueringe Flanders from the bondage of Spaine (as he alleadged) broughte this heresie into that Countrie, which was the cause of all the troubles of Flanders for the spate of 60. yeares, but by what dissimulation, periurie, and deceite the said Prince of Aurenge did infect Flanders with this heresie, the Chanceler of Louaine doth witnesse. I was present (saith he) when the Prince of Aurenge (the cause of all the troubles of Flanders) made a protestation at Mons, that his drifte was not to disturbe or vexe any priest or religious person, or to offend the Catholicke Church in any thing, but to deliuer Flanders from the slauerie of the Spaniardes. This verie oathe he made before Mathias Arch-Ducke of Austria, vnto whome he was made lieutenante generall, but this lewed companion neuer kepte his worde, as the histories of Flanders doe relate, but became a most cruell persecutor of all ecclesiasticall and religious persons, spoiled Churches, violated and abused sacred virgins, destroyed Alters, troad vnderfoote the holy sacrament of the alter, tooke away all the ornamentes, which he prophaned, robbed all Churches and Monasteries of their Challices, and other sacred implements dedicated to the seruice of

*Epistola Michaell Baysane Loua. de vnione statuum. An. 1578.*

of almightie God, embrewed his filthie murtheringe handes with the inocent blood of most vertuous priestes and religious men, not sparinge any order of personnes though neuer soe holy, wher-vpon many of the nobility beinge offended thereat, with many Citties, as Mastrick, Mõs, Douay, Arras, & others forsooke him, and yealded themselues to the Prince of Parma.

5. Of the like falshoode, deceite and periurie was the bastard of Scotland called Iames detected, base brother to the last Queene of Scottes, by whome also he was made Regent of Scotland, and aduanced by her meanes, to the greatest dignitie and wealth that Scotlãd could yealde. Notwithstanding for all these kindnes and obligations, aswell by nature, as by such singuler promotions, benefittes and desertes, yea his vowe and promise soe often iterated and solemlye confirmed with wicked oathes, yet beinge infected by Iohn Knocks an Apostate Friar, and afterwards a minister & instrument of Caluine, to enkendle the flames of that most wicked and damnable Heresie in that Countrie (the Author and instrument of all the rebellion of Scotland) he conspired againste that sacred soueraigne, murthered her husbande, and appeached her with the ymputation of that murther, who beinge most innocent

thereof,

thereof, plotted, and ſtirred vp ſuch ſtronge rebellions by her ſubiectes (himſelfe beinge the cheefe Captaine of this combuſtiō) as ſhe was taken and caſt into a moſt filthie priſon, where her death was threatned vnles ſhee would reſigne the gouernment of her kingdome vnto that ouglie monſter. And beinge deliuered out of that priſon, ſhee was faine to flye into England, where by the procuremente of that baſtard, ſhee was caſt into priſon, which ſhee ſuffred the ſpace of xx. yeares, and at lenghte, beinge Queene of France and Scotland, notwithſtanding was putt to death.

*Hollenſ in hiſt. ſcholaſt. pag. 500.*

6. This baſtard and the reſt of his Caluinian Confederates, ſought nothinge at the beginninge (as they pretended) but libertie of their conſcience: which beinge graunted, they proteſted and ſwoare all dutifull allegance to the Queene and ſtate. But after they obtained what they ſoughte for, they tooke perforce the whole ciuil gouernment into their owne handes, and by their faction and combination, ſodainlie grewe ſoe ſtronge and inſolente, that they denied the ſame libertie of conſcience vnto her; & her husband. And as Buchanan in his Scotiſh hiſtorie ſayeth, when vpon all ſainctes day the Queene would in her Chapple haue had Maſſe after a ſolemne manner, the miniſters of the Ghoſpell (ſaith this auctor) encenſed the nobility againſt her, that by force and

*Lib. 16. pag. 590.*

and violence they should compell her to leaue off: so that she was enforced to obey a crewe of Caluinian ministers, which could doe more in Scotland at that time, by their newe heresies (neuer in any requeste in that Countrie before) then their aunciente and Catholicke religion, by which they were conuerted from gentyles to be Christians, which they professed soe many hundreth yeares before, or the dutie of subiectes to their Prince, or the power of the Prince her selfe, or any feare of God, or respect of his lawes, diuine, naturall, or any humaine honestie or Ciuill modestie. Where yow may perceaue what libertie this wicked and licentious heresie giues, how turbulente it is, what garboyles it bringeth with it, vnto which dissolute and wanton youthes are most enclined: wherof a number of that Countrie being in France to trye their wittes, or to raise their fortunes, they brought with them from Caluine this poysoned doctrine, that infected all that Countrie.

7. Not vnlike vnto this hypocriticall pretence of Conscience, Caluine, Beza, and his ministers vsed, to gett footinge in France, although not with the like successe. After they had most solemly protested that they intended nothing but onlie libertie of their conscience. And soe in the assembly of Poyse, they did sweare obedience

to

to Charles the nynth, and his succeſſors, and vttered theſe, wordes. Wee ſweare before God and your maieſtie who are our soueraigne, that if any of vs hereafter ſhall misbehaue himſelfe in kindlinge any ſturr in France, that wee will ourſelues perſecute him with fire and ſworde. This proteſtation was made by Beza, which not withſtanding was the only author and fire-brand of all the miſerie, and calamities of France (as Iohn Knockes and Buchanan in Scotland) by whoſe plottes, and pollices, all France was in an vprore, al the nobilitie deuided by faxions, the ciuill gouernment and politicall lawes of the kingdom vtterly deſpiſed, the eccleſiaſticall lawes and Cenſures of the Church quite reiected, all ſacred thinges prophaned, Churches and monaſteries burned, ſacred Virgins defloured, many preiſtes, and religious perſons with moſt vnuſuall torments, murthered and maſſacred, the nobilitie deſtroied, their howſes ranſaked, by whoſe cruell handes moſt of the blood Royall of France was extinguiſhed, as the kinge of Nauare at the ſiege of Roane, the Duke Monepenſer, Roſorgomus. The Prince Dellphine. The Duke Memoroſe, the Duke of Longauile. The Dukes Niuer, the father, the ſonne, and the ſonne in lawe, the Conſtable of France, And manny Marſhalls thereof, Saincta Derane, Mount Moranſius, Mattugon,

gon, Dauillan, Brisarus, Touanus, Byron, Francis Duke of Ioys, besides manny thowsandes in the battells of Drintts, Saint Dennys, Iernan, and Mount Counter, and at many other townes, as Roane, Rochell, & Saincte Angell, soe as in one yeare more then a hundred thousande Frenchmen were slaine, yea Beza who made the said speach before the kinge, said that such as were killed in these Battells (beinge rebells) were blessed Martyres, because (saith he) they were the first that shedd their blood for the restoringe of the ghospell in France; And yet he with his fellow ministers, gaue a solemne oath as before is recited, to be true to the King, Crowne, and Countrie. How many thousand were also killed at other tymes in France, in other Ciuill warres, soe often renewed by these fellowes?

*Beza in prefat. noui testamenti ad Reginam Angliæ. An. 1564.*

8. Luther alsoe saith, that in seauen weekes betwixt Easter and Whittlontyde, were killed of the Peasants of Germanye, more then one hundred thousand; besides many millions of people in other warres of that Countrie, especially when Albert the Marques of Bramdeburge did destroy with fire and sworde all thinges that came within his reache. Besides the destruction and desolation he caused in many places of Germanie. In Norriberge he burned a hundred villages, Townes and Castles, and shutt vp in them men and women, with children and

*Luther tomo in ser. f. 270 An. 1553.*

Surius. An. 1553. and olde people which the firy flame consumed, viz. at Alterfum and Laufum. Againe did not Christiernus kinge of Denmarke, execute the like crueltie vpon those of Stocholum the cheefe Cittie of Suethlande, after that he inuited all the nobilitie with the two Archbishopps viz. Sarcen and Stringeron, and then murthered them euerie one, and afterwards all the rest of the Cittizens, notwithstandinge he had giuen his royall worde to the contrarie: in the Surius. An. 1517. execution of which murther, he continued for many dayes.

*That heresies are the cause of Reuolution of Countries, and destruction of state.*

## CHAPTER IV.

1. SAincte Gregorie sayeth that the conseruation of the Common wealth, doth depende of the peace of the Church, and that for two reason; for that the lawe of God commaundes vs, that wee should obey our kinges and princes in thinges that are not contrarie to the said lawe of God, soe that he that obeyes God, he muste needes obey his lawfull Soueraigne, because God almightie soe commaunded, for that obedience wee owe to the kinge, is parte of that wee owe to God. But when

when men doth cast away this bridle by heresie, or by anny other occasion of their vnbridled and incorrigible humors, as they haue no feare of God, soe bear they noe dutie to their Prince, or Soueraigne. Wherfore Constantius Clorus, father to Constantyne the greate, a most prudente and valiante Prince, intendinge to assay and proue the loyaltie of some Christian souldiers, he said vnto them, that if they would renounce their faith, and sacrifice to the Idolls, they should abide with him and possesse such honors, and promotions as they had receaued of him: otherwise such as would refuse soe to doe, they should departe from him. Some there were who for to gaine the Princes fauor did as he comaunded, and renounced their religion, others refused soe to doe. But Constantius putt awaie such as did sacrifice to the Idolls, and kepte with him such as refused soe to doe, saying that they were his best subiectes, for (quoth he) he that is a Traytor vnto God, will alsoe be a Traytor vnto his Prince.

*Euseb. de vit. Const. lib. 1. c. 11. Zozo. lib. 1. cap. 6.*

*Carol. Sig. lib. 2. de occiden. imperio.*

2. The like alsoe did Theodoricke being an Arrian hereticke killing a Courtier of his owne, whome he loued intirlie, for that from a Catholicke he became an Arrian only to please the kinges humor, sayinge, that he could neuer keepe touch with man, that was not faithfull vnto God; Also the most valiant Martyr S. Hornusta said vnto the kinge

*Carol. Sig. lib. 16. de occid. imp. Theodor. histor. l. 5. cap. 36.*

kinge of Persia, who comaunded him to denye his religion, and become an infidel, that if he should denie Christe, that was Lord and Redeemer of the worlde, he shoulde more easilie denye him that was a mortall man. Through want of faith therefore and good religion, rebellions are stirred vpp against their Princes and Soueraignes, as alsoe insurrections of subiectes, spoyles and garboyles of Traitors, combustion and confusion of Common wealthes, and all other enormities and trespasses are committed. And as Aristotele saith: *Cuius vsus est optimus, eius abusus est pessimus*, the more excellent and eminent a thing is if it be well vsed, soe the more mischeefe it ingenders, and the more ruine it bringeth with it, if it be abused. For as nothinge in this world is comparable in goodnesse to the Christian Catholick faith: so when the same is abused by sectes and diuisions, nothinge did euer more trouble the Christian Comon wealth: for that discordes in matters of faith, doe procure and ingender discordes and differences in the hartes and mindes of them that professe the same, from which discords and variances proceedes soe manny mischeefes and reuolutions of Countries and kingdomes: and kingdomes deuided (as our Sauior saith) cannot longe endure. Therfore Theodosius the yonger, beinge at Constinople, and seinge his Empire deuided

deuided into sectes by the heresie of Nestorius, he wrote an Epistle to that most vertuous and holy man Symon Stylites, which at that tyme did florish with most rare example of sanctitie, by which epistle he requested him verie earnestly, that hee should aske of God peace and vnion for the Church; and added these wordes. Because that its diuision doth soe afflict vs, that it is the roote and fountayne of all our euills and calamities. Wherefore whosoeuer will read the Chronicles of kingdomes, and the ecclesiasticall histories of the sainctes, he shall finde this to be true, by the warres that the Catholicks had in the Easte with the Arrians, and in Africke with the Donatists, and the Gentiles and Iewes against the Christians in all places.

*Act. Conc. Ephes. edi. tom. 5. Ces. Baro. tomo 5. An. 432.*

3. And neither Iewe nor Gentile are soe infestuous and pernitious againste the Churche and Christian Comon wealth, as hereticks, and especially those of our vnhappie times, and of all sects the Caluinistes, which are flames of sedition and destruction of Church and Comon wealthe, an infernall fire-brand that burnes wheresoeuer it takes place, which consumes to ashes all states and Citties where it is nourished, not vnlike the Cancker that eates and gnawes the body that feedes it: thus much you shall knowe by readinge a booke called *Incendium Caluinisticum*, printed 1584.

*Hollensen. hist. Angl. Anno 1554. idem in histo. Scot. Anno 1567.* Allso the histories of the troubles of France lib. 1. Anno 1565. The historie of Flanders Anno 1555. in the additions of Surius 1585. Stanislaus Rescius Ambassadors and Treasure, for the kinge of Poland in Naples, did write a booke 1596. *De Atheismis & Phallerismis Euangelicorum nostri temporis, videl.* of Atheismes and Phallerismes, I meane cruelties of the Euangelistes of our tyme, neither onlie doe they destroie kingdomes, but allsoe seeke to depriue Princes of theyr liues, that oppose themselues againste their doctrine, for some of them conspired to kill Queene Marie, and one of them confessed the same at his death, which was at Tiborn the 18. of May 1554. Norman Lesby, Iames Meluine, and other Caluinists in Scotland murthered the Cardinall of S. Andrewes in his owne howse and chamber the yeare 1546. and this by approbation of Iohn Knockes Buchanan and others, of the Geneuian Consistorie.

*Stow c. 1554.*

4. Buchanan in his most wicked and vngodly declamation made at London against his dread soueraigne the last Queene of Scottes, incensed both English and Scottes against her, to depriue her of her life and of her kingdome, whose wicked desires, and desigmentes was putt in execution by the English in the moneth of Ianuarie 1587. which was a wonderfull president and a mise-

*Doctor Bancraft in his booke of dangerous positions. lib. 4. c. 1. & in historia. lib. Lesley ep Rosse.*

miserable spectacle to the whole worlde. Knocks and one Lindesay another reprobate assistinge him, by their secrett combination with the Earle of Morton & others, set vpp the Bastard of Scotlande who after he was promoted to the Earldome of Moraye and Regencye of that kingdome, he went about to aduannce himselfe vnto the Royall Scepter of the kingdome, boasting himselfe to be borne in lawfull weadlocke, and therfore that he was the only legittimate sonne of his Father Iames the fift. These impudent mates write in their bookes, that by godes lawes women shoulde not be admitted to the gouernmente of kingdomes: that the people of the ghospell should not be tied vnto the lawes of kinred: that kingdomes should not be giuen vnto the nexte degree of fleshe and bloode: and that it stoode in the power of the people to create kinges, to depose or punish them at their pleasure, if they giue cause of offense: and this to be not onlye lawfull for all the people, but for euerie one: that he is prayse worthie whatsoeuer priuate person he be, that shoulde kill any kinge that misgouernes himselfe: that the supreame authoritie consisteth in the people and not in the kinge, and this they did write only to take awaye the last Queene and her issue (as it is related by Adame Blackwoode) who beinge big with childe, was pittifully ama-

*Knox in the Scotish historie said that if princes be tyrants against God, subiectes be freed from their obedience. Cal. in ep. Daniell. ver. 22. aleadged by kellyső. Replie to Sutcliffe the hugonots of France in their congregation. ar. 34 Luther also as Sleydan hath l. 8 Chro. Zuing. lib. 4. Epist.*

*Blacuodeus Apolo pro regibus cap. 2.3. & 4. Buchan.*

zed and terrified at the bloodye cruell and most horrible murther of her Secretarie Dauid Rice (a man of an innocente life and a most deuoute Catholicke) without lawe, reason, or any iustice, which was practised by these mens procurmente and sinister deuises, in her owne sight and Chamber of presence, callinge for her helpe, who was not able to releeue him, her selfe beinge in the like danger, as being straite conueide to close prison, and there taxed with an infamous reporte and imputation of her honestie (shee beinge most innocent therof) which was diuulged and spread abroade by their calumnious practise of slaunderous libells, reportes, and letters to all Princes.

5. Did not these lewed mates, as soone as they reuolted from the Catholicke Church, rebelle alsoe against their Princes, and at one instant become enemies of priests & Princes, soe Stephen Bosgaie the Hungarian, and the Emperor Rodolphe, his page, noe sooner became a Caluiniste, then he made all Hungarie for the most parte to ioyne with the Turcke, and to rebell against the said Emperor. Geneua noe sooner opened the gates for Pharell and Caluine, but they shutt them againste their lawfull Princes. The Princes of Germany reuolted from Charles the 5. Emperor, as soone as they forsooke their faith and became Lutherans. Flanders hath done the like especially such

*The rebellion of the low countries is knowen by their owne edic. printed at Francfort. 1583.*

as

as embraced these newe sects, who rebelled against their lawfull kinge and against all his gouernors, as againste Margaret Duches of Parma, and gouernesse, of the same, who was threatned to be murthered if shee should in any thinge gainsay them. In the same danger was her sonne, the Duke of Parma by gunnpouder & vilde fire, which was prepared for him in a vaute to destroy him and all his traine at Antuerpe, and before him, Dom Iohn de Austria by the treacherie of one Boniuetius a frenchman, who was suborned by the Prince of Aurenge to murther him, and missinge of their purpose, they deuised his death by many other miscreantes; Alsoe 1560. at Geneua Caluine and Beza conspired and combined together to murther the kinge, and to ransake and destroye all the Courte of France, and persuaded Spifamius to be the Architecte of this detestable practise beinge backt and entised therin by Otoman the Turque: the cheefe instrumētes & compassers of which plotte, were punished the 24. of March of that yeare. They set vpp and crowned alsoe Lodouicke the Prince of Conde kinge, and called him by the name of Lodouicke 13. the firste Christian kinge of the Franckes, against the trewe kinge thereof, this is proued by Peter Carpenters booke a hugonot, who writeth that to noe other purpose were intended all the deuises and machina-

*Surius hist.*

*Surius 24*

*Lodowick the 13. Surius. 1567.*

tions of the Causaries (soe he calles the hugonotts adiected to this cause) then to abolishe and destroye the Queene mother with all her whelpes, and therfore said he; Beza chargeth and accuseth the lompishnes and slowe indeuors of the causaries, through their quiett rest and peaceable disposition, relented in their rancor and malice againste the papistes, and the kinge, and that he accused he Hugonott princes for not destroyinge and killinge the Princes of France, and that in all their assemblies and meetinges they neuer once make any motion of peace, of God or his religion, but rather of warres, troubles, tumultes and sedition: they alsoe complotted the kinges death at Amboise, before the edict of pacification which was anno 1561.

6. The like is read of that vnluckie Luther who wrote and wished the Citizens of Hall, and the subiectes of the Bishopp of Mongontia, to putt away, or murther their Archbishoppe. And called Cæsar, and all Christian Princes Traitors, Tirantts and reprobatts: he exhorted all those princes to wash their handes in the bloode of the people and Cardinalls. Did not Farnar the kinges gouernor at Rochell, betraie that towne assone as he was infected with Caluinisme, and made the same to rebell againste their kinge by the instigation of North? Beza commended deceite, and that it is

*Sur. hist.*

*Idem ibid*

*Sur. hist. 1568.*

it is good to embrace it ſometimes, videlicet, to faine one thinge, and to doe another. Alſo they ſoughte to murther Herreſtus Archbiſhop of Coline, and the Prince Ferdinand his brother. What ſhall I ſpeake of the two kinges of France, Francis and Charles the 9. how often haue they rebelled againſt them, and how often haue they ſoughte to murther them, as they haue don Frances Duke of Guiſe by the inſtigation of Beza, and by the treacherie of Poltrot, for they neuer ſpare to plott the like tragedie, when they can bringe the ſame to paſſe, by whatſoeuer meanes of diſsimulation, deceite and hipocriſie as they write in their owne Bookes? Were not the Miniſters of Scotland in the fielde with the Earles of Anguiſh and Marre, and others againſt his maieſtie that nowe is? was not their deteſtable plott of betraying their Countrie and Prince, detected by the Earle of Gory, before his death? For that conſpiracy did not Patricke Galoway miniſter of S. Iohns, on Andrew Pollard ſubdeane of Glaſco, Iames Carnihel miniſter of Haddington, Andrew Hea perſon of Panfroe, Andrew Meluin profeſſor of diuinity in S. Andrewes, and diuers others cheefe miniſters of that Contry, flye into England, and for this traitrous fact were there receaued and cheriſhed? Did nott Robert Pont and walter Baquanquell miniſter, by the inſtigatiō of Iames Lanſon cheefe preachers oppose themselues against his maiesties edict that now is, publickly at Edenborough? Did not these ministers demaund of his maiestie, also to be admitted in parleamẽt aboue their bishopps? Is it not one of their cheefe articles, that it is heresie for any kinge, to call himselfe head of the Church within his realme?

*A prosecution of the laste Chapter, that heresies are the causes of troubles and disquiettnes.*

## CHAPTER V.

THe other reason of these reuolutions, is the fauor that kinges & Princes doe giue vnto heretickes, when they doe not in time punish them, or at leaste ridde their Countries of them, because that kinges or Princes, growinge forgettfull of God, haue a more respecte to their temporall commoditie, then vnto the will of God, or the good of his Church, thinkinge by their owne industrie and reason of estate, themselues and their estate to be sure and secure: yet God almightie doth often suffer them to fall into great miseries, and calamities, and their kingdomes to be ouerthrowen and ruynated. Valent. an Arrian Emperor did send against the Goathes his great Captayne, and a deuout Catholicke, who was called Traian, and was ouercome by them, when he re-

*Tripert. hist. lib 8 cap. 13. Theod. l. 4*

he retourned he reprehended him, & called him Couard, he answered, it is you, and not I that haue lost the victory, for that you haue forsakẽ God, he gaue the victory to the Barbarians against thee. Also the said Emperor in his iourney against those Goathes, was mette by the holy Monk called Isacius, who said vnto him whether doe you goe hauing God against you, for against him thou makest this warre &c. giue ouer thy warres against God, and he will giue ouer his warres against thee.

*Theod. l. 4 cap. 30. Metaf. in vita Isacij*

2. Valentinian the younger who being deceaued of his mother Iustine, did fauor the Arrians, was put to flight by Maximus the Tyrante, who made himselfe Emperor, and soe Theodosius the great did write vnto him, that is was goods iust iudgment, that he should suffer that infamy, for that he forsooke the trewe Christian catholicke religion, and fauored the enemyes thereof. So Winceslaus the 12. kinge of Bohemia by his false reason of estate, giuing tolleration vnto the hereticks, was both by them depriued of his life and kingdome.

*Theod lib. 4. cap. 14.*

*Carol. Sig. lib. 9.*

*Eneas Syl. hist. Bohemia. c. 35.*

3. Boleslaus Prince of Polland, did suffer the people of Prusia to renounce their Christianitie, and liue in Idolatrie, for which they sent him a verie riche present but was after ouerthrowen by them, with the ruyne of all the kinges and the nobilitie of Polande.

*In Chron. lib. 6. hist. Polo.*

Nice-

Sabel. Æneas 8 c.6 Carol. Sig de regu Genebr. in Chron. An. 607.

4. Nicephorus Cōstant for that he fauored secrettly the Manichees was ouerthrowen & slaine by the Bulgares. The like example wee haue of Gessulte Duke of the Lombardes, who for fauoringe the Arrians, his armie beinge ouerthrowen, was slaine himselfe by the Auoros, whose wyfe betraied the Cittie wherin shee and her husband liued, to the captaine generall of them, thinkinge to marry him after: but shee first was dishonored in her bodie, and then hanged a liue vppon a Gibbett.

Num. 16. 4. Reg. 17. Geneb. in Chron.

5. Not without cause did God say vnto Moyses, departe from the Tabernacles and tentes of wicked people, and touch nothinge that belonges vnto them: God sent liōs amoungst the people of Samaria for hauinge Idolls, both to kill and destroy them, wherfore the Cittie of Parris hath this for a monumente engrauen vppon her gates, one God, one kinge, one faith, one lawe.

2. Reg. 11. Isa. 39.

6. Hence it is written by the holy Ghoste in these woordes. All the kinges, besides Dauid, Ezechias, & Iosias sinned, and that the kings of Iuda forsakinge God, and his lawes, were with all their kingdomes deliuered vnto others, and their glorie to strangers: and although Dauid did committ adulterie, and soe Ezechias alsoe offended by his ostentation, yet because they forsooke not their faith, and religion, nor made shippwracke thereof, it is not counted

that they sinnned, for that to forsake our faith, is the greatest sinne that is.

*That God doth extende the rodde of his wrath vppon Princes and Common welthes infected with heresies.*

## CHAPTER VI.

1. THe sore punishmente and affliction, by which almightie God, doth prosecute this wickednes, many authors doe treate therof, especially the ecclesiasticall histories, and of late Thomas Bozius. For none are more prone to wantones & riotous misdeameanors, which euerie Heresie bringes with it then Princes, because commonly they are brought vpp without due chastisment and correction, and because each man soothes them to flater and misreporte the truth. As also because they are loath to submitt themselues to the ecclesiasticall discipline and censure of the Church, or to acknowledge anny spirituall power in the Church of Christe, to constraine them as it doth heretickes, of whom it is said by the prophet and proued by experience, that the nation and people that serueth her not, shall perish: whosoeuer obeieth her not must be accounted as Ethniques: & yet (to mantaine their absurde heresies) they doe labour to deface

*De signis Eccl. lib. 5 cap. 11. signo 16.*

deface and infringe her authoritie as wee see in all ages, yea onlye the disobeinge the authoritie of the Church, and the censure of S. Peter, and his successors, is the cause of all the heresies, that euer were, and the Princes that hearken vnto them, and forsooke the Church, by defendinge them, were vtterly destroyed with their states. For what punishment doth he deserue, that vnder the pretence of Christianitie, makes warre against Christ, and he that shall call himselfe the childe of the Church, destroies and rayses a flame therein? all which examples it were to long for me to repeate, for I will not alleadge here, the dolfull and ruynous example of Constans and Valens Emperors, who were enemyes of the Church; neither of Hunericus kinge of the Vandals; neither of Basiliscus the capitall enemie of the Councell of Chalcedon, who was depriued of the Empire by Zenon; neither of Zenon himselfe, which was buried aliue by the comaundement of Ariadne his wife, nether of Heraclius which in the beginning was a catholicke, and a valiant Prince, but after became an heretick, and lost soe many noble Prouinces in the Easte, and dyed of a most shamfull disease; nor of Anastasius, vnto whom a vision did appeare of a terrible and dreadfull man, with a booke in his hande who opened the booke, in the which the name of the said Anastasius was written, and

*Ionas 1.3. ibi. Ion & Paulus Diaconus lib. 7. c. 1. Carol. Sig. lib. 7. de occid. imp.*

and ſaid theſe wordes, vnto him; For thy errors and peruerſe faith I will cutt ſhorte of they life 14. yeares, & blotted out his name, who a little afterwardes, was ſlaine by a thunderbolte; neither will I handle the miſerable end of Conſtantius Copronimus, who was ſoe forſaken of God, that he cried out and ſaid, I am caſt into a fire, which ſhal neuer be quenched; neither of Philip, who impugned ſacred Images, degraded and put from the Empire, and his name taken out of the Coyne, and publicke Roules, yea and blotted out of the Maſſe; neither of Leon Iſaurus Emperor alſo, who loſt the occidental Empire, and was the cauſe that Gregorie the 3. did transfer it to Germanye, and the ſame tranſlation confirmed by Leo the 3. Nether of George Pobibratius, who perſiſtinge in his obſtinacie, and perfidiouſnes, was excomunicated by the Pope, and loſt both the kingdome of Bohemia and his life. The like did happen alſo in our dayes, to Chriſtiernus kinge of Denmarke, who forſakinge the Catholicke faith, was depriued both of his kingdome and libertie. For omittinge more exāples, it is well knowen, that God doth not only puniſh wicked Princes with woefull endes, but alſo their kingdomes and Prouinces, who embraced hereſies. And although the inconſtāt courſe of this chaungeable worlde is ſuch, that noe kingdome or monarchie can houlde it ſelfe

*Sigib. An. 776.*

*Iou. lib. 7. de vitis illuſt. Geneb in Chron. Cedrenus & Zonaras greci ſcriptores. Mich. ab Iſelt hiſt. Surius hiſt.*

ſelfe ſtedfaſte, or firme, or free from reuolutions, yet fatall chaunce, and alteration for the moſt parte proceeded of hereſies & diuerſitie of ſectes in religion, and this you ſhall know by hiſtoricall diſcourſes, if you will rippe vpp and peruſe the anciente beginninges of theſe diſaſtorous euentes.

*The reuolutions of of the Romane Empire began by the Goathes.*

2. The Goathes were the firſte, that made their inundation in the prouinces of the weaſt Empire, and made alſo hauock of the auncient monumēts of the Romans, the monarkes thereof abuſinge their powerfull force and ſtrenght, accordinge to their owne ſenſuall affections, and beaſtlie concupiſcence: eccleſiaſticall cenſures beinge not obeyed, for that the moſt parte of the Chriſtian Princes, held in contempte (by the inſtigation of heretickes then ſpringinge vpp) all ſpirituall regiment and iuriſdiction of the Church. The Goathes themſelues as longe as they were Catholikes, were moſt valiant conquerors, but by the inſtigation of their Buſhopp called Vlfillus, an Arrian hereticke, they were preſentlie deuided by ſectes and diſcordes, and ouercome by the Hunnes. Atilla their kinge like a moſt raginge ſwifte ſtreame ouerunning, and deſtroying all where he came till, he had diſpoſſeſſed thoſe Goathes of all the Prouinces they had taken. And when thoſe Goathes came to Spaigne and ouercame it, the heretické called the Priſcillians, infected it. When the

*The Goathes brocken by hereſie.*

*Carol. Sig. de occid. imp. l. 8.*

*Libr. 2. ſacræ hiſt. epiſt. 93.*

the Vandalles destroied Affrike and made themselues Lordes of the same, the hereticks called the Donaitstes, peruerted and sowed their heresies there. *Africi abundantes immensa multitudine Donatistarum quibus pracipites se dederunt in gurgitem turpitudinum, vnde Dei vindicta factum est, vt dedignantes sanctis obtemperare sacerdotibus &c.* As Saluianus Bishopp of Marcell and Cæsar Baronius seteth downe, when Affricke did abounde with infinite swarmes of Donatistes, by which they were owerwhelmed in the gulfe of all filthines: by meanes whereof, and for not obeyinge the holie priestes, the wrath of God was executed vppon them, and by the iuste iudgment of the almighty, they were rendred vp to the mercilesse and bloodye handes of the Barbarians. Likewise when the Franckes breakinge out of Germanie, wasted all France, the heresie of Vigilantius tooke footinge therin. And when the Longobardes occupied and spoiled Italie, diuers sortes of heresies were embraced there, especially against the councel of Constantinople, and Chalcedon. As also when the Normanes violentlie rushed into France, the French shewed litle obedience to the Churche.

*Africque confounded by heresie.*

*Ann. 427. & 428.*

*France destroied in time of heresie.*

*Italy destroied by heresie.*

3. But what shall I say of that wreatched and miserable tyme, when the Sarasins breakinge out of Arabia, despoiled and wasted the most notable partes of all Asia, with

*The Easte in a miserable estate by heresie.*

soe many sharpe stormes and troublesome garboiles? Was not this pestilente generation, first set abroache by the instigation of wicked Mohomett, borne for the ruyne and destruction of mankinde: whose force (the diuision and heresies of Nestorius in the easte encreasinge) more, and more encreased? Was not Sergius, for that he was exiled out of Constantinople for that heresie of Nestorius, the helper of this Mahomett against the Catholicke religion, as Luther and Caluine doe now a daies helpe and further the Turcks and other reprobates of that stāpe and liuerie, against the Catholicke Church? Was not such a tumultuous broyle and confuse disorder made at Constantinople by the procurement of the heretickes, the verie tyme when Nestorius hatched his heresie, as that Marcellinus doth reporte, 445. that the sedition was soe greate, that many kild themselues? yea such a slaughter was comitted, that the streates did stincke with dead carcasses, famine, & pestilence, disease, & wreacke of all thinges, which did happen there, the chefe Church of that noble Cittie beinge burned: soe as no sooner did that ougly blossome bud forth, but that noble Cittie of all Citties (before that heresie) most florishinge, was become most lamentable and desolate, for heresie euer bringeth with it abhomination, and desolation, as the sacred scriptu-

*Marcell. in Chron. Cesa. to 6. An. 445.*

*Marc. 24. Daniel. 9.*

res proue. Afterwardes in the yeare of our Lord 1453. the said Cittie was distroyed and taken by the Babylonian and Turkish Pharao, for that they held diuers heresies against the holly Ghoste, and for that they did breake from the determination of the Councells of florence, wherein they were reunited vnto the Romaine Church, their Emperor Iohn Paleogus, and their Patriarche consentinge thervnto. And as longe as religion did florish in Greece, their Empire alsoe did florish, and when religion failed, their Empire was tourned vnto a perpetuall moorninge and pittifull slauerie of vnsufferable tyrantes, and Sathanicall crewe of Turkish burden. And in the yeare 1558. the Prouince of Libonia which was of the knightes of our Lady de Teutonica, was taken by the Duke of Muscouia, when they loste their faith and ymbraced the heresie of Luther. Hungarie and Trasiluania may to their great cost beare wittnesse also that this is true, who forsakinge their Catholicke faith, are ouerwhelmed with the infernall thraldome of turkish Pharao.

*Constantinople taken.*

4. Wherfore should I not spreake of great Brittaine, sith Gildas that most eloquente and aunciente trewe writter of that tyme, saith. The Brittaines brought for their aide the Englishmen againste the Pictes, and Scottes, at which time it was altogether destroied by the heresie of Pela-

gius a Moncke of Bangor: for chastisment wherof, almightie God suffred the Englishmen to turne the edge of their sworde vppon those that sent for them, for their defence, and dispossessed them of their Countrie, and made themselues Lord thereof, & called Brittanie Englande by their owne name: soe that heresie did soe increase in that kingdome about the tyme that S. Gregorie did send S. Augustine, and other holy mounckes thither to preach the Catholick faith therein, that 9. hereticall busshoppes beinge there before them, no one catholick bishopp was found. Ireland allsoe when the Englishe in kinge Henry the 2. gott footinge therein did little esteeme the sacred censure of holly Church, and the noblemen of that kingdome did vsurpe Church liuinges as may appeare by S. Bernard. Edward the 3. beinge a most glorious kinge, his end was pittifull, his heire kinge Richard after infinitt sedition, contention, and blood-shedd of the nobilitie and others was deposed and made away, the bloody diuision of the howse of lancaster, & yorcke came in, and endured almoste one hundreth yeares, with the ruyne not only of the royall lyne of Lācaster, by whom especially Iohn Wittcliffe a peruerse hereticke condemned in the Councell of Constance, was fauored at the beginninge, but with the ouerthrowe of many other Princes and familie,

*Vortiger was the leader of the Church when old Britans weare destroyd.*

*Bern. in vita Malachiæ. Dolman. Lib. 2.*

milies and most pernicious warres and garboyles continued both at home, & abroade with the losse of all the states and Prouinces of France. Thomas Walsingham settes downe the Commotion of King Richard the 2. his time, againste the nobilitie and Cleargie vnder their seditious Captaines, Iacke Strawe, Watt Tyler, and the rest, & soe againe vnder other kinges whilest this heresie lasted, and namly against the two most valiant Catholicke Princes Henry the 4 and 5. his sonne: in the first yeare of whose rayne, to witt kinge Henry the fift, Iohn Stowe wryteth thus. That the fauorers of Witcleefe his secte did nayle vpp scedulles vpon the Church doores of London containinge, that there were an hundreth thousand readie to rise against all such as could not awaye with their secte. The first tumultes of Pollardes and Wicliffians in England were Anno 1414. and hereon followed the open rebellion of Sr. Iohn old Castle and Sr. Roger Acton and others in S. Giles filde by Holborne, neuerthelesse this secte could neuer take hold or preuaile in England, neither then or after: vntill foure pointes thereof, beinge renewed by Luther and Zuinglius, the later, I meane Zuinglius his secte, was admitted in kinge Edward his dayes.

5. Did not the kinge of Denmarke bringe the people of Thretmarse which were a

free ſtate,into a vilde thraldome, after they were Lutheranes? whereas,as longe as they were Catholicks they were a free ſtate of their owne. S. Ambroſe alſo doth proue the ſame as Cæſar Baronius doth alleadge, and ſaith: *Vna cum hæreſi in regna cladem inuehi,& cum fide catholica ſalutem ferri &c.* that noe ſooner hereſie was broughte in, then preſentlie the kingdomes where it crepte in, were ouerthrowen, and quickly deſtroied: and were againe reſtored and eſtabliſhed by Catholique religion. This he ſpake of the Empire of the eaſte, *ſicque in occidente accumulari victorijs Gratianum*: that in the weaſt by the Catholique religion, Gratianus the Emperor did encreaſe in many victories. *Cum in caſtris excubant cum gratia atque precibus Sacerdotum ſancta religio*, when the prieſtes in the Campe did watch in prayers and other exerciſes of ſacred religion. Contrariewiſe you ſhall ſee the happie and floriſhinge Empire to decay and caſt topſie, turuie when the Emperor did fauor heretiques, or at leaſte when they were ſlacke in defendinge the Catholicque religion, *adeo*, ſaith he, *vt perſpicuè intelligas claram victoriam religionem penitus conſequi, hereſes triſtes erumnas euocatas ab inferis ſecum ducere*, ſoe as you may plainly perceaue, that by religion victorie was gotten, and alſoe by hereſie woe and wreake, and all other dolfull calamitie and helliſh confuſion was broughte

*Ceſ. to. 4. An. Chriſti 379. S. Amb. in libris ad Gratianũ. Cæſ. Baro. to. 4. 379.*

to

to the worlde. The like assertion hath holie Basill, *quod enim comune est ciuitatibus omnibus vt cum semel hereticis aurem præbent, mox vna cum heresi dissentiones, rixæ, ac mala omnia fugata recta fide paceque subintrent, ita planè Neocesarientibus accidit*, that which is incident to all Citties, when once they giue eare vnto hereticques, presently trewe faith beinge once abandoned dissentions, debates, and all other mischeefes will creepe in, as wee see an euident example to those of Noecessaria, what heresie, saith he, but which was contraire to the traditions of S. Gregorie the greate, his wordes be these, *aduersaria traditioni magni reuera Gregorij.* *Basil. ep. 69. Cæs. Bar. to 4. An. Christi 363.*

6. The like miserie yow may read by the Epistles of those holy Sainctes videlicet Mileuitanus, Eusebius and Basilius to the Bushoppes of Italie and France, and related by Cæsar Baronius, in which he wrote as followeth. *Miserandus status orientalis ecclesiæ &c.* The state of the Easte Church is to be pitted, for not onlie two or three Churches haue fallen vnto this dangerous tempest, but that mischeefe of heresie hath extended her selfe from the bondes of Illiria vnto Tebaira, the seede of which was first sowed by Arrius, and afterwarde was gathered by wicked people, who haue broughte forth wicked and pernitious fruites: and discipline and doctrine of pietie and goood life is ouerthrowen, all bondes and obligation *tomo 4. An. Christi 371. many heresies in the East.*

of honeſtie and charitie is confounded and decaide, none hath ſway ouer others, but he that is moſt wicked: whoſe rewarde is the gouernment of others, and he that exceedes others in blaſphemies, exceedes all in the epiſcopall dignitie. The grauitie of Biſhopps is loſt, the honeſtie of Paſtors is gone, the holy Canons of the Church are troade vnderfoote, the releefe of the poore is altogether abuſed to their filthie vſe. The occaſions of all ſuch miſcheefes are laide open by Sainƈte Optatus Mileuitanus, who hauinge reckoned the bloody and cruell aƈtes of the heretickes called Donatiſtes, he applied that place of the ſcripture vnto them. *Veloces pedes eorum ad effudendum ſanguinem*, their feete are verie ſwifte to ſhedd blood. And then addeth *In Maritaniæ ciuitatibus &c.* In the Citties of Mauritania by your procuremente they were affrighted with many garboiles, Children were kilde in their mothers bellies, men were murthered and torne in peeces, matrons were violated, infantes were ſlaine by riping vp their mothers bellies, behould this your Church which was mantained & vpholden by cruell and bloody Biſhoppes, whoſe greateſt furie, and vildeſt faƈte, although in their eſtimation it ſeemed the lighteſt, was extended vnto that which was moſt ſacred & holie, which thoſe ympious ſacrilegious, and Sathannicall Biſhoppes haue violated, they

*Cruelty of heretiques Mauritaniæ videl. the ſea coaſt of Affrique next vnto Europe.*

they caſt the Euchariſt vnto dogges, not without manifeſt tokens of Godes diuine reuenge, for thoſe dogges beinge enkendled with rage and madnes, inſulted vppon their maiſters. *Hi ſancti corporis*, guilty of the holy body, and toare them in peeces, and ſome of them did caſt forth out of a windowe a boxe of holy Chriſme to breake it, but the angelicall hande by Godes protection preſerued it from beinge broken, amoungeſt the ſtones; The like ſacriledge the hereticks of our daies beinge miſled by the ſame Sathanicall ſpirite doe cōmitt and perpetrate. And hauinge recorded other wickednes of thoſe hereticques in all theſe execrable procedinges, ſaid this bleſſed Author, the Biſhoppes, and prieſts felt their greateſt ſmarte, ſoe that the Biſhoppes, and prieſtes beinge taken away, the people would be vtterlye and eaſilye deluded, and ouercome, for how can the flocke defend themſelues when a multitude be gouerned without a rector, noe otherwiſe then the Paſtor beinge taken awaye, the ſheepe would be a bootie for the wolfes: by your wicked aduiſe the faithfull are diſarmed, the prieſtes are diſhonored and ſpoyled of that reuerence, which ought to be giuen vnto them in honor of his holy name, by whome they were ordayned. For they were made perfecte by him and worthie of all reuerence; and therfore you abuſe Godes vocation, and with all hostilitie you proceede vtterlie defacinge Godes worcke, destroyinge by the engines and inuentious of your malice, Godes diuine ordinance, and therfore of you it is said. *Quoniam quæ tu perfecisti, ipsi destruxerunt*; for whatsoeuer thou (ô God) broughtest to perfection, they brought to destruction. What is more wicked then to exorcise the holy Ghoast, to breake altares, to cast the Eucharist vnto brutish beasts? And in the 9. booke he saith; *Quid enim tam sacrilegum est quam altàre dei in quibus vos aliquando obtulistis, frangere, radere, & remouere.* What is more sacrilegious then to breake, to cutt, and remoue thoses altares, vppon which somtimes your selues did offer, in which the suffrage of the people, and the members of Christe are caried, in which the omnipotent God is called vpon, in which by your praiers the holy ghoast comes, and descendes? *Vnde à multis pignus salutis æternæ &c.* from whence comes the pleadge of euerlastinge saluation, the safeguarde of our faith, the hope of our resurrection is receaued; for what is the alter but the lodginge and seate of the body and blood of Christ? All these you in your furie and rage haue either torne, or brocken, or remoued: wherein hath Christe offended you whose bodie and blood dwelled there for certaine momentes? You haue brocken Challices which carried the blood of Christe,

*Psal. 10.*

Christe, and conuerted the vse therof and forme into Lumpes, exposinge them to a wicked sale, and haue herein redoubled your villanie by sellinge them to filthie women, pagans haue boughte them to tourne them for to make sacrifice to their Idolls. O wicked acte, ô vnspeakable villanie, to take from God, that which you haue dedicated to Idolls, to robbe Christe to the end you might exercise more sacriledge. What horrible feates haue you practised towardes sacred Virgins, consecrated and dedicated to almightie God, from whome you haue taken away they veyle of their dedication? Thus farre this blessed Sainćte, Optatus Milleuitanus, as Cesar Baronius doth relate. The like tyrannie was exercised and atchiued by Iulian the Apostate Emperor, for he made an edićte, which he diuulged in all places, to robbe, and spoyle Churches, againste whom S. Nazian. framed his speech thus. Your edićt was aswell priuatlie and aćtually executed, as it was publiquely diuulged, and proclaymed against sacred and religious howses. For that I should let slippe, the spoylinge and ransakinge of Altares, takinge awaye of all religious ornaments, and donatiues from sanćtuaries, and holy places, which were a bootie vnto his vnsatiable and greedie desire, which was putt in execution by wicked instrumentes, his impietie

*Cæs. tom. An. Christi. 362.*

*Naz: oratione prima in Iul.*

pietie and couetousnes instigatinge him thereunto, he determined alsoe to depriue the Christians of all libertie, and trust in the common wealth, and to inhibitt them of all Councells, marcketts, assemblies, and iudgmente: neither could any haue the benefitt of thies thinges, but such as woulde sacrifice to Idols. O lawes and law makers and kinges, who as the beautie of the heauens and splendor of the sunne, yea as the brething of aire, by common clemencie exposed, to all; and that truly superabundantly, do you so make the vse of lawes equall to all free men, and reuerenced of all, that you decree to depriue Christians of it, that beinge euen tiranically oppressed, they may not be able to exact the penalties, nor to sue any one for any wronge or extortion done against them. *For to practise these thinges, the hangman, yea that homicide* (said, the said Sainct) pretended iustice, and did vse a
*Matt. 5.* collorable defēse of scripture, in soe doinge.
*Rom. 12.1* For he alleadged the places of scripture
*Cor. 6.* that Christians ought patientlie to beare
*Matt. 10.* all wronges, to suffer al iniuries, rather then once offend any. That wee should possesse nothing or haue any propriety, and that we should despise, and sett at naughte all thinges, that either the eare doth heare, or the eye doth see, or the flesh can feele, that wee should render good for euill, if a man would strike vs vpon the one cheeke, wee should

should turne the other, and that wee should possesse nothinge but our Cloake, or our Coate, with many such places.

*Ruff. lib.1 cap. 32.* *Annianus lib. 22.*

7. But that of all most to be deplored, he inhibited Christians the schooles of Rhetorique or Grāmer, wherfore the said Naz. did most bitterlie inueigh against him sayinge: what reason haue you of all men most incōstant, to goe about, to take away from Christians the vse of learninge, thus far S. Naz. against Iulian. Alsoe in the yeare of our Lord 366. when the Arrian heresie was promoted by the fauor of the Emperor Valens, the said holy man made a most eloquēt Oration, the title whereof is called (*Ad sancta Laminia*) when that heresie (said he) was guarded and adorned with the ymperiall crowne of Valens, and soe like a sawsie princocke grewe soe insolente, not vnlike the daughter of Herodiades, beinge not contented with the gift of the head of one S. Iohn Baptist, was made droncke with the bloode of many Bishoppes and holy people, in the repressinge whereof, the blessed Sainct shewed his great desire, and as in the state of the Easte Church in those daies if the Lord of hoastes, *non reliquisset nobis semen &c.* had not left some seede with vs, wee had bene like to Sodom and Gomora, and as they had S. Naz. and holy Basill, so we haue most vertuous holy and learned Doctors to represse this wicked heresie, which as it doth

doth exceede all the heresies that euer were in ympietie of Doctrine and wickednes of life, so it doth alsoe surpasse all Heretiques, Infideles, Turcks, and Iewes in all bloody feates, cruell exploites, Babilonian confusion, tragicall designmentes, diuelish purposes and plottes, yea and strange inuented lawes newer heard of before, with their most rigorous execution.

You see the fruite of heresie the complotters and compassers thereof, the cheefe Architects of her detestable practise, her effiminacye & luxurious wantones, her inducementes to all abhominable pleasures and licentious libertie, her bloodie imbrumentes and lamentable tragedies in euerie countrie, where shee was nourished and inuented, which brought a masse of miserie and calamitie with it to those places that receaued her, the shipwracke of whose opulente and aboundante fortunes, can beare wittnesse thereof, obstinate pride, presumptuous and turbulent spirittes, dislike and disdaininge of good order and sound discipline, contempte and despising of authoritie, curiositie and affectation of noueltie, discontentment and disquietnes of mindes, through ympatience of filthie luste, and other malignante priuate humors, which were neuer inspired by the spirite of God, but by the suggestion of the diuill who was the cause thereof.

*Of the*

## *Of the miseravle death and endes of such as deuised and defended the protestant Religion, as also other heresies.*

## CHAPTER VII.

1. THe first plotter of this heresie was Martine Luther, whose life as it was most wicked, soe his ende was noe lesse miserable. He after that he had surfeyted through one nightes gossopinge, himselfe beinge fild intemperatlie vpp to the throate, was found dead in the morninge with his wife, and as it is suspected was choaked by her. Henrye Zuthphan, which was the first that brought Lutheranisme into Breame, was afterwardes burned at Meldorphe in Thretmarsse Anno 1524. Hulderique Zuinglius, an Apostate Priest, in a furious skirmish, beinge leader of the Tigurians, whome he brought to that dolefull battle, animatinge them to the combatte, as surmountinge their aduersaries in multitude of souldiers, were all ouerthrowen, and he himselfe was found dead amoungest the dead carcases, and was cast into the fire, soe as he suffred a double death by fire and sworde. Of whome the Epitaph was made thus.

*Luthers death.*

*Occubuit patrio bellator Zuinglius ense,*
*Et gressa est armis gens populosa suis.*

*Zuinglius death.*
*Conrad. in Theolog.*
*Fox. pag. 444.*

Zuin-

Zuinglius the Warior was slaine in the fielde
And the sword of his Countrie did pierce,
His side by many bloody batles fought:
His Country vnto ruine he brought.

*Genebrardus in Chron. 2. fol. 72.*

Cōradus a Lutheran protestant writeth, that God manifested his iudgmente vppon Caluine, euen in this world, whom he visited in the rodde of furie, and punished him horribly before the dreadfull hower of his vnhappie death; for (saith he) God by his powerfull hand did soe stricke this heretique, that beinge in desperation, blaspheminge, and cursinge the name of God, and calling vppon the diuills, he yelded vpp his wicked ghoaste, hauinge an vglye and filthie apostume in his priuie partes, out of which there issued such a number of loathsome and stinckinge woormes, that not any could abide to come nere him: this farre the said Author; Carolastadius was slaine by the diuilll, as the ministers of Basill themselues doe witnesse. Oecolampadins also a married Mounque of the order of S. Brigget, and one of the firste and principalest Architectes of the protestante religion, was founde slaine in his bedd, by his wyues side, and that by her or rather, by the diuill himselfe, as Luther thincketh. The Duke of Saxonie, and the Lantgraue of Hesse, which were the cheefe promotors and Patrons of lutheranisme, were in battell vanquished by Charles the fifte, depriued of

*Caluins dreadfull death.*

*Carolostadius his death.*

*Epistola de morte Carolastadij.*

*Oecolāpadus death.*

*Luth. lib. de Missa priuata.*

of their dominions and kepte in prison by him many yeares. The Prince of Condye, and the admirall of France, which were the Patrones of the secte of Caluine, or hugnottes in that Countrye, were alsoe vanquished and ouerthrowen in the field with their kinge, after many other ouerthrowes and slaughter of their adherentes, the one, I meane Condie, was slaine in the battell of Iarnan, the other was kild in a triumph at Paris, his carcase beinge caste from the topp of a high howse, his necke beinge broken and his body torne, was drawen by a rope through the streates, and hanged not much vnlike to Iezabell, where also the Prince Montgomery was beheaded, beinge a great defender of Caluinisme.

*The prince of Condys death.*

2. The same miserable end they tasted alsoe that were the patrones of this wicked ghospell in England as Queene Anne Bullen Thomas Cromell, the Duke of Somersett, and Thomas Cranmer Bishopp of Canterburie. The first was accused, arraigned and conuicted of a filthie incest, her supposed Father beinge the iudge thereof, and by his sentence putt to death, who was so besotted of her filthie loue. The next was condemned and putt to death for heresie and high treason by kinge Henry the eighte vnto whom he yealded himselfe both soule and bodie before, by the lawe he made himselfe videlicet, whosoeuer should be cast without

*The death of such in Englãd as were patrons of Protestancie.*

into the tower, he ſhould be put to death without examination. Fox act and monuments 563. whome he called the wall and defenſe of the proteſtant Chruch. The third which was the Duke of Somerſett, beinge vncle vnto kinge Edward, his vicar generall in all eccleſiaſticall cauſes and protector, and as it were kinge of the whole Realme, was depriued of all auctoritie, and publiquelie beheadded. The laſt which was Cranmer, after abiuringe his wicked hereſie at Oxford by Queene Marie. Robert Barnes, Thomas Gerrard, William Ierom, beinge the firſt cheefe inſtruments that Kinge Henry the 8. had to perſwade the people touching the kinges ſupremacie in eccleſiaſticall cauſes, were by the ſaid kinge Henrye burned afterwards, and the ſaid Barnes beinge there at the ſtake, and the flame readie to lay hould vppon him, ſaid theſe words. By our meanes the kinge was made abſolute kinge of England, whereas before, he was but halfe a kinge, and for our paynes, this is the rewarde wee haue. Anno Domini 1540.

*Prince of Aurengs death.*

3. The Prince of Aurenge that was the author and enginer thereof in flanders, was ſlaine with a piſtole in his newe wyues lappe, by Balthazer Gerard.

Ludouicus Naſconius, brother to the ſaid Prince, and the cheefe author of the rebellion of the ſaid lowe Countries, in the battle

battle of Mokens which he lost, the Spaniardes hauinge gotten the victory, was burned in a little cottage aliue, whether he fledd for safeguard. In that battle also, his Brother Henry perished, as his brother Adolphus, did perishe a little before in Frislād, William Lumenus the Earle of Manssil, after defilinge his murtheringe hands with the cruell death of many religious persons, priests and Catholiques in Holland and Zeland and other places, was kild by an Englishe dogge that himselfe brought vpp.

4. The Bastard of Scotland, Iames Earle of Moray, that troubled Scotland with the same heresie in his greatest triumphe beinge accompanied with 500. horsemen at Lith, was shott by a gunn, by which he was slaine, the author therof escapinge harmles: & notwithstanding he was admonished the night before, that there was such a plot laid for his destruction, yet he did not shunn it. Iames Duglas Earle of Morton, a great defender of Caluinisme and persecutor of the Catholiques, was beheaded at Edenborough for treason against his maiesties Father.

*The Earle of Moray his death.*

5. The first that broughte it to Denmarque, was Christiernus king of that Countrie, who was depriued of his kingdome, and banished by his subiectes, and beinge by the intreatie of Charles the fifte, and Henry the 8. his kinsmen retourned home,

was apprehended of his subiectes and caste into a filthie caue, where he ended his life most miserablie.

*The first who preached protestancy in Ireland.*

6. The first that euer preached protestancie in Ireland, was George Browne, who in kinge Harries daies was made Archbishoppe of Dublin, the capital cittie of the kingdome of Ireland, and the first sunday he preached the protestant religion at Dublin, he made a Catholique sermon at Christs Churche, and desired his audience neuer to beleue him, if (through frailtie of the flesh, feare of the Prince, or loue to temporall interesse) he should preache the contrarie: and the verie next sonday ymediatly followinge, he preached protestant religion, which was nothinge els then a deniall of that which he preached the sonday before. Vnto whom some of the Aldermen of that Cittie said. My lo. doe you not remember that yow wished vs not to beleue you, if happilie yow should preach the contrarie of that yow preached the sonday before? To whom he answered sainge, I must needes haue done soe or else haue lost my liuing. This man, when Queene Marie came in, vpon his recantation, was restored to his liuinge, & the night that his Bul came ouer, he was found dead in the morninge. Some said he died for verie great ioy about mid-night when vppon the suddaine he receaued newes that he was restored to his

Arch-

Archbisshoprique.

7. The Duke of Norfolke which gaue his verditt for the supplantinge of Catholique religion, and for the aduancinge of the protestancye with Queene Elizabeth in her first parleament assembled for that purpose beinge therunto solicited by his Brother in lawe the Earle of Arundell, vnder pretence to marrie the said Queene, vnto whome shee made a promisse of mariadge, if the said Earle with his faction would helpe her, for the alteringe of religion, was arraigned, condemned of highe treason, and was beheaded for the same, which a certaine matrone meeting him goinge from the pleament prophesied, tellinge him that he should neuer haue a better ende or rewarde of them, for whome he gaue his voyce and suffrage against the Catholique religion. And the said Earle beinge frustrated of his purpose, and deceaud of his hope, died soone after for verie greefe, and without issue, and perhapps if he should haue liued longer, he should haue tasted that Cuppe for his labour that his brother in lawe had done before him. The said Duke his eldest sonne called Philip Howarde and Earle of Arundell, was arraigned condemned of highe treason, and died in the Tower of London.

*Norfolks his death.*

*Sanderus de schismate Angliæ.*

8. Sr. Iohn Perott, when he was Lord presidente of the Prouince of Mounster in

Irelande, was the first that caused the parish priests, and other incombents of porte Townes in that Prouince, to ymbrace the English seruice, which when they tould him they could not vnderstand the English, his aunsweare was, that they should chatter like Geese. He putt to death a prieste called Sr. Thomas Coursie, vicar of Kinsale by marshall lawe, for that he went to perswade Sr. Iames fitz-Morice to restore the praye which he had taken frō Kinsale. This man in the middest of his greatest honor beinge lorde deputie of Ireland, and one of the preuie Councell of England, was apprehended, arraigned, and condemned of high treason, and died verie miserably in the tower, his landes and goodes beinge all confiscated.

Deut. 31. 9. *Laudate gentes populum eius, quia sanguinem seruorum suorum vlciscetur & vindictam retribuet in hostes eorum.* Let the gentiles praise gods people, becaule he shall reuenge the blood of his seruants, and will pay home, their enemies with a reuenge: as may appeare by the horrible and dreadfull punishment of all other persecutors and heretiques. As of Pharao the first persecutor of Gods Churche Exod 14. Of Dathan and Abiron the first Scismatiques Numeri 16. of Iezabell 4. Reg. 9. of Antiochus 2. Machab. 9. Of Pilat who killed himselfe, as Euseb writes lib. 2. c. 7. & declares the destruction

of

of the Iewes which Iosephus setts downe *lib. de bello Iudaico.* Of Herod Ascolonita who was eaten by woormes after he had slaine his wyfe and Children and went about to slay himselfe as Iosephus declareth lib 17 antiquita cap.9. Of Herod the Tetrach who lost his kingdome liued in perpetuall banishment accordinge to the said Ioseph. lib. 18. cap. 14. of the daughter of Herodiades read Nicheporus lib. 1. caput. 20. of Herod Agrippa read Act. 12. Nero Domitian and other wicked Emperors who persecuted the Church, eyther slewe themselues or else were slaine by others as all histories doe wyttnes. Dioclesian for that he could not destroie the Church, for verie greefe gaue ouer his Empire, the Emperor Maximianus and Maximine were chasticed with such a horrible disease, that the Pagan Phisitians said it was the plague of God, as Eusebius wrieth in Chronico. & lib. 8. hist cap. vlt. & lib. 9. cap. vlt.

10. As touchinge old heretiques, they tasted the like dreadfull death. Simon Magus when he would flye, by the praiers of S. Peter, he fell headlonge downe and was kilde Egesippus lib. 3. caput. 1. de excidio. Also Arnobius l. 2. con. gentes. Manicheus the heretique was flaid aliue by the kinge of Persea, because intendinge to cure his daughter, he kild her. Epiph. heres. 66. Montaine, Theodotus & their prophets, hanged

themselues Euseb. lib. 5. hist, cap. 19. The Donatistes that cast the Eucharist vnto dogges, were torne in peeces by the said doggs. Optat. lib. 1. Parmenianum. Arius goinge to Church, went to purge nature when together which his excrementes, he did cast fourth all his intralles and presentlie died, as S. Athanasius wittnesseth, oratione cont. Arrianos & Ruff. lib. 10. hist. cap. 13. And although there may be some hereticall Princes or Common wealthes that haue not felt as yett any of these calamities, and perhappes they bragge and boast of their great pleasures and prosperitie, noe otherwise, then the woman doth in the Apocalipes, *sedeo regina & vidua non sum, & luctum non videbo*. I sitt as a Queene, I am not a widdowe and I shall not bewaile, trulie at lenght after all their great security they shall haue a sudden fall, and let them take example by the dolefull ouerthrowe of others that haue lead their liues in pleasures, and haue abused their power againste godes Church, and the members thereof, let all men knowe that all heresies be fatall, ominous, and vnfortunate, especially to the first professors thereof. *Vltio sanguinis seruorum tuorum qui effusus est introeat in conspectu tuo gemitus compeditorum.* Psal. 7.

*Whether there be nothing that the Protestants affirmatiuely beleeue, confesse, and professe, but the Church of Rome doth beleeue the same, and cannot be denyed by Catholiques, but that they are most auncient and consonant with the word of God.*

## CHAPTER I.

1. ALl Heretiques say (as Lactantius reportes) that their owne religion is verie good and agreable to the word of God, and better then others. It is naturall to euerie beast according to Pliny to thinke his owne shape more beautifull then the rest, yea such as are most deformed, thinkes themselues most beautifull, as the Apes doe, which though they do counterfeit mens shapes, or gestures neuer so much, cannot be said to haue the forme of men: so these sectaries, though they like Apes in imitation, haue taken from vs some, partes out of the Masse as may appeare; and in their spirituall courtes, visitations, conuocations, and excommunications (although in deede none ought to excommunicate, but he that can absolue, they by their owne doctrine cannot absolue therfore they cannot excommunicate) yet for all that, they

*Lib. 4 diuinist. cap. vlt.*

*Plin. lib. 8. cap. 4.*

*Plin. ibid.*

cannot be said to haue the trewe forme of Religion, or the trewe Church, for the ecclesiasticall forme, and gouernment of your Protestantes is reiected by the Puritantes, contemned by the ministers of Caluine and Beza, and other Hugonottes of France, as part of the reliques of Antechrist, your common praier booke being called by them in contempt, the missall of England. Yf such as yow yourselues cales protestants, do disprooue your Religion to be altogether against the woord of God; how much more will the Romish Church, say the like who doe differ from yow almost in euerie point?

2. In the Booke of dangerous positiōs in the 9. chapter set forth Anno 1593. by Doctor Bancraft of Canterburie, it is alleadged, that the Puritants do say of the comon booke of publick praiers videlicet: that it is full of corruption, and that many of the contentes thereof, are against the woord of God: the sacramentes wickedly mangled, and prophaned therin; the Lordes supper not eaten but made a pageant, and stage play: that their publique baptisme is full of childish superstitious toyes: & so many Puritants did write against it, that England will neuer do well vntill that booke be burned. Also the superintendēt of Rateburge, and the cheefest ministers in Germanie hauing read Caluines woorckes printed Anno

*1. admonitio ad Parla. pag. 9 41. 43.*

An. 1592. at Francfort. *In timore Domini* saith he, *legi & relegi, dico in Christo Iesu &c.* I haue read and perused them the space of 23. yeares, I auoutch it before IESVS Christ, saith he, that all the Caluinistes do nourish in their breastes the Aryan & Turkish ympietie, and that they open windowes and gates, for Arianisme and Mahometisme, as our bookes publickly set forth do manifest the same; and so brought an example of Adam Newser, the cheefe Pastor of the Church of Hedelberge, who from a Zuinglian, be came an Arian, and afterwardes a Turcke: which three sectes I meane Caluinisme, Arianisme, and Mahometisme, another protestant Doctor calles them three briches of one cloathe, and that fellowe hauinge gone vnto Constantinople Anno 1574. did writt that none became an Arian which first was not a Caluinist, and brought example of Seruetus Blandrata, Alciatus, Franciscus Dauidis, Gentilis, Gribaldus, Siluanus and others.

*Caluinistarum lib. 3. in pref. Apost. lib. 1 a 2. fol. 9.*

*Vid. f. 9.*

*Iohn Schutz in lib. 50. Causarum causa 48.*

3. There was printed a booke 1586. at Iena in Saxony by a Lutheran minister, the Tittle whereof was. An admonition from the woord of God, that Caluinistes be not Christians, but Iewes, and baptized Mahometts. Also 2. yeares afterwards, another was setfourth at Tubinge by Philipp Nicholas minister; the tittle whereof was a detection of the Caluinian sect to agree with the

the Arians and Neſtorians in the groundes, and foundations of their religion, and that no Chriſtian can ioyne with the Caluiniſtes, but that he muſt defend the Arians and the Neſtorians. Bernardinus Ochinus being the firſt principall Apoſtle of England in kinge Edwardes his dayes, with Peter Martyr, Martyne Buzer, and Paulus Phalangius, vnto whoſe direction both the vniuerſities of England were comitted, did oppugne the bleſſed Trinitie, the deitie of Chriſt, and of the holy Ghoſt, ſo as Beza called him the fauorer of the Arian hereſie, and a ſcoffer at all Chriſtian religion: yet neuertheleſſe one Iohn Bale, ſomtimes Biſhopp of Oſſorie in Ireland, calles this Bernardin, and Peter Martyr, the light of the Ghoſpell of England, and Caluine ſaith that the ſaid Bernardine was borne for the happines of England. It is ſaid alſo in the ſuruey of the pretended holy diſcipline printed at London, that the ſect of Caluiniſtes is a cancker, and another Thalmud, which by their wicked rebellion againſt their lawfull Princes, haue founded their ghoſpell, and Church, which by their intollerable arrogancy do oppoſe themſelues againſt all ſacred Doctors, againſt all venerable Councells, and againſt all the floriſhing Churches, that euer were from Chriſt his tyme vntill our dayes, & that there is no place of Scripture, which they do not wreſt from the lawfull ſenſe

*Sleid. hiſt. lib. 19. An. 47.*

*Okinus in lib. dialog. Zanchius de vno Deo.*

*Beza ep. 1. par. 11.*

*Bal. in pref. act. Rom Pontific.*

*Calu. lib. 1 de ſcandalis pa. 136*

*An. 1593. pag. 44.*

ſenſe thereof neuer before knowen by the Church of God, and that it had beene good for England, that none brought vpp in the filthie ſchoole of Geneua or Scotland, had euer entred into England.

4. Conradus a Proteſtant, writeth that Caluine ſayeth, that the merittes of Chriſt cannot preuaile againſt the iudgment of God; Alſo he affirmed Caluine to write, that the blood of Chriſt was of no force to blott out ſinnes, and that aboue 1500. yeares it was putrified fo. 84. 85. 87. Curæus in ſpongia fol. 250. Eraſt. pag. 29. Fridericus Boruſsius pag. 45 Oſiander in confeſſ. haue written the like impietie, with many other blaſphemies which yow may read in the Caluini Turciſmo lib. 4. c. 22: Other Lutheran writters, make bookes of the contradictories and contradictions of Caluine, the tittle whereof is called *Laberinthi inextricabiles contradictionum*. The intricatt Laberinthes of contradictions. Luther ſaith that the Zuinglian doctrine and ghoſpell was from the diuill, & that the diuill made an inſtrument of him, and that by him he did gouerne and raygne. In another place he called him. *Perdiabolatum, indiabolatum, & ſuperdiabolatum, ſceleratum cor, & mendax os habebat.* That he was perſathaniſed, inſathanized, and ſuperſathanized, and that he had a wicked harte and a lyinge mouthe. So Zuinglius calles Luther, a falſe prophett, an incor-

*Caluini. Theolog. lib. 1. f. 85*
*Luth. lib. de Sacrament. fol. 376.*
*Orthodox. Conf. en le Tigurine tract. 3. fol. 127.*
*Luth. tom. 6. Ienueſ. Germa. fol. 257.*

*Zuinglius tomo 2. in exegesi ad Luth & in corresponsione ad Luth. lib de Sacra. Ort. conf. eccles. Tiguri trac. 1. f 35. Ibid. fol. 106.*

incorrigible heretique, foolish, arrogant, blasphemous, and lyinge, a diuell, a beast, a deceauer, a seducer an Antechrist. Luther also said of him againe. I had rather burne, then to hold the opinions of Zuinglius and Oecolampadius and all other wicked bedlam companions, & cales them Archdiuills, and so he saith. I that am nowe readie for the graue, God is my wittnesse, and this will be my glory before his tribunall, that I haue labored the condemnation of all these hellish people, videlicet, Carolastadius, Ziuinglius, Stinckfeld, and those that are at Tigur and Geneua; yett these are the cheefe pillers of the protestant religion. Luther also did diuorce a certaine wooman beinge married to a Zuinglian, and bid her to marry whome shee listed, for that saith he, it is not lawfull for yow to marrie an infidel. Agaihe, It is said of Luther and Melancthon that there is asmuch difference betwixt them as betwixt Sumer and Winter. Zuinglius said, that nothing did greeue him so much, as for being called a Lutheran. Brentius saith, beinge a kind of a Lutheran, *nos Zuinglianam* &c. Wee cannot ymbrace with a safe conscience, the heresie of Zuinglian and Osiander. Do not the madeburgenses inueigh against the Zuinglians, for denyinge the reale presence? and doth not Luther saye, that the holy scriptures are corrupted of the Zuinglians? In the Duchy of

*Colloquiũ Altẽburg. elect. 3. resp ad Saxo. Zuingl. tomo 1 in exempl. ar. 18.*

*1550 Cẽturici 4 Elizab Reg. dedicata.*

of wittenbergue where Brentius was superintendent, an edict was proclaimed against the Sacramentaries. The ministers of Ienua did exhibit a petitiō to the Princes there, to haue an assemblie, to the end they should condemne the Sacramentaries and the Ziuinglians as aduersaries. And in the yeare 1560. in that Towne, Hesutius printed a boooke against the Sacramentaries. Caluine did also writt a booke against Hesutius. William Clebitius did writt against the Lutherans with this tittle. The ruyne of the papacie of Saxonie videlicet, Lutheranisme. Also Iohn Sturmius writt against the Lutheranes. Brentius writt against Bullenger. The Lutheranes of Saxonie in their Conuenticle, did condemne Albert Hardenburg a Zuinglian of heresie. In Transiluania Lutheranes are against the Sacramentaries, and the Sacramentaries against them. The people of Breme in Saxonie after they were in Lutheranisme, fell to Caluinisme and banished all Lutheranes,

5. Neither can they excuse themselues their debate or strife to be of thinges indifferent, or of ceremonies, or such like smale and trifling thinges, but of the cheefest pointes and articles of our faith. For Nicolas Gallus a protestant preacher of Ratisbon, doth declare the same, saying. *Non sunt leues inter nos &c.* Betwixt vs ghospellers, it is not in light thinges wee differ, nor

*In suis Thesibus ita scribit.*

nor our variances are not of thinges of ſmale moment, but concerninge the cheefeſt articles of Chriſtian religion, videlicet, of the lawe of the ghoſpell, of iuſtification, of good worcks, of the Sacraments, of the vſe and order of ceremonies, which by no meanes can be decided or compoūded. Wherfore Luther ſaith wee eſteeme ſeriouſlie & in good ſadnes, all Zuinglians, heretiques, and alliens from the Churche of God. Beza calles Lutheranes, Eutichiās, and Neſtorians. And Caluiniſtes doe count Lutheranes no better thē Manychees, Marcioniſtes, & Monotholites who were oulde heretiques, Illiricus ſaith, *Caluiniſtarum liturgia non vno ſacrilegio viciata eſt*. The liturgie of Caluiniſtes, is not ſpotted with one only ſacriledge: the like cenſure Conradus giues of the ſame liturgie. Oecolāpadius moſt bitterly writes againſt Lutheranes, and alſo in the like bitternes Lutheranes write againſt him by Brentius. Iohanes Pomeranus did allſo write againſt Brentius. Did not the Duke of Saxonie puniſh moſt ſeuerely Zuinglians, by the inſtigation of Luther? Did not the kinge of Denmarcke expell Caluiniſtes out of Denmarke? and did not Caluiniſtes expell Lutheranes out of Count pallentine his Countrie? did not Weaſtphalus write moſt bitterly againſt Caluin, and Caluine againſt him 1557. intituled, An admonition vnto Weaſtphalus,

*Luther. Theſ. 77. 1545.*

*Illir. in confeſſ. Ang. 17.*

which

which if he ſhall not obey, he ſhalbe counted an heretique? and the ſaid Weaſtphalus hath theſe woordes: no doctrine is more ſpatiouſly diſperſed, none with greater deuiſes and hipocriſie defended, none that ſeduceth more people with greater errors, then the falſe doctrine of the Sacrament of the Euchariſt. Oecolampadius ſaith theſe woords of Luther and his ſect. Lutheranes, ſaith he, they haue a kind of ſhewe of the woord of God, but the right word of God they haue not, and herein they followe other heretiques who relies, althogether on the woord of God. Did not (after that Caluiniſme was admitted and ymbraced in Tranſiluania, and Hungarie) Arianiſme, and Sabellianiſme take place there? Doth not Lannoy ſay that the cheefeſt point of all theſe fellowes doctrine is, that Chriſt is not God, nor by any meanes begotten of the ſubſtance of his Father? Did not Brentius ſay: that the doctrine of the Zuinglians and Caluiniſtes, tendeth directly to Athiſme, Iudiſme, and Mahometiſme? Some others ſay, that this ſect of Caluine, tendes to Ethniſme, others to Atheiſme, as Iohn Whitgifte affirmeth, with which ſaith he, England aboundes. And Bullenger writeth, ſuch is the diſſention betwixt Zuinglians and Lutheranes, that none hereafter will beleeue ought, but what it pleaſeth him.

*En la reformation des fauſſes ſuppoſitions lib. 2*

*Brent. in recognit. prophetici & Apoſtolici, item in Bull.*

*def. tract. 3. cap. 6. pag. 278.*

*Bullenger. contra Brent. c. 1.*

6. Doe not Proteſtantes ſay, that the Engliſh-

*Admonitio 2. ad parla vide act in Comitijs parla. Londini. An 1593 f. 10. 11. 12. 13.*

Englishmen as longe as they be of this religion, which they professe, that they are not baptized, nor ought to be counted Christians, the ecclesiasticall regiment therof to be as vnlawfull, as that of antechrist, and that the Church of England is so prophaned, and like Babell gouerned by the power of Sathan, and not by the order of Christ, that none in which there is any sparcke of Godes grace, or any feelinge of conscience can liue in England, and that all that liue in England, and that goes to their Churches, and whosoeuer that heares the sound of their belles, ioynes with them in their Churches, are conuocated thither by the name of Antechrist, and are addicted

*Ibid. f. 15.*

vnto the slauerie of Babylon and Egipt. And a great protestant minister, in a supplication sent to the last Queene, said that shee was one of those Princes which made profession of the ghospell, but opposed her selfe against the ghospell, and that they are flatters that tell her the contrarie: and if that shee could get the crowne without the ghospell, it is doubtfull, whether euer the ghospell would haue footing in England. Stanchares said, that Caluin iumped very well with Arrius, and that both of them makes the Sonne of God to pray in the diuine nature, that he is a minister, a Bishopp, and a mediator in that nature, and that the ministers in Germany, Hungarie, Transiluania,

uania, and Polonia, haue celebrated many Councells and sinodes to take away our Catholique faith of the Trinitie and mediator, and haue made many bookes full of Arrian blasphemies to that effect. In Heluetia the ministers of the Church of Tigure, do professe the Arrian faith. Tiguri epist. ad Polonos, Anno 1560. And all those that are of the Church of Geneua and Tigurie are Arians, thus fare the said Stancharus. Many saith Iosias Simlerus, (*in pref. lib. de eterno dei*) that are brought vpp in Geneua, are become Turckes, for they came vnto Polonie and so they did ymb ace Mahometisme, as Ochinus, Alamanus, Blandrata, Paulus Alciatus, and Gregor. Paulus, minister of the Church of Cracouia, who hauing denied the Trinitie, became a Turcke, as Gonesius and Gribaldus, and Franciscus Dauidis, for this last was superintendent of Hungarie. So did Adam Nimser the cheefe superinten. of Heydelberge in Palatyne of Rhene, with his fellowe Iohn Syluanus, who of Caluinistes, became Turckes and went to Constantinople, where they made open profession thereof, and protested that the religion of Caluinistes, tended directly to Turcisme, and before these people went out of Palatyne, they subuerted many great preachers, who by their meanes became Turckes, and taught publickly the Alcoran in Germanie. Also Iohn Socius being brought vpp at Ge-

*Tiguri ep. ad Polonos Anno 1560.*

*Stan li. de mediatore fol. 38.*

neua did not only preach the Turkish religion, but also published bookes confirminge the same. So did Volanus beinge brought vpp in that place not only become Turcke himselfe, but also set foorth bookes defendinge Turcisme, and auoutched, that he learned the groundes of his doctrine from Caluine and Beza. Lucas Sternebergerus, a minister of Morauia did the like, for 1. he preached against the Trinity, tooke away all inuocation thereof, because saith he, there is no mention thereof made in the Scripture. 2. that Christ was not God but man, but more excellent then all the prophetts. 3. that the holy Ghoast is not God 4. that wee must not keepe holy dayes to Sainctes. 5. that wee must keepe Saterday holie, and not Sonday, because saith he, God so comaunded in the scripture: and by the same argument he brought in Circumcision.

*Prateolus in Elench. Alphabetica lib. 10 c. 12.*

7. And did not some of the familie of loue, publishe these articles at London, that Christ is not equall with his Father, as by Caluine his interpretation they proue it, and that Christ in no sort is God. 3. That there is no Trinitie, & such as calles God, the Father, God the sonne, and God the holy Ghoast do speake blasphemouslie, for, say they, this is to professe there are three Godes. Did not Thomas Lyth, Cartwrites companion, for puritanisme in the weast part

part of England, as the other in the North part (being brought to Ireland by Sr. Iohn Dowdall to Yonghull a Towne in Mounster in Ireland) say that the Angell Raphaell was a witch, and that the blessed Virgin Marie was not blessed amoungest all woomen: with many other such blasphemous speechees? And lastlie, did not this Turkish doctrine, infect many Northern Prouinces by the infection of one Lastus, which was a cheefe superintendent of England in king Edwardes dayes? This man being a Disciple of Zuinglian, did labour in Polonia to abolish the blessed Trinitie, and the Deitie of Christ, by whose instigation Nicholas Badzudius the Duke of Olice and Palatine, did of vilanie send one Martyne Secouitus with letters to Bullenger and Caluine, to ioyne with them in this wicked doctrine of taking away the Trinitie and Deitie of IESVS Christ.

*A further Confirmation, that these new gospellers, tende directly to Turcisme.*

## CHAPTER II.

1. THe first and cheefest of the Protestants did affirme, the religion of the Turckes to be far better then that of the Papistes, and when the Turcke inuaded Austria, Lu-

ther writt bookes, that the Germanes ſhould not take part with the Emperor againſt him, as *Eraſ. in epiſt. ad fratres Germaniæ inferioris*, ſaying. I had rather fight for a Turcke not baptized, then for a Turcke baptized: meaninge the Emperor Charles the fift. The rebelles of Flanders in the begininge of their inſurrection, againſt their lawfull Prince, Phillipp the 2. of Spaine, in their ſtandart, gaue the enſignes and Armes of the Turck, videlicet a ſiluer figure of the encreaſe of the Moone with this enſigne. *Plutoſt Turckes que Papaux*. Wee will rather be Turckes then Papiſts. How many proteſtant Princes did ſollicitt Amurate, and other princes of the Ottoman howſe, to come to Hungarie, Auſtria, and other places? Alſo, anno 1575. the Prince of Códe, being broken with France, and at Baſill conſulting with the miniſters there, what were beſt to be done to renewe the warres againſt his kinge and country, they gaue him counſell to ſubmitt himſelfe to the Turckes, and that by that meanes, the warres would be reinflamed againe. Did not in the ſecond rebellion of France the Hugonotes by many meſſengers ſeeke to bring in the Turcke to the ruyne of France & the reſt of Chriſtendome An. 1589. for ſaid they, our religion, is neereſt vnto your religion, vnleſſe that yow obſerue more faſtinge, and praying, vnto which our religion doth not tye vs: alſo that wee haue giuen

*Math. de Iannoy en la. repliq lib. 2. c. 13*

giuen a great impediment by the Princes of Germany who followed our Councell against Charles the fift: also wee dissuaded our kinges of France, not to giue helpe to his brother the kinge of Spayne in the warres of Millan seas against you, for the kinge of Spaine had the possession of those landes which he had lost about that sea, had not our Bretheren the gospellers of France dissuaded our kinge from helpinge him: also wee promise vnto you, whensoeuer it shall please you, that wee will be redie to broach any sturr or insurrection in Germanie and in France.

*Ex literis Constanti. ad Venetū patrium in fine libri de fucoribus Gallicis vide Surium 1568.*

Did not the English Ambassadour, labor to putt away the Iesuittes out of Constantinople, which are there for the releefe of poore christiās, whisperinge into the Turckes eares, that they would bringe his monarchie vnto great perill? And that the said English Ambassadour, sollicited the great Turcke to make warres vppon Spaine, the cheefe reason he moued, was it not that the kinge of Spaine was the Cheefe defender of the Romish Idolatrie, infestiue and offensiue to both of their religions, I meane the Protestant and Turkishe religion? And the said Ambassadour concluded, that if those Idolaters were ouerthrowen, all nations would become Turckes, and so both they and themselues would reuerence one God.

*Resp. ad iustā Britanicum. pag. 167. Par. 1584*

*An. 1567. Pet. Saxonius lib. inscriptio admonitio ad fideles Germanos caueant à Caluinistis*

## De Elemosina eroganda Sacerdotibus.

*Whether Papist Priestes do amisse in taking any thinge for their Masses.*

## CHAPTER III.

1. S. Paule did receaue offeringes (as the Church doth for their iust liuelyhood) from the Philippians, *bene fecistis*, (*inquit*) you haue done well communicating to my tribulation; and you allso knowe, O Phillippians, that in the beginninge of the Ghospell, when I departed from Macedonia, noe Church commmunicated vnto me in accompt of guift and receipt, but you onlie: for vnto Thessalonica allso once, and twice yow sent to my vse: not that I seeke the guifte, but I seeke the fruicte aboundinge in your accompt. He counteth it not meere almesse, or a free guift, that the people bestoweth on theire Pastors or preachers, but a certaine mutuall trafficke, as it were an enterchange, the one giuinge spirituall thinges, the other rendringe temporall thinges in lieu thereof: for so it putteth one the condition of an oblation or sacrifice, offred vnto God, and is most acceptable & sweete in his sight.

*Phil. 4.*

2. Behould the Apostle receaued of them

them godlie and charitable helpes, and meanes, and least he should only preach or pray for them, in lue of those corruptible guiftes, he avouched: *non quia requiro datum*, not that I ayme at any temporall guift or reward, but that I may perceaue the fruitt of your deuotion. Priestes are worthie of a double honnor, especially such as do labour in woord and doctrine, and by this comandement wee are bid, *vt boui trituranti, os non claudamus ac alligemus*, that wee should not stopp, or moosell the mouth of the Oxe that treadeth out the corne, for according to the counsel of our Sauiour, the workman is worthy of his wages, *D. Hiero: Homilia lib. 2. Comentar. in cap. 15. Math.* and as Waldensis saith against Witcliffe, he did not comaunde to sell spirituall thinges, *sed bouem edere de tritura*, but that the ox, or cowe should eat of his thresinge and labour. Hee doth not seeke herein the proffitt of him that receaues, but of him that giues, as S. Paule saith: yf wee giue vnto you spirituall foode, it is not much if you giue vs corporal St. Paule sought helpes for the Sainctes at Hierusalem, sainge. Now I go to Hierusalem to minister vnto the Sainctes: and as S. Hierom saith. *Si spiritualium &c.* why should not the Gentiles ymparte theire corruptible goodes for theire releefe, by whose dispensation they are made partakers of spirituall graces, and therfore the aboundance

*1. Cor. 9.*

of the one, ought to ſupplie the want of the other. And as the Apoſtle S. Paule ſaith. 2. Corinth. ca. 8. Exod. 16. & 28. Let in in this preſent tyme, your aboundance ſupplie theire want, and their aboundance alſo may ſupplie your want, that there may be an equalitie, as it is written, he that had much abounded not, and he that had little wanted not: his meaninge herein is, that ſuch as abound in worldly riches, ſhould communicate for ſupplie of other their bretherens neceſsities whatſoeuer they may; that on the other ſide thoſe whome they helpe in temporall, may ympart vnto them againe ſome of their ſpirituall riches, as praiers, and ſome other holly woorckes, & graces which is a happy change for wealthie people.

3. In the ix. Chapter of this Epiſtle, he exhorted the Corinthiãs verie earneſtly to giue their Almes for the releife of the Saincres, ſaying he that ſoweth ſparinglie, ſparinglie allo ſhall reape, and he that ſoweth in bleſsinges, of bleſsinges alſo ſhall reape, as it is written, he diſtributed, he gaue to the poore, his iuſtice remaineth foreuer. Almes is compared to ſeede, for as the ſeede throwen into the grounde, though it ſeeme to be caſt away, yet it is not loſt, but is laide vp in certaine hope of great increaſe. Reade the x. Chapter of S. Math. the x. and 16. of S. Luke. S. Ambroſe vppon the ſecond

cond epistle & 8. chapter, saith that the Corinthians had no more priuiledges, then other Churches, auouchinge that the laborer was worthie of his wages. Where behould that it is neuer granted to any nation to haue the Ghospell freelie preached vnto them, without giuinge reliefe to the preachers thereof, our Sauiour confirminge the same; *dignus est operarius mercede sua*; the labörer is worthie of his hyre.

4. But the heretiques of this time do imitate the Donatistes, to preach pouertie to others, when they gather riches to themselues, fayninge pouertie, but most falslie, as S. August. writes lib: 2. against Petilian, who saith. *Nos spiritu pauperes &c.* Wee (saith Petilian) beinge poore in spiritt, and careles of wealth, wee abhorr riches. Iohn Witcleffe (as Thomas Waldensis writtes of him) did obiect to the religious priestes, and preachers, that they did administer the Sacraments, and preach for gaine. *Waldensis de Scramentalibus cap. 99.*

5. S. Paule in the 6. to the Galathians saith. He that is catechized in the word, doth communicate to him that catechised him in all goodes, addinge, for what thinges a man shall sowe, those alsoe shall he reape. The woorcks of mercy be the seede of life euerlastinge, and the proper cause thereof. Loe here S. Paule shewes the great dutie, and respect that wee ought to haue to such as preach,

preach, or teach vs the Catholique faith, and not in regarde onlie of their paines taken with vs, but that wee may be partakers of their merittes, wee ought especially to do good to such, or (as the Apostle saith) communicate with them in all our temporall goodes, that wee may be partakers of
*1. Cor. 9.* their spirituall. Wherevpon. S. Aug. lib. 2. Euangel. 48. Knowe you not (saith he) that they which worcke in the holy place, eate the thinges that are of the holy place, and they that serue the alter, participate of the alter? So also our Lord ordeined for them that preach the ghospell, and such as labour at the alter, whose sacrifice, and oblations redoundes to the comfort of the Christian flocke, as also as are dedicated to serue God in recollection, praiers, and contemplations, or any other spirituall, and godly functions which also is beneficiall to the Church, and the faithfull ought to be releeued, and mantained by the liberalitie, and deuotion of them.

*Hiero. lib. 5. vig. Cap. 5.* 6. S. Hierom vpon that place of S. Luc. 16. saith. *Make vnto your selues frindes of the mammon of iniquitie, that when they shall fayle, they may receaue you into the heauenly tabernacles*. Which cannot be ment of the comon vulgar sorte of poore. *Num isti &c.* shall their pouertie (saith he) in the middest of their filth and nastines, whose raginge concupiscence is nothinge the lesse abated, pur-

chase,

chase vnto thẽselues those heauenly tabernacles, who do neither possesse thinges present, nor thinges to come? for it is not euery poore that is called happy, but the poore in spiritt of whome it is said. *Beatus qui intelligit super egenum & pauperem &c.* Blessed is he that hath a respect to the poore and needie, for in the euill day our Lord will deliuer him: which is vnderstood of the poore in spirit, who is ashamed to receaue what is offred vnto him.

*Psal 40.*

*Of prayinge vnto Sainctes: And whether the Church doth offend in praying vnto them.*

## CHAPTER IV.

1. DIcit Dominus ad Elephaz Themanitem &c. I conceaue a great displeasure against thee, and against thy two frindes, because thou hast not spoken right before me, as my seruãt Iob hath done. Take therfore 7. Bulles and 7. Rames, & go vnto my seruant Iob, and offer sacrifice for your selues, and my seruant Iob shall praie for you, and for his sake this fault shall not be imputed vnto you. The same Iob saith. Turne vnto some one of the Saincts. Iudas Machabeus did see Onias lyfting vpp his handes to pray for all the people of Iewrie 2. Mac. 15. The old fathers, and the children of Israell did praye

*Iob. 42.*

*Dan. lib. 4 cap. 16.*

in

Gen. 48. in the name of Abraham, Isack and Iacob, when it was said. *Inuocetur super eos nomen meum &c.* That is to say. Let my name and the name of my fathers, Abraham and Isack be called vppon these children. Afterwards they did call on the name of Dauid. And Christ by the intercession of the Apostles did heale the mother in lawe of S. Peter,
Act. 9. being attached with a great feuer. The said S. Peter at the intercession of the poore widdowes that were releeued by Tabita, did raise her from death to life, so as wee see the praiers of our Almes-folkes, and beades men, may do vs great good after our departure.

Ioh. 11. Did not the faith of Martha helpe her brother Lazarus dead, sayinge, did not I say to thee that if thou beleeue thou shalt see the glorie of God. S. Cyrill Hyerosoll: saith, *tantum enim, inquit, potuit illa sororum fides, vt mortuus à porta inferi reuocaretur*, the faith of the sisters liuinge was of that force, that the dead was brought back againe from the gates of hell.

2. When poore miserable sinners can pray, and be heard, what absurditie is it, that the blessed Sainctes nowe in heauen may be heard of God, and also prayed vnto, otherwise wee should denye them perfect felicitie, which is to be able to helpe, their poore frindes subiect to many calamities in this miserable lyfe. The old hereticke Vigi-

Vigilantius, and allo these newe heretickes of our tyme, do answere vnto this: the Sain&ts beinge lyuing in this world, and not when they be dead may pray, and be heard for the liuinge. But S. Hierom in the 3. booke that he made against the said Vigilantius, doth sufficiētly conuince them, sayinge. *Si Apostoli, &c.* yf the Apostles liuing in their bodies could pray for others, how much more now being crowned for their victorius Tryūphes. One man Moyses, obtayned pardon of God for 6000. armed men. S. Stephen the true follower of Christ, and his first Martyr, did desire pardon for his persecutors, and shall they be of lesse force, and their prayers lesse heard of Christ, enioyning his familiar and blessed presence? The Apostle S. Paule auouched that God at his intercession gaue vnto him 28. soules that were sayling in one shipp with him, and now being receaued to euerlasting glorie, shal his petitions and prayers be reiected in the behaulfe of them, that receaued the Ghospell of Christ?

3. Vigilantius (ympairinge the glorie, and felicitie of the Saincts) said, that a liuinge dogge is better then a dead lyon; but God doth declare vnto vs, that neither S. paule, nor other Saincts are dead in spiritt, which are not said to be dead, but at rest, and as it were sleepinge. So Lazarus which was to be raysed, was not said to be

be dead but a sleepe; did not Onias, and Hieremias after this life praie for the people? Soe Noe, Iob, and Daniell after this life, were appointed intercessors by God for the people. Did not S. Ambrose writt that the Emperor Theodosius after this life, was both a prelate, and a tutor with Christ, in the behaulfe of his children Archadius, and Honorius, and for their Empire which they possessed after their Father? Was not Abdias and Amos, intercessors vnto God for the younge heires of their succession Iosue & Asaph? who then can be in doubte but that Theodosius is a protector with God, in the behaulfe of his children, so as by the fauour of God, and the intercession of Theodosius, Archadius is nowe a valiant Emperor?

4. Wee must therfore honnor the saincts as the frindes of Christ and the heires of God, as the learned diuine S. Iohn the Euangelist saith cap. 1. As many as receaued
*Ro. cap. 1.* him, he made them the children of God wherfore not seruants, but children, and sonnes, if sonnes, then heires, yea heires of God, and coheires of Christ. And Damasus saith, when you call on the Saincts in your prayers, you must esteeme of them, as the shining light, more bright then the beames of the sun, which do see all good thinges by contemplatinge the vision of God: as in another place S. Aug. saith, *quid est quod non videt*

*videt, qui videntem omnia videt*; what is it, that he seeth not, that beholdeth him that behouldes all thinges? And S. Hierom saith. *Si propheta sunt, &c.* if there be prophetts, and that the word of our Lord be in them, lett them withstand the Lord of Hoastes: vpon which place S. Hierom sheweth, that a true prophett by his prayers may resist, our Lord, as Moyses stoode in the persecution against our Lord, that he might turne, and appease the wrath of his furie. Samuel did the like, & our Lord said vnto Moyses. Suffer me, said he, to strike this people for when he said suffer me, he giues vs to vnderstand, that by the intercession, and suffrages of the saincts, he may be appeased, and retained from putting his wrath in execution. *Lib. 5. Coment.*

5. S. Ambrose doth sett downe very larglie, the vertu, and maruelous effect of the intercession of the sainctes, and of the great victorie gotten by Theodosius by their prayers, and therfore he said, he had rather haue the prayers of the poore, then a stroung Armye, sainge that they are far stroung, because they as it were, bynde God himselfe. When wee direct our prayers vnto the Saincts, wee direct them vnto Christ, and as wee followe or reuerence no other in the Saincts but Christ, so wee do not inuocate, or pray any in them or by them, but Christ, which as he lodged in them *Lib. 5. epistolar. clero & populo Thess.*

*Gal. 1.* them when they were charged with their
*Ephes. 3.* corporall lumpe, soe much more nowe whē they are exempted from it. So as wee direct our prayers, and petitions vnto Christ in his Saincts, and by his Saincts, whether they remayne with vs in earth or whether they Triumphe with him aboue in heauen, vsinge the one as our intercessors, and acknowledging theother the bountiful giuer, for benefitts are asked of Saints, not as the authors, and giuers thereof, which wee reserue for God alone, but as intercessours onlie, as by our daylie Littanies wee say to God, *miserere nobis*, be mercifull vnto vs, but vnto Sainctes we say, pray for vs.

6. Secondarilie we say, that Saincts are our intercessors vnto God, but yet by Christe, and by the meritts of his death, and passion. And so the Church in all her collects, and prayers saith and concludeth without intermission. *Per Dominum nostrum*
*Dan. 3.* *Iesum Christum &c*. The three children in the fornace of Babylon did praye vnto God, *propter Abraham dilectum tuum*: for the intercession of Abraham thy beloued, and Isacke thy seruant, and Israell thy holie one. So
*Isayas 63.* prayed Isayas saying. Turne vnto vs O Lord by the intercessiō of thy seruants. So prayed
*Hester. 13.* Hester by the intercession of Abraham. Soe
*Psal. 131.* prayed Salomon by the meritres of his Father. *Memento Domine Dauid & omnis man-*
*1. Paral. 29.* *suetudinis eius*. Soe prayed Dauid himselfe, naminge

naminge Abraham, Iſaac, and Iacob, for his interceſſors, ſo prayed Elias ſo prayed Moyſes ſaying. *Recordare Domine ſeruorum tuorum Abraham, Iſaac, & Iacob*: ſo prayed Iacob callinge, and interpoſinge the name of his father Iſaac, when he did pray vnto the Angells to bleſſe his children, meaninge noe doubte but he ſhould obtaine godes bleſsing for them.

*Elias 2. par. 5.*
*Deut. 9.*
*Geneſ. 48.*

7. This the ancient fathers doe likewiſe teſtifie, ſayinge. *O ſancti Dei* (ſaith Origines) *vos lacrimis ac fletu plenis obteſtor*, with ſobbinge teares, and mourninge eies, I beſeech you that you will proſtrate your ſelues at Godes mercifull feete for me a wretched ſinner. *Heu mihi pater Abraham deprecare pro me ne definibus tuis aliener.* O bleſſed Abraham pray for vs miſerable ſinners. S. Gregorie Nazianzen neuer writts all moſt of any Martyr or Saincte, but praieth hartelie vnto them. So writinge the life of S. Cyprian the Martyre, before he was conuerted to Chriſtianitie, he firſt ſheweth that the Martyr finding himſelfe tempted with the beautie of Iuſtina the Virgin afterward martired with him, prayed moſt humblie, and deuoutlie to aſsiſt him in that combate againſt the fleſh, addinge moreouer, that he did aſsiſt himſelfe by faſting, & aflicting his bodye. S. Gregorie Naz. did pray alſo vnto him, ſayinge. *Tu nos è Cælo benignè aſpice*, behould vs from heauen moſt charitablie.

*Orig. lam. l. 2. in Iob.*

*S. Eph. Sermo. de sanctis martirib. Nect. orat. de Sanct. Theodoro.*

The verie like prayer maketh he to S. Athanasius and S. Basill deceased a little before him. S. Epiphanius writinge the life of certaine Martyres praied vnto them. S. Nectarius Archbishoppe of Constantinople, writinge an oration of Theodorus Martyr, prayed vnto him.

*Hom nat. apollog. c.*

8. After these men liued S. Iohn Chrisostome, who praied vnto S. Peter, and S. Paule: he praied vnto S. Peter also for the Emperor that then liued. S. Chrisostome in his liturgie hath these woordes. Apostles, Martires, Prophetts, Priests, Confessors iust men, and woomen which haue ended your fight, haue kept your faith, and obserued your promise and fidelitie to our Sauiour, pray for vs. &c. S. Cyrill Archbishopp of Alexandria did pray vnto S. Iohn the Euangelist in his sermon made in the festiual dayes of him in the councell of Ephesus. The Generall councell of Calcedon did affirme, that the holie Bishoppe S. Flamianus, Archbishoppe of Constantinople and Martyr, whose death was procured by Dioscorus Bishoppe of the same Sea, did pray for them vsing these woordes. *Flamianus post mortem viuit, Martyr pro nobis orat.* S. Hierom wrote the lyues of S. Hillarius and Paule and others, and prayed vnto them. Paulinus Bishopp of Nola wrote the lyues of S. Celsus and S. Felix. The same is confirmed by Prudentius in the Himnes of

*Cyrill. homil. in die Iohn. Concilij. Ephe. 428*

*Conc. Calci. 17. Au. 453. Socrat. lib. 7. histor. cap. 32.*

S. Laurence, that glorious Martyr of Spaine. And by S. Hipolitus. I pray read S. Gregorie Turonensis, and S. Gregorie the great to this effect. This is likewise auouched in the councell of Orleance in France, held vpon the yeare 512. the councell of Gerundia in Spaine, held the next yeare after. The fifte councell of Tolleto likewise in Spaine held vpon the yeare 640. the councell of Bracaren the second, held two yeares after that. Againe the councell of Ments in Germaine, held vnder Pope Leo. 3. and Charles the great anno 613. All these councells, I say, ordaininge Littanies and inuocation of Saincts to be vsed in solemne procession vpon certaine dayes in the yeare, as namely in the rogation weeke, three dayes before the Ascention The Greeke Church in the yeare of Christ 663. cap. 7. doth sufficientlie sett downe the sense of both Churches in these woordes. *Soli Deo Creatori adoratio &c.* Let adoration be giuen to God alone, but yet let a Christian inuocat the Sainctes, that they may intercede the diuine Maiestie for him. Of the heretiques called Albigenses S. Bernard saith. *Irrident nos hereticici quod sanctorum suffragia postulamus.* Heretiques scoffe at vs, because we craue the suffrages of Saincts. The said S. Bernard did pray holie S. Victor to helpe him.

*Can. 27.* *Cap. 3.* *Cap. 1.* *Cap. 9.* *Ber. hom. 6. in Cãt.*

9. Next wee ought to knowe, that amoungest all the Saincts there is none

whose petition is sooner heard, then the petition of the Blessed Virgin, at whose intreatie our Sauionr did worcke his first miracle, which is declared vnto vs by S. Bernarde, *O homo securum accessum habes apud Deum &c.* O man, thou hast secure accesse vnto God, thou hast the mother to the sonne, and the sonne to the father, the mother shewing her sonne her breast with her pappes, the sonne shewing vnto his father his side, and his woundes. Againe did not
*Tob.* 12. the Angell saie vnto Tobias, I haue offred thy prayers vnto God? Did not the Angell
*Daniel*. 7. also saie vnto Daniell, from the tyme that thou purposedst to chastice thy body before God, thy prayers were heard, and I being moued by them came for thine assistance. And your selues in the Comunion booke, doe auouche the same, hauinge translated the Collect which the whole Catholique Church in her masses doth vse vpon S. Michaell the Archangells day: which Collect is sett downe by your selues in your booke of Common prayers, the words are these. *Euerlastinge God which hast ordayned and constituted the seruices of all Angells, and men in a wonderfull order, mercifully grant, that they which alway do thee seruice in heauen, may by thy appointment succour and defend vs in earth,*
*Mat.* 18. *through Iesus Christ our Lord. &c.*

10. Did not Christ bid vs that we should not despise any of these little ones for I say vnto

vnto you, that their Angells in heauen alwaies do see the face of my father which is in heauen. Two manner of wayes S. Thomas sayes wee offer our prayers to any, *primo vt sit per eum petitio implenda, secundo vt per ipsum impetranda*, first that our desire by our prayers may be by him accomplished: secondarily that our desire may be obtayned by him. In the first manner wee offer our prayers vnto God onlie, because that all our prayers, and desires ought to ayme att godes graces, and glorie which none can giue but God alone: In the second manner wee offer our prayers vnto the holie Angells, and Saincts, that by their intercession, God almightie may be moued to take commiseration on vs; as it is alleadged by S. Iohn, saying. And there ascended the smoake of the incenses of the prayers of the Saincts before God. This also is proued by so many apparitions of Saincts made vnto the liuing, ymploring their helpe and protection as are registred by the holy doctors. S. Euthimius did appeare vnto Phillipp Deacon being cast away in the mediterranean Sea, and hauinge prayed vnto that holy S. for ayde, he tooke him by the hand, and brought him safe to the shoare. S. Bernabas did appeare vnto Anthemias Bishopp of Salamina thrice, beinge sore vexed by the Heretiques that were then rising vp. S. Peter did appeare vnto the widdowe Galla,

*D. Thom. 1 2. q. 83. ad 4.*

*Apoc. 8.*

*Apparitions of saincts.*

*Cæsar. Baron. An. 477. apud.*

*Cæsar. Baron. An. 485.*

*Ibid. 604.*

confortinge her, that her sinnes were forgiuen her. So the blessed Virgin Marie appeared vnto Seueriana, about her death, with many other apparitions which we both read and heare daylie &c. but I cannot omitt that which S. Gregory of Niss. relateth in the life of S Gregory Thaumaturgus, how that the blessed Virgin Mary, together with S. Iohn the Euangelist appeared vnto the said S. Gregory Tha. and did instruct him in the mistery of the blessed Trinity. S. Gregory of Tours declareth that the blessed Virgin appeared vnto the master carpenter that was set to woorck by Constantine the great to buyld a church in her honour, which was so huge as it was hard to be builded, but shee instructed him the manner how to bring the same to perfection. The like apparitions of other saincts do wittnesse. *S. Basil. in oratione de Sancto Mamante. S. Greg. Naz. in orat. in Iulian. S. Sulpitius in vita S. Martini. Theodoretus lib. 5. hist. cap. 24. Paulinus natal. sancti Felicis. S. Aug. lib. de cura pro mortuis habenda cap. 16.*

*Lib. de Anglia martyrum cap. 9.*

*Whether Papistes doe err in worshippinge and adorninge the reliques of Saincts, & whether they sell their Masse and prayers for temporall gaine.*

## CHAPTER V.

1. I Answere, that the holy reliques of of Christ, or his Saincts, are not vsed

vsed for temporall gaines, but for the spirituall consolation of the faithfull, which by those blessed reliques haue receaued great comforts and blessinges, as you may read, that the Iron chaines, the Napkins, yea the verie shadowe of the holy people, and Apostles did releeue many, and reuiued some. And if the deuout Christians doe offer any thinge at the Alter where those blessed reliques are kept, the same beinge *prætium peccatorum*, the price of their sinnes, and the releefe of the poore, they were not principally instituted for that purpose. *Act. 12. Act. 5. Mat. 5.*

2. This verie obiection against the Catholique Church, was first inuented by Iohn Witcleffe in England in king Richard 2. his time, as that most learned man Thomas Waldensis, then prouinciall of the or-order of the Charmilitts writeth, & his answere may serue aswell for you as it did for Witcliffe, which you shall read in the 2. booke. As for the Adoration or woorshippinge of Relicks, or Images, wee must consider that this adoration doth signifie honor, and reuerence which is comonly vsed both vnto God, and to his creatures, as S. Hierom saith. *Veni Bethlem, præsepe Domini & incunabile adoraui*. I adored the Cribb, and Craddle of our Lord when I came to Bethlem. Abraham adored the Angell that appeared vnto him, so did alsoe Moyses & Iosue, Nabuchodonoser adored Daniell. *Lib. de Sacramēt. tit. 12. Hieron. li. contra. Genes. 8. Exod. 3. Num. 22.*

S. Hierom alleadgeth the fact of Alexander the great in kneelling at the feete of Ioyda the high priest of the Iewes.

3. So Iacob dyinge did blesse his children, and adored the topp of his rodd. *Adore yee his footstoole*. Which rodd did signifie the holy Crosse. In the Apocalips it is also said. I will make them come before thy feete; which is mente of the Bishopp or Angell of Philadelpha. Againe the Temple, the Arcke, the Tabernacle, the Propitiatorie, the Cherubins, the Alter, the bread of proposition was adored, and because Vigilantius gaue not vnto the Saincts and Images, their due reuerence, he was condemned as an heretick of the Church of God.

*Psal. 98.* *Apoc. 3.* *Psal. 5.6.* *3. Reg. 8.* *Iohn. 7.* *Hier. contra Vigi. 2 syno. Nyceni.* *Aug. de ciuit. c. 8.*

4. It was a custome of holy people to adore great men, and Dauid adored Ionothan fallinge downe vpon the earth. So Abigall adored Dauid. Wee adore saith S. Augustine, those good people with Charitie, not with seruitude. So Iosue adored not the man that he sawe, but the Angell which he vnderstood. Elizeus hauinge receaued the new spiritt of Elias, did suffer himselfe to be adored of the children of the prophets at the riuer of Iordan. Balaã adored the Angel. Saule adored the soule of Samuell. Abdias honoured Elias. Porpheri an old enemie of Christiã religiõ, whom Iohn Witcleffe did obiect vnto the Church saith, that against the olde lawe of God, shee doth adore

*1. Reg. 20.* *Io. 5.* *Regum 2.* *Num. 22.* *3. Reg. 18.* *4. Reg. 2.*

adore the Angells, the lawe prohibitinge any adoration to be extended towardes any besides towards God, saying. *Deum tuũ adorabis, & illi soli seruies*, vnto whome saincte Augustine answereth, that wee liuing in this miserable peregrination, honor and reuerence the Angells, as the most blessed Citizens of heauen, neither doth the lawe of God prohibite the same, but rather commende it, the lawe only forbides that the due reuerence and adoration which is due to God, should not be transferred vnto any other creature, or that wee should offer sacrifice vnto it, which belongeth vnto God, which God did forbid the Hebrewes, sayinge. *Sacrificans dijs alienis eradicabitur.* He that offereth sacrifice to strãge godes, shalbe rooted out.

*Aug. lib. 10. de Ciuit. Dei, cap. 20.*

5. For wee must note, that the sence of adoring the creature may be considered either in the creatures themselues, or else as they be in the first patterne or example. Creatures in the first rancke as they are in themselues, they are neuer adored with that diuine honor, which is due to the Creator, and therfore the Image of any, or the Crucifix of Christ in it selfe, without a reflection made vpon the first paterne, or example that the same represẽteth, must not be adored, or reuerenced either by externall ceremonie, or internall affection or cogitation, as no kinge doth euer reuerence the legate, but

but only for the kinges ſake as our learned diuines do auouche. Alexander. 3. p. q. 30. nu. 3. ar. 3. &. 1. D. Th. 3. p. q. 25. ar. 3. 4. S. Caſtantis and others in that place. Albert. in 3. d. 9. ar. q. Bonauentura 3. diſt. art. 1. q. 1. Capreolus. q. 1. ar. 1. cond. 2. & 3. and others: alſo the councell of Trent. ſeſſ. 25. *Decreto de ſacris imaginibus*, alſo the 7 generall Councell beinge holden at Niſſe doth declare the ſame action.

6. Another reaſon that thoſe learned Doctours do giue, is that the Image without the paterne or example, cannot be adored: *Nulla res inanima aut irrationabilis &c.* noe irreaſonable, or inſenſible thinge without reaſon can be capable of any reuerence, worſhipp, honor, or adoration: but the Image in it ſelfe without the exemplar, or reflection, or relation to it, is inſenſible & without life, therfore without the exemplar, it muſt not be adored; For adoration, which is here meant, is accordinge to *S. Damaſcen. oratione 1. de imaginibus pag. 5. ſignum ſubmiſsionis & honoris*, a token of honor, and ſubmiſsion, and as Anaſtaſius Biſhopp of Theopo. beinge alleadged in the 7. councel. act. 4. Adoration is nothinge elſe, ſaieth he, then *Significatio honoris alicui exhibiti veluti* Emph*aſim* 1. (*ſimbolum*) then an expreſſe ſignification of honor, or worſhipp exhibited towardes any, which adoration is performed by two meanes videl.

*Antoninus Turrianus Caſtro. Alma.*

What adoration is.

by

by externall tokens, as the inclination of the body outwardlie, and internall will, and affection inwardly: for the outward appearance of this honor must be correspondent to the inward affection, so as by one act of adoration, wee reuerence the Image and the exemplar, so as the Image cannot be reuerenced but by the example.

7. This is the sense, and meaninge of saint Augustine, sayinge, who will adore the purple robe of the kinge beinge not vpon his backe, but when the kinge putteth it on his backe, he that will not reuerence the same with the kinge, shall incurr the danger of death. So in Christ I do not adore his humanitie alone, but ioyned to his diuinitie, and whosoeuer disdeyneth to adore the same, shall purchase the paynes of euerlastinge death, this saint August. This is also proued by Leontius, related in 4. action of the 7. councell, sayinge; *Si & ego &c.* In adoringe the Image of Christ, I doe not adore the matter, or colour thereof, God forbid. But I adore the liuelesse charecter and figure of Christ. S. Hierom also hath the like speeches. Why do yow reproue vs, saith he that wee should adore the dumbe stones, and wood eaten of wormes? Do you esteeme them to be blinde, which by these thinges doe Contemplate the Lord of our faithe? Doth not the Psalmist saye. Inclininge to the earth, wee adore his foote stoole

*August. de verbis Domini ser. 59.*

*Leont. in 4. Dialog. contra Iudæos.*

ſtoole which is the earth? And ſainɫ Thomas beholdinge the woundes of Chriſt, & the printe of the nayles, did forth with adore Chriſt, and ſo he did adore the creature with the Creator, ſayinge. *Dominus meus & Deus meus.* My Lord and my God. And if the diſhonor offered vnto his fleſh redoundes vnto God, why ſhould not the honor, done vnto the ſame fleſh redounde alſo to the perſon of God, being aſwel vnited in reſpect of the one, as of the other?

8. Neither is the humanitie of Chriſt onlie to be adored, but his Cribe, his Croſſe, and euery thinge that are ordayned to repreſent & expreſſe Chriſt vnto our vewe and vnderſtanding. Wherfore S. Damaſcen. ſaith. *Adorandum ſignum Chriſti &c.* Lett vs ſaith he, adore that which repreſenteth Chriſt, wher his ſigne ſhall be, there Chriſt himſelfe wilbe. Let vs therfore adore euerie thinge that are adioyned and adiacent vnto him, vnto whome herein wee yeld the reuerence. And therfore this holie ſainɫte ſaith, that Chriſt is preſent where his ſigne, or repreſentation is. And although he be not in bodie vnited vnto the Croſſe, or vnto the Cribbe, or vnto the nayles, as he was when he ſuffred vpon them, yet by a ſpeciall eminent vertue diffuſed into them, they ſhewe and declare his preſence more then any other thinges, and are expreſſe ſiggnes and tokens ordained, and inſtituted

to

to expoſe Chriſt to the vewe, and conſideration of the deuout chriſtian, betwixt whome and the harte of him that doth adore them, ther is both vnion and relation, different from any other thinge.

9. You will ſay with Iohn Witcleefe, that we ought not to worſhipp any but God: *Quia ſolus Deus adorandus.* S. Auguſt. doth anſwere you in his Enchirid. *Imo*, ſaith he, *ſolus Deus colendus eſt; & tamen homo colendus & terra colenda*, and in another place he ſaith, *Soli Deo, honor & gloria*: vnto God alone be honor and glorie. Euen as the heate of the fire though the wood be neuer ſo much cannot be infinite, that is to ſay, it can not be ſo much but it may be more, & more, ſo the adoration of honor that is giuen to any creature cannot haue any proportion with the adoration due vnto God. And although he ſhould adore a thing more then he ſhould haue done, it is not materiall, for a falſe adoration is nothinge as ſaincte Paul ſaith. *Idolum nihil eſt.* Therfore wee muſt conſider, that the word (*Solus*) alone, or onlie accordinge to the ſenſe of the ſcripture, and the interpretation of the Catholique Church, doth exclude thinges of another kind, for that thinge which is proper to that alone, cannot be common to manie, neither doth it expell all other thinges in another faſhion, *vt ſolus Deus adoretur*, that God alone ſhould be adored with that

*In Enchiridion.*

*De ciuit. lib. 10.*

kinde

kinde of adoration which is Latria, which is onlie due to God, and not to any creature, and soe nothing in that kind of adoration is adored *per se*, videlicet in it selfe as God, as in the Hymnes of the Angells, the Church doth sing of Christ: *Tu solus Sanctus, tu solus Dominus, tu solus altissimus, Iesu Christe.* Thow only art holly, thow onlie art Lord, and thou only art most high, but the Father and the holy ghost are included in that kind of adoration, and as S. Augustine saith: *Non est cui alteri*, none can challēge vnto himselfe that which Virgilius translated out of Sybilla her verses.

*Te Domine, si qua manent sceleris vestigia nostri,*
*Irrita perpetua, soluent formidine terras.*

By thee alone wee be released
From dregs of filthie sinne.
And eke the earth receaued peace,
From foe, and dreadfull feind.

10. Although God is said to be only good, onlie holie, only Lord, the onlie giuer of grace, all these perfections, and attributts be giuen vnto him, *per essentiam, & per se, & per naturam suam independenter ab omni alio*; by his essence, nature, and beinge independent of any other, yet there are manie soe called, videlicet, holie, Lordes, &c. who are so called, not by nature or essence, *sed participatiuè, & dependenter ab authore gratiæ*, but haue the same grace dependinge of God,

and

and so are made partaker of his grace, and iustification, of which iustification, God is the vniuersall, & efficient cause. The bloode and pasion of Christ, is the meritorious cause, the Sacraments are the instrumentall causes, the Priests are the administeriall causes, and gods glorie is the finall cause thereof. And although God is said to remitte sinne, because as the Philosopher saith. *Illi tribuitur actio, à quo dependet operandi virtus,* he is the worcker of the act, by whose vertue, and influence the same proceedes, yet other causes do concurr for the remision thereof in their owne kind, and operation, although god hath the cheefest stroake therein, of whome those causes principallie do depend, and so wee adore God with the word Latria. And as God doth communicate his goodnes vnto good men, and holie people, and neuer doth ymparte vnto them the excellencie of his goodnes; so wee neuer giue vnto them the excellencie of Latria which is diuine adoration, but wee giue vnto them, accordinge to their goodnes correspondent titles of woorshipp, and reuerence. So the holy Saincts wee worshipp with the stile and title of Dulia, which accordinge to *S. Thomas, est obseruantia qua maioribus honorem deferrimus.* Is an obseruation 2.2.q.102 q.103. by which wee offer honour to our elders, and betters, by which wee reuerence the Saincts in God: for he that honors the Mar-

tyr

tyr in God, doth honour God in the Martyr. The blessed Virgin is honored by the title of reuerence which is called *Hyperdulia, quod idem est, quod excellens & eximia dulia,* because that as in meritts of grace, and sanctitie, beinge the mother of him. *De cuius plenitudine nos omnes accepimus;* frō whose fulnes all grace did springe into the world, shee exceeded all the creatures that euer were: so her honor, and respect of reuerence ought to excell the honors and reuerence which wee exibite to any other creature whatsoeuer.

11. *Ioannes Catacuzenus in Apologia. 3. & 4. contra Mahometanos, credimus inquit.* Wee beleeue saith hee, that no man like to Marie was euer borne nor euer shalbe vnto the end of the worlde, & though accordinge to humane nature shee is inferior to the Angells, yet accordinge to her holynes, and sanctitie she surpasseth the Angells. S. Epiph. saith, that by the misterie of the Incarnation she is more honorable then all other saincts.

*Epiph. hæres. 79.*

*S. Bernard in sermone 1. de natiuitate beatæ Mariæ & 1. de assumptione,* doth call her Aduocate of the Church, calleth her *spes nostra* our hope, as also the same S. Bernard: *ser. illo. 1. de natiuitate.* Holie Ephrem *in oratione de laudibus Virginis gaudium & salutem mundi ipsam esse prædicat.* And though these titles of honor may seene proper vnto God, yet there are other titles due vnto God, and so proper

proper vnto him, that they can neuer be giuen to any other, as that God is infinite, omnipotent, and eternall: there are other titles which are common to God, and his saincts, as the title of Pastor, Maister fundation, and rocke, which are not accomodated to the blessed Virgin. *Naz. in tragedia de Christo.*

12. Where you say that wee comitt Idolatrie in giuinge all these titles of honor vnto the saincts in reuerencinge their relicks and so you call Images Idols, Epiph. doth answere such people, sayinge. *O insanientem linguam, quam instar macheræ veneno imbutæ possident.* O furious and raginge tounge, which is like a sharpe poisoned sword, which calles the deuout and innocent faith of Christians, Idolatrie. No Christian vnder the heauens did giue the worshipp of God which is called Latria vnto any image. *Latria nostra*, saith he, *in spiritu est*: our adoration is in spiritt. *Eph. tomo 4. & 2. contra hæreticos. S. Aug. lib. 20. contra Faustum arguit, si per cultum qui latria dicitur &c.* If as S. Aug. doth argue against Faustus, how by the adoration of Latria which is due vnto God, do wee serue rather the creature, then the Creator, when our purpose, and meaninge is to serue God therein? For our thought therein beinge referred to God, & not the creature, wee honor God only, and not creatures. And therfore he is condemned as an heretique in the 7. generall *7. Synod.*

H Coun-

Councell, that calls Images, Idolls. *Qui venerandas imagines idola appellant, Anathema sit.* Whosoeuer calls the venerable Images, Idolls. Lett him be cursed.

*Read the 26 of Leuit. wher idolum is said*: Non facies vobis idolū.

13. Origenes declaringe that of Exodus. *Non facies tibi sculptile*, which the 70. called Idolon saith, *aliud est facere idolum, aliud similitudinem*. It is not all one to make an Idole, and the likenes of any thinge, for an Idole doth represent a thinge vnto vs otherwise then it is, as the Gentiles made an Idole of the Image of Iupiter, thinking him to be God, which he was not. An Idole is such a thing as is not God, & is reuerenced as God, whether it be a similitude or any thinge, which wee thincke to be God. But an Image is the similitude of any paterne, or exemple, which if that similitude doe represent vnto our vewe, any thinge worthie of veneration, is reuerenced and honored with the example: so as an Image is not a verie similitude, but which is putt, and ordayned to represent and expresse this thinge or that thinge and ther- Thomas Waldesis saies, *Idolum à dolo dictum est*, that is to saie of deceite.

*Tomo 3. de Sacramentalibus.*

14. Doctor Sanders doth saie, that the old heretickes, Marcionists, and Manychies, after the Euthichians were the first ympugners of Images, imitatinge herein the Hebrewes, Sarrecens, Gentiles, and Samaritans, as Heretiques doe. Amoungst the

the Emperors the first that opposed himselfe against Images was Phillipp, as Paulus Diaconus doth relate in his life: this Emperor beinge at Constantinople, did see a picture, wherin was written the acts, and monuments of the 6. generall Councell, which he comanded to be taken awaye, in which Councell there was two wills defined in Christ; this is related by Paulus Dianius. Next vnto him was Leo Isauricus, who by the instigation of some Iewes, comanded Images to be broken, as Paulus, Zonarus doth relate, and so he is called Leo the Image breaker, his sonne called Constantinus, Capronimus, did the like after him Leo Armenius the Emperor. So in France the Albigences certaine Hereticks in the tyme of Pope Innocent the third, and Frederick the second Emperor, waged warre against Images. After them Iohn Witcliffe Anno 1372. and now in this last miserable age Iohn Caluine lib 1. institut. cap. 2. said that in the first 500. yeares, there were no Images in the Temples of Christians. How false it is, lett the Reader peruerse *Eusebius lib. 3. & 4.* of the life of Constantine the great, who saith that there were great stoare of Images in the temples that were made by Constantine the great, *Sozomenus lib. 5. cap. 20. Nicepho. lib. 5. c. 30.* doe write, that the Image of Christe in the time of Iulian the Apostate, was brought into the temple by the Christians, see *Tertulian. in lib. de pudicitia. Naz. ad Olympium. Damasc. in vita Siluestri. Basil. in vita Barlaam. Chrisost. in mißam, quam Erasmus latinam reddit. Euodium lib. 2. de miraculis S. Stephani. Prudentium in libro de sancto Cassiano. Paulinum epistola ad Seuerum. August. lib. de consensu Euangelistarum cap. 10.* and a little before him, Carolastadius in this heresie was the first that opposed himselfe against Images.

15. That there were manie Images of Christ from the beginninge of the Church it is well knowen, and in the life tyme of Christ himselfe there were two Images. The first himselfe takinge a napkin, & rubbinge his face with all, in the which he drewe his owne picture, and did send it to the kinge of Edessa, called Abagarus, which to this day is kepte in a certaine Church. Of this verie Image Euagrius makes mention and Damascenus, and Symon Metaphrastes, and others who also doe confirme the said historie to be true, as Stephen and Iuo doe declare *4. parte decreti cap. 83.* and Adrian *in script. de Imaginibus ad Carolum magnum.*

*Euagr. li. 4 cap. 16. Damasc. oratione 1. de Imag. Metaphr. in vita Constant Leo. in 7. Synod. act 4.*

16. The second was the picture that the wooman of Paneades made, after that shee was heald from the yssue of blood, in token of her thankful minde for receauinge such a benefitt. And as manie, receauinge great benefitts of great potentats, in remem-

bringe

bringe their benefactors, they put vpp, and keepe their pictures in their howses: so the Church of Christ, which ought to be most thankfull vnto Christ for sufferinge death for her, doe embrace and putt vpp his picture in her Churches, and Chappells. Of this picture *Eusebius*, *Sozomenus*, *Damasce.* and S. Gregorie make mention. It is also recorded that in the Vatican Librarie at Rome in hande writinge, in the tyme of Tiberius Emperor this Image was brought to Rome.

*Euseb.l. 7. hist.c. 14. Sozome. lib. 5. cap. 1. 20. Damasc. oratione 1. de Imag. Gregor. Papa epist. ad Germa. quæ habetur 7. Syn.*

17. Also it is recorded by S. Athanasius that the Image of Christ which was made by Nicodemus, beinge brought by a Christian to a Cittie called Beritho in Syria neere Antioch, was crucified by the Iewes in horrour, and hatred of him, (whom the same did represent. This historie is avouched in 7. Synd. act. 4.) and euen so hereticks doe now in the countries where they rule, wher with their cruell hādes, prophane thoughts, and blasphemous acts, they pollute, defile, deface, cast downe, burne and massacre all sacred Images, and reliques, as the Iewes haue don at Beritho, and in all places were they can laye handes vpon the Image of Christ. Was not that a most lamentable president comitted at Showards, alias Swards in Ireland, within six miles of Dublin, by one Hewson an English minister of that village, in the first yeare of the kinges raigne,

*Athanas. lib de passione Ima. cap. 4.*

in the Monthe of Maye, who rushed vehementlie vpon one of the village called Horishe, and tooke from him the Crucifix, which he held in his handes, and did hange the same vpon a gallous, not in despight of the Catholiques, as he himselfe said, but rather in hatred of him the same did represent, writing this poesie. Helpe all strangers, for the God of the papistes is in dāger: the poore man Horish bringinge with him the said picture so defaced by the said minister, that it was a pittifull thinge for a Christian to behold the same, went before the Councell of estate of that miserable Countrie, & tould them the dishonor offred by such a base fellow vnto the Image of Christ. One of that Councell called Sr. Geffrie Fenton Secretarie to the state, insulted vpon the poore fellowe most furiouslie, snatched the Crucifix from him, and cast it on the ground vnder his feete, and the poore fellowe for complayning against the said minister of that abuse, was cast into pryson.

18. The said Sr. Geffrye Fenton did sett a poore fellowe on the pillorie in the markett tyme at dublin with the picture of Christ about his necke for carienge the same before a frind of his that was dead at that tyme. Loys de Perusiis in his booke, *discours des guerres*, writinge of those tumultes which were stirred vpp by the Hugonotes

gonotes in France aboute Auignion in Prouince, reporteth that in one place they tooke an Image of the Crucifix, bound it vpon an Asse backe, and so went leadinge the Asse whippinge and scourginge the Crucifix through the Towne. I aske of this sorte of people, if any should hange the kinges picture vpon the gallous whether he should incurre the kinge and his subiects ill will, or no, yea and perhapps suffer death for soe doinge, referringe herein the iniurie, and indignitie of abusinge his picture, to the kinges owne person? I praie was it not the cheefest article against O Roerke a noble man of Ireland, as you may read in the Chronicles of England, that he was charged that he did hange Queene Elizabeth her picture at a horse tayle, so as the said noble man was hanged drawen and quartered at Tyborne Anno 1592. and he that hangeth Christs picture, shall rather be fauored, and countenanced then punished for the same, and poore zealous Christians for findinge fault with him, or for declaringe their griefe for that indignitie shalbe be aflicted. Woe be to that age wherein this wicked fact is done and suffred with ympunitie. Was not the people of Thessalonica punished by the edge of the sworde of the Armye of the Emperor Theodosius the great, for that they at their gate in despighte of the Empresse did hange her picture, for which that holy Bishopp S. Ambrose did excommunicate, the said Emperor. All these Princes did esteeme the iniurie done vnto themselues, which was done vnto their Image: for in Persia they haue this customè, what punishment they inflict vpon malefactors, the same they ympose vpon their Images, and as the Image of God or his saincts, or their relicks, is not capable of honor, or estimation, but all the honor due vnto the same is related and referred vnto the example, or paterne: so the iniurie, or irreuerente handlinge of them, redoundes allso vnto them: this is proued by Nicephorus the Patriarch of Constantinople *in dialogo cui titulus est orthodoxus*, as Turrianus translated. *Liquet Christum &c.* It is lawfull for Christ to be a patterne, or example of his owne Image, forasmuch as in all thinges he ought to resemble his brethren: although it be not written in plaine woordes; and when the Heretique shall aske, where is it written, that wee must adore the Image of Christ? I answere, that in the same place it is written, where wee read that wee must adore Christ, seinge his shape and likenes is inseparable from himselfe.

*Turri. lib. 1. pro Cā. apost. c. 25.*

19. And as D. Sanders said, as dead thinges haue there denomination from the the thinges vnto which they haue their reference, or relation so such thinges vnto whome any sanctitie belongeth are called holie.

*Sand. li. 2. de Imag. cap. 1.*

holie. *Terra in qua stas locus sanctus est*. *Dies* Exo.3.12
*Paschæ*. Easter day his called holie. Sainct Exod. 28.
Paule called the Scripture holie; in as much as it is holie wee must reuerence it, forasmuch as veneration is due vnto holynes. 2. Tim. 3.
And so the Angell said vnto Moyses. *Terra in qua stas &c.* the land whereupon you stand it is called the holie land, and therfore he bid him to put off his shoes in token of reuerence. And so as thinges without life, cannot be called holie, but in order, reference, or relation to another, and being ioyned with him, vnto whome honor is due can be, and ought to be adored, as S. Paule saith. *Cui honorem honor &c.* Let vs giue honor, vnto whome it is due: Euen so in the same order, and obseruation, Images are holie, and venerable, when they be referred, and related to their examples, forme, or patterne with which only they are to be adored, no otherwise then the Image of the kinge is reuerenced for his maiestie: therfore the Image of the sainct, for his sanctitie is to be reuerenced. Turria.li. 1. epistolis Cano.

20. The venerable vse of Images is proued by the cannons of the Apostles, by the 52. cannon of the sixt generall councell, by the Romane councell vnder Greg. the 3. as Sigibertus setts downe, by *Amoinus*, *Adonienensis*, *Regino in suis Chronicis*, *Anno 766.* by Paulus Emilius, by another councell at Rome vnder pope Stephen. 3. as Sigibertus setts Sigib. An. 1733. Amoi. in animalib. li.4.c.67. Emil. lib. 20. de gestis francorum.

ſetts downe, Ænead. 2. lib. 1. by Sabellicus Ænead. 8. lib. after all theſe councells, the ſame is proued by one of the 7. generall councell of the world, which was the 2. of Nice. of which *Paulus Diaconus*, *Cedrenus*, & *Zonaras*, & *Photius Patriarche* who in this councell was the Popes Legate, and the legates of three Patriarches, Alexandria, Antioche, and Hieruſalem, and the Patriarche himſelfe of Conſtantinople. This is proued by the councell of *Trent. ſeſſ. 25. in decreto de reliquijs.*

21. This is proued alſo by the miracles that God doth daylie worcke by the Images, and reliques of his ſaincts, by which miracles. S. Iohn Chriſoſtome amoungeſt other argumentes proues the God head of Chriſt, for had he not bene God, how could his Image and the Images of his ſaincts do ſuch wonders, as the Image of Chriſt which was peirced with a launce in diſhonor of Chriſt, caſt forth peſentlie ſtreames of blood as S. Athanaſ. and Leontius ſetts downe, how the Image beinge thruſt with the launce of a Iewe that dwelt at Beritho a cittie nere Antioch, did the like; he recordeth moreouer the miracles of Coſma & Damiã; other miracles are recorded in the 7. 2. generall councell *actione* 5. and that miracle which Euſebius. lib 7. cap 9. de Homorriſſa which our Lord healed, who made the picture of Chriſt in token to remember him

*Ath. lib. de paſsione Imagi. Chriſti & Leont.*

*Act.* 5.

him for his benefitts, vpon the place where the picture was, there grewe an hearbe which did reach vnto the hemme of the Image, which did cure all diseases. Sozomenus saith, when Iulian the apostate did remoue the Image from that place, and put his owne picture in the rome, a fyrie flame came from heauen and cast of the head thereof. But what should I register old examples, when wee haue so many daylie at home before our eies? *Sozo lib. cap. 28. Theoph. in c. 9. Mat.*

22. When the earle of Essex tooke the castle of Cahire in the Prouince of Mounster in Irland, one of the gallants whome he left in garrison therin, went to a dissolued monasterie in that place, cast downe, and burned the Image of our Sauiour Christ, the next night after he was cast into madnes, and cast himselfe, headlonge from the toppe of that castle downe into the riuer that runneth vnderneathe. In the towne of Yonghull in that prouince 3. soldiors that were there in garrison, one serued vnder Captaine Peers, another serued vnder Captaine Tanner, another vnder Sr. William Morgan a welshe knight, which were left there in garrison in the warres of Gerrot Earle of Desmond, did insult vpon the holie Roode that at that tyme stoode vp in the Abbey of S. Dominicke, which is called in that Towne the North Abbey, and castinge it downe did burne the same in the markett *An. 1600* *Godes punishment inflicted vppon Image breakers.* *2. of them were caled Clough & Pocd.*

markett place of that Towne. One of the principall actors therin was taken with a raginge madnesse, by which, he was so tormented, that he could neuer sleepe or take any rest, cryinge out and sayinge, that the holie Roode was following him, of which furie he died at night tyme in the streete. At Yonghull within a seauennight after that cursed fact, his second companion died, eaten vp with lice and vermine. The third was kild by the earles sentinelle in a sallie out of that Towne, and all this happened within one seauē night: which I proteste to be true, & wherof many liuing yet in that Towne were eye witnesses.

23. In the countie of Wexford in a countrie there called the Morrowes, in a certaine Church dedicated to S. Iohn Baptist, called Castle Elice, one Sr. Iames Deuereux an apostate priest keepinge court there, for the Bishopp or superintendent of that Diocesse, and findinge the Image of that glorious sainct at the alter ( for the Caluinian prophane Common table neuer came to that place ) and seinge the poore people offringe little pence, and beades vnto the Image, ranne to the Image in a rage, saying what a superstition is this, and threw downe the Image : and thinckinge to carry it out of the Church, he was presentlie strocken dead vpon the ground, nor neuer went out of the church-yard of that Church; And with

with much a doe could any abide to ſtand by him, when he was ſtript of his apparell to be buried, by reaſon of the loathſome ſtincke, and ſmell that iſſued from him: this is moſt true, as all that countrie can auouche, being done in ſuch a generall aſſemblie, of which many of the beſt ſort are yet liuinge to teſtifie the ſame, and happened in the yeere anno 1600.

24. I could bringe many examples that do dailie happen, as the Catholicks can tell, and the Proteſtants do dailie ſee before their eyes. *Sed vt videntes non vident, & audientes non intelligunt.* But you are thoſe of whome our Sauiour ſaith, ſeinge you doe not ſee, and hearinge you doe not vnderſtand, you may ſaie with the Prophett: *Defecit in me virtus mea, & lumen oculorum meorum non eſt mecum.* Grace doth fayle you, and the power, or ſence of ſeinge is not with you, and although many of you haue withno leſſe deſpightfull indignitie then Samaritans, Iewes, and Mahometts with your curſed handes, and blaſphemous lips, polluted, and defaced the Image of Chriſt and of his Saincts, and haue not receaued condigne and worthie puniſhment in this life, yet you ought not to bragge of godes mercie, in ſparinge you, for as S. Auguſtine ſaith, if God ſhould puniſh euerie wicked man in this world, it ſhould be an argument for you, that there is not a place of puniſhment

for

for transgressors besides this world, & therfore he doth not inflict punishment vpon all in this life, but reserues the same vnto the other, that wee may assure our selues, that our wickednes and trangressions, which wee our selues do daily perpetrate and practize, and which are rigorouslie punished in others, shall not escape the damnation of godes iudgment, whose mercifull forbearinge with vs will increase his wrathe, and augment our woe, which wee ought to preuent by other mens ruyne.

*The manner how to reuerēce Christ his Image.*

25. The manner how to reuerence Christes Image, Gregorius lib 7. as Vasquez Cites in his second booke *de adoratione, disputatione. 8. cap. 13.* and in the councell of Rome vnder Pope Stephen the 3. his wordes be these. *Et nos quidem &c.* We truly, saith he, not as it were before the diuinitie, prostrate our selues when wee come before the Image of Christ, but wee doe adore him, which by the Image, either in his birth, passion, or sittinge in the Throne of Iudgment wee contemplate, and behold. Read the verses which Sabellicus wrote l. 8. Æneade 8. and as some do thincke were cōposed in the 7. generall councell and are written with letters of gould at Venice ingraued in an old wall.

*Nā Deus est, quod imago docet, sed non Deus, ipse*
*Hanc videas, sed mente colas, quod cernis in ipsa.*

Christs picture humblie worshipp thou,

Which

Which by the ſame dooſt paſſe,
Yet picture worſhipp not but him,
For whom it pictured was.
Nor God, nor man this Image is,
Which thou doſt preſent ſee,
Yet whom this bleſſed Image ſhewes
Both God and man is hee.
For God is that which the Image ſhewes
But yet no God it is.
Behold this forme, but worſhipp that,
The minde beholdes in this.

26. The ſame doth Hieronimus Auguſtus ſett downe. *Hic eſt colendi modus, publicis concionibus ſedulò inculcandus*, this is the order of reuerencinge Images, and in pulpitts wee muſt inculcate the ſame to the people, that by the Image wee maye worſhipp in ſpiritt, and trueth, and eleuate our mindes and wills excitated by them to God, and to direct our prayers, and petitions vnto him, and to his holie Saints. Where wee muſt conſider, that wee ought not to giue the prayſes of the patterne to the Image, neither thinck the ſame capable of any prayers, for it being a dead thinge, it is not capable thereof; and although the Church in the paſsion Sonday hath theſe wordes.

*O crux aue ſpes vnica*
*Hoc paſsionis tempore,*
*Auge pijs iuſtitiam*
*Reiſque dona veniam.*

O Croſſe of Chriſt, our onlie hope, and healpe

healpe in tyme of neede, In tyme of these bitter paines voutchase, to helpe vs with releefe, the godlie to confirme in grace and sinners to forgiue. Wee meane not to apply to the Crosse it selfe, but vnto Christ figuratiuely, *per figuram prosopopeiam*, which is common to poets and Orators. When wee speake to dead thinges in the person of the liuinge; and also by the figure called Metonomia, when the Crosse is taken for Christ, *vt continens pro contento*, as the author of the Crosse for the Crosse it selfe, so that to the Image it selfe, our petition hath noe relation beinge not capable thereof. And therfore the councell of Trent saith, that in the Images themselues there is no vertue or excellencie for the which they should be reuerenced, or praide vnto, or that wee should repose any hope in them, neither sacrifice is offred to Images, which can be offred to none but to God, for it is a protestation of the omnipotent power and maiestie of God as he is the author and Lord of all, neither are oblations properlie offred vnto them, because that oblation is offred only to God vnto whome all sacrifice and oblations do belonge, as S. Thomas 2. 2. q. 85. ar. 3. and 3. teaceth. And although the 7. generall councell hath these woordes. *Merito nos ad Imagines reuerenter accedere debemus oblationibus suffultum & luminarium*, Wee ought to aproach reuerentlie

*Sess. in decreto de Imag.*

*7. Synod. act. 9.*

lie before the Images with oblations of incense, perfumes and lightes. The holie doctor did not thinke those thinges to be properly oblations as they were offred vnto Images, neither that generall counsell saith that the oblations should be offred to Images, but saith that wee should approache before Images with oblations: for the councell intendeth, that those oblations offred vnto Images should be properlie offred vnto God, vnto whom principaly they haue their reference, and not vnto Images, vnto whome adoration and not oblation belongeth, vnles you will call those thinges that are offred before Images Donaria, videlicet guiftes which are hanged about Images.

*Whether Papists do committ Idolatrie, in worshippinge the Crosse of Iesus Christ.*

## CHAPTER VI.

1. THe first heresie touchinge the adoration of the Crosse, was of Claudius Bishopp of Thaurum, as Iuo Carnotensis auoucheth. The second heresie was, of a certaine sect called Pauliciain, as Photius the Patriarck doth alleadge, and as *Euthimius in sua panoplia*, declareth. The third heresie was, in the time of S. Bernard, by one Pe-

trus Brius, against whome Petrus Cluniacensis did write. The fourth was, of those that followed Iohn Witcleeffe, as *Thomas Waldensis declares, homil. 3. cap. 160.* The first heresie was, of Caluine in his booke of Institutions the 11. chapter q. 7. his argumēt is. The crosse of Christ was the instrument of the greefe & death of Christ: therfore we ought not to honour the same, neither the reliques of his other passions. This Caluin was he, who threw downe the Image of Christ, and permitted his owne Image to be reuerenced and worne about mens neckes. And when a certaine familiar frind of his owne, tould him that the people did so ymbrace his Image; he answered him scoffingly and said. If any man be offended therwith, ether let him not behold the same, or lett him pull out his eyes, or goe hange himselfe.

2. Wee for our parts do not reuerence the Crosse of Christ, in respect of the torments of Christ, and of his paynes, but as those torments and passion were a remedie for mankind, and a sacrifice gratefull vnto God: as also an euident argument of his affection, loue, and charitie towardes mankinde, and as the Crosse was the standarte of our redemption by which he destroyed him, *qui mortis habuit imperium*, that had the comand of death: *pacificans omnia sanguine crucis*, appeasinge godes wrathe by his death

vpon

vppon the Crosse, which he conceaued against mankinde. Caluine herein doth imitate Iulian the Apostate, who obiected vnto the Christians the adoration of the Crosse, sayinge. *Crucis lignum adoratis, imaginem illius in fronte, & ante domos pingentes*. Yow adore the crosse of Christ, you make his Image in your fore-head, you paint his picture before your howses: who therfore may not whorthilie hate your wisest men, or pittie your ignorant and silly sorte, who at lenght are fallen into that callamitie, that hauing forsaken the eternall God, you passe vnto a dead Iewe, thus far the said Apostate, against the Christians. *Apud Cyrill. Alex. lib. 6. in Iulianum.*

3. As for the catholick doctrine it doth teach, that not only the crosse, *in qua Christus mortuus, sed quacumque crucis figura &c.* in which Christ suffred, but any other figure of the crosse, is to be honored & reuereced: this is proued by the seuenth generall councell the 2. of Nice. act. 7. where the councell defined honor, & reuerence to be giuen to the tipe and forme of the holie Crosse, much more to the Crosse it selfe, for both of them are the signe of Christ crucified. This is proued by S. Paule, sainge. Christ wyped out the hand writinge of decree that was against vs, and the same he hath taken awaie, fastning it to the Crosse, and spoilinge the principalities and potestates. And in the first *2. Coloss.*

1. Epist. Coloss. epistle he saith, he reconciled all thinges by himselfe, pacifyinge by the blood of his Crosse, I meane his death which he suffred vpon the Crosse. And as S, Peter saith.
1. Pet. 2. Christ himselfe did beare our sinnes in his bodie vpon the tree. Why should not then that blessed Crosse be reuerenced, as the sacred Altar of that sacrifice, & the instrument of so great a triumph and redẽption? And as Leontius said, any thinge that belonges to our father or freind whome wee desire to behold, wee reuerence and esteeme, and wee kisse the same, yea somtimes with weepinge eyes, why then should not wee also with reuerence kisse the tree and Crosse, which was the instrument of our redemption, and approach vnto it with weepinge eyes? If a captayne had frought a combate for the common wealth, the ensigne or standart by which he had ouerthrowen his enemies, would be houlden for a great monument, and why should not the standart of Iesus Christ be highlie reuerẽced by which he hath owerthrowen that enemie of mankind, and obtained victorie against the power of Sathan? *Triumphans eos palam in ligno &c.* as hath bene written in the old greeke translation, bringinge the Princes of darknes in a triumphinge manner, vnder the standart of the Crosse?

Cyrill. Epist. ad Const. Au. 4. This reuerence belonginge to the holie Crosse is proued by the inuention thereof

thereof by S. Helena as S. Cyrill of Hierusalem S. Ambrose. *Chrisost. Rufinus Paulinus, Sulpitius, Socrates lib.1. cap. 17. 1. Iustinianus imperator in nouella cōstit. 28.* do write. Truly had not that holie Crosse bene worthie of reuerence and honor neither Helena should haue bin moued with diuine inspiration to search for it, neither by godes diuine prouidence should shee haue found it, neither yet in the findinge of it, those miracles should euer haue byn wrought, as also since in all ages as the holie doctors doe auouche. *Damascenus, Cyrillus. Hierosolimitanus. Nyscenus, Paulinus. Chrisostome. Homilia quod Christus sit Deus. in.5.Homil.Hierom epist. 17.* which not only made mention of the Crosse, but of other relicks of Christ. S. Gregorie in the 7. booke epist. 126. did send a parcell of the Crosse vnto Recaredus kinge of Spaine. S. Augustine doth testifie that a parte of the earth of the holie land, beinge brought into Affricke, did great miracles. S. Ambrose doth declare that one of the Nayles of Christ his Crosse, was fixed in the helmett of Constantine the great, the same is testified by Eusebius.

5. The veneration of this Crosse, is proued by the wonderfull victorie gotten by Heraclius the Emperor in recoueringe the holy Crosse from the Persians, which whē it was restored to its former place, many miracles were wrought therby, as

*gust. Amb. de obitu Theodo. Chris. ho. 84. in cap. 19. Ioh. s. Ruf. li. 12. hist. c. 7. Euir. l. 11 Paul. Epi. 11. ad Seuer. Sulp. l. 2 sacræ hist. c. 18. Theod. l. 1 hist. c. 18. Sozom. l. 2 cap. 1. Damasc. 4 de fid. c. 12 Cyrill. 10. & 13. Nyse. in vita Marcinæ soror. Paul Ep. 11. Hiero. Aug. l. 22. de ciui c. 8 Amb. in orat. de obitu Theo. Euseb l. 1. vita Cōst. cap. 25.*

*Paulus Diaconus, Zonaras, & Cedrenus* make mention, and *Sigibertus in Chronica*; for which cause the feast of the exaltation of the Crosse was instituted by the Church: Againe the signe of the Crosse is proued by S. Mathewe in the daie of Iudgment, the signe of the Sonne of man shall appeare, as *Origines, Chrisostome, Theophilactus, Euthymius, Hillarius, Beda, Cyrill. Hieroso. & S. Aug.* doe declare, and all the rest doe testifie the same. S. Cyprian doth teach, that the signe of the Crosse is so expedient, as in old tyme the signe Tau. Ezec. 9. which place S. Hierō expoundinge saith, that in the beginninge the letter Tau was like a Crosse. Origines, Tertulian, and Cyprian holde, that such as were liuinge in any battayle, were sett downe by this letter T. and such as were dead were described by this letter. O. The reuerence of the Crosse is proued also, by the reuerence that Constantine the great, and other Christian Emperors did exhibite towardes the same, as stamping it in their monies and gould, puttinge it in their ensignes, carryinge it before them, and as holie Doctors doe say, that in thinges naturall it is of great vertue, as *Iustinus Apologia. 2. Ambr. ser. 56.* for the signe of the Crosse serueth to the mariners to saile, to the birdes to flie, and as Rufinus doth write, the figure of the Crosse with the Egiptians in their Hieregtiphes, doth signifie life euerlastinge.

*In vita Heraclij.* *Mat. 24. Cyrill. Aug. ser. 130. de tempore. Damasc. l. 4 ca. 12. Cypr li. 2 ad Quir. cap. 1. & Amb. ser. 56. Ruf li. 12. hist. 2. cap. 29.*

6. And

6. And wee must obserue, that when wee expresse the signe of the Crosse vpon any thinge, wee doe not meane by that signe, to ympart any vertue vnto the same, but only by the signe of the crosse expressed vpon the same, wee implore the helpe of Christ crucified, soe that it is an impudent lye of Heretiques to say, that the signe of the crosse is superstitious. Heretiques cry against the catholique church for makinge the signe of the crosse or the picture of Christ, saying. Confusion be to all those that doe worshipp any engrauen thinge, & *qui adorant sculptilia*. I answere that it is ment to worshipp it as God: and so, Cassiodorus doth interpret it an Idoll or to make an Idol of it. For as in the Téple of Salomõ there were pictures & grauen Images: soe in the Téple of the Christians; yet neither the one nor the other are Idolls, for the picture of Christ & of his Saincts, of which we doe not make godes, are but signes to bringe vs to remember the true God. If to painte the picture of Christ were Idolatry, why should S.Luke, *Comes Sancti Pauli in euangelio*, the fellowe of S. Paule in the ghospell, painte both the Image of Christ and his Mother as wee reade in the fourth booke of the Sentences ca. 5. and as learned Saincts doe write? *Damascenus* said as *Thomas Waldensis reportes*, *Accepimus, Lucam Euangelistam &c.* Wee haue receaued, that Luke the Euangelist

*S Lucke painted the Image of Christ.*

painted Christ and his mother, and that the famous Cittie of Rome hath the same picture. Origines declaring in his 8. homilie vpon Iosue, how that the kinge Hay was hãged vpon a double tree, saith. It followeth that the crosse of our Lord, was a double crosse, the one a visible crosse, wheron the sonne of God was crucified in flesh: the other was an inuisible crosse, wheron inuisibly the diuill with all his power and
*1. Epist. Coloss.* Princes was Crucified, as S. Paule saith, he ouerthrewe the power and mightie Princes of darcknesse, & tryumphed ouer them on the tree of the crosse: so as this crosse hath two singuler considerations. The first is, that which S. Peter saith, that Christ was crucified, leauinge vnto vs an example to followe his stepps. The second consideration, wherin he gott the victorie ouer Zabull, wherin he was crucified: therfore S. Paul saith, woe be vnto me saith he if I glorie in any thinge, but in the crosse of Christ, by which the world is crucified vnto me, and I vnto the world. Soe as you see two effects which he doth alleadge, for he saith that two contrarie thinges are crucified, the vertuous liuer, and the sinfull sinner, the mortified bodie, and the wicked world, accordinge as Origines saith of Christ and of the deuill. *Thomas Waldensis* and others here vpon doe say, that the crosse is called both the woode, and Christ, as Hieremias saith,

*venite*

*venite mittamus lignum in panem eius*. Lett vs cast woode into his bread, soe as he meaneth by the woode the crosse, and by his bread, his tender flesh. Christ himselfe auoucheth the same: *panis quem ego dabo &c.* the bread I shall giue, is my flesh. S. Hierome saith, he hath not lefte his crosse vpon the earth, but he carried it with him vnto heauen, and soe he shall come with his crosse, so as he meant by his crosse his bodie and flesh and himselfe. Of which crosse Sybilla said. *O ter beatum lignum in quo Deus extensus est*. O thrise happie wood vpon which God was eleuated.

7. S. Ambrose speakinge in the person of Hellena, hath these wordes. *Quomodo me redemptum arbitror, si redemptio ipsa non cernitur; video quid egeris ô diabole, vt gladius quo percussus es, destrueretur.* How shall I knowe my redemption if the redemption it selfe be not seene, I know ô diuill it is thy crafte to hide the sword by which thou wert ouerthrowen. It is written in the booke of wisedome. *Benedictum est lignum per quod fit iustitia.* Blessed be the wood by which Iustice is don, cursed be the hand by which an Idoll is made, and also him that makes the same, behold he did blesse the wood of the crosse, and did curse the Idoll of impietie. Was Iosue an Idolater, when he said to the sunne, thou shalt not moue against Gabaon, neither the moone against Haylon? for

wee

wee knowe that Iosue did speake vnto the Creator of them. The 3. children also did singe and say, *benedicite sol & luna*. O sunne and moone, day and night, blesse yee our Lord, and so did Dauid saie to all creatures; and will you charge the Church of God with Idolatrie for honoring God in his creatures? And so wee saie the like vnto the greene wood, and to the blessed crosse, not adoringe the nature of wood herein, but the liuinge crosse of him that was crucified, whose grace and fauour in the same wee implore.

*Epistola* 140. 8. S. Bernard speaking of the holy crosse, *Confessio sanctæ crucis, non nisi crucifixi confessio est*, the confession of the holie crosse, is no other then the confession of the crucified. Therfore *Thomas Waldensis* speakinge of the inuention of this holie crosse. *Quid in hoc festo infestum sit*, what harme is in this feast, but that wee giue God thanckes, which procured that gratious wooman, and as S. Ambrose saith. *Infudit ei spiritus vt lignum requirat*. Inspired her with his spirit to search the wood. S. Iohn Chrisostome addeth in his booke of the crosse these woordes. *Si scire desideres charissimè virtutem crucis &c.* Most deere, if you would knowe what vertue the crosse hath, and how much I could speake in the prayse thereof, know that the crosse is the hope of the Christian, the crosse is the waye for

people

people in desperation, the crosse is the resurrection of the dead, the crosse is the guide vnto heauen, the crosse is the staffe for the lame, the crosse is the comfort of the sorrowfull, the crosse is the bridle of the rich, the crosse is the destruction of the proude, the crosse is the paine of the enuious, the triumphe of deuills, the tutor of youth, the patience of the poore, the pylott of mariners and saylers, the wall of those that are beseeged, the father of orphanes, the defence of widdowes, the comfort of martyrs, the chastitie of Virgins, the solace of priestes, the victorie of the Romans, the bread of the hungrie, and the fountaine of the thirstie, thus much sainct Iohn Chrisostome, and much more of the glorious crosse. And in his homilie vpon S. Mathewe 16. *Læto animo crucem Christi circumferamus &c.* Lett vs with a willing mind carrie the crosse of Christ, the same beinge the badge of our saluation, by which it was effected, without whose presence wee cannot be regenerated, when wee be fedd and susteyned with the holie foode of life, or consecrate the same; the enseigne or standarte of the victorie must stand by. Wherfore lett vs fixe, and place it in our chambers, on the walles, in the windowes, yea lett vs signe our foreheads and our harts withall, for that is the collizen and marke of our saftie, of our comon libertie, yea of the

*Iohn Chri-sost. homil.*

the humilitie and lenitie of our Lord. And in the same homilie, he saith: *Hoc signum nostris & priscis temporibus clausas ianuas reserauit, &c.* this hath opened the dores that were shut, hath abated the force of poyson, hath tamed wilde and cruell beastes, healed deadly bitinges of serpents, broken the gates of hell, opened the gates of heauen, renewed the waie to Paradise, it also did breake the serpents head: what should wee wonder that the same ouercame cruell beastes and pestiferous poisons. This signe conuerted the whole world, and reuiued it, tooke awaie feare, and brought truthe and tranquillitie againe, restored the earth vnto heauen, and made of men Angells.

9. S. Hierom writinge vnto Letham said. *Quicquid comederis, quicquid biberis, muni semper signo Crucis.* Whatsoeuer you eate or drinke, putt the signe of the crosse vpon it. And as S. Gregorie doth witnesse S. Benedict, by the signe of the crosse did breake a glasse full of poysoned licoure. Iuliã, though otherwise a wretched Apostate, with the signe of the crosse did chase away diuills. Cassiodorus vpon those wordes of S. Chrisostome. *Crux mortuorum resurrectio, Crux claudorum baculus &c.* the crosse is the resurrection of the dead &c. said that he did vtter them by diuine inspiration, and he added these wordes himselfe. *Crux est tuitio humilium &c,* the crosse is the safeguard of the humble,

humble, the destruction of the diuil, the victorie of Christ, the ouerthrowe of hell, *vita iustorum & mors infidelium hæreticorũ*, the life of the iust, and the death of vnbeleeuinge Hereticks. And in confirmation of the historie of Constantine the great and Heraclius, he did interpose the victory of the Romanes: now are these wordes, & confirmation of those glorious saincts touchinge the crosse to be reputed Idolatrie? Cassidiorus saith, that S. Iohn Chrisostome made crosses of siluer which were carried with waxe guilte with Gold and siluer at the expenses of Eudoxia the Empresse, wherfore the Arrians repininge against those crosses, insulted vpon them. thus Cassiodorus. Eusebius writeth, that when the Emperor Constantine the great gathered his Armye against Maxentius the Tyrant of Rome (for at that tyme he was a fauorer of Christian religion) he saw in his sleepe in the ayre towardes the east, the signe of the crosse shininge with a fierie flame, and beinge astonished with such an vnusuall aspect, he sawe two Angells sayinge vnto him. Constantine in this signe thou shalt ouercome. And as Isayas saith, *Ecce leuo &c.* behold I wil carrye my strenght to the Gentiles, and I will exalt my signe towardes the people, & they shall with a lowe countenance towards the earthe adore thee, and shall licke with their tounge the dust of thy feete, and you shall

*Lib. Tripart. c. 10.*

*Lib. 9. Eccles. hist.*

*Leuo ad gentes manum meã. Isay. 49.*

shall knowe I am your God, what signe I pray then is this, but the crosse of Christ which is his only signe as S. August. saith? *Ipsam crucem suam signum habiturus es, ipsam crucem de diabolo superato tanquam tropheum in frontibus fidelium positurus*, it is his crosse saith he, that was his signe, it is the marke and badge, I meane his crosse by which he triumphed ouer the diuill, as the ensigne of his victorie which he fixed in the fore-head of euerie Christian, as the Apostle saith. *Absit mihi gloriari &c.* Woe be vnto me, if I glorie in any other thinge then in the crosse of Christ.

*Super Iohn homil. 36*

10. Vpon these wordes. *Adorate scabellum pedum eius, quia sanctum est*. Adore yee his foote stoole because it is holie S. Hierom saith there are many opinions touchinge this foote stoole, verie like it is, it is meant by his bodie, in which the maiestie of his diuinity stoode as vpon a foote stoole, which ought to be adored, his foote stoole, saith S. Hierom is his bodie, his foote stoole is his soule, his foote stoole is his crosse. S. Ambrose saith, *iam ergo aucthoritatem habent &c.* now therfore saith he, they haue the ecclesiasticall authotitie, and the aucthoritie of the Apostles, and also the aucthoritie of so great fathers by whom they may carrie the signe of Christs crosse, amoungst the people in ecclesiasticall processions and conuents, in assemblies of pre-

*Psal. 98.*

*De fide. Gratiam.*

lates

lates, in the ſtandarts and crownes of catholique kinges, to the end that his foote ſtoole might be humblie worſhipped and adored, thus much S. Ambroſe. *Signatum eſt ſuper nos lumen vultus tui Domine*. O Lord thou haſt imprinted the impreſsion of thy light in our fore-heads. Caſsiodorus ſaith vppon that verſe. *In Crucis impreſsione lumen eſt vultus Dei, quia ſemper in eis noſcitur radiare*. Gods gratious fauor is extended towards them that are marked with his ſigne, becauſe he is knowne allwaies to ſhine in them. S. Gregorie wrote vnto Secundinum, that he would ſend vnto him two Images & a croſſe, that ſo he ſhould be defended from malignant ſpiritts, *& in reſcripto ad eum duas tabulas:* wee haue ſent vnto you two tables the Image of our Sauior, of the bleſſed Virgin his mother, and S. Peter and S. Paule, by our ſaid ſonne or Deacone, *pro benedictione*, for a benediction, that by it you may be protected from euill ſpiritts, by whoſe bleſſed croſſe you ſhall be ſure to be defended from euill ſpiritts. *Cap. 4.*

11. This is that bleſſed croſſe, of which our Sauiour ſpake ſayinge, when he ſhould be exalted from the earth, he would drawe all thinges to himſelfe. If the Adamant ſtone with its vertue draweth Iron vnto it, the fiſh called Remora being ſo little, holdeth faſt the greateſt ſhipp that euer was, notwithſtandinge all the deuiſes both of *Ioh. 12.*

nature

nature and arte indeuor to put her forward,
if the ſtone in latine called Gagates, in Engliſh Agat-ſtone, by a certaine hidden vertu
chaſeth awaie deuils, how much more this
bleſſed Croſſe, by the vertue of him that
died therupon doth, and ſhall chaſe awaie
deuills and euill ſpiritts? And as the Apoſtle
ſaith, the word of the croſſe to them in deed
that periſh is fooliſhnes: but to them that
are ſaued is the power of God, for it is written I will deſtroie the wiſedome of the wiſe
*1. Cor. 1.* and the prudence of the prudent I will reiect, for that which is the fooliſhe of God,
is wiſer then men, and that which is the in-
*Iſa. 33. 18* firme of God, is ſtrounger then men: and
as God almightie comanded Moyſes when
he would deliuer his people, from the ſer-
*Exod. 4.* uile yoke of Ægipte, to take into his handes a peece of wood, that is to ſay his rodd,
by which he was to worke all thoſe miracles that he wrought, ſo when our Sauiour
*Exod. 7. 8. 9.* was to deliuer mãkind from the thraldome
of the deuill, he tooke this wood which is
his croſſe, of which Moyſes rodde was a figure, by which our Sauiour hath redeemed
vs, and by which both he and his ſpouſe the
Church doe worke miracles, of which the
*Cant. 7.* ſpouſe in the Canticles ſaith. *Aſcendam in al-
tum & apprehendam fructum eius.* I will climbe
vpp into the toppe thereof, and I will take
ſome of the fruicte. The fruit of this noble
croſſe is the mortifications of our paſsions,
the

the bridlinge of our filthie concupiscense, the crucifienge of our luxurious carcase, the restraint of our vnsatiable appetites. The fruitt threreof, are all the vertues both morall and supernaturall. The fruicte thereof is a chast bodie, a contrite hart, an instant prayer, a feruent spiritt, a sounde religion, a quiett conscience, a perfect life, a pure intention, and a contemplatiue mind; the foundatiõ of all these vertues, is true humilitie, which was neuer knowen in the worlde, before the crosse was exalted in worlde: which as the Apostle saith, as vnto *1. Cor. 1.* the Iewes certes a scandall, vnto the gentiles foolishnes, so now adayes vnto the heretiques of this tyme is Idolatrie, but glorie and saluation vnto the vertuous catholiques, who doe learne daily by this signe of the holy crosse, the principall misteries of our faith which are two.

12. First, the misterie of the vnitie and trinitie of God; secondlie the incarnation and pasſion of our Sauiour. Wee make the signe of the crosse in the name of the father, and of the sonne, and of the holy ghost, and in this forme: Puttinge the right hand vnder the foread, when wee say in the name of the Father: then vnder the breast, when wee say, and of the sonne: lastly from the left shoulder vnto the right, when wee say, and of the holie ghoast. And saying in the name, and not in the names doth shew

the vnitie of God, and the diuine power and authoritie which is one onlie in all the three persons, these woordes of the father, of the sonne, and of the holy Ghoast, doe shewe vnto vs the trinitie of persons: the signinge in forme of a crosse representeth vnto vs the passion, and consequentlie the incarnation of the sonne of God: the passinge from the left shoulder to the right, signifieth that by that passion of our Sauiour, wee were transferred from sinne vnto grace, from transitorie thinges vnto eternall, from death to life: and wee that for our demeritts were to be placed with goates vpon the lefte hand, he transferred vs with his sheepe vnto the right, where wee
Matt. 15. may heare that blessed voice. Come yee blessed of my Father, possesse the kingdome prepared for you &c.

13. This signe also is made, to shewe that wee are Christians, to witt souldiors of Christ, because this signe is as it were an ensigne or liuerie which distinguisheth the souldiors of Christ, from all the enemies of the holie Church, videl. Gentiles, Iewes, Turckes, and Heretiques: besides, this signe is made to call for Godes helpe in all our woorkes, because with this signe the most holie Trinity is called to helpe by meanes of the passion of our Sauiour: and therfore good Christians vse to make this signe when they arise from bed, when they goe

to

to ſleepe, and in the beginninge of all other thinges. Finally this ſigne is made to arme vs againſt all temptations of the diuill, becauſe the diuill is afraide of this ſigne, and flieth from it as malefactours doe when they ſee the ſigne of the Officers of iuſtice, and many tymes by meanes of this ſigne of the holy croſſe, a man eſcapeth many dangers.

14. S. Gregor. Nazianzen, writeth of Iulian the Apoſtate. *Ad crucem confugit, ac ob timorem ſignatur, adiutorem facit quem perſequebatur &c.* He flieth vnto the croſſe, he ſignes himſelfe therwith, he doth aske his helpe, whome he perſecuted: the ſigne of the croſſe did preuaile, the diuills are ouercome. Theodoretus, moſt famous amoungeſt the Grecians, ſaith alſo of him. *Apparentibus demonibus &c.* When the diuills did appeare vnto him, he was compelled to ſigne his fore-head with the ſigne of the croſſe, and preſentlie the diuills at the ſight of the ſigne of Chriſts enſigne, remembringe their ouerthrowe, they preſentlie vaniſhed away. And Zozomenus ſaith of him thus. *Ex conſuetudine priſtina, ſymbolo ſe Chriſti clanculum obſignauit, ſpectra illi ſubito euanuerunt.* Accordinge the old cuſtome he did ſigne himſelfe ſecretlie with the badge of Chriſt, and the ghoaſtes forthwith diſappeared.

*Naz. in oratione priore quã ſcripſit aduerſ. Iulianum.*

*Theod. li. 3. hiſt. eccle.*

15. Tertulian alſo, wiſheth euerie true

*Tert. de corona militis.*

soldiear of Christ, to defend and arme him-selfe with the signe of the crosse. *Quamobrem ad omnem progressum &c.* Wherfore it was vsed, that euerie one should make the signe of the crosse in his fore-head, at his progresse and promotion, at his goinge in, and cominge forth, in apparellinge him-selfe, in puttinge on his shoes, in washinge himselfe, at the table, at the lightes, at his goinge to bed, at his rest, in all his actions and conuersations. Vnto which agreeth S.

*Chrys. in demonstr. aduersus Gentiles quod Christus sit Deus. to. 3.*

Chrisostome saying. *Neque sic regia corona ornatur caput, vt Cruce: subinde omnes ea se signant &c.* The crosse is a better ornament for the head of a Christian, then the Diademe or crowne of a kinge, when as all men do signe themselues therwith, in their cheefest and principalest member, which is the fore-head, beinge the piller in which the same is engraued: soe it is vsed in the Eucharist and in the holy Orders of priesthood: likewise it shineth at Christs bodie, at his misticall supper, at home and abroade, aboue and in companie, in your iourney, at sea, in the shipp, in your apparell, in your weapons and armes, in the bodies of beastes ill at ease, in the bodies of men possessed by the diuills, so as all men ought to be greedie of this maruailous and pretious good, of which they ought to be verie carfull: thus fare S. Chrisostome of this noble crosse, of which none that is a good Chris-

tian

tian is ashamed, but the Heretique is confounded therwith.

16. The same also S. Augustine insinuated, saying. Let him delude and tryumph ouer Christ crucified, *insultat ille Christo crucifixo &c.* I may behold the crosse of Christ in the fore-head of kinges, that which he despiseth, is a saluation to me, none is so prowde as the diseased man, that scornes his owne cure, if he will not scorne it, he should himselfe receaue it, and therwith be healed: the signe of the crosse is the signe of humilitie, but pride will not ymbrace the meanes by which her loftinesse may be remedied. And in another place he saith. *Quid est quod omnes nouerunt signum Christi? &c.* What is the cause that all men doe knowe the signe of the holy crosse, which signe if it be not vsed in our fore-heades, or in the water by which wee be regenerated, or in the holie oyle by which wee be anointed, in the Chrysme or in the sacrifice by which wee are nourished, nothinge of all these is well done. Againe in another place he saith. *Crucis mysterio rudes cathechisantur &c.* By the misterie of the crosse, the ignorant are cathechised, the fountayne of our regeneration is consecrated, by imposition of handes the baptized receaue the guift of graces, Churches are dedicated, Altares are consecrated, Priestes and Leuites are promoted vnto holie orders, and all ecclesiasticall Sacraments

*Aug. in Psal 141.*

*Idem trac. 118. in Ioannem.*

*Idem ser. 19. le sanctis.*

cramenents by the vertue of the croſſe are perfected and conſumated. Abdius that was diſciple vnto the Apoſtles, who wrote their liues, and their acts, doth alſo obſerue, howe often at all occaſions of dangers they made the ſigne of the Croſſe on their foreheades, which euerie Chriſtian alſo doeth obſerue in all ages, in all dangers and perils: all Chriſtian Churches, in euery kingdome and Prouince, from age to age, from poſteritie to poſteritie, are framed and ſhaped in likenes of this bleſſed Croſſe, in which
croſſe S. Paul did glorie ſo much, that he
*Gal. 5.* ſaid the world was crucified vnto him, and
*1. Pet. 5.* he alſo crucified vnto the world, by which
*Gal. 2.* *Gal. 6.* S. Peter ſaith he himſelfe was ioyned and
faſtened vnto Chriſt.

---

*Whether Papiſtes blaſpheme againſt God, in ſayinge that any man can meritt.*

## CHAPTER I.

1. THe cauſe, wherfore you will not haue merittes in man, is becauſe you ſay, that no man though neuer ſoe iuſt, or by any grace of God a man
may haue, can keepe, or obſerue his com-
*Ioſue. 11.* mandements. Which is moſt falſe, for in
*3. Regum.* the holie ſcriptures, manie godlie men are
prayſed becauſe they haue kept and obſerued
godes

godes comaundements, as may appeare in diuers places. Was not Zacharie and Elizabeth iuste before God, because they did walke in the comaundements and iustifications of our Lord without blame? This is confirmed by Ezech. *Spiritum meum ponam;* I will fixe my spiritt in the middest of you and I will cause you that you shall walke in my precepts, and that you shall obserue and keepe my comaundements. And although without godes grace, the comaundements cannot be performed, yet by the grace of the holie ghost which is promised to the iust, they may be kepte, for by that grace the yoke of Christ is made light, and his burden sweete, and as S. Iohn saith, his comaundements are not heauie. This is proued by the holie fathers, especially S. Augustine. *Non igitur Deus impossibilia iubet &c.* Therfore God doth not comaunde thinges impossible, but comaunded you to doe, what yow may doe, and to aske of him what of your selfe you coulde not doe. And according hereunto holie S. Hierom saith. *Execramur (inquit) eorum blasphemias &c.* Wee execrate their blasphemies, because they said, that God comaunded any thinge impossible, and that Godes comaundemēts may be kept not onlie of some, but of manie. The same verie wordes S. Augustine hath, vnto which agreeth S. Basill, sayinge; It is a wicked sayinge, that preceptes of the

*Luca 10.*

*Ezec. 36.*

*Matt. 11.*

*Iohn. 5.*

*Aug. lib. de natur. & gratia. cap. 43.*

*Symbo. ad Damas.*

*Aug. ser. 100. 91. de tēpore.*

*Basil. in oratione super illud. attende tibi.* spiritt are impossible. Wherfore by the holie councell of Auransica in Affrique, and of Trent, the contrarie is defined as a matter of faith, for if men coulde not obserue the *Con Trid. sess. 6. Cano. 18.* preceptes of God, it should be no offence to transgresse them: for noe man offendeth in that he cānot shunne. And therfore almightie God without cause and most iniustlie should punishe transgressors, either in this world or in the next, but he doth not iniustlie punish offendors, but iustlie, for the offences which they could haue auoided, and for not doinge the good which they could haue done.

*Obiection.* 2. But the heretiques obiect against this catholique doctrine, that by the comaundement, thou shalt loue thy Lord thy God, withall thy harte &c. and thou shalt not couett, wee ought so to direct and ordayne all our actions, thoughts, and affections vnto God, suppresinge, and mortifyinge all concupiscence of our proper desire or comoditie, as the Apostle saith. *1. Cor. 10. & 16.* Referr all your actions vnto God, and lett all you actions be don in charitie: but noe man can performe this thinge, for as longe as a man liueth in the flesh, he doth couett against the spiritt. Wherfore in all our actions though neuer so iust, those two precepts are violated, touchinge the loue of God, and not to couett any thinge.

3. Wee answere that the precepte of louinge

louinge God is affirmatiue, and neuer bindeth any man allwaies, and at all tymes, so as wee should neuer cease from louinge God actually, that is to say, in euerie time or moment to shew and declare the effects of our loue, by externall signes and tokens, but by that precepte wee are bound, to shewe our loue outwardlie, and to putt it in due execution, when iust opportunitie and fitt occasion shalbe offered, and neuer to preferre any creature before God; For, to thinke of God allwaies, and to direct all our actions vnto him, is not meant or comprehēded in the obligation of this precepte, but is a good councell, and a thinge which shalbe accomplished in the state of blisse & euerlastinge felicitie, as S. Thomas and S. Augustine doe declare. *D. Tho. 2. 2. q. 44. art. 6. Aug lib. de perfect. iust.*

4. Secondarilie wee answere, that the precepte, thou shalt not couett, byndes vs that wee should not obey or yelde vnto the filthie motions of concupiscence which are called, *motus primo primi*, by free delectation and consent, which comandement the Apostle inculcateth in other, sayinge: *Non regnet peccatum in vestro mortali corpore, vt obediatis concupiscentijs eius*. Lett not sinne raigne in your corruptible bodie, that you shold yeld or consent therunto, so longe as the concupiscēce of the same doe not raigne, that precepte is not violated, for to feele the vnbridled motions of concupiscence is *Rom. 6.*

Aug. li. 1. de nuptijs & concupis. c. 23. & lib. 5. contra Iulianum. D. Greg. & Ozius in confess.

not a ſinne, but to yeld conſent therunto is a ſinne; for it is manifeſt that many doe not yeid vnto filthie cõcupiſcence, but with all ſpeedie meanes and force, they reſiſt the ſame by the grace of God, which is readie to be offred to euery one that will imploie his beſt endeuour. Soe auoucheth S. Auguſtine and S. Gregorie, Ozius and other holie fathers. To the intent therfore that you may take awaie all good indeuours, from man in the buyſines of his ſaluation, and that wee ſhould doe nothinge therin, you take away all cooperation of man with godes grace, and that grace it ſelfe without which wee can doe nothinge in the worke of our iuſtification, you take it quite awaie, ſayinge that man hath not this grace inherent in him. To this purpoſe you ſay with Luther in his ſecond booke of the captiuitie of Babylon, that to teach that good workes are neceſſarie to ſaluation is deuiliſhe. You ſay alſo with Caluine, that neuer any good workes were done of any ſaincte, which did not deſerue reproache. And a little before, he ſaid, that all our workes are pernitious, and whoſoeuer doth them is curſed. And the ſaid Luther in the 30. articles condẽned of Leo the Tenthe ſaith: all the euill that wee doe is by the inſpiration of God, and that by ſinninge wee doe well, God beinge the cauſe of all euill, as Caluine ſaith, in ſo much ſaith he, that not to ſinne,

2. lib. de capt.

Calu 3. de inſtit. c. 19

lib. 1. inſt. cap. 28.

is sinne, and to restraine any appetite or motion of any thought, is to resist God and to sinne. And so Luther saith in his booke, the more wicked you be, the neerer you are to purchase godes fauour. How damnable these articles be, lett any Christian iudge that will open his eares to heare them. I would euerie one would stoppe his eares from hearinge such horrible blasphemies, so contrarie to holie scriptures, and all honestie. Noe prophane Philosopher or wicked heretique though neuer so damnable, euer said the like. And therfore these blasphemous and wicked articles, are condemned by the whole Senate of Christianitie, in the councell of Trent, & most worthilie: because they be against comon honestie, and against the holy scriptures, in which many tymes the workes and endeuours of good people, are comended and praysed as good and holie, in which works there was noe sinne, as it is said in Iob. In all these thinges Iob hath not offended: and in the Ghospell of S. Luke it is said of Zacharias and Elizabeth, that both of them were iust before God, walkinge in godes comandements and righteousnes without grudge. And as S. Paule saith: if a virgin should marrie, therein shee shoulde not sinne, and in many other places wee are comaunded not to comitte sinne, therfore the holie scriptures doe meane that wee may doe, many

*Lib de ser. arbit.*

*Con. Trid. sess. c. 11. & cano. 28. & 21.*

*Iob. 1.*

*Luca 1.*

*1. Cor. 7.*

many good works by godes grace without sinne.

5. Hereticks answere vnto these scriptures sayinge, that the cause wherfore the scriptures saies that there are many good works of iust persons, is, because it is not imputed vnto them to damnation for the faith of Christ, although say they, they be sinfull. I replie against that, for the scriptures doe distinguish betwixt this which is to sinne, and that which is to remitte sinnes, or not to impute vnto vs the sinne which wee haue comitted, as it is playne; *Scribo vobis vt non peccetis:* I write vnto you that yow should not sinne, for if any man shall sinne, wee haue an aduocate with the Father &c. this trueth is confirmed by the tradition of the Church, and the holie fathers. It is also defined against Pelagius, that without the grace of God, a man cannot liue iustlie without sinne: yet saith the councell by the grace of God wee may liue without offence. Therfore S. Hierom saith. *Hoc (inquit) & nos dicimus, posse hominem &c.* And this selfe same wee saie also, that a man maye liue without sinne, if it please him accordinge to the tyme and place, accordinge to the frailtie of his nature as longe as his mind is well disposed &c. And the same he teacheth vpon that place of S. Paul: *Vt essemus sacti & immaculati*, as S. Amb. sup. Luc. S. Aug. and other saincts doe teach the like.

*1. Ioh. 2. Conc. Aurauc. c. 9. 18. & 20. Hier. li. 3. contra Pelag. In Proemio super epist. ad Philomen. Ephes. 1. Aug. sup. Luc. 1. Amb. de Spiritu & litera. cap 36. De natura & gratia reg. super Cõc. Trid.*

*Pro-*

*Protestants saie, that a Christian though neuer so vertuous, or so acceptable to God, hath noe grace, or vertue inherent in him; because they would haue noe good acte to come from man, by reason of that grace.*

## CHAPTER II.

1. THe generall Councell of Trent against this your heresie saith; The onlie formall and intrinsicall cause of our iustification, is the iustice of God, not by which he is iust himselfe, but by which he makes vs iust, by which wee beinge endued, and inuested, wee be renewed by the spiritt of our soule, and not onlie that wee be soe reputed, but that wee are trulie iust, not only by name, but by deede; and the said holy councell hath these words. Whosoeuer shal saie that men are iustified, either only by remission of our sinnes, or only by the imputation of the iustice of Christ, excludinge & takinge away grace and charitie, which is diffused in their hartes, by the holie Ghost, which is giuen vnto them, and by which the same grace doth lodge in them, *Anathema sit*, let him be anathema. Thus farre the councell. This also is proued by reason; for when wee see a man to change his wicked life, and vngodlie custome of sinne,

*Cōc. Trid. sess. 6. c. 7.*

finne, and to putt on the newe man, which accordinge to God was created in sanctitie and iustice, wee see so palpable a change in him, that wee say. *Hæc est mutatio dextræ excelsi*. From the right hand of the highest comes this alteration, from bad to good, from impietie to iustice, from spirituall death to spirituall life: but this true alteration and mutation cannot be without some feelinge or sparke of grace in man inwardly inherent in him. The Maior proposition is proued by the gospell. Wee are translated
*1. Ioh. 3.* from death to life, and Ezeech. I will giue
*Ezec. 36.* vnto you a newe harte, and I will put into the middest of you hart a newe spiritt, and
*Coloss. 3.* I will take away a stonie harte, and S. Paule saith. Spoile yourselues of the old man with his actes, and putt one the newe, that is renewed in knowledge accordinge to the Image of him that created him. And to the
*4. Ephes.* Ephesians, he said, be renewed in the spiritt of your minde, and putt one the newe man, which accordinge to God is created in iustice and holynes of trueth, I meane in true holynes and iustice, and not in feined
*Iohn. 4.* imputatiue iustice. This is proued by S. Iohn of whom it is said of the grace, and iustice by which wee be ordained to life euerlasstinge, there will be in him a fountaine of
*Ioh. c. 7.* water issuinge to life euerlasting. And in another place he said, whosoeuer beleeueth in me, there shall flowe fountaines of water
of

of life out of his bellie: this he said of the spiritt, that the faithfull should receaue, I meane of the spiritt that should sanctifie & iustifie vs inwardly, and further vs to worke, and to fructifie to life euerlastinge. And as it is said, he that is borne of God doth not comitt sinne against him, because his seede remaynes in him, which is the grace of God fructifyinge, and buddinge forth to life euerlasting. Bellarmine, & Ozius bringe many places to proue this amoungest many I will alleadg a fewe. S. Basill. *Gratia Spiritus in eo qui recipit illam est &c.* the grace of the spiritte, who so receaues the same, is as the eye-sight in a sound eye, and as an arte in him that workes by arte: and S. Ambrose doth compare that grace to a figure or a beautified Image. Wherfore he saith. Doe not blott any beautifull picture, not framed in waxe but in grace: and as S. Cyrill saith that the iust is framed by grace to be the child of God. In the same manner doe speake Ireneus, Cyprianus, Hieron. S. August. and other fathers.

*Ioh 3.*

*Basil lib. de Spiritu sancto. cap. 29.*

*Cyrill. lib. 4. in Isay. oratione 2.*

2. This is confirmed by verie reason, for if a man be not saued by godes grace inherent in him, but only by this that God doth couer and hide our offences, and that he doth not impute vnto vs our said offences and trespasses, then it followeth that that they be not blotted or taken away by the merites of Christs passion: which is

most false, and against the scripture, for
*Ioh. 1.* S. Iohn saith, beholde the Lambe of God
*Hebr. 9.* that takes away the offences of the worlde: and in another place. The blood of Iesus Christ doth clense vs from all our sinnes; and S. Paule saith, the blood of Christ doth purge vs from deadlie workes, that is to say, from wicked desires, to serue the liuinge God which was offred to abolishe our offences. This is proued, for the passion of Christ should be of greater excellencie and efficacie to disroote, blott and take away altogether our sinnes and the blemishes therof, restoringe vnto vs by grace an inherent qualitie of godes inspiration, then if he should couer, or hide them onlie, therfore in not grauntinge this, you derogate from the passion of Iesus Christ.

3. Another absurditie doth followe, that one iust parson hath no more iustice or grace then another, and that all in the kingdome of heauen, shall haue equall glorie which is against S. Paule sayinge, that as one Starr excelleth another in brightnesse, soe one iust doth excell another in iustice and grace. Hence followeth also, that noe iust man by godes grace, meritts by any good worke that he doth, and that those that are predestinated, neuer comitt any deadlie offence: all which notwithstandinge so great absurdities and damnable heresies, yet hereticks doe graunt them, and builde their beleefe vpon them.

In

*In that heretiques reprehend the Catholick Church, yea condemne her of great folly, for endeuouringe her selfe to receaue godes grace: they by this meanes take away free will from man, and all due preparation, and disposition to receaue godes grace, and diuine influence.*

## CHAPTER III.

1. LVther (as the holy Martyr Roffensis said) in his 36. articles doth barke, and speake many blasphemies against contrition, the feare of hell, the endeuours in his saluation: yea he said the more wicked you be, the neerer you are to gett the fauour of God, *Lutherus de piscat. F* and if you adorne your selfe with good workes, you preuaile nothinge with God. But the holy catholique church hath condemned these wicked propositions as damnable and execrable heresie, both repugnant, not onlie to the holie scriptures, but also contrarie to good manners & ciuill honestie. For God doth exhorte and comaund sinners, that they should conuert themselues vnto him, and that they should prepare their hartes, that he might confer his grace and his iustice vnto them. *Conuertimini &c.* *Zach. 1.* Turne vnto me with all your harts and I will turne vnto you: the Councell of Trentt saith, when God saith, turne

you vnto me, and I will turne vnto you:
Seß.6.c.5 wee are admonished of our owne libertie in this matter, and when wee saie. Turne vs to thee, wee are putt in minde that God by his grace doth preuent and helpe vs, and as it is the worke of Gods grace, to rayse and eleuate our soules to receaue the influence thereof: soe it pertaynes to the wil of man so raysed and eleuated, by godes motions and inspirations, to consent therunto, and
3.Reg.7. to turne to God almightie. And as it is said, if you will returne from your harte, take awaie strange godes from your hartes, and prepare your hartes to our Lord. And it is
Prou.16. said allso; *hominis est præparare*. Lett man prepare his soule: *qui timet &c.* Whosoeuer feares God, they shall prepare their hartes, and in his presence they shall sanctifie their
Ezech.18. soules. *Cum auerterit se impius ab impietate sua &c.* when the wicked man shall turne from his impietie, and shall doe iudgment
Iohn.6. and iustice, he shall sanctifie his soule. And, make to your selues a newe harte and a newe spiritt. All you that haue heard the the Father and learned from him, let him
Ad.Phi.2 come vnto me. Worke your saluation
Cant. with feare and tremblinge. My sister, and
Apoc.3. my spouse come vnto me &c. Behold I stand at your doore, and knocke at your gate, if any man will open, I will enter &c. In which, and other places wee are bidd to turne to God, and to clense our hartes from

from the filth of sinne. And as God giues vs his helpe soe wee receaue the same without resistance, and yealde our harts and resigne our thoughts vnto him. Wherfore S. Augustine saith, the beginninge of our saluation wee haue from the mercie of God, but to condiscend to his hoalsome inspiration, it is in our owne choise or power. And in another place, in all thinges godes mercie doth preuent vs, but to condescend to godes vocation, or to disagree from the same, it is in our will. It is in mans power to change his will into better, but that power is nothinge vnlesse it be giuen of God. And the same holie doctor comparing Pharao with Nabuchodonosor said, that in all thinges they were all a like, and that both of them were equallie preuented by godes diuine mercie, yet notwithstandinge they had different endes, because Pharao against godes mercie did oppose his free will. Nabuchodonosor beinge touched with godes discipline, bewailed his owne impietie; And in another place, he saith, that if two persons had equall graces, and equall temperature, both of bodie and soule, one of them may behaue himselfe well by his free will, another by the same free will may behaue himselfe ill.

*Aug. li. de ecclesiasticis dogmatibus cap. 21. lib. de Spiritu & litera cap. 34. & lib. 1. retract. cap. 22.*

*Aug. de prædest & grat. c. 15. Aug. li de ciuit. c. 6.*

2. That a man must dispose himselfe to receaue godes grace S. Thomas proues it by naturall reason, for the forme can neuer

*D. Tho. q. 1. 2. q. 113*

uer be receaued into the subiect, without aswell the disposition of the forme, as of the subiect, especially when the subiect hath alreadie a disposition repugnant to the forme: but a miserable sinner is loaden with sinne, then the which nothinge is more repugnant to godes grace, by which wee be gratefull vnto him: therfore that this may be introduced, there must be a conuenient disposition, which ought to be correspondent vnto man. This is proued, for as sinne was voluntarilie comitted, therfore a man must haue a voluntarie disposition to forgoe sinne: almightie God would haue al men to be saued, therfore man is in faulte, and not God that he is not saued. Otherwise if this doctrine had not bene true, in vaine did the Prophetts, Apostles, and preachers in their sermons, admonitiōs and exhortations crie vnto the people, that they should turne them vnto God, and prepare themselues with due pennance and other blessed workes, to reforme themselues, and to dispose themselues to serue God, to obtaine his grace and remission of their sinnes, by meanes of those vertues which are giuen vnto man to saue him. It is proued likewise by the holie councelles, and namlie by the *Aurans.* councell of Auransican, of which Celestine *Celest.* pope makes mention to the Bishoppes of *epistola. 1.* France; It is defined, saith he, that wee ought to cooperate with the helpe of godes grace

grace in these thinges that appertayne vnto our saluation, that by the meanes of our cooperation and disposition, wee may be saued before God.

3. This is also proued, for that wee haue alreadie proued that sinners are iustified by a certaine forme or grace inherent in man: therfore there must be some disposition in respect of the free will to receaue that forme or grace. For accordinge to the ordinance of God, noe subiecte receaues any forme, without a disposition in the subiect, accordinge to the naturall inclination of the subiect: but naturall subiects are disposed naturallie, therfore free subiects are to be disposed freelie, accordinge to the exigence and condition of their nature.

4. Heretiques doe obiect against this doctrine, that of the Romaines. *Non volentis neque currentis &c.* It is not of him that willeth, nor of him that runneth, but of godes mercie. Not of the workes of iustice, that wee haue done, but accordinge to his mercie, he saueth vs. Man in respect of his owne iustification is as it were a masse of claye in the handes of the potter, or els a deade instrument without any proper motion, as Isayas saith, shall the axe glorie or boast against him that cuttes with the same, or shall the sawe lyft it selfe vpp against him that draweth the same? otherwise it should not be said that man is iustified freelie, but

*Ad Titum. 3.*

*Isa. 64.*
*Hier. 18.*
*Rom. 9.*

*Isa. 10.*

for his, good woorks, and rather that he ſhould iuſtifie himſelfe.

5. Wee anſwere that the whole worke of our iuſtification is attributed vnto God, becauſe he is the principall doer and agent thereof, not onlie by powringe his grace vpon vs, but alſo in diſpoſinge our wills to receaue the ſame by a ſpeciall motion of his diuine grace. Notwithſtādinge it is aſcribed vnto man alſo in that wee cooperate, and that wee doe ſomthinge in the worke of our iuſtification, as I haue allreadie alleadged out of ſcripture: otherwiſe they ſhould not be prayſed that with all their harts ſhould turne vnto God, neither ſhould they be diſpraiſed that doe reſiſte godes vocation, otherwiſe they ſhould contradict the prophett. *Expandi manus meas tota die ad populum incredulum & contradicentem mihi.* I haue ſtretched my handes all the whole day to an incredulous people and contradictinge me. And alſo it ſhould not be ſaid. *Vos duræ ceruicis reſiſtitis Spiritu ſancto.* You ſtif-necked people, you reſiſte the holie ghoaſte.

*Seſſ. 9. c. 5* 6. Therfore the Councell of Trentt hath damned thoſe heretiques that ſaid, that wee haue noe free will in the worke of our iuſtification, and that wee are dead & without life in thoſe actions. For though a man beinge lefte to his owne naturall forces and ſtrenghte, hath noe actiue force to to obtaine the grace of God or yet any disposition therevnto, notwithstandinge as a man is holpen and moued of God, and eleuated aboue his owne nature by Godes helpe, he doth cooperate actiuelie, freelie disposinge himselfe to receaue the same. And therfore S. Paule saith. *Non ego, sed gratia Dei mecum*; not, I in respecte of myne owne nature and force, but in respect of the grace of God with me. And to that which you obiect out of S. Paule videlicet: wee should not be said to be iustified gratis or freelie. I answere it is not soe taken, but in respect of meritts, which is called *meritum de condigno*, that is to say, that a man hath done woorks before Gods grace worthie of Godes grace, which catholiques doe not say; and that gratis takes not away the freedome of man, neither doth it followe that a man can iustifie himselfe, yet may it be said that a man maie dispose himselfe to receaue Gods grace, as 2. Eccl. *In conspectu illius sanctificabunt animas suas*. And Ezech: in his sight they shall sanctifie their soules: and, he hath quickned his owne soule.

7. This is proued by naturall reason as also in all supernaturall actions, for the meanes by which man doth turne vnto God, is by the acts of faith, hope, and charitie, and a penitent harte, but it should be an implication against all reason, that a man should beleeue in God, hope, and loue God,

and be penitent for offendinge God, and that he should doe nothinge therein, or that when a man doth pennaunce, or loueth God, it should be said he loues not God or doth noe pennaunce: in which wee see two contradictories true, which cannot be, for one must be false when the other is true, for if it be true that a man hath faith, or beleefe in God, therfore the contradictorie is false, that man hath no faith, nor doth not beleeue in God: euen as it is false that the fire doth burne, and the sunne giue light, and yet that none of them doth any thinge. For to beleeue, or to hope, or to loue, in man are called vitall, and immanent actions, which cannot be supplied by any other cause, then by such principles out of which they be produced; but to beleeue, or to loue, are produced out of the two principles of man, I meane vnderstandinge and will, for it is not the action of God immediatlie, but the action of man of whome immediatlie and next it is produced, for it is not said that any other creature doth loue God, but man when man doth loue God: and therfore you must not saie, that man beleeuinge, hopinge in God, and louinge God, are not the actions of man when he hath the principles, I meane vnderstandinge and will out of which they procede.

*Whether*

*Whether wee derogate from the merittes of Christ, in making our meritts partakers of his meritts.*

## CHAPTER IV.

1. GOd forbid that the merittes of the iust should derogate from Christs B. passion, or should be iniurious vnto him; they rather are a great glorie vnto Christe, beinge the fruicts of the merittes of his passion, which of themselues haue noe valour or excellencie, but as they are bedewed and sprinckled with the blood of Christe, vnto whome wee owe the merittes of them by his grace, and not vnto our selues, as *Albertus magnus* saith. *Iustitia meritorum Christi, fulget in virtutibus sanctorum.* The iustice of the merittes of Christ, doth shine in the vertues and woorks of the Sainctes. Take awaie this iustice from them, and they may be condemned, yea they cannot be saued. Therfore wee saie that a reward is giuen vnto them, not as they come from vs, but as they come from his grace, which worketh in vs. And he himselfe saith. *Merces vestra copiosa est in Cælis:* your reward is great in heauen, which reward is giuen vnto our workes by Christ, whoe makes our workes worthie thereof.

*Albert. ar. 3. q. 2. in 29. d.*

*Matt. 5.*

2. This argument is weake. Christ sufficientlie

ficientlie merited for man, therfore a man ought not to meritt anie thinge himselfe, Christ prayed, Christ suffred, Christ preached, Christe fasted, and offred himselfe vnto God for our sinnes; therfore wee should not merite; wee should not praye, nor suffer; nor preach; nor faste; nor offer our selues to God. Whereas Christ merited, prayed, fasted, suffred, and offered himselfe, that I should merite, fast, praie, suffer &c. When as the actions of Christe are our instructions, and although Christ suffred for all, yet he left vs, as S. Peter said, an example to followe his stepps. And though the meritts of Christs passion are of themselues sufficient to purchase, and merite life euerlastinge for all men, yet he would not haue the efficacie thereof to be applied vnto vs, vnlesse wee would endeuour by his grace, to ioyne also our meritts therunto; which yet derogates nothinge from the passion of Christ, for it is more excellent to obtaine glorie by deserts, then without the same: and therfore our meritts are not required for the insufficiencie of the meritts of Christ, but rather are required for the great excellencie of the meritts of them, and of his great loue, and charitie towardes vs.

3. Wee saie with the whole catholique church, the good workes of iust persons, if they proceede of the grace of God, doe deserue

deserue and meritte life euerlastinge which
doth consiste in the cleere vision, and frui-
tion of God, this is proued by many places
of scripture. Gode giues euerie man accordinge to his workes: and in the Apocalips. I
come, and my reward is with me to giue
euerie man, as his worke shalbe: & with the *Psal. 65.*
Apostle; Euerie man shall receaue accordin- *Matt. 16.*
ge to his owne labour: where in trueth, he *Rom. 2.*
spoke of the reward of life euerlastinge. And *1. Cor. 3.*
when our Sauiour saith, blessed be the
poore in spiritt, blessed be the poore in hart,
he concludes, reioice and be glad, for your *Matt. 5.*
reward is great in the kingdome of heauen:
in another place he saith. Come yee blessed
of my father, I haue bene hungrie and you *Matt. 25*
gaue me to eate, come and possesse the kingdome of heauen. And as the Apostle saith, *Gal. 8.*
*qui seminat in Spiritu*, he that soweth in the
spiritt or spirituall workes: he shal purchase
life euerlastinge: if you will enter into life,
keepe the comaundements. Euerie one that
shall forgoe howse &c. he shall receaue an
hundreth fould, and he shall possesse life
euerlastinge. Blessed is that man that suffers *Matt. 19.*
tentation &c. when he shalbe tried he shall
receaue a crowne of life which God promised to those that loue him. The Apostle
saith pietie is profitable to all thinges hauinge promise of the life, that now is, and
of that to come.

4. Some heretiques aunswere these
places,

places, that God giues life euerlastinge to those that worke well vnto the end, but not that our workes deserues the same. Vnto this I replie, when it is said that life euerlastinge is the reward of good deedes, and that by the promise of God it is giuen to those workes, it is sufficiently explicated, that good workes doe merite life euerlastinge. Merites and rewardes are correlatiues which are said to be the promise, hire, or recompence that are giuen for works, the
*Heb. 13.* verie woord is declared by S. Paule. And beneficence and communication doe not
*Eccles. 16.* forget, for with such hostes God is promerited; and it is said in another place, all mercie maketh place to euerie one accordinge
*Con. Arã. cap. 16.* to the merittes of his woorks. It is auouched by the counsells. *Debetur merces bonis operibus si fiant, sed gratia, quæ non debetur, præcedit, vt fiant.* Reward is due vnto good workes if they be done, but grace which is not due doth goe before that they may be
*Lateran. sub Innocent. 3.* done. By the councell of Lateran. *cap. firmiter de summa trinitate. Omnes iusti cuiuscunque conditionis sunt & statim per opera bona prælucentes Deo merentur ad æternam vitam peruenire.*
*Con. Floren. in decreto de purg.* All iust men of whatsoeuer condition they be, shininge by theire good works before God, they deserue to come to euerlastinge life. The councell of Florence saith, that by
*Con Trid. sess 6. cap. vlt.* diuersitie of workes, one sees God more cleerer thẽ another. This is proued by al the fathers.

fathers. *Ignatius, Ireneus, Iustinus, Origines, Basil. Chrisost. Nazian.* and *Nisse: Tertul: Cyprian: Hillar: Ambro: August: Paulinus: Prosper: Gregorius Papa: & Bernard: as Cardinall Bellarmin cites.*

5. S. Augustine saith; *Sicut merito peccati tanquam stipendium redditur mors, ita merito iustitiæ tanqum stipendium redditur vita æterna.* As sinne is rewarded with death, soe iustice is rewarded with life euerlastinge: and as Celestinus saith. *Tanta erga homines est bonitas Dei, vt nostra velit esse merita, quæ sunt ipsius dona.* Soe great is the goodnes of God towardes men, that he would haue to be our desertes, which are his guifts. He that laboures in the seruice of any man, whatsoeuer he is promised by his bargaine, he ought to receaue the same accordinge to the promise made: but the iust people doe labour in godes seruice by a bargaine to receaue, *denarium diurnum*, the daylie hire which is life euerlasting, accordinge the exposition of the Doctors vpon S. Mathewe: therfore almightie God ought to giue vnto iust people accordinge to his promise, and accordinge to their desertes, which deserts are called. *Merita de condigno*, condigne meritts as S. Paule saith, I haue fought a good fight &c. there is layde vp for me a crowne of iustice &c. Glorie is called a crowne of iustice, because it is giuen as the debt of iustice, and because it is giuen by the

*Ad Episc. Galliæ cap. 12.*

*Matt. 20.*

*2. Timoth.*

the iust iudge in the daie of iuste iudgment.
*Eep. 6.* And in another place God is not iniust that
*Psal. 17.* he should forget your workes; God will
*Apoc. 3.* retribute vnto me accordinge to my iustice.
*Thes. 1.* They did walke with me in white because
*Luc. 10.* they were worthie. That you may be made
*Luc. c. 10.* worthie of the kingdome of God, for the
*Sap. 3.* which you suffer. The workman is worthie of his wages. They shalbe worthie of that world and the resurrection from the dead. And in another place. God did assay them and found them worthie of himselfe. For life euerlastinge is giuen to iust persons as the reward of theire workes, accordinge to the 20. ghospell of S. Mathewe, where *denarius diurnus*, is the daylie pennie or wages, that is giuen vnto euerie one for his worke: but it is certaine that those labourers did deserue by iustice the daylie pennye, as it is manifest that the husband man said in that gospel to one of the laborers; frind I doe you noe wronge, did not you bargaine with me for a penny? take your owne and depart in peace, that is to say; so much must I giue you as I promised and bargained, and vnto that, and to nothinge else you haue right, and if I should denie you that, I should doe you great wronge.

*Aug. li. de nat & grat ca. 2. lib 4. aduers. Iul. cap. 3.*

6. S. Augustine, saith. *Non est iniustus Deus.* God is not iniust, that he should deceaue the iust of the reward of iustice. In another place he saith. God should be vniuste,

iuste, if he should not admitte iust people into his kingdome. And S. Bernard saith. *Promissum quidem ex misericordia*, that which was promised by his mercie, must be perfourmed by his iustice. Vnto this agreeth S. Basil sayinge. All wee that frame our life accordinge to Christs ghospel, wee are as marchants, & by the woorks of the comandements we purchase vnto our selues celestiall possessions. Therfore it is lawfull to labour, for to purchase the kingdome of heauen, as the prophett saith. *Inclinaui cor meum &c.* I enclined my hart to keepe these comaundements for retribution or recompence. It is lawfull also to repose hope and confidence in our proper meritts secundarilie, although principallie, and cheeflie wee must repose our hope in God, as in the cheefest cause, who gaue vs grace and vertue to worke well, as S. Thomas saith. For if our workes done by godes grace, had not bene meritorious, why should the Apostle saie, in doinge good lett vs not faile, for in due tyme wee shall reape, not faylinge. And therfore saith he, whiles wee haue tyme, lett vs worke good to all, but speciall to the houshould of faith: these be the workes that are done of a man, that is in godes fauour. *Qui seminat in Spiritu &c.* he that soweth in the spiritt, he shall reape life euerlastinge. I beseech you brethren, saith he, that you will walke worthilie, plea-

*Bern. de grat. & lib. arb.*

*Basil. in oratione super prouerbia Salomonis.*

*Psal. 18.*

*D.Tho. 2. 2.q. 17.*

*Ad Gal. 6*

*Coloss. c. 1.*

*Rom. 10.*

pleasing God, fructifyinge in all good workes. For these blessed workes done of the good, doe not only redounde to the saluation of man, but also to the glorie of God, as it is said in the ghospell. *Sic luceat lux vestra coram hominibus, vt videntes opera bona vestra glorificent &c.* Let your light soe shine before, men that seing your good worckes, they may glorifie your father which is in heauen. So heretiques condemning the woorks of good men, take away godes glorie, the good example that wee are bound to giue vnto our neighbors, and Gods promise to giue life euerlastinge for them, and consequentlie take awaie mans endeuour and labour in the exercise of them, which is against S. Peter sayinge. *Fratres magis satagite, vt per bona opera &c.* Wherfore brethren endeuor the more that by good woorks you make sure your vocation, and election. And finally take away all christian religion, which is nothinge else then precepts, admonitions and councells, to imploie our life and our lymmes in the exercise of them. Vnto the riche people Christ biddeth them to make vnto themselues freindes of the Mammon of iniquity, that when they faile, they may receaue them into the eternall tabernacles. Vnto all sortes of christians he proclaimeth and diuulgeth, that vnlesse their iustice abound more then that of the Scribes and Pharisies, they shall not

*Petr. 1.*

*Luc. 16.*

*Matt. 5.*

not enter into the kingdome of heauen.

7. Wherfore the puritie and sanctitie of life in the professors of this christian catholique religion, which not onlie with subtile arguments and craftie deuises rather suggested by the diuil then inuented by man, heretiques impugne, but also with al the straungest lawes, the seuerest policies, and the cruellest persecutions that euer were, or could be inuented, or imagined, or apprehended by any creature, they goe about to ouerthrowe and confound, the reformation of their manners, the mortification of their passions, their angellicall conuersation in in their behauiour, their blessed and heroicall resolutions in suffringe all exquisite torments in the defence, testimonie and confirmation thereof, their morall life adorned and replenished with all morall and supernaturall vertues, their eminent learninge and science, tempered with all humilitie of spiritt voide of pride or ambition, their admirable and incomparable workes of charitie, pietie, and deuotion, which is the life and fruictes of true and vnblemished religion, haue bene motiues vnto the gentiles, pagans, yea and to the stiff-necked Iewes themselues to abandon their idolatrie, and to imbrace this christian religion.

8. That these blessed endeuours and works of charitie are the badge and distinctiue token of the true religion of christian

Catholiques by which their conuersation should be acceptable vnto God, gratefull vnto their neighbors admirable to pagans, terrible to the diuills, and offensiue, hurtfull or scandalous to none. S. Paule auoucheth

*Ephes. 4.* the same. I prisoner, saith he, in our Lord beseech you, that you walke worthie of the vocation in which you are called with all humilitie and midlnesse, with patience, supportinge one another in charitie, carefull to keepe the vnitie of the spiritt in the bonde of peace. And in the same chapter he saith, I testifie in our Lord that nowe you walke not as the Gentiles walke in the vanitie of their sinne, hauinge their vnderstandinge

*1. Pet. 4. 3. Rom. 1. 21.* obscured with darcknes, alienated from the life of God, by the ignorance that is in them, who dispayringe haue giuen vpp themselues to impudicitie, vnto the operation of all vncleannesse, vnto auarice, but you haue not soe learned Christ. Lay you awaie accordinge to the old conuersation the old man which is corrupted accordinge to the desires of errour. For before the catholique christian religion came into the world, it was nothinge else, then a dungeon full of all filth, a denne of theeues, and most wicked liuers: a fayre or markett where there was nothingto be bought but all kind of crafte, deceite, & diuilish inuentions: a schoole where there was nothinge else to be learned, but to lett loose the raynes

nes

nes to all voluptuous pleaſures, beaſtlie appetites, and inhumane concupiſcence of vnſpeakeable and ſhamles impudicitie, of beaſtiality, and Sodomiticall riotouſnes, not only of the gentiles; but alſo of the Iewes themſelues, who had the knowledge of God. Therfore Iſayas the prophett did compare the people of thoſe ages, with dragons, ſerpents, woolues, lyons, beares, and Baſilisks, and for that cauſe he called the world at that tyme the land of waſt, dried, ſterrill, without tyllage, which was nothinge elſe then the denn of wilde beaſts, the caue of ſerpents, the brothell howſe and ſtewes of all filthie liuers: but the chriſtian religion and preachinge of Chriſts goſpell, not only by miracles, but by the ſanctitie and holines of the liues of the prechars, did conuerte wolues into ſheepe, lyons into lambes, ſerpents into doues, and wilde fruitles trees into moſt floriſhinge braunches, bearinge euerlaſtinge fruicte, as the ſaid prophett ſaid, that there ſhould be a tyme, that the deſert ſhould be tranſlated into a pleaſant orchard, and the drie withered ſoyle voyde of trees or hearbes, into a place of pleaſure, which doe ſignifie by this comparison the pulchritude and the beautie of the ſanctitie of ſuch as ſhould floriſh in the world by the chriſtian catholique religion, and the true preachinge of his religious ghoſpell, and ſoe the ſonne of

*Iſa. 35.*

God did appeare that he ſhould diſſolue the the works of the diuill. Iob. 1. Ioh. 3. which he hath done by his owne paſsion and death, as alſo by the preachinge and vertuous life of his ſeruaunts.

9. If any man will knowe further of this matter, lett him reade eccleſiaſticall hiſtoris which doe treate of the ſame, relating the liues of the holie Sainctes and fathers, which liued in the wildernes, and the Chronicles of the holy orders of religion, where he ſhall haue aboundante ſtoare of holy Biſhoppes, Confeſſors and Virgins (which haue crucified their fleſh with the vice and concupiſcence thereof) innumerable ſtore of bleſſed Moncks, whereof ſome liued in their conuents, ſome other ſegregated and eſtranged from humanie ſocietie, where they liued rather like angells then like men, whoſoeuer I ſay ſhall reade ouer the liues of theſe people written by the beſt wyttneſſes that euer were, he ſhal there behold, howe they haue ſpent whole nightes in deuoute prayers, aſwell vocall as mentall, without ſleepe, hauinge noe other bedd then the earthe. He ſhall ſee that the Cells of theſe fathers were ſoe narrowe, that they ſhould ſeeme rather ſepulchers then Cells. He ſhall vnderſtand that many of them had noe other meate then bread and ſalt with water and with Rootes of hearbes, that as Saint Hierom writes, to taſt

*In vita S. Paul Eremitæ.*

tast of any thinge boiled vpon the fire was counted riotuousnes, he shall perceaue such pouertie in their attire that it cannot be more, such was their recollection and retired life wherein they were estranged from all inordinat affection and passion, in which they vsed such wonderfull mortification, as they would not suffer their neerest in blood to approach vnto thẽ. What should I declare their constant abidinge and perseuerance in continuall prayers without wearines, their spiritual exercise without loathsomnes, their discomfortable sollitarines without gruding, hauinge noe other company then that of wilde beasts, vglie serpents and fierce lyons, which with a confident hope fixed in God, they tamed and ouercame. This life was so admirable and soe supernaturall, as they without supernaturall helpe and grace of God could not endure it. What should I speake of their constant sufferinge of all kinde of exquisitt,, and cruell torments, how many battells they fought, howe gloriouslie they haue triumphed ouer the world and the diuill, and all their wicked instruments, and ministers.

10. When our Sauiour gaue vs a caueat of false prophetts, he gaue vs noe other token to discerne them, then by their fruicts, and woorks. Doe men, saith he, gather grapes of thornes, or figgs of thistles, euen so euerie good tree yeldeth good fruicts, and *Matt. 7.*

the euill tree yeldeth euill fruicte. Are not you those falſe prophetts whoſe religion is moſt falſe, in aſmuch as noe good fruicte came euer into the world by it, noe reformation of our manners, noe amendment of our liues, noe mortification of our paſsions, noe reſtraint of our filthie appetites, noe motiue or impulſiue meães that ſhould ſtirr vs vpp vnto any deuotion, but rather giuinge vs all libertie to diſſolution, and to all wanton exerciſe? Haue you not taken awaie all the Euangelicall Councells of our Sauiour in his ghoſpell? Haue you not forbidden all vowes and votaries, all Sacraments and ſacrifice? Haue you not quite aboliſhed confeſsion of our ſinnes? inward contrition in our harte? and externall ſatiſfaction, and reſtitution outwardlie? charitie from our harte? and mercie from our workes? pietie from our ſoules? and humilitie from our ſpiritt? and conſequentlie all conſolatiō from our aflicted conſciences, with the damnable libertie of your wanton and laſciuious ghoſpell as is auouched by the cheefeſt profeſſors thereof? For after this manner doth Smidline ſpeake. *Vt totus mundus cognoſcat eos non eſſe papiſtas nec bonis operibus quidquam fidere &c.* That all the world may knowe that they be not papiſts, neither that they care for good works, they exerciſe none at all. And hauinge reckened infinite wickedneſſe of them, this kinde of life

life (they say) the ghospell hath taught thē: thus he. Erasmus in his epistle ad Neocomum, saith. *Profer mihi &c.* Tell me I pray thee, what man was euer made any thinge the bettter by that ghospell: was there any epicure or gurmandizer made sober or temperate, or any vnchast or shamlesse fellowe, become chast, or honest, or cruell made gentle, or extortioner persuaded to become liberall, or the cursed to become blessed, but I can shewe you many made worse then themselues.

*Episto. Eras. ad Neocomū. 1529.*

11. Luther the roote of all these Rugamuffines hath these wordes; *mundus indies fit deterior &c.* The world (saith he) is euerie daye worse and worse, now men are more greedie of reuenge, more couetous, more remote from all mercie, more immodest, more indisciplinable then they were in poperie. These be Luthers owne wordes. As touching their learninge or knowledge in diuinitie, Francis Stancarus witnesseth one of their prophetts, one Petrus Lombardus is more worthie then one hundreth Luthers, two hundred Melancthons, three hundred Bullingers, foure hundreth Martyrs: fiue hundreth Caluines. Who all if they were pounded in one morter, there could not be beaten out of them one ounce of true diuinitie, especiallie in the articles of the trinitie, incarnation, mediator, and sacraments.

*Luth. in postilla super 1. Dominic. aduentus.*

*Stanc. lib. de trinitate & mediatore.*

12. You ſee what teſtimonie your owne prophett doth beare againſt you, looke to all thoſe countries where they haue ſtirred vpp their tragedies, was there any countrie the better for this ghoſpell, or was the wicked life of any one reformed by it, or were the profeſſors themſelues amended any thinge in their wicked liues by it? Compare the wicked life of the profeſſors of this newe religion, with the vertuous life of the holie fathers that haue planted the religion that wee profeſſe. Haue they not ſhined in all holines of life, in all heauenly conuerſation, by which they haue allured the hearts of faithles and ſtiffnecked gentiles, did they conuerte any kingdome vnto Chriſte by the ſword, haue they euer ſurpriſed citties or ouerthrowen kingdomes, or euer brought with them armies into the fielde, no, not by the ſword but by godes word and humilitie of ſpiritte haue they ouercome the deuill. Was not Luther a profeſſed Fryar many yeares, who beinge giuen to looſenes of life, did tranſgreſſe the lawe of God in breakinge his vowe by which he conſecrated himſelfe to ſerue God in holines of life and continencie of body all the dayes of his life, whoe rann awaie and tooke a Nunne with him out of her Cloiſter? Was not Iohn Caluine the fire brād of France and Scotland and other countries alſoe, he being a prieſt, for Sodomitticall wickedneſſe bur-

*No kingdome gained vnto thirst by the woord*

burned in the backe, and continewinge his wicked life stil, in that filthie sinne surprised Geneua; Was not Beza his next successor giuen to that wicked and abhominable sinne with a boy called Andebertus, and that manifestlie. And to defend their wicked liues and filthie sensualitie, they cast forth poisoned doctrine, as that vowes and votaries are not made by the lawe of God, that wee are not iustified by works done by Gods grace, and that the same be not meritorious before God, but that wee are iustified by faith only, & that all our woorkes though neuer soe good are sinfull before God: that to bridle or restraine our filthie desires, is to resist Gods ordinaunces, that God is the cause of all euill, and that from him all mischeefe comes. Therfore they take away free will from man, saying that man doth not concurre to his owne iustification, with many such damntble heresies which were to long to relate, and whether these be false prophetts who bringe into the world such poisoned doctrine, lett euerie man iudge, at least lett him take heede that his soule be not poisoned therwith, in followinge their liues or imbracinge their cursed heresies, out of which as our Sauiour wittnesseth noe good fruicte can bud forthe, and consequentlie noe meritorious works of religion or charitie can wee euer expect at their handes.

*The*

*The absurditie of this doctrin, that euery one should assure him selfe that he is predestinated vnto life euerlastinge, and that wee ought to be soe certayne therof as wee should not once feare the contrarie, or to misdoubt the same, is discussed.*

## CHAPTER V.

1. THis doctrine is most false, wicked, and hereticall, sith the holie scriptures saie. *Cogitationes*
Sap. 9. *mortalium timidæ & incertæ prouidentiæ nostræ.* The thoughtes of men are fearfull, and their prouidence is vncertaine, by reason that the bodie which is corrupted doth aggrauate the soule, beinge in great danger by reason of the inclinations of the flesh, occasions of the world, and tentations of the deuill, and wee being in the countrie of our enemies, wherevpon S. Bernard saith, *faciles sumus ad seducendum, debiles ad operandum, & fragiles ad resistendum*: wee are easilie to be seduced, weake to worke and labour well, and fraile to resist manfullie and couragiouslie. And soe our Sauiour said to
Luc. 10. the Apostle. *Neminem per viam salutaueritis.* You shall salute none by the waie, as S. Vin-
Ser. 11. post trinit. centius expoundeth. *Saluum dixeritis viatorem*, to him that is a poore pilgrime or stranger, you cannot assure his saftie without

out danger, nor ſecuritie without feare, for the ſhipp is not ſafe without feare in dangerous ſeas, otherwiſe wee ſhould not be admoniſhed. *Lauda poſt mortem, magnifica poſt conſumationem*; prayſe none before his deathe, nor magnifie any before his end. The ſcripture confirminge the ſame. *Nèmo ſcit vtrum odio, vel amore dignus ſit, ſed omnia in futurum ſeruantur incerta:* None knoweth whether he be worthie of hatred or loue, when all thinges are reſerued in tyme to come. And therfore the Apoſtle which was one of the greateſt Saintes that was, ſaith. *Nihil mihi conſcius ſum, ſed tamen in hoc non iuſtificatus ſum*: I am not guiltie in conſcience of any thinge, but I am not iuſtified herein. The Apoſtle durſt not aſſure himſelfe that he was iuſtified, neither would he iudge whether his thoughtes were pure or noe, but the trial thereof he left to Gods iudgment. And for this cauſe wee are wild to worke our ſaluation with feare and tremblinge.

*Eccle. 9.*

*1. Cor. 4.*

2. As for predeſtination which is almightie God his election, foreſight, purpoſe and decree of his deare children, as alſoe his other actes touchinge their vocation, inſpiration, illuſtration and illumination of them, and conſequentlie their iuſtification, and laſt of all their glorification, wee doe not denie but it ought to be reuerenced, and embraced of all men with tremblinge, feare and

& dreadfull humilitie; but that wee ſhould not caſt our ſelues with headlonge fall into any precipitat madnes, and preſumptuous malipartnes; for this hath bene the gulfe, wherein manie proude perſons, aſwell at this tyme, as before haue by godes iuſt iudgment periſhed: groundinge thereon moſt execrable hereſies, and damnable blaſphemies againſt godes mercie, good life, free will, humble behauiour and religious chriſtian modeſtie. S. Paule hath theſe wordes
*Rom. 8.* of predeſtination, whome he hath forknowen, he hath alſo predeſtinated to be made conformable to the Image of his ſonne, that he might be the firſt borne in many brethren, and whome he hath predeſtinated, them alſo he hath called, and whome he hath called, them alſo he hath iuſtified, and whome he hath iuſtified, them alſoe he hath glorified. S. Auguſtine anſwereth thoſe that are curious of Gods fore-knowledge and decree, who ſaith. *Si quæras &c.* If any man will aske wherfore God doth make choiſe more of this man, then of that man, lett him ſearch godes inſcrutable and vnſearcheable iudgment, and in that ſearch lett him take heede of a headlonge fall. It is true
*Rom. 8.* that God hath elected his people before the conſtitution of the world, accordinge to the
*Ephe. 1.* Apoſtle, but he ſaid afterwardes that they ſhould be holie and imaculate in his ſight in charitie: for in godes predeſtination are implied

implied and inuolued, good life and works of mercie done by godes grace; It is an infallible and theologicall rule, when God ordaines any end, he ordaines meanes with out which wee cannot come to that end, as God hath ordained his glorie to be the end of man, soe he ordained grace, and the works done by that grace, to be the meanes to obtayne it.

3. If a kinge will make any of his noblemen gouernour or deputie of any prouince or kingdome, it must be vnderstood that he must obserue iustice, although it be not expressed in his pattent: if God doth predestinate vs, it must be vnderstood that he should giue vs his grace wherby wee should be iust, and worke by that grace and our endeuours, our iustification, & therfore S. Peter; 1. *Pet.* 1.
saith. *Fratres magis satagite vt per bona opera certam vestram vocationem & electionem faciatis &c.* Wherfore brethren, labour the more that by good works you may make sure your vocation and election, for in doinge these thinges you shall not sinne at any tyme. Was not S. Iohn saued by his innocencie, and Peter also saued by his pennaunce, for the end of man was neuer ordained withour wayes or meanes to come to the said end; And therfore you must not saie God hath ordained my end, and I will not endeuour my selfe to come to that end otherwise you take awaie the one halfe of pre-

predestination, that is to say, the waie and meanes appointed for the same. And therfore S. Gregorie saith. *Ipsa perennis regni prædestinatio &c* That euerlastinge and endles predestination of godes perpetuall kingdome, so it is of the omnipotent God disposed and determined, that vnto the same the electe may approache by their owne labour, that they maye aske by their desertes that which the omnipotent God before the world, was disposed to giue, if you will not goe to hell, take away your sinnes and amend your wicked life, and thither you shall not goe, otherwise, *ve impis à malo,* woe be vnto the sinfull through his wickednes, and confusion be vnto him for his iniquitie.

*Greg 1. Dialog. & ponitur d. 23 q. 4. 2.*

4. Neither ought wee to saie, almightie God knoweth all thinges to come, & whether I shalbe saued, therfore I ought nor to labour my selfe for my saluation. God knoweth that this daie you shal dyne, therfore you ought not to prouide for dinner. God knoueth that you shalbe cured of your disease, therfore you ought not to prouide any medecine for your cure, God allso knoueth that the kinge shall haue the victorie against his enemies, that the husband shall haue a good haruest of corne, that the mariner shall ariue safe in Spaine, that Christ should escape the bloudy handes of Herod, therfore neither the kinge should le-

uie an armie, nor the husband man sowe the seede or till the grounde: euen so the meanes are to be vsed to purchase the victorie, and to fill the barne with corne, and to ariue safely in Spaine, and to be secure from Herod. Vnto this agree the holy sc iptures, that predestination and godes foreknowledge, takes not away mans free will and endeuours. *Deus ab initio constituit homiminem & reliquit eum in manu consilij &c.* God from the beginninge made man and lefte him at his owne choyce. He hath putt before vs his precepts and comaundements, if we will keepe the comaundements they will keepe and preserue vs; he hath putt before vs fire & water, vnto which of them we list we may stretch forth our arme, for before vs he hath placed both good & euill, life and death, of any of which man may take his owne choyce. *Eccl. 5.*

5. S. Paule was predestinated, yet spareth not to say. *Castigo corpus meum &c.* I chastice my bodie and I bringe the fleshe in seruitude to the spiritt, least that preachinge to others I should become reprobate my selfe, therfore wee may see, that our owne good endeuours, which godes holie grace doth worke with vs, are not excluded from our election, but those workes are both the meanes, and effects thereof, and therfore it is a desperate follie, and a great signe of reprobate and damnable persons to saie, if I be

be predestinated, doe what I will I shalbe saued. Did not Christ promise and assure his disciples of the cominge of the holie ghoast, notwithstandinge did not those disciples with the deuout weomen and the blessed Virgin, continewe together in prayers and fastinge, disposinge themselues to
*Actor. 1.* receaue the same? Neither in their prayers or fastinge did they misdoubt the cominge of the holie ghoast, accordinge as our Sauiour promised the same, notwithstandinge they knewe that they ought to prepare themselues to be cleane vessells fitt for the receipt thereof. Yf the Pope should promise vnto you to fill your vessell full of Balme or Chrisme, which are most pretious liquores, if you will bringe an vnclean vessell vnto him, he will not giue vnto you what was promised, for in his promise was included that you should bringe a fitt and cleane vessell to receaue the same. Soe Christ notwithstandinge he promised to fill their consciences, vnderstandinge, memorie, and will with the balme of the holy ghoast, yet the Apostles ought to haue their consciences and their soules withall the powers thereof, cleane and voide of all filth of sinne and wickednes to receaue the same, for such as are predestinated are written in a white paper in golden lettres as S. Vincentius saith: neither only the persons soe predestinated are written there, but also the

the works and meanes by which they are ſaued and predeſtinated, videlicet that ſuch people ſhalbe baptized, that they ſhalbe mercifull, patient, chaſte, godlie and penitent: euen ſoe ſuch as are damned are written in a blacke parchement, not only the perſon but their works, by which they be damned and reprobate, that is to ſay, that he is cruell, leacherous, impenitent, proude, couetous. &c.

---

*Whether the holie ſcriptures be for proteſtantes, and not for papiſtes, and whether we relie vpon Traditions, not warranted by holy Scripure.*

## CHAPTER I.

1. S. Cyrill doth anſwere this obiection ſaying. *Omnes hæretici de ſcriptura diuinitus inſpirata, ſui colligunt erroris occaſionem*: all heretiques do founde their errors vpon the Scriptures which were infuſed by God, which wordes were pronounced in the 7. generall councell, and are inſerted in the councell of Calcedon. S. Auguſtine alſo doth confirme the ſame ſaying. *Non aliunde natas eſſe hæreſes, & quædam dogmata peruerſitatis illaquentia animas, & in profundum præcipitantia niſi cum ſcripturæ bonæ intelligantur*

*Epiſt. 18.*

*Aug. trac. 18. in Ioh.*

*tur non bene, & quod in eis non bene intelligitur, etiam temerè & audacter asseritur:* heresies and other peruerse opinions, infectinge and intanglinge our soules, euen to the deepe pitt of confusion, doe springe of noe other roote then when good scriptures are ill vnderstoode, and the badd vnderstandinge therof, is bouldly and rashlie applied. S. Ambrose doth likewise declare the same, sayinge. *Hæretici per verba legis, legem impugnant.* by the wordes of the lawe it selfe, the heretiques doe impugne the lawe. S. Hillarius allso saith. *Neminem hæreticorum esse qui se non secundum sacras scripturas prædicare eas quæ blasphemat, mentiatur,* there is noe heretique that doth not alleadge falsy the scriptures, for his blasphemies. Allso he saith, *de intelligētia heresis sit, non de scriptura, sensus non sermo fiat crimen:* heresie is of the vnderstāding, not of the scripture, the fault is in the sense, and not in the word, vnto which agreeth S. Hierom. *Neque sibi blandiantur &c.* Lett them not flatter themselues, if they alleadge or affirme any thinge of the scriptures, when euen the deuill hath alleadged the scriptures for his purpose. The scriptures saith he, doe not consiste in readinge of them, but in vnderstandinge of them. Origines allso declareth the same, saying. *Non raro &c.* Somtimes the diuill doth wreast godes wordes from many, for that there is nothinge soe holie but the enemie of mankinde, doth abuse

*Ambr. 3. ad Titū.*
S. *Hil. in lib. ad Const.*
*Lib. 10. de Trinit.*
*Hiero ad Lucif.*
*Orig hom. 9. in Exo.*

buse the same to the destruction of man. Tertulian also saith, *de scripturis agebant, de scipturis suadebant &c*. They pleade the scriptures, they persuade the scriptures, they inculcate the scriptures, vnto this they moue some at the first dashe, they wearie the stronge, they confound the weake, and men of indifferent iudgment they dismisse with scrupules. Thus far Tertulian: soe the Arian heresie, the Macedonian, the Nestorian, Eutichian, and all other old heresies, would allowe nothinge but scripture: and last of all, these newe phantasticall heresies, doe grounde all their turbulent spirittes, and singuler, maleperte, and headie deuises, vpon holie scriptures. *De prescript. her.*

2. For example, Luther in his first booke against Zuinglius saith that amoungest Zuingilans, the Zuinglians themselues concerninge these 5. wordes there arose tenn seuerall sects of different religion I meane, *hoc est enim corpus meum.* Stanislaus Rescius hath deuided the hereticall sects of this tyme into two hundred and 70. different heresies, euerie one alleadginge scripture for his owne fancie. Theodorus did reckon 76. heresies in his owne tyme. S. Augustine also did reckon 88. heresies vnto his owne tyme. And vnto Luther his tyme there were 290. sortes of heresies, all which did alleadge scriptures. Yea was there euer any heresie that did alleadge more scriptures for her

*270. sects of heresies in this time.*

*Lib de here. fabulis.*

*Aug. lib. de heres.*

her selfe, then that of the Arians; did not the Iewes alleadge scriptures against Christ, that he should not be holden for a Prophett?
John. 7. saying. *Scrutate scripturas, & vide quia à Galilea propheta non surgit*, search the scriptures, saie they, and behould that a prophett doth not arise from Galile: and by scripture they did endeuour to proue that he was
Iohn. 19. worthie of deathe. Wee haue a law say they, and by our lawe he ought to die, because he made himselfe the sonne of God. Did not Iulian the apostate alleadge scripture as S. Cyrill saithe, lib 10. in Iulianum for visitinge Martyrs Reliques, alleadginge that place of S. Mathewe 23. that the Scribes, Pharisies, and Hipocritts are like to white monuments, and they ought not to visitt them &c. Also he alleadged many places of scripture as Math. 5. Ro. 12. 1. Cor. 6. Math. 10. against the christians for repininge against him for takinge away their goodes, but to beare all tyrannicall oppresions patientlie. Did not Osiander a cheefe secretarie alleadge 20. different opinions touchinge the article of Iustification, and at last he cited his owne opinion, contrarie to them all?

3. Of all these sectes it is saide. *Obscurum est insipiens cor eorum, dicentes se esse patientes, stulti facti sunt.* Their foolish hearte is darkned, sayinge themselues to be wise, but they be made fooles; for heretiques can neuer

neuer haue the knowledge of the ſcriptures. *In maleuolam animam non introibit ſapientia, nec habitabit corpore ſubdito peccatis*, true knowledge ſhall not enter into a wicked ſoule, nor lodge in a bodie ſubiect to ſinne. Therfore the prophett ſaithe. *Diſcam in via immaculata*: I will learne in an vnſpotted waie, and when heretiques through pride, and malice, haue moſt maliciouſlie, oppoſed thẽſelues againſt the catholique church, the piller, and foundation of all trueth, and haue ſought by all wicked and malicious meanes to deface the ſame, wee muſt not thinke they haue had any true knowledge or perfect wiſdome, for if once a foundation of a houſe or a rocke (vpon which are builded manie chambers) do fall, all thoſe chambers cannot ſtand vpp: the catholique church is the firme rocke, vpon which the faithe of euerie chriſtian is builded, if he once fall from the church he hath no faith, nor any vnderſtandinge of the ſcriptures, and therfore S. Auguſtine ſaith, he would not haue beleeued the ghoſpelll, without the authoritie of the church, which beinge inſpired by the holie ghoaſt, hath taught thinges, which the ſcritures haue taught the contrarie: as that wee ſhould not obſerue the old lawe, nor obſtaine from thinges ſuffocated or ſtraungled and ſuch like: for the letter ſaith S. Paule killeth, but the ſpiritt quickneth. And as the letter in the old

*Sap. cap. 1*

*2. Cor. 3.*

lawe, not trulie vnderstoode nor referred to Christ, did by occasion kill the carnall Iewe, so the letter of the newe testament, not truly taken nor expounded by the spiritte of Christe, which only is in his church, killeth the heretique, who also being carnall, and voide of spiritt, gaineth nothinge by the scriptures, but rather taketh hurte by the same; as S. Augustine auoucheth, for in the newe testament (saith S. Peter) are certaine thinges hard to be vnderstoode, which the vnlearned, and vnstable deprave, as also they do the rest of the scriptures to their owne perdition: of whom S. Paule himselfe saith; alwaies learninge and neuer attayninge vnto the knowledge of the truth, men corrupte in mind, reprobate concerninge the faith, but they shall prosper noe further, for their folly shalbe made manifest to all, and as Iames and Mambres resisted Moyses, soe they alsoe resiste the truethe.

*Aug. to. 10. de tēpore & li. de Spiritu & litt. c 5. 6.*
*2. Pet. 3.*
*2. Tim. 3.*

4. If Daniell, after that God had reuealed vnto him thinges to come, concerninge the militant church, saith. *Ego audiui & non intellexi*, I haue heard, but I vnderstood not, the Angell said vnto Daniell, *vade quia clausi sunt, signatique sermones vsque ad præfinitum tempus*: Goe your wayes for these speeches are shutt vpp and sealed vntill the time appointed, if soe great a Prophett heard and vnderstoode not what he heard, what

what will heretiques and wicked arogant presumptuous people, make glosses vpon euerie sillable of holie scripture? Wherfore S. Augustine saith. *Sacra scriptura &c.* The holie scripture are not knowen to the proude, nor manifest, or playne to boyes; in the begining therof it is easie, but when you enter into it, it is loftie and couered with misteries, and I was not of that capacitie that I might intermedle therin. And in another place, he perswaded a yonge man learned in humanitie, and Philosophie and other liberall sciences, that he should not rashlie reade holie scriptures, sayinge to set vpon Maurus a Comedian, or Terẽce, because thou hast noe skill in poetrie, thou darest not without a master, and to vnderstand him beinge a comon poett thou searchest the commentaries of Asper, Cornutus, Donatus, and infinitte others: and darest thou without a guide, or iudge venture vpon holie scripture? which as S. Paule speaketh, *in ijs qui pereunt velatum est*, in them that perishe is hidd, *in quibus Deus huius seculi excæcauit sensum incredulorum*, in whome the God of this worlde hath blinded the myndes of the infidles, that the illumination of the ghospell of the glorie of Christe, might not shine in them, and as S. Iohn saith, the light shined in darcknes, and the darcknes did not comprehende it, the heretiques hauinge not the light of Christes

*Aug. Con. ep c. 4.*

*Aug. lib. de vtil. cred. c. 7.*

*2. Cor. 4.*

*Ioh. 1.*

ſpiritt which is giuen to the church, nor true humilitie by which they ſhould obeie the ſame, cannot haue the ſhininge light of Chriſt his ghoſpell, nor the true vnderſtandinge thereof. *Credite & intelligetis*, ſaith the Prophett, beleue the church and you ſhall vnderſtād the ſcriptures, vnto whom
*Eſa. 7.* almightie God hath giuen the true interpretation thereof, and to noe particuler ſpiritt.

5. S. Hierom beinge ſoe well learned as he was, and furniſhed with the knowledge of all the tongues, did ſtumble in many
*Lib. 1. de Doctr. chr. c. 6.* thinges, for he ſweateth in explayninge the prophetts: the ſame difficultie S. Auguſtine had as he himſelfe declares, when he would expounde that place of ſcripture of the ſinne againſt the holie ghoaſt, and when he alleadged many places, he was not ſatiſfied in them: all ſo he ſaith that many obſcure places be in the ſcriptures, almightie God ordayninge the ſame, to abate the pride and arrogancie of man, and to ſubmitt his priuate ſpiritt, to the vniuerſall ſpiritt of Chriſt his church, & therfore Tertul. ſaith. *Fides te ſaluum fecit, non exercitatio ſcripturæ*, it is thy faith that ſaueth thee and not the readinge, or exerciſe of ſcriptures, the miſteries wherof are hidden from the wicked, for they be like Margarittes, and pretious ſtones, and which ought not to be giuen to ſwine, noe more ought they to be common to euerie one,

one, and as a holy man saith. *Non intelligendi viuacitas, sed credendi simplicitas te saluum fecit*: it is not the quicknes of vnderstandinge, but simplicitie of beleeuinge that shall saue thee. *Omnis prophetia* (saith S. Hierom) in Ezech 45. propherts are obscure, what the disciples doe heare inwardlie, the comon people knowes not what is said in them: and accordinge to this the prophett saith, *tenebrosa aqua in nubibus æris*; obscure water in the cloudes of the aier, the ordinarie gloss in that place hath, *obscura doctrina in prophetis*, the prophets are full of darke, and difficult doctrine.

6. Was not the Eunuch Threasurer to the Queene of Ethyopia, exercised in the scripture, and yet he confessed he could not vnderstand them? Act 8. Did not Christe interpreate the scriptures to the Iewes and his disciples Luc. vlt? S. Iohn Chrisostom vpon that place, *scrutamini scripturas. Christus*, saith he, *Iudeos &c*: Christe did not referr the Iewes vnto the bare, and naked readinge the scriptures, but vnto the diligent examination and inuestigation thereof. S. Hierō saith, that all the Epistles of S. Paule to the Romaines be verie obscure and intricate. Luther himselfe vpon the Psalme 88. *Thronus eius sicut dies cæli*: his throane is like the daie of heauen saith; I would haue noe man to presume in my behalfe, that I can vnderstand the Psalmes in their lawfull sense,

*Act. 8.* *Luc. vlt.*

*Lib. 1. præf. comment. in epist. ad Alga. q. 2.*

ſenſe, which was neuer performed of anie, though neuer ſoe learned or ſoe holie, for the ſcriptures muſt be conſidered,either litteralie in themſelues, or accordinge to their methode and ſenſe, for in themſelues they ſpeake, and containe things ſupernaturall and miſticall, which are hidden from the capacitie of the vulgar ſorte: or if they ſhould be conſidered accordinge to their methode or ſenſe, they ſhould be deuided into foures kindes of ſenſes, & vnderſtandinge as, ſenſus *Anagogicus* which is called the celeſtiall ſenſe, *Allegoricus* which is the ſpirituall ſenſe, *Tropologicus* which is the morall ſenſe, and *Hiſtoricus* which is the litterall ſenſe. Therfore the prophett cried out vnto God ſayinge, *da mihi intellectum &c.* giue me vnderſtandinge and I will ſearche into thy lawe; *faciem tuam illumina ſuper ſeruum tuum Domine*. Illuminate my vnderſtandinge with thy grace ô Lord: that I may vnderſtand thy word; *ſacræ ſcripturæ* (ſaith Hylarius) *non in legendo ſed intelligendo, non in præuaricatione ſed in charitate*: the holy ſcriptures doe not conſiſte in readinge of them, but in the true ſenſe and meaning of them, not in corruptinge or in preuarication of them,but in the charitable interpretation of them. And when S. Auguſtine did ſee the manifeſt and falſe applyinge of them by the Pellagiãs, he did appeale to the Biſhopes both of the eaſt and weaſt.

*The ſcripture hath 4. ſenſes or vnderſtanding.*

*Lib. ad Conſtan.*

7. Caluine saith of the protestantes that they would haue the scriptures to patronize and support their errours, sayinge. *Ibi quid non inuertunt, quid non deprauant,* what is there but they peruert and depraue? Luther would not admitt any translation of scripture but his owne translation: noe more would Zuinglius his aduersarie. Luther was offended with the printer that did send him Zuinglius his translation, who would not once peruse it, and so Zuinglius with Luther. Kinge Henry the 8. after he made himselfe head of the Church, he caused the scriptures to be translated into English, which afterwards he suppressed and inhibited. Afterwardes he caused another translation to be made by the authoritie of the parlament Anno regni sui 34. and proclaymed vnder paine of death, that noe other translation should be vsed but that, and this he did to mantayne his opinion. Also when his children, kinge Edward and Elizabeth came to the Crowne and held contrarie opinions, they caused contrarie translations to be published. Vulgar translations of scriptures profitts nothinge, vnlesse wee knowe the true sense of them, & as for the true sense, the protestantes giue vs no rule at all for the same. For in England they cannott iudge of the controuersie of religion by the scriptures, because they are boūd by their lawes to beleue according to the will

*In præfat. ad lectores ex Phyco.*

*Lutherus in hist. Sacrament. foll. 22.*

*Zuingl. to 2. resp. ad Luth.*

*Fox. in Henri. 8. in fine hist.*

*Fox. ibid.*

will and decree of the parleament howse and of the kinge. And in other protestant countries, where the parleament or the wil of a prince is not of force, there are so many sects and heresies, as they cannot be reclaymed, euerie one wreasting the scriptures, to his owne priuate, and fantasticall opinions; for the Protestants, doe not care for the vulgare translation: vnles they may peruert the sense thereof, according to their owne turbulent braines.

8. Neither is there any people, that doe reuerence, and honor the scriptures more then those of the Catholick religion. Which
2. Cor. 4. as S. Paule saith, doth renounce the adulterating of the word of God, wicked constructions, deceitfull interpretations, and sinister application thereof, & which is common to heretiques (as Luther affirmeth) that the roote of all heresies hath bene the scriptures, yea he added that the scriptures ought to be called the booke of heretiques. There is neither iott, nor sillable in the scripture, but the catholique church doth imbrace, & allowe the same as written, and sett downe by the holie ghoast; and although the priuate spiritt of some haue thought some bookes of the sacred scriptures not to be canonicall, yet the whole catholique church hath receaued them; & hath taken awaie that doubte. Touchinge the bookes of the old testament videlicet Iudith, Tobyas, the booke of wisdome,

dome, Ecclesiastes, the two first bookes of the Machabees, and of Baruch, as alsoe of the newe, as the Apocalips, the Epistle of S. Paul to the Hebreues, the Epistle of S. Iames, the 2. of S. Peter, the 2. and 3. of S. Iohn, and therfore the heretiques of this time doe not allowe those, for that some in tymes paste haue doubted thereof. Did not S. Tho: doubt also of Christs resurrection, and therfore ought he or wee doubt thereof still, Christ hauing manifested his scarres and his woundes vnto him? Euen soe though some learned men haue doubted of those bookes, yet by the vniuersall consent of the church these bookes were made knowen to be Canonicall scripture. As concerninge the booke of Iudith, the councell of Carthage vnder Aurelius Bishopp thereof, Innocentius the first, Gelasius with 70. Bishoppes, the councell of Florence vnder Eugenius the 4. haue pronounced it to be canonicall, as also of the booke of Tobie, Ecclesiastes, and wisdome. As for the two bookes of Machabes, the Canons of the Apostles (the author whereof is said to be S. Clemēt) in the ende thereof the two bookes of the Machabees, are inserted as Canonicall, those two bookes are confirmed by Innocentius the first and by the councell of Carthage, and confirmed by the 6. Generall councell, in such like manner the said 2. bookes are cōfirmed, both by the two generall councells, of

*Aug. li. 18 de ciuit. Dei c. 16. con. Gaud. epist. lib. 2. cap. 23.*

of Florence, and Trentt, and as S. Augustine saith, that the Churche and not the Iewes, doth allowe the Machabees for canonicall: and not onlie S. Augustine, doth produce wittnesse out of them, but also Ireneus, Tertul. Cyprian. Chrysost. and others, soe as to doubte of these bookes, is rather the infidelitie of the Iewes, then the faith of the Christians, especially when the Church hath once decreede the same, and soe are all the rest of the said bookes made Canonicall by the Church, and by her determination, which is of greater force to allowe, or disalowe of them (as also of the true interpretation of them) then all the priuate spirittes in the world, vnto whome all priuate mens iudgment ought to submit themselues. Basill the greate, and S. Gregorie: Naz. being the cheefest diuines amoungest the Grecians, and hauinge cast awaie all other bookes, they recollected themselues, to studie the holie scriptures, the true meaninge and interpretation thereof, as Ruffinus testifieth, they gathered out of the authoritie and comentaries of their predecessors, & not of their owne priuate presumption or proper imagination.

*Ruff. lib 2. cap 9. in Eccl hist.*

*Gal 2. Aug. lib. 28 in Faust. c. 4.*

9. Did not S. Paule beinge an Apostle, before he preached the Ghospell, goe vpp to Hierusalem, that he might confer with S. Peter, Iames, and Iohn, and especiallie with Peter touching the preaching and expoun-

*Lucc. 22.*

poundinge of the Ghospell, for that our Sauiour did praie particulerlie for S. Peter, that he should not faile in his faith, vnto whome he promised the assistance of his holie spirite? If this soe great a doctor beinge illuminated by Christe, and receauinge his ghospell frō him, did neuerthelesse conferr the same with S. Peter, the foundation of the ecclesiasticall Hierarchy, the Pastor of Christs sheepe, the captaine of his armie, the sonne that shineth in this hemispher of christendome, and heade of the misticall bodie of Christe, which is his church, how much ought others to doe the like, which haue not so much securitie, nor soe good a warrant to be fauored and inspired of God, as he had? Howe can wee thinke or beleeue, that heretiques can vnderstand the scriptures, who haue not the spiritt of God to instruct them in the knowledge thereof? For as no member of the bodie, hath the spiritt of the bodie, vnlesse it be vnited and ioyned to the bodie; soe noe member of the misticall bodie of Christ which is his church hath the spirite thereof, that is separated frō the same. Wherevpon S. Augustine saith; *nihil magis debet christianus formidare &c.* there is nothinge that a christian ought to feare more, then to be separated from the bodie of Christe, for if he be separated and disunited from the bodie of the church: he is not a member thereof, and if he be not a mem-

*Aug tract. 17. in Iohn.*

member of the ſame, he is not quickned by her ſpiritt, and whoſoeuer hath not the ſpiritt of Chriſte, as the Apoſtle ſaith, he is not his, it is the ſpiritt that quickneth, the fleſh auaileth nothinge. Therfore you beinge not in the Church, vnto whome the ſpiritt of God is promiſed, to direct her in all trueth, and to guide her from all errors and hereſies, wee ought not to beleue that you haue the knowledge of the ſcriptures, or the true vnderſtandinge or interpretation thereof, for it cannot ſtande with any reaſon or rule, that this ſpiritt of trueth can be in turbulent mindes, or malicious heades,
Iſa. 66. as hetiquees be, *qui non requieſcit niſi ſuper humilem, & manſuetum & trementem ſermones ſuos*: neuer reſteth, but vpon the humble, and meeke, and tremblinge at his wordes and ſpeeches.

*Whether euery man ought to be iudge of the ſcripture, and to rely altogether vpon his owne iudgment touching the interpretation thereof, being inſpired by the holly ghoaſt concerning the ſame.*

## CHAPTER V.

1. THis is the aſſerſion of william Whitakers in his booke againſt Cardinall Bellarmin, for that ſaith he, councells, fathers, and popes

popes be men. And the ſcripture auerreth, all men to be lyeares, and ſo no man can be aſſured his faith to be certaine and infallible. Wherto I anſwer, that no priuat man can be aſſured of the certitude of an infallible faith, and therfore nott of the good ſpiritt, rather then of the badde, by whoſe ſuggeſtiō many are intoxicated with dangerous and damnable opinions, for according to the Apoſtle. Sathan often times tranſfigureth himſelfe into an Angell of light, *2.Corint.* and therfore the holy ſcripture willeth vs, to be very carefull in diſcerning of the ſpiritts, and nott to beleue euery ſpiritt, for it *1 Ioh.4.* *Th 4.* is the holy catholicke church that wee ought to beleue and obey, which the ſcripture beareth wittneſſe to be the piller and *1. Tim. 3.* firmament of trueth: but it giueth no certitude or euidence of any priuat ſpiritt, or pecular iudgment of any one in particuler, and therfore the holy councell ſaith. It ſeemeth good to the holy ghoſt and to vs, *Act.15.* which holy ghoaſt is ſaid to be nott with euerie particuler mān, but with the church in generall, and with thoſe that haue charge and direction therof. *Ero vobiſcum vſque ad conſummationem ſeculi,* euen to the conſummatiō of the world. And vnto S. Peter & his *Matt. 28.* ſucceſſors is ſaid. I haue praid for you that your faith may not fayle; and ſeeing this priuiledg is giuen to S. Peter for the good of *Luc. 22.* the church, as the firſt and cheefe paſtor

O therof

therof vnder Christ, and to no other in particuler, as long as the church shall continewe, the praiers and intercession of Christ shal not be frustrated. And therfore S. Cypriã affirmeth the fountaine of all heresies to haue proceeded, for that one priest for the time being, & one iudg for the time being, vnder Christ, is not regarded. For which way, saith he, can heresies be preuented that they spring nott, or being sprong already, that they be nott extended or encreased, wher there are so many masters as disciples, & so many iudges as barristers? And for this cause S. Hierom saith against Iouinian, amoungest 12. one is chosen, that a cheef being ordained, occasion of scisme should be taken away.

2. The tables of both the testaments referred vs ouer to no particuler iudgment, but altogether to the finall decree and arbitrement of the high priest, as it is saied. If
*Deut. 17.* there be any hard or doubtfull iudgment amongest you, goe to the priest of the Leuiticall stocke, and to the iudge that shall be ordained for that time, and he shall enforme you of the trueth. Whose lippes,
*Mal. 2.* according to Malachias, shall keepe wisdome because he is the angell of the Lord of hoastes: if he will not hearken vn-
*Matt. 18.* to the Church, lett him be vnto you an ethnick and a publican. And in the newe testament our Sauiour appointed one pastor

aboue the reſt, vnto which he hath committed the feeding of his flocke, which ſhould haue beene friuolous if the flocke would nott receaue food from him; Afterwards he ordained paſtors and doctors in his church which ſhould be alſo a friuolous ordinance, if euerie one ſhould be a proper paſtor and doctor to him ſelf. And although councells, fathers, and popes are men, ſo the teſtimonies of the ſcriptures may alſo be taxed with the imputation of humane errors: ſo were the Apoſtles and prophets men alſo, yett wee ought to beleue them becauſe the holly ghoſt was not a lyar that ſpake in them; And ſo the eccleſiaſticall councells, fathers, and popes being lawfully aſſembled together and aſsiſted by the holly ghoaſt, which in ſuch a caſe is promiſed vnto them, did not erre. *Epheſ.4.* *Matt. 28.*

3. Another obiection they bring, ſaying S. Peter was nott promiſed vnto the Church to direct the ſame, butt the holly Ghoſt which ſhould direct and inſtruct all the Apoſtles, and nott S. Peeter. I anſwer that God promiſed the holie ghoaſt as an inuiſible and internall doctor and director. S. Peter his viſible and externall doctor he left in his church. And therfore S. Auguſtine ſaith, after promiſing the holly ghoaſt lett no man thincke that he ſhall ſo giue the holly ghoaſt vnto his church in his owne place, as though him ſelf alſo would nott *Ioan.14.* *Aug. in Ioh. 14.*

be with the ſame, for he auowtched he would nott leaue them orphanes, but would come vnto them.

4. And althoughe the holy ghoaſt was promiſed to inſtruct the Church in all trueth, yett not without the Father and the ſonne for their externall worcks, are indiuiſible: for there is but one indiuiſible ſubſtance, and becauſe the Church is a viſible body, ſo it ought to haue a viſible viccar vnder Chriſt the inuiſible head therof. And therfore he ſaide vnto S. Peter Ioh. 11. Simon of Iohn, loueſt thou me more then theſe, feed my lambes, which he repeated thriſe, firſt commending vnto him his lambes, afterwards his litle ones, the third time his ſheepe, and ſo expoundeth. S. Ambroſe in cap. vlt. Luc.

5. Nowe the power and iuriſdiction which was promiſed vnto S. Peter Math. 16. that the Church ſhould be builded vpon him, that the keyes of the kingdome of heauen, ſhould be alſo giuen vnto him, is accompliſhed and performed in the 21. of S. Iohn, feed my ſheep, of whom he is actually made the generall paſtor and viccar.

6. And although the reſt of the Apoſtles were lightes and prieſts, and had authoritie alſo in the 20. of S. Iohn, yet theirs was extraordinary which ſhould end with them ſelues, and whatſoeuer authority they had, was by the ſacraments by which they remit-

remitted sinne. S. Peter had authoritie to bind and loose immediatly, and by him the the Apostles as depending vpon him as S. Thomas saith in 4. dist. 19. q. 1. art. 3. and so he maketh a distinction of the two powers videl. of order, and iurisdiction, the first was equally giuen to all the Apostles. Iohn. 20. and consequently to all priests, but the secōd power was principally giuē to S. Peeter, and from him to be deriued vnto the rest of the Apostles.

*How heretiques would faine take awaie all tradition, alleadginge for their purpose that of S. Math. 15. In vaine you worshipp me, teachinge for doctrine mens precepts.*

## CHAPTER III.

1. THis is it saith S. Augustine that all heretiques doe bragge of, if I should aunswere all such trifles, I should neuer make an ende saith he, soe as he would not aunswere to this place, for he saith that the traditions of the Apostles ought to be of as great force as the holie scriptures. But to those wordes of our Sauiour, S. Basill doth aunswere, saying. *Nihil aliud ijs recepi verbis intelligi, quam quod humanis traditionibus ad mandatum Dei reprobandum, obsequendum non sit*, that nothinge else is meante by those wordes,

*Lib. contr. Maximin.*

*Bas. in Ethicis.*



then

then that wee ought not obey ſuch traditions as are repugnant to Godes lawes ; as many obſeruations of the Iewes, and allſoe of the phariſies were then, and the like traditions of heretiques are nowe: yet we ought to obey the cuſtome of the church, otherwiſe wee ſhould be counted by the wordes of Chriſte, as Ethnicks and Publicans. But the traditions deliuered to vs by the paſtors and fathers thereof, which are the foundation of our faith, and which are not repugnant to Godes precepts, nor to his lawes, or ſcriptures, but doe rather confirme the ſame, are not meant by thoſe wordes: for Godes worde doth not conſiſte onlie of the ſcripture, but allſo of tradition, for ſuch as were old heretiques did not gainſaie the written word, but becauſe they did not beleue the tradition of the church, and the definition thereof, they were ſoe counted, and accurſed.

*Vppon what occaſion hereſie did growe.*

2. That the ſonne is of the ſame ſubſtance with the father, the catholique fathers haue defined by godes word: but becauſe the heretiques did not finde the ſame written, they would not beleue the church, which did grant it was nor written, but deliuered by tradition. Soe as you may ſee the difference betwixt the heretique, and the catholique. *Felix Pontifex*, writinge to *Benignum* 130. yeares before the councell of Nyce ſaith, that it was an Apoſtolicall tradition,

dition, that the sonne was of one substance with the father, and that the holie Ghoast is to be adored, as the father and the sonne, and that he is of the same substance with the father; and when the same heretiques did aske where it was written, the church did answere them, that it was deliuered, vnto them by tradition which two pointes continued afterwardes by the 2. councell of Nyce and Constinople. Also in the councell of Ephesus, that the blessed Virgin Marie should be called the mother of God. In the councell of chalcedon, that there are two natures in Christe. In the 3. councell of Constantinople, that there are in him two wills, and two operations. In the second councell of Nyce against heretiques, that the church should vse Images. In the generall councell of florence, that the holy ghoast proceedeth from the father, and the sonne; And when heretiques did relie all vpon the scripture, the catholique fathers did conuince their interpretation of scriptures, by tradition of the succesiue doctors and fathers in all ages. The tradition also that easter daye should be obserued vpon the sondaie next after vnto the 14. daie of the new Moone (as some doe write) S. Peter and S. Paule ordained; so as in all pointes of doctrine wee recurr to the tradition of our ancestors: and when you teache that all thinges are don by necessitie, & not by the free will

*Articles of faith by traditions.*

of man, wee recurr vnto the succeſsiue age, and wee find out, that the firſt author was *Symon magnus*, next vnto him was Marcion, next vnto Marcion, was Manichæus, next vnto him, was Petrus Adelhardus. Next vnto him, was Iohn Wicklief. Next after whome followed your great maſter Martyne Luther: ſo that we find in all antiquitie of tymes, that this doctrine was deteſted by the holy doctors, that liued in thoſe ages.

*Tradition of proteſtantes.*

3. Againe when you obiect vnto vs your tradition of your imputatiue iuſtice: where you ſay that our faith is imputed vnto vs by the iuſtice of Chriſt, as if it had bene our owne iuſtice, as alſo that euery one vnder paine of damnation is bounde to beleue, and to be certaine that his ſinnes be forgiuen him, & that he ſhould not miſtruſt his proper infirmitie therein; alſo that not any one is inſtified, but he that beleues for certaine that he is iuſtified, and that his iuſtification and abſolution of his ſinnes, is effected by faith onlie, without any relation to the Sacraments, and that euerie one is bound to beleue, that he is in the number of thoſe that are predeſtinated, and that by all infallible certitude he hath the guifte of perſeuerance to be the true ſeruante of God vnto the laſt gaſpe of his life: this and ſuch like wee can not find in the ſcriptures, nor in the fathers, nor in the doctors of the

the churche, but rather the contrarie; and that which the holie catholique churche calles pennaunce, you call terror of conscience, and that which she calles Sacraments and sacrifice, you call it the Lords supper: wee search the fathers, and wee can finde noe such wordes, and although somtimes they make mention of the supper, yet more often doe they call the same a sacrifice. Did not S. Paule wish Timothy to keepe his depositum & to auoide the prophane nouelties of voices and oppositions of false tearmed knowledge? For the scripture is not subiecte to loftie skill, or arrogant or presumptuous mindes; who I pray hath greater skill or knowledge and vnderstandinge of the scriptures then the deuilles, and yet it auaileth them nothinge, because their mindes are possessed with malice, and their hartes are emptie of charitie, soe as men doe not sinne so much by the ignorance of the vnderstanding, as by the malice of the will, and accordinge to S. Augustine the summe & scope of all the scriptures is charity: whosoeuer saith he that seemes to vnderstād the scripture or any parcell thereof, soe that his vnderstandinge doth not edifie that knott I meane the loue of God and our neigbors, he hath not as yet vnderstoode the scriptures.

*All things peruerted by the protestants.*

*Aug. de doctrina Christi, an. cap. 35.*

4. Now all your manner of administration, and ministerie, is your owne tradition

and

and inuention, without ſcripture or warrant of godes worde, but the traditions of the Apoſtles and ancients, and all the preceptes of holie churche, were comaũded to be kepte, and they are not preſcribed by man only, but are made by the holie ghoaſt, ioyninge
*Luc.* 2.37. with our paſtors in the regimente of the
*Matt.* 18. faithfull, where Chriſte ſaith; he that heareth you, heareth me, and he that deſpiſeth you, deſpiſeth me, they are made by our mother the churche, which whoſouer obeieth not, wee are warned to take him as a heathen. S.
2.*Cor.* 3. Paule willed the people to keepe the decrees that were decreede by the Apoſtles and auncientes at Ieruſalem, he commaunded the people to keepe the precepts of the Apoſtles. You are, ſaith he, written in our hartes, not written with Incke, but with the finger of the holy ghoſt. S. Paule wrote many thinges not vttered in any epiſtle, as ſome of the Apoſtles wrote the chriſtian religion in the hartes of their hearers. Wherfore Ireneus
*Iren.l.*3.4 ſaith, what if the Apoſtles alſo had lefte noe ſcriptures, ought wee not to followe the order of the tradition? which was then deliuered vnto them, to whome they comitted the church, to the which many nations of thoſe barbarous people that haue beleeued in Chriſte, doe conſente without letter or inke, hauinge ſaluation written in in their hartes, and keepinge diligentlie the tradition of our elders, and ſoe S. Hier. ſaith
cont.

cont. Heref. 9. The creede of our faith and hope which beinge deliuered by tradition from the Apoftles, is not written in paper and Incke, but in the tables of the hearte: and this is in the church booke alfo, wherby & wherein fhee keepeth faithfully all trueth in the hartes of thofe to whome the Apoftles did preach. And therfore S. Paule faith, Brethren ftande & hold the tradition which you haue learned, whether it be by worde or by epiftle, not only the thinges written and fett downe in the hollye fcriptures, but all other truethes and pointes of religion vttered by worde of mouthe, and deliuered and giuen by the Apoftles to their fchollers. And fo S. Bafil faith thus. I accompte it Apoftolique tradition to continue firmlie euen in vnwritten traditions: and to proue this he alleadgeth this place of faint Paule in the fame booke cap. 17. and faith, if wee once goe aboute to reiecte vnwritten cuftomes, as thinges of no importance, wee fhal ere wee beware endamadge the principall partes of our faith, and bringe the preachinge of the ghofpell to a naked name. and for example of thefe neceffarie traditiōs, he named the figne of the Croffe, prayinge towardes the eafte, the wordes fpoken at the eleuation or fhewinge of the holy Euchariste, with diuers ceremonies vfed before and after baptifme: with three immerfions in the fonte: the wordes of abrenunciation

*2. Thef. 2. 15.*

ciation and exorcismes of the partie that is to be baptised; and what scripture saith he taught these and such like? None trulie, all cominge by secret and silent traditions, &c. S. Hierome reckneth vpp diuers, such like traditions, willinge men to attribuit to the Apostles, such customes as the Church hath receaued by Christians of diuers Countrie.

*Hieron. in dialogo. Lucife. c. 4. & epist. con. Luci. 28.*

5. S. August. ad Genn, saith. Let vs holde faste those thinges that are not written, but are deliuered vnto vs, which beinge generally obserued in all places of the worlde, wee must thincke them to come from the Apostles, or from the generall councells, which oughte to be of greate authoritie in the churche of God, and whosoeuer will dispute, hereof ought to be counted of most insolent madnes. S. Hier. ad Luc. wee must obserue the traditions of our Ancestors. S. Paule comaunded vs to submitt our selues to our pastors and teachers. S. Augustine saith, wee learne by tradition that children in their infancie shoulde be baptized de gen. ad liter. 101. 23. Tradition caused him to beleeue that the baptized of heretiques should not be rebaptized, by tradition onlie he and others condemned Heluidius the heretique for denyinge the perpetuall virginitie of our Ladie, and without this noe Arrian, noe Macedonian, noe Pelagian, noe Caluin will will yealde; Wee must vse tradition saith Epiph. for the scripture hath not all thinges,

and

and therfore the Apostles deliuered certaine thinges by tradition. S.Iren. lib.3.14. saith that in all questions wee must haue recourse to the traditions of the Apostles, teachinge vs withall that the waie to true apostolicall tradition, and to bringe it to the fountaine, is by the apostolicall succesion of Bishoppes, but especially of the apostolicall church of Rome, declaring in the same place that there are manie barbarous people simple for learninge, but for constancie in the faith moste wise, which neuer had scriptures but learned onlie by tradition. Tert. lib de corn. reckoneth vpp a great number of christian obseruations or customes (as S. Cyprian in mannie places doth) whereof in fine he concludethe of such, and such, If thou require the rule of scriptures, thou shalt finde none, tradition shalbe alleadged, the author, custome the confirmer, and faith of the obseruer Orig. homil. 5. proueth the same, Dyonisius Areopag. referreth the oblation and prayinge for the death in the lyturgie or Masse, to an Apostolicall tradition. Soe doth Tertull. Aug. Chrys. Damasc. alleadge; Also wee mighte add that the scriptures themselues, euen all the bookes of the Byble, be giuen vs by tradition, elfe should wee not take them as they be indeede, for the infallible worde of God, noe more then the worcks of S. Ignat. S. Aug. S. Dion. and the like.

6. The true sense alsoe of the scriptures which

which Catholiques haue, and heretiques haue not, remayneth still in the Church by tradition, the Creede is an Apostolicall tradition. *Ruff. in expo. simb. ad principium. Hier. Epist. 61. cap. 9. Ambr. ser. 38. Aug. de Simb. ad Cath. lib. 3. cap. 1.* Alsoe it is by tradition wee hould, that the holie Ghost is God, & therfore Macedonius was condemned in the 2. councell of Constantinople for an heretique, for that he denyed the same, because in the scripture this name is not giuen vnto him, for in the scriptures, manny thinges are said to be such by Metaphors, which are not soe indeede, as that God is a sleepe, that he is angrie, that he is sorrye, although noe such thinge is in God, as alsoe manny thinges that are such and yet are not mentioned in the scriptures, God to be ingenitus, with manny such attributes, as Trinitie, parson, consubstantialitie *hypostasis, vnio hypostatica,* homousion, and because the Arrians did not yelde vnto the same, not findinge them in the scriptures they were in the councell of Nyce condemned for heretiques. And althoughe the verie wordes be not in the scripture, yet they be collected of the sence of the scriptures. And soe S. Cyrill, of that place of scripture: *Ego sum qui sum,* I am the same that is, doth gather, that the sonne is consubstantiall with the father, although the worde consubstantiall is not founde in the scriptures. So the catho-

*Naz. lib. 5. Theol.*

*Cyrill. l. 1. dialogorũ de trinit.*

lique

lique Church in all ages, out of the ſenſe of the ſcripture, doth gather, that wee oughte to pray vnto Sainctes, to pray for the deade: that there is a Purgatorie, althoughe the verie wordes themſelues be not there; And when S. Paule did ſpeake of the holy Eucharist, he broughte noe ſcriptures to proue it; I haue receaued of our Lord, ſaith he, that I deliuered vnto you, he alleadged nothinge but tradition, which he had receaued from our Lorde, that a woman ought not teache in the Churche, that a womā ought to be couered, that the man oughte to be bareheadded, that the Biſhoppe ought to be huſband of one wife, he alleadginge nothinge but the cuſtome, if any man would be captious, or contentious, he did oppoſe againſt thē the cuſtome of the Churche, ſaying, wee haue noe ſuch cuſtome, nor the Church of God, and whoſoeuer deſpiſeth theſe thinges, he doth not deſpiſe man but God. And therfore wee are referred by the holie ſcriptures to our aunceſtors, to aske knowledge of them. *Interroga patres tuos, & dicent tibi &c.* aske thy Fathers, and they ſhall declare vnto thee, and thy aunceſtors, and they will tell thee. *Non te prætereat narratio ſeniorum, ipſi enim &c.* Omitt not to heare thine elders, for they haue learned of their parents, that of them you may learne vnderſtandinge: *Non tranſgrediaris terminos antiquos quos poſuerunt parentes.* Doe not you tranſ-

*Deut. 32.*
*Eccleſ. 8.*
*Eccleſ. 8.*
*Prou. 22.*

transgresse the old limittes which your parẽts haue prescribed? Are not the Rechabites praised for followinge the tradition and preceptes of Ionadab? *Hæc dicit Deus exercituũ, pro eo quod obedistis præcepto Ionadab patris vestri &c.* Thus saith the Lord of hoastes, because that you haue obeyed the precepte of Ionadab your father, and haue kepte all his commaundements, therfore the Lord of hoastes the God of Israell saith, there shall not faile one of the stirpe of Ionadab, the sonne of Rechab that shall stande in my presence.

*Hier. 35. 18.*

7. In the dolfull and damnable debate and discorde that Martyne Luther, Caluine and others haue raised vp, by which they plunged themselues and the worlde into such an intricat laberinth of errors and heresies, where shall the poore silly sheepe haue resolution of their doubts, but of their parentes and pastors, which God hath placed in his churche to gouerne and directe his flocke, from all errors? shall not the children beleeue their fathers, and the sheepe their pastors? Wee must not only flie vnto the scriptures as S. Vincentius Lyrinensis saith, but vnto traditiõ of the catholique church, notwithstandinge saith he in that place, that the scriptures are of themselues sufficient, yet saith he because all men doe not conceaue the loftines of the scripture a like, but accordinge to euery mans phantasticall censure

*Vincent. 9. heres. c. 1.*

censure and humorous passion, as soe many heades, soe many mindes; for men as they be deuided in sects or factions, soe they deuide the sense of the scriptures, *Nouatianus, Photinus, Sabellius, Donatus, Arrius, Eunomius, Macedonius, Apollinaris, Priscilianus, Iouianus, and Pellagius*, haue eche of them grounded their proper heresies vpon the scripture. *Nam videas eos volare per singula quæque sanctæ legis volumina sacræ scripturæ.* You may see them flie ouer all the bookes of the holie lawe, both in publique and priuate, in their sermons, in their bookes, in their banquettes, in tauernes, in the streate, nothinge did they euer produce which was not shadowed by the scriptures, for they knewe verie well, that their errors coulde neuer be pleasing vnto the people, without the scriptures, with which as with sweete water they sprinckle the same, euen as soure drincke is tẽpered with sweet honny; so as when children drincke therof, hauinge once felte the sweetnes, they haue noe loathsomnes of it though neuer soe bitter; But the more scripture they bring the more wee ought to feare them, saith S. Vincentius, and to shunne them: *Magnopere curandum est in ipsa Ecclesia Catholica, vt id teneamus quod vbique, quod semper, quod ab omnibus creditum est.* For in the catholique church, wee must alwayes beware, that wee keepe that which is beleeued, alwayes, euerie where, and of euerie

P body;

body: *& hæc est verè & propriè Catholica*, which is properlie and trulie catholique. And in the 9. chapter he saith. *Quo quisque religiosior est, eò promptius nouellis adinuentionibus contrariatur*, the more vertuous, that a man is, the more prompte & ready he opposeth himselfe against newe inuentions: and soe he saith, our maister S. Stephen in his epistles to the Bishoppes of Affricke touching rebaptisinge of infants that were baptized by heretiques, *nihil innouandum est nisi quod traditum est*, the good and religious man would haue vs children to inuente noe religion, but what wee haue receaued of our fathers, and whose steppes he would haue vs to followe in all thinges.

*Apud Cypri. li. 2. cap. 7.*

8. This said author expoundinge, *1. Timoth. depositum custodi*; keepe in depositum what I haue left in your custodie, the religion and the obseruation thereof, that I deliuered vnto you, shunninge prophane noueltie of voices; he doth not saye, shunn antiquitie, or ancientie, or continuance, but noueltie and innouation of thinges, *nam si vitanda est nouitas, tenenda est antiquitas &c.* For if wee oughte to auoide noueltie, wee shoulde imbrace antiquitie: if noueltie be a prophane thinge, antiquitie is a sacred thinge, keepe the depositum saith he, which is giuen vnto thee and to the whole church, to be kepte from theeues and enemies, least they should sowe cockell or darnell amongest the cleane wheate

wheate. The depositum which you haue receaued, not which you haue inuented. The depositũ, which is not coyned by thy witt, but deliuered by my doctrine. Not any mans priuate vsurpation, but the common, and vniuersall tradition: in which you are not the author, but the keeper: not the institutor, but the follower: not the mayster, but the disciple. The depositum, saith he, *Catholicæ fidei talentum*, keepe the talent of the catholique religion, vnspotted, inuiolable, and vndefiled by you saith he, the rosarie of the spirituall tabernacle: *Pretiosas diuini dogmatis gẽmas exculpe fideliter & comptè, adorna sapienter, adijce splendorem, gratiam & venustatem*, do you garnish, turne faithfully, and adorne with the pretious Iewell of the diuine decree, doe you add therunto, splendor grace and beautie.

*Exod. 36.*

*Vincẽtius cap. 27.*

6. All this I haue alleadged out of *Vincentius Lyrinensis* word, by word; for his whole booke against heresies hath noe other obiecte but the tradition of our auncestors, by which he confuteth and conuinceth the prophane noueltie of heretiques, and their arrogant insolent ostentation of scriptures, vpon which they grounde all their hereticall cauillation, which as all our forfathers before vs, soe wee after them doe finde by experience, that the interpretation and meaninge thereof as they doe produce them, is of greater difficultie, then the con-

trouersie it selfe, the fathers did vrge them with a shorter way by askinge, *quid prius & posterius?* what is first and laste? for that heresie is grounded in noueltie, and euer cometh after the Catholique trueth first planted. And for that euerie heresie pretendeth his heresie to be auncient and from the Apostles, the fathers doe alleadge that this trueth muste not onlye be eldeste, but also must haue continewed from tyme to tyme, at the leaste with the greatest parte of Christians. And therfore Tertulian saith lib. *De præscriptione: quod apud multos vnum inuenitur, non est erratum sed traditum*, that wherin moste men doe agree vppon, it is not an erronious opinion, but a common tradition. For the Church of God is a most liuely ghospell, for with the Apostles there was the Church of Christe before the ghospell was written, sith none of the Euangelists did write vntill 18. yeares after Christs assention. With Abraham Isaacke & Iacob was a true Churche in the faith of one creator and redeemer to come, when there was noe scripture, for Moyses was the first that comitted the word of God to inke and paper, hauinge written the same in the Hebrewe tounge, which was the first that inuented characters or letters as Eusebius doth wittnesse, & euen by the testimony of prophane writers themselues, and haue taught the people beinge rude and ignorante

*Hil. 2. ad Const. Aug lib. 1 de trinitate cap. 3.*

*Tertul. li. aduers. prax. c. 20*

*Moyses the first that wrot. Euseb. li 9 c. 4 & li. 10 cap 3 præparationis Euangelicæ.*

rante to vſe them; Moyſes beinge dead Cadmas in the daies of Ioſue did firſte inuente greeke characters.

10. The holy ſcriptures doe teſtifie, as alſo prophane hiſtories, that learninge and philoſophie came from the Phenicians, Aſſirians, Chaldeans, and Aegipte vnto Greece, and the ſame doth Ioſephus teach. The firſt vniuerſitie that euer was, was Cariath Sopher in the lande of Canaan in Aſiria, it was called the cittie of learninge, neere vnto the cittie of Hebron, longe after the Gretians begann to haue lettres and learninge: and Origines ſaith, none amoungeſt the Grecians did regiſter or write any thinge of the actes or monuments of the Grecians before Homer, and Heſiodus, which were 400. yeares after Moyſes, and if there were any thing written of the Aſſyrians, or of the Phenicians before Moyſes, they did periſhe, the holie ſcriptures by godes diuine prouidence beinge reſerued ſafe, and before any ſcripture there was the Church, for betwixt Moſes and our firſt Father, was more then 2. thowſand yeares, in all which time there was noe lawe written, but the lawe of nature, the word of God which he ſignified vnto Adam, Noe, Abraham, or what otherwiſe he did inſpire into the hartes of the Patriarches, by tradition onlye it came to the poſteritie, and to Moyſes himſelfe, ſoe as tradition was before the ſcripture

*Ioſeph. 1. Apionem grammaticam.*
*Ioſue c. 15*
*Iudic. 1.*

more then 2000. yeares; the lawe of grace, which was by a liuely voice deliuered by Christe to his Apostles, was not written by him, nor commaunded by him to be written, and therfore shall not the Christians beleue the same, because he commaunded not it should be writtẽ? or should the Christians which did beleue the Apostles before the same lawe was written, be reputed fooles for beleeuinge the same before it was written? For our Sauiour did not say: *Scribite Euangelium, sed prædicate Euangelium omni creaturæ*, write the ghospel, but preach the ghospel to all creatures, how many thowsandes be there in the worlde that cannot write nor read the scriptures, and yet shall they not beleue them deliuered vnto them, by the tradition and prea-
1. Cor. 15. chinge of the church? *sicut prædicauimus, sic credidistis*, saith the Apostle, as wee haue preached, soe you haue beleued, he did not
2. Tim 3. say as wee haue written. *Tu vero, &c.* Doe you abide in those thinges, that you haue learned, knowinge of whome you haue
Act. 15. learned them, soe it seemeth good to the
1. Cor. 11 holly ghoaste and vs, if any man be contentious, wee haue noe such custome. He did not obiect scripture but custome, and tra-
2. Thes 2 dition, therfore he said, *state in fide*, stande
Horm. in diacetis Cap 25. q. 1. fast to your faith and keepe the traditions. Therfore it is inserted in the Cannons of Hormista, *prima salus est rectæ fidei regulam custo-*

*custodire, & in constitutis patrum nullatenus deuiare*; it is the beginning of our saluation to obserue and keepe the rule of right faith, and not to goe one steppe away from the decree and ordinance of our ancestors.

*Certaine obiections answered against traditions, taken out of the first Chapter of S. Paule to the Galathians.*

## CHAPTER III.

1. ALthough saith S. Paule, wee, or an Angell from heauen euãgelize beside that which wee haue euangelized to you, be he anathema or accursed. This verie place is cited by S. Athanasius in the defense and confirmation of traditions, sayinge. If any man will cite out of scriptures any texte against the decree or determinations of the churche and councells, let him be accursed, and although he alleadge all the scripture in the worlde against that which alreadie wee haue receaued, wee must not beleeue him, for children, as Athanasius saith ought not to iudge of the decree of their parentes, vnles they would haue themselues to be bastardes. *Galat. 1.*

2. Yet notwithstandinge wee must distinguishe the wordes of S. Paule which may be vnderstoode two manner of wayes as S.

Aug trac 96 super Iohn.

Augustine hath vnderstoode the same, saying. *Aliud est euangelizare preterquam quod accepistis, & aliud est euangelizare plusquam accepistis, euangelizare preterquam accepistis, est transgredi regulam fidei & recedere a via euangelij semel per Apostolos prædicata,* for it is not all one to say to euangelize otherwise then you haue receaued, and to euangelize more then you haue receaued, for to euangelize otherwise thē you haue receaued, is to transgresse the rule and limittes of faith, and to departe from the decree of the Apostles, which is a detestable thinge: and therfore to euangelize more then you haue receaued is not S. Paules meaninge, otherwise he should be repugnante to himselfe, who desired to come to Thessalonica that he might supply what was defectiue and lackinge of other mens faith; For when the Apostles vttered these wordes from Ephesus to Galatia, the ghospells of the 4. Euangelistes were not written, and specially the ghospell of S. Iohn. For it is not all a like the ghospell, and the writtinge of the ghospell, the first that was written was the ghospell of S. Mathewe, and S. Luke did supplye what was wanting of the same, and S. Iohn in his ghospell did add in many thinges which was not writen in the other 3. Euangelistes. And soe S. Paule himselfe in his Epistles did expresse many thinges, which were not soe plaine in anye of the

the 4. Euangelistes.

3. Lastlie accordinge to the declaration of all the doctors of the church, especially Ireneus, Tertulian, Cyprian, Hierom, Augustine, and others, many thinges were deliuered vnto vs by the tradition of the Apostles, which are not expreslie and manifestly in the scriptures. And therfore S. Basil saith: *Te paratum reddat traditio, Dominus ita docuit, Apostoli prædicauerunt, patres custodierunt, confirmauerunt martyres &c.* Let tradition please thee, wee are soe taught by our Lord, the Apostles haue soe preached vnto vs, the fathers haue soe kepte the same, and the same was confirmed by the Martyrs. And in another place he further saith: *Fidem nos neque ab alijs scriptam nobis recentiorem suscepimus, neque ipsi mentis nostræ germina tradere audeamus,* wee neither receaue a later faith written for vs by others, neither doe wee presume to deliuer euerie phantasie that springes out of our owne braine, least matters of religion should be thoughte to be mens fictions or inuentions.

*Basil. in homil. Sabel. & Arc.*

*Basil. ep. ad Antiochenum. Ecclesiæ.*

*Whether*

*Whether we prohibit the scriptures to be translated into the vulgar tounge.*

## CHAPTER IV.

1. TRulye the Catholique Church doth nott altogether forbide vulgar translations of holly Scriptures, althoughe shee would not haue euerie bodie at his pleasure to read the same or to make glosses thereon. The councell of Trentt in the table of prohibited bookes, and 4. rule, permitted the vse of the vulgar translations to them, whome the Bishopp or inquisitor, with the licence of the pastoure, shall thinke to be such as will reade them to their edification, and not to their damadge. Malmsburie affirmeth out of S. Bede, that there was somtimes permitted vulgar translations in Englande. The French alsoe had their French Bibles a long time: and soe the Englishe catholiques by permission from Rome, had the newe testamente in English.

2. After the retourninge of the children of Israell from Babylon, the diuine office & the holly scriptures were read vnto the people in the Hebrewe tounge, not withstandinge the Siriac or the Chaldean language was their vulgar tounge, for the Hebrewe was not al that time vulgare, otherwise the people

people ſhould not haue had neede, of an in-
terpretor when the lawe was read of Eſ- *2. Eſd. 8.*
dras;as alſoe when Moyſes, and Ioſias did *13.*
propoſe the ſame vnto the people. Againe
the Apoſtles did write their ghoſpell in noe
other languadge but in Hebrewe, Greeke,
and Latine; for Peter and Iames did write
vnto the Iewes diſperſed throughout the
whole world in the greeke tounge, as S.
Iohn did write vnto the Perſians.

3. In Affricke as longe as the Chriſtian *Aug. de*
religion was there, the latine tonge was in *doctrina*
vſe as S. Aug. and S. Cyprian doe wittneſſe, *Chriſtiana*
who alſo ſay that the pſalmes were ſounge
in that languadge,and in the Maſſe. *Surſum*
*corda, habemus ad Dominum, gratias agamus*
*Domino Deo noſtro &c.* That the latine tonge *Iſid lib. 2.*
was vſed in Spaine in their churches it is *de diuinis*
wittneſſed by S. Iſidorus aboue 900. yeares *officijs*
a goe, it was alſo decreed in the councell of *cap. 2.* *Conc.*
Toller that order ſhould be obſerued in ſin- *Toll. 4.*
ginge the ſpalmes.In englande aboue, 1000. *Bed. lib. 1.*
yeres the ſeruice was in latine as Beda, and *hiſt. ſuæ*
Thomas Waldēſis doe wittneſſe.In Fraunce *gent.*
alſo the ſame tonge was in vſe in their *VVal. to.*
churches, as *Alcuinus de diuinis officijs*, doth *3. de ſa-*
wittneſſe, and *Amallaricus Treuirēſis de officijs* *cramenta-*
*eccleſiaſticis*, who ſaith that in all the weaſt, *libus.*
the office of the church was in latine. In *Rab 2. de*
Germanie the ſame alſo was obſerued, as *inſtit. Cler.*
Rabanus doth wittneſſe and Rupertus. *Rup. de diuinis officiis.*

4. The Apoſtles as Iuſtinus Martyr doth
obſerue

obſerue, did celebrate and ſinge the pſalmes to the gentiles conuerted to the faith in the greeke tonge, notwitſtandinge there were diuers tounges, as of the Parthiás, Medes, Elamitans and ſuch like, neither yet in the vulgar greeke, but in the Atticke which was the more common and more learned, ſoe that the languadge which the greeke prieſts doe vſe at Maſſe & ſacrifice, is not the ſame, that the vulgar ſorte did vſe. Gregorie the 7. denied the kinge of Bohemia licence to tranſlate the holy Bible into the vulgar tonge, ſoe denied Innocentius the 3. longe requeſted therunto by the Biſhopp of Mentes, for theſe good fathers would not haue ſuch profound miſteries of the ſcripture, to be in contempte and ſubiect to the croſſe ſenſe of the vulgar ſorte, for ſome ſimple religious perſons readinge the holy ſcriptures, did read of godes eyes, armes and feete, and ſuch like, which indeede ought to be vnderſtoode not litteraly, but metaphoricallie, and therupon thought God to be a corpulent bodye or palpable ſubiecte.

*Caſsiod. colla* 10. *c.* 2. 3. 4. 5.

5. Dauid George the Hollander, by readinge the ſcripture alſoe in the hollandiſh languadge, found that the trewe Church ſhould neuer fayle, and becauſe he found by experience that noe other church continewed ſoe longe, as the Church of Rome, he denied Chriſt to be the true Meſſias: ſo that beinge ſubuerted and carried away

away by the sectaries of these daies, he thought the Church of Rome not to be the true churche, vnto which rather then he would yelde any beleefe, he denied Christ to be God, and soe denied the church of Rome to be true the churche. And a certaine wooman in Englande hauinge heard the 25. Chapter of Ecclesiasticus read by the minister against women, said it was the word of the diuill, and not the word of God. *Bell. to. 1. l. 2. c. 15.*

6. Who can giue greater euidence of the inconuenience of readinge the scriptures more then the heretiques of this time, euery one groundinge their heresies and absurdities vppon scriptures, falslie applied, and ill vnderstoode, wherfore reason it self without other authoritie, should perswade the church to haue the scriptures and her seruice in a certaine languadg, otherwise there could be noe vnitie or communication of churches, for none either learned, or vnlearned should frequent any churches, or heare seruice, but in his owne Countrie, where he should heare his owne vulgare languadge; neither could there be generall councells, for all the fathers that comes thither haue not euerie one of them the gifte of tonges, and therfore this is the cause that the Apostles for the moste parte did write all in greeke, for that at that tyme it was the commonest languadge of all, as Cicero saith, *Oratione pro Archia poeta*, the greeke tounge is read

is read almoſt amoungeſt all nations, but the latine, is reſtayned within her ſmale bondes and limittes, but when the Romaine Empire beganne to floriſh, the latine alſoe floriſhed, eſpecially amoungeſt the learned, as in Italie, France, Spaine, Affrique and in other nations, and therfore in reſpect that it is now the cōmō language, the ſcriptures and ſeruice of the Church ought to be in the ſame.

7. If any reaſon ſhould moue the church to haue the ſcriptures in the vulgar tonges, it is for that the ſimple people ſhould vnderſtande them, but they cannot vnderſtande the pſalmes nor the prophetts, nor many other bookes of the ſcripture, neither by readinge them take much fruite thereby, but rather great harme, for if they ſhould read in the prophett Oſee, Goe and make vnto your ſelues children of fornications, the adulterie of Dauid, the inceſt of Thamar, the lies of Iudith, and how that Ioſeph made his brethren druncke, and how that Sara, Lia, and Rachell gaue their hand-maides as concubines to other men, they would ether deſpiſe the Patriarches, or imitate them in thoſe thinges, and when they ſhould ſee ſoe many contradictories accordinge to the litterall ſenſe which the rude cannot reſolue, they woulde be in a confuſion, or bringe the ſcriptures to manifeſt contempt.

8. Alſo in reſpecte that kingdomes and nations

nations are subiecte to conquestes, and inuasion of strange nations, which alwayes for the most parte bringe with them their languadge, vtterly defacinge the languadge of the country conquered; soe also in these countries, there muste be alterations of trãslations of scriptures, which cannot be done without great danger of the corruption thereof, either in respect of the ignorance, or malice of the trãslators, especiallie if they be heretiques, which neuer translated the scriptures trulie being carried away by their passionat affection of their heresie; And therfore S. Hierom founde great faulte, that the scripture should be soe common and in contempte, for saith he talkatiue ould women and doting ould men, the cauelinge Sophiste, all men doe presume to speake of scripture, they rent the scriptures in peeces, they teach it before they learne it. When S. Basil heard the cheefe cooke of the Emperor, in his presence to speake of scriptures, he reprehended him, sayinge: *Tuum est de pulmentis cogitare, non dogmata diuina decoquere,* it is thy office to thincke vppon thy cooquerie, & not to play the Cooke in diuine misteries. I am sure if these fathers were liuinge in this wicked age, to see the Cobler the Tailor, the Tapster speake and dispute of scriptures, and alsoe to preach in the pulpitt, they would sharplie reprehend them.

*Hier epist. ad Paulinum.*

*Whether*

*Whether we forbid the ignorante to pray in a languadge which they vnderstand.*

## CHAPTER V.

1\. Cor 14. 1. THe heretiques obiect vnto vs, the wordes of S. Paul saying, he that speaketh with the tongue let him pray that he may interprete, for if I pray with the tonge, my spirite prayeth but my vnderstandinge is without fruite. I answere that although it be not fruitfull for his vnderstandinge yet it is fruitefull for his deuotion, for here is noe mention made of any other tonges, but of such as men did speake in the primitiue churche by miracle, as of spirituall collations and exhortations which the christians were wont to make to praise God, and not of those lãguadges which were then common to all the world, as Hebrewe, greeke and latine, in which the scriptures both olde and newe were written. For it is a palpable and grosse deceit and cogginge of the heretiques, to say that the vertue, and efficacie of the Sacramentes and sacrifice, oblations, prayers, and religion dependeth vppon the peoples vnderstandinge, hearing or knowledge, the principall operation and force therof, and of the whole misterie of the Church, consistinge especially in the verie vertue of the

worcke,

worcke, and the publicke office of the prieſtes, who are appointed by Chriſte to diſpoſe the miſteries to our ſaluation. The infant, innocente, idiott, and vnlearned, takinge noe leſſe fruite by baptiſme, and all other diuine offices then the learnedeſt clearcke, yea more, if they be more humble, charitable, deuoute, and obedient, and perhappes wee ſee more often the ſimple to be more deuoute, and the learned more rechles and more colde, for deuotion doth not conſiſte in the vnderſtandinge, vnles the will be well affected.

2. S. Auguſtine ſaid of the common people, *non intellgendi viuacitas, ſed credendi ſimplicitas tutiſsimum facit.* It is not quicknes of vnderſtanding, but ſimplicitie of beleefe that ſhall ſaue vs; And in another place he ſaith. *Si propter ſolos eos Chriſtus mortuus eſt qui certa intelligentia poſſunt quæ ad fidem pertinent diſcernere, penè fruſtra in Eccleſia laboramus.* If Chriſte had died onlie for ſuch as can vnderſtand well the miſteries of our faith, in vaine wee ſhould labour in godes church, for God doth rather reſpect your ſimple beleefe, then your deepe vnderſtandinge, the affection of the will concerning your faith, then the hawtie knowledge of your loftie minde. *Charitas ædificat, ſcientia inflat*, as the Apoſtle ſaith: charitie doth fruictifie to edification, when ſcience ſerueth for the moſte parte to oſtentation, ſoe as our Sa-

uiour did ſpeake vnto the common people in parables, whoſe ſimplicitie and godly affection did proffitt more therby, then the wordlie wiſdome and proud knowledge of the arrogant and ſwellinge Scribes and Pharesies.

3. Doe you thincke that the children of the Hebrewes did vnderſtande when they cried in the Temple. *Oſanna filio Dauid?* Or that our Sauiour was diſpleaſed therby for that they vnderſtoode it not, but the prieſts and ſcribes were much confounded therby, ſaying. *Audis quid iſti dicunt*, truly our Sauiour was not diſcontented at the prayſes of thoſe littles ones, for then the propheſie was fulfilled, *ex ore infantium & lactentium &c.* thou makeſt an inſtrument of the tender infante and ſuckinge babe to magnifie, and praiſe thy name, to the confuſion and ouerthrowe of thine enemies, ſeinge the ende of all the ſcriptures, and of the lawe of God and man, and of the ſcience and knowledge thereof, is true and perfecte charitie, inflaminge and inkendlinge our hartes with the firie loue, both of God and our neighbors, flowinge and floriſhing abondantlie with all fruitfull exerciſes and worckes of mercie, pietie and religion, as the Apoſtle ſaith: *plenitudo legis eſt dilectio*: the fulnes of the lawe is charitie.

4. The experience of the catholique flocke in agreeing and ſubmittinge themſelues

ues to the seruice of the church in the vniuersall and common languadge thereof, and of their great increase and charitie, pietie deuotion & religion therby, as their shining resplendent vertues of their godly conuersation and their externall worckes of mercie, may wittnesse and confirme the same, and the example of the contrarie practise in fewe yeares paste of these new euangelistes or pretended reformers, as in disagreeing from the common vse and custome of the whole churche and reuoltinge from the obedience thereof auoucheth no lesse, as also the smale or noe fruite at all that their vulgar and confused translations haue brought both vnto themselues and to their miserable and scabbed flocke, which like giddy heades and itchinge braines, were not contented nor setled therein, but conceaued great loathsomnes thereof, like the children of Israell who hauinge soe earnestlie sought vnto themselues a kinge, yet when he did raigne ouer them, nothinge was more toilsome vnto them; soe as nothinge is more troublesom vnto your carnal appetites then any sett prayers or seruice in your vulgar translations, which the puritantes doe protest to be collected out of the Popes portuis & Masse, and consequentlie verie distastfull vnto them. Admonition parl. pag. 45. and for this cause by the protestants of englande, are censured as scismatickes. Was

*Puritants cares nott for prayers.*

*Admonitio parleamenti.*

euer their ſtinge more venemous, or their bookes more exaſperatinge or more vehement againſt the ſeruice of the church in the latine tounge, then it is this day againſt the booke of comon prayer, ſet forth in the engliſhe tonge, and ſet ſeruice in your owne churches? I haue reade the ſlanderous and bitinge booke of Thomas Cartwrithe oppugninge the ſame, againſt doctor Whiteguifte Biſhopp of Canterburie for defending it: there you may ſee with what inuectiue ſtiles, redoublinge withall oprobrious tearmes, they doe entertaine one another, and what a generall reuolte wee ſee nowe a dayes from this vulgar tranſlation of ſett prayers, & order ſett downe in that booke, and comaunded to be putt in continuall practiſe, into Caluiniſme and Puritaniſme (yea and at laſt vnto plaine athiſme) who will haue noe ſet prayers or common ſeruice at all, ſauinge ſome laſciuious and wanton pſalmes of Geneua, rather for faſhion ſake, or ſome carnall delight, then for any ſpirituall deuotion. I haue ſeene a pamphlett in printe which was exhibited to the parlament, that it was not lawfull for chriſtians to ſay our pater noſter, or the creede, yea not in our vulgar tongue.,

8. God doth knowe and wee ought not to be ignorant, that your vulgar and falſe tranſlation of ſcriptures or ſet prayers, is not for ediſication, but rather for cauillation

though

though you inculcate the same soe oftē, your selues not restinge therein but slidinge from it againe. In the kingdome of Ireland you comaund the englishe Bible, and the english common prayer booke, to be obserued in all the churches of that poore kingdome cō-pellinge the prisoners to buy those bookes which themselues coulde not vnderstande, yea not one person amoungest 40. when that comaūd was giuen forthe, could speake or vnderstande the english tonge. And now in the kinges raigne you cause those bookes to be set forth in the Irishe tonge, compel-linge euerie parish church to pay 10. shil for an Irishe Bible, when one amoungest a 100. cannott read them, or vnderstand them, and therfore an Irish protestant Bishopp, did laugh at this strange kinde of alteration, and said to some of his frindes: in Queene Elizabeth her time wee had englishe Bibles and Irish ministers, but nowe said he, wee haue ministers come out of england vnto vs, and Irish Bibles with them.

6. Are not for the most parte all the benefices and church liuinges of that kingdome bestowed vpō English & Scotish ministers, not one of them hauinge three wordes of the Irish tonge, and although in the English pale, and in porte townes, the inhabitants, especially the best sorte, cā speake Englishe, yet fewe of the common sorte, except it be betwixt Dublin and Drodach

and in 3. barronies in the country of Wexforde can ſpeake any worde of Engliſhe, and truly I thinke that the Iriſh Bibles haue as many faultes & errors in thẽ, as the tranſlation Martine Luther made of the Bible, in which Hieronimus Enſer found more then 1000. errors, which he ſet downe in the tranſlation that he made 1522. And not only catholiques haue charged him with thoſe errors, but alſo Zuinglius who made another kind of tranſlation diſagreeing from that of Luther. The ſame is alſo witneſſed by your variable trãſlations of your Engliſh Bible, the firſt not agreeing with the laſt, nor with the ſeconde. In the conference had at Hampton courte, the Engliſh Bible was cenſured to be ill tranſlated, and containing very partiall, vntrue, and ſeditious notes, and too much fauoringe of dangerous and traiterous conceites, and ſoe order was taken to make a newe tranſlation. How can the true ſenſe and meaninge of the oracles of God be imbraced, if they be toſſed and corrupted with euerie vulgar tongue, which oughte to be a ſufficient cauſe that it ſhould be preſerued, in thoſe languadges in which it was firſt ſet forth by the Apoſtles and fathers of the primitiue church.

*Cor.* 14. *7.* S. Paule did forbid a womã to ſpeake in the church: but nowe euerie woman amoungeſt the proteſtants, is a miſtris of ſcripture, are all men Apoſtles, all Euangeliſts

lists, all doctors saith the Apostle but nowe? this vulgar translation, or rather corruption or prophanation, all Shoomakers, Coblers, Tailors, Tauernors, yea and lasciuious wanton women, yea the most ignorant of all are Apostles, prophetts, euangelists and doctors, so as they take away all order and forme of discipline from godes church, and in the place of Hierusalem which ought to be a cittie well ordered withall vnformitie both of doctrine and discipline, there is a Babilon builded, where there is nothinge but a sauadge and barbarous confusion. Soe as wee may perceaue, that this inordinate desire of knowinge the hidden and secrett misteries of God, which he woulde not haue to be abused, by these contemptuous spirittes, brought such fruite vnto the worlde, as that disordered greedines of our first parentes touching the knowledge of good, and euill, therfore wee are warned not to knowe to much but rather to feare, least wee should abuse our knowledg, and therfore the holly ghoast doth aduise vs, not to be curious in searching things aboue our capacitie, and beyond our reache. *Eccle c. 3.*

8. The beginninge and end of Ezechiel as S. Hierom wittnesseth, was read by noe man before he was 30. yeares of age, Baptisme was vealed in the read sea, the Eucharist in the paschall lambe, in manna, and in Melchisedeks, bread and wine, the trinitie *Hier. in proemio Ezech.*

was not knowen to any, but to the prophetts and the highe priesties. S. Paule calleth the incarnation, *misterium absconditum à sæculis*. A misterie hidden from ages, for the word *misterium* is not to be made knowen or diuulged to euerie one, as Dyonisius and Origenes doe counsel. Did not the Apostles forbide to write the creede, that noe man might learne it but by word of mouth of the Christians? S. Ambrose alsoe saith *lib. de ijs qui initiantur cap. 9. lib. 6. de Sacra. c. 4.* that ineffable misteries must be kept silent. And therfore, in the latine translation of the scripture, wee retaine many Hebrew wordes, and not without great cause are they reserued in the very hebrew it selfe, which cannot be soe well translated into the latine, much lesse to any other languadge as, *Alleluia, Osanna, Amen, Emanuell, Rabbi, Abba*, as also greeke wordes, *Kyrie eleison, Psalmum, Christum, Baptismum, Episcopum, Diaconum, Eucharistiam, Euangelium*, which are greeke voyces, and when the Pope doth celebrate the Ghospell and the Epistle are read in greeke before the latine in the churche of Constantinople those were read first by the grecians in latine and afterwardes in greeke, and soe the latine was interpreted, by the greeke, and this as Remigius declareth, was done to shew the vnitie of faith in those two churches, and that greeke in which the priests in Grecia doe celebrate

*Dion lib Ecclef. Hier. c. 1. Orig hom 5. in cant. Hier. ep. 81. ad Pamachum.*

or

or ſay Maſſe, is not the ſame which the vulgare people doe vſe, but farr different from it, which only the learned ſorte of people doe vnderſtande: euen as the latine tonge is not the vulgare tonge of the latines, but the Italian tonge, for the latine is only knowẽ to the learned. For as S. Baſil ſaith, it is not a miſterie if it be commõ to the vulgar ſorte, for in the olde lawe all the veſſells of the tabernacle were couered leaſt they ſhould be ſubiect to the viewe of the people: by which Origines did ſignifie, that the miſterie of the ſacrifice, ought to be hidden from the common people and vnworthie perſons: and ſoe Dionyſ. ſaith when our holly princes did inſtitute publiquely the holly ſacrifice, they haue neuertheleſſe deliuered the ſame in ſecret manner.

*Baſil. lib. de Spiritu ſancto.*

*Num. 5.*

*Lib. Ecclesiæ Hierarch.*

9. Were not the Bethſamites puniſhed for beholding the Arcke curiouſlie? was not Oza alſoe puniſhed by death for touching it? Was not Balthazer plaged for prophaninge the holly veſſels, and for drinckinge out of them? were not the ſheapeeds caſt downe with a thonder bolte in the fields for ſinging the holly wordes of conſecration, as Innocentius the 3. doth reporte, & therfore he comaunded that thoſe wordes ſhould be very ſecretly vſed in the church? Therfore S. Baſill ſaith, that many thinges are deliuered vnto the churche, which are not writtẽ, leaſt the cuſtome of ſuch thinges ſhould

*Baſ. ibid.*

ſhould breede contempte, and ſoe ſpeaking of Moyſes he ſaid, that he would not ſuffer euerie thinge that was ſacred to be common to all, for he knewe accordinge to his wiſdome, that the thinges common to euerie bodie, are not in that requeſt as thinges that are ſecrette, therfore of theſe miſticall things the Apoſtle S. Paule comaunded Timothy, that he ſhould comend thē to men of faith and ſanctity, which are fitt for the ſame. Soe Tertulian ſaith, *non nimium eſt de Deo loqui neque omnibus, neque omnia ſunt propalanda*, it becomes not all men to diſpute or reaſon of God, and diuine thinges, for all thinges are not to be made publicke to all men, neither in all places. *Ignorare pleraque inquit ille nequum quod non debeas, noris quia quod deberis noſti*: for it better ſaith he to be ignorante in thoſe thinges which you ought not to knowe, becauſe it is ſufficient to knowe what you are bound to knowe. Soe Hilarius ſayes. *Habet non tam veniam quā præmium ignorare quod credas, quia maximum fidei ſtipendium eſt ſperare quæ neſcias*, you ſhall not onlie haue pardon, but a reward to be ignorant of that you beleue, for it is a greate meritt of faith, to hope that which you knowe not. Soe Clemens Alexandrinus ſaith: not ſuch as are wiſe accordinge to the word, but ſuch as are wiſe before God haue the poſſeſsion of their faith, which is learned without learninge, the written booke of

*2. Timot.*

*Tert. lib. 1 Theologia.*

of it is true charitie, which is the diuine decree pertaininge to the ſimple and humble of harte. Yea, ſeuenty the two interpreters which were choſen of the beſt that could be found, alſwell for their learning and vertue, as alſo for knowledge in the ſcripture, choſen by Eleazer the high prieſt, at the requeſt of Ptolomeus Philadelfus king of Ægipt, & inſpired by the holy ghoaſt to tranſlate the ſcriptures, yet in the miſterie of the bleſſed Trinitie and the coming of the Meſsias, for that they were miſteries moſt profound, they placed but a little marke without any other expoſition, for that they durſt not interprett them.

*Whether a man ought not to praie, either by himſelfe, or by another, but in a languadge he vnderſtandeth.*

## CHAPTER VI.

1. ORigines doth aunſwere to this point, ſaying. *Non parum ex hoc ipſo vtilitatis animæ conferri &c.* he teacheth although the woordes of the ſcriptures be obſcure which wee heare, yet they penetratinge and pearcinge our hartes and mindes, doe receaue great conſolation therby: if wee may beleeue that amoungeſt the gentiles ſome verſes which they pronounce at their charminge and inchauntinge, be of

be of that force and efficacie when they be whiſpered into mens eares, which thoſe people themſelues that doe repeate or ſaie them, are ignorant of them, and at the only voice or ſounde of them, the ſerpentes are either lulled a ſleepe, or driuen out of their hoales and caues; how much more ought wee to beleue that the words of the holie ſcriptures, and the prayers of the catholique church ſhould be of greater force and vertue, though they be pronounced in any languadge, then any charminge whatſoeuer? And as our Sauiour ſaith of the children of the church, that their Angells doe aſsiſt thẽ before godes throne, they doe offer our prayers, and whatſoeuer appellation or inuocation wee make, they exibitte and prefer it before his diuine maieſtie. And althoughe wee doe not vnderſtand *Kyrie eleiſon &c.* yet the Angells vnderſtand it, and not onlie manie vertues are aboute vs, but they alſoe doe lodge, and dwell in vs, as the prophett ſaid, *Benedic anima mea Dominum &c.* Let my ſoule prayſe God, and alſoe all my interior partes praiſe him, vid. all that is within me, which are the angelicall vertues vnto whome the care of our ſoules and bodies are committed: whoe are the more delighted, if wee pray or vtter any verſe of the ſcriptures, if wee ſpeake with our tounge though the ſenſe be without fruicte, yet
1. *Cor.* 14. the ſpiritt doth pray, and ſoe S. Paule ſaith it to

it to be a kind of misterie , that somtymes the spiritt which is within vs doth praye, & yet the sense hath noe fruicte, and soe he said that the spirits doth praye, which are the blessed Angells resident in vs, and are made ioyfull and refreshed by our prayers, though wee doe not ourselues vnderstand them: and not onlie the Angells, but God the Father, God the sonne, and God the holy ghoast, accordinge to S. Iohn, *ad eum veniemus & apud eum mansionem faciemus*: wee will come vnto him, and dwell with him: thus farre Origines, and much more touchinge this subiect which were to longe to repeate.

2. Yf a man ought not to pray or not to heare any thinge in the Church which he doth not vnderstand, you will take awaye from her the vse of the psalmes, which none though neuer soe learned can attaine to the full vnderstandinge of them in any knowen tounge whatsoeuer, yea our Lords prayer which wee call the *Pater noster*, though it be translated in to euerie language, how many shall you finde that cannot vnderstand the same? For amoungest the common sorte, one of an hundred cannot comprehende the litterall meaninge of it, much lesse the true sense of these wordes; *Giue vs this day our daylie bread &c.* which few amoungest your cheyfest ministers, can expound; as also these other wordes. *Et ne inducas in tentationem*, and leade vs not into tenta-

tentation. Wherein not three amoungest you all, will agree in one and the selfe same exposition. Soe as if you will neuer haue any prayers in the Church, but what you vnderstand, you shall haue but fewe or none at all.

3. Our deuotion therfore doth not consist in the vnderstāding, but in the will, if the wil be furnished with charitie, it skilleth not whether the vndestandinge be replenished with great science, or much knowledge. It is charitie, saith S. Paule that doth edifie; but an heretique can neuer edifie though he haue neuer soe much knowledge, being the author of separation, deuision and schisme, sith there is noe greater token of charitie, then vnanimitie. *Quia multitudo &c.* Because the multitude of such as beleeue, ought to be one harte and one soule, and soe one languadge comon to them all, especiallie in the seruice of the church and administration of the sacraments: for confusion of tounges, haue hindred the worke of the Tower of Babilon, and before that confusion, there was but one languadge, and soe before your heresie and diuersitie of religion, the church of God was, *terra vnius labij sermonem eorundem:* of one lip, of one speech: and as there was but one God adored of all, soe there was but one faith embraced and professed by all, one administration of the sacraments, and one order of ceremonies amoun-

amoungeſt all ; There was vnitie of beleefe, without deuiſion of ſects; ſimplicitie, without duplicitie; pietie of religion, without impietie of hereſie; one paſtor, and one flock the execrable and dreadfull blaſphemies and hereſies of this wicked age were not heard of, all were called chriſtians, and not Euangeliſtes, nor Apoſtles, nor Lutherans, nor Caluiniſtes, nor Hugonotts, nor Geues, nor Adamitts , nor Anabaptiſtes, nor Papiſtes: children were obedient to their Parents, the ſheepe did acknowledge their Paſtors; the laſciuious and pratlinge woman, was not a Miſtres of the ſcriptures; the pope was not called antechriſte : his authoritie was not called in queſtion; The church was feared and obeied of her ſubiects, againſt which there was noe rebellion, or inſurrection of carnall, filthie, inceſtuous and abhominable Apoſtates ; men were of honeſt & ſimple diſpoſition , without contention or debate, touchinge their religion, euerie one referringe himſelfe to the catholick church, whoſe faith and meritts was communicated and diffuſed to al her bleſſed members. They had noe newe ghoſpell, but that which was dictated by the holie ghoaſte, and deliuered by the Apoſtles to the Church, and which the Churche propoſed to the faithfull to beleeue. And now ſince they had diuerſitie of tounges, they haue alſo had diuerſitie of faith , and diuerſitie of hereſies.

4. But

4. But to aunſwere more fullie this obiection, the catholique churche doth not forbid any one to praye in any tounge he thinkes good priuately to himſelf, although in the publique and comon ſeruice thereof, ſhee would haue the comon languadge to be practiſed & obſerued, to preuent confuſion of tounges, and corruption both of wordes and ſenſe. And as in the Church of God there is one ſacrifice, one order of ceremonies and adminiſtration of the ſacraments, ſoe wee haue but one languadge comon to all church men. For if you goe to Spaine or America, or to any other cōtry, you ſhall haue the common languadge by which you may vnderſtand them, and they you. Otherwiſe if in one church there were fortie different languadges, you muſt haue fortie portuſes and fortie Maſſe-bookes, and ſoe in the like caſe wee muſt haue infinitt bookes and portuſes and infinite Maſſe-bookes which cannot be without great inconuenience, and I pray you which way can an Iriſh man ſaie Maſſe or mattens, who hath no printe in his Countrie to printe thoſe bookes in Iriſhe? I am ſure the proteſtant printer at Dublin would not printe Maſſe-bookes in the Iriſh tounge, or if the Iriſhe or Engliſh had gon to Spaine or other Countries, he could neuer ſaye or heare Maſſe and exerciſe the rites of his religion, if it could not be don but in his owne languadge

guadge. Therfore blessed is that order that taketh awaie this disordered confusion and inconuenience of these fond heretiques.

5. As for priuate prayers, you should not charge her, for her blessed doctors in all ages haue replenished the world with infinite books of prayers, of deuotion and pietie in all languadges, which haue wrought such maruelous effects and strange conuersions of notorious sinners, such contempt of wordlie honor, such despisinge of all wordlie vanitie, such heroicall resolutions in mens hartes, such collections for releeuinge the poore and the distressed, and such an ardent loue to our Sauiour, Creator, and Redeemer, as the like was neuer brought to passe, nor neuer shalbe by any of Luther or Caluines followers. Who can be ignorant of the most godlie prayers of S. Augustine and all the fathers of the churche? S. Gregorie, S. Bernard, S. Fulgentius, S. Thomas S. Bonauenture S. Anselme, and in our owne age those of Dionis. Carthusianus, Laurentius, Surius, Stella and Loartes, translated into all vulgar tounges, with infinite others which were to longe to rehearse? But I cannot passe with silence that most famous, renowmed, reuerend and religious father Lewis de Granada, whose godlie works of deuotion and prayers, are translated into seuerall tounges. I neuer hearde of anie booke of deuotion or religion, sett forth

by any of these sectaries, any way comparable vnto his, whose workes and bookes serue only to ouerthrowe deuotion, pietie, prayer, and religion, I haue seene many godly bookes violated and defiled by them: It is strange then that you will picke out a certaine languadge for prayers and yet banishe awaie all kinde of prayers, sauinge the wanton Psalmes of Geneua, corrupted by your false translatiō, wherein you praie to keepe vs from Pope, Turcke, and Papistrie, yea I my selfe haue seene a supplication exhibited to the last Queene, and to the parleament house wherein it was auerred, that it was not lawfull for christians to saie our Lordes prayer. To conclude therfore, deuout prayers doe proceede from the ardent loue of God, which is diffused into our soules by the holy ghoaste which is giuen vnto vs, and inwardlie doth dwell and lodge in vs, *Rom. 8.* by which wee saie and crie out Abba pater: our father, and by which wee prostrate our selues with our sighinge hartes and dolefull groanes before the throne of the almightie God, and by which wee enioye his familiar and blessed presence.

*Whether*

*Whether the Church vniuerſall can be charged With errors, contrarie to the firſt inſtitution of the bleſſed Sacrament of the Euchariſt.*

## CHAPTER I.

1. THe church of Chriſt did neuer alter the matter and forme of any of her ſacraments, much leſſe of this, beinge the greateſt of the reſt, in which Chriſt hath ſhewed his wonderfull great loue vnto the church his only ſpouſe, in feedinge and ſanctifiinge the ſoules of her children with his owne pretious bodie and blood, that beinge fedd by Chriſte, ſhee may be purified and clenſed by him in that fearfull and dreadfull Hoaſt, which doth exceede the capacitie of any earthlie vnderſtandinge. Of this wonderfull loue of Chriſte it was ſaid by Iſaias, *Quid eſt &c.* what is it that I ought to doe vnto my vineard, and haue not don it? meaninge therby, that in this Sacrament he manifeſted the bowells of his charitie, and loue towardes his churche, which loue is magnified by S. Iohn Chriſoſtome, ſayinge. *Nam parentes quidem alijs ſæpè filios tradent alendos &c.* For parents doe often deliuer their children to others to be nouriſhed, but

*Iſa 5.*
*Chryſ homil 61. ad populum Antiochenū.*

I doe not soe, for I nourishe you with the fleshe of my owne bodie, and I putt my selfe before yow, giuinge yow the same flesh and bloode by which I was made your brother. And as you take away Christ altogether from the sacrament, denyinge it contrarie to Christs plaine, certaine and manifest trueth to be his bodie and blood, so you diminishe and extenuate godes loue towardes vs, and our affection, loue, reuerence, and deuotion towardes him, and take awaye both the substance, matter, forme, order, ceremonies, valour, estimation, respect and reuerence from so great, so dreadfull, and so incomprehensible a Sacrament.

2. But the church of Christe doth not take away any valour, or forme from this Sacrament, and shee beinge instructed by the wisdome of godes spirite, and by the instruction of Christ and his Apostles, accordinge to tyme and place, for godes iust honour and greater reuerence of the Sacrament, and the christians most profitt and fruicte, therby disposeth not of the forme or substãce of the order and obseruatiõ in receauinge the same which himselfe (said S. Augustine) did not comaund, that he might comitt that to the Apostles, by whome he was to dispose the affaires of his church, though both he and the Apostles at Emaus, and the fathers in the primatiue church re-

*Epist. 118. ad Ianuarium.*

ceiued

ceiued vnder one kinde, in giuinge the blood onlie to litle children, and in reseruinge most commonlie the bodie onelie, as Tertulian doth reporte, in houselinge the sicke therewith as Eusebius doth affirme. This is knowen by the holie Ermittes that receaued and reserued the bodie, and not the blood in the wildernes, as S. Basil doth wittnesse. You ought therfore to consider, that there is noe liuinge fleshe without the blood, and whosoeuer receaueth the bodie, receaues the blood alsoe. Yea Luther himselfe was of this faith, after his reuolte from the Churche; and for that the Christian people be nowe increased, and manie receaues often, and at once, soe much wine cannot be consecrated without eminent danger of sheddinge: as also when in manie countries vnder the North pole they haue not wine at all, it cannot be without great charges to giue euerie man wine, asmuch as should serue for consecration: and besides it would be offensiue to the poore, if they themselues should be excluded from the chalice more then the rich. And therfore the Church in regard of Christian charitie, to take away all murmure and occasion of offence, hath ordained that all should abstaine from the challice, when aswell Christe is receaued vnder one kinde, as vnder both kindes, neither in the meane time is Christs institution violated; The priests therfore

*Luc. 24. 25. Act. 2. 20. 7. Lib. de lap n. 10. Tertul li. ad vxo. nu 4. Euse. hist. eccles lib. 6. cap. 36. Basil ep. ad Cass.*

to whom it was commaunded to doe that which Christ hath done in his last supper, they doe both consecrate and offer, receaue and take, noe otherwise then Christ himselfe hath done, who did consecrate and offer, receaue and take, and hath giuen vnto them also to be taken vnder both kindes, and this when the priest saith Masse, & noe otherwise, because he must expreslie, represent the pasion of Christe, and the separation of his blood from his bodie in the same, and soe vnto the priestes is said, doe this in remembrance of me.

3. And although he said. *Bibite ex hoc omnes.* Drinke you all of this, yet it is manifest that in the house of Simon the Leaper, there were many others where he consecrated this blessed hoaste, & yet onlie the twelue Ap stles satte downe, whome he instituted newe priestes, for to consecrate this newe Sacrament. And although the Sacrament of Christ pertaynes to all, yet vnto the priestes onlie pertaines the chalice. But the laye people and the Clergie also, when they doe not execute their function or say Masse themselues, are to receaue vnder one kind, beinge therby noe lesse partakers of Christ his whole person and grace, then if they receaued vnder bothe. For our Sauiour receaued and consecrated two distincte matters of this sacrament, vid. bread and wine, and hath vsed two distincte formes

formes therein, therfore euerie one of those kindes hauing a distincte matter, & a distinct forme, is a distincte Sacramtē, especially they being cōsecrated in two distincte tymes, vid. at supper and after supper, therfore the consecration of the bodie and distributiō which for some tyme went before the Chalice was a perfect worke of God, for the worckes of God are perfecte and not defectuous: for after the consecration and distribution of each of these kindas, he said. *Doe this in remembrance of me.* In which he declared an euident distinction of both these diuine actions, for these wordes were not vttered after both the kindes, but a parte after eche of them, therfore these two actes are a part and separated when ech of them haue their proper determination. For as the Ciuill Lawyers saie. *In cunctis actibus & dispositionibus, eos articulos, quorum quilibet habet suam propriam determinationem & clausulam concludentem, pro separatis esse habendos.* In all actes of pleadinges, of which euery article hath a distincte & proper limitation by distincte clauses, wee must consider of them, not in generall, but a parte by themselues.

4. For Christ would by his distinct institution and distribution, giue power to his churche to dispense or giue, either the one kind, or the other, accordinge to her wisdome and discretion: wherevpon. S. Bernard saith when our Sauiour arose from the table,

*Bern. ser. in cæna Domini.*

table, he washed all the disciples feete, afterwardes returning to the table, he ordained the sacrifice of his bodie and blood, the breade a parte, and afterwardes deliueringe the blood a parte. The same is also proued by Pope Iulius the first, whose wordes were afterwardes related in the councell of Brach: with sundrie other proofes which I could produce vnto this purpose.

*Iul. epist. ad Episc. Ægipt. con. Brac. c. 3. 1. Cor. 10.*

5. But you will vrge against the church, the institution of Christ who did institute this Sacrament vnder both kindes. I aunswere that Christs example doth not binde vs, but in those thinges wherein he intended to bind vs, for in many thinges which he did in that sacrament, he did not binde vs, as it is manifest, otherwise wee should alwaies celebrate in the toppe of a house as he did, and after supper, and vpon thursdaie, and amoungest noe more nor lesse thë twelue, and they twelue Apostles, and also a Iudas amoungest them, and noe wooman should communicate, for noe wooman was there, wee ought alsoe to take the body, before the bread by benediction should be consecrated, as our Sauiour did at that supper, vnto which the churche is not bounde. And as in these thinges we are not bound to imitate Christ, soe that the laitie should receaue vnder both kindes, they are not bound to followe the example of Christ, for as the lawyers

lawyers ſaie, wee muſt not iudge by examples but by lawes; As for the prieſtes repreſentinge the perſon of Chriſte, vnto whome the precepte is giuen, *Doe this &c.* they receaue Chriſt vnder both kindes, and yet the greekes doe not vſe the Chalice in lent, and the latines vpon good fridaye doe receaue Chriſt vnder one kinde.

6. I aunſwere further that many thinges are inſtituted by Chriſt, which doe not bind vs to accompliſhe them, as matrimonie, holie orders, vowes and votaries, to ſay maſſe, virginitie, and euangelicall councells are inſtituted by Chriſte, and yet wee are not obliged therunto, for it is in euerie mans owne election to marrie, to receaue holie orders, to vowe, to be a virgin: it was alſo inſtituted of God that wyne ſhould be vſed for drinke, and yet wee are not comaunded to drinke it: it was alſo appointed by God, that the firſt fruictes of wyne ſhould be offred vnto the prieſts for their drinke, yet they were not comaunded to drinke it. Trulie you ſhould followe Chriſt and imitate him, had yow bene obedient to his church accordinge to the example of himſelfe, who did ſubmitt himſelfe to his mother, the Sinagoge, and her preceptes. For wee muſt vnderſtand, that ſuch thinges as our Lord hath ordained by himſelfe, cannot be altered in his Church, nor be diſpenſed withall, as the morall preceptes, and the

the articles of our faith, which are immutable, and ſuch as pertaine to the ſubſtance of the ſacraments: but ſuch as are poſitiue precepts, as the rites of the ſacraments not eſſentiallie pertaininge to the ſame which Chriſte himſelfe hath not inſtituted, by occaſion of time and place and other circumſtancies, the churche beinge directed by the ſpiritt of God, may alter them, becauſe herſelfe hath inſtituted them: as this obſeruation of communicatinge either vnder one or both kindes, and therfore it may be changed by the churche.

7. The holy doctors haue diuided the church into three ſtates of times, as Nicolaus de Luſſa Cardinall, related by Alfonſo Salmeron hath obſerued. The firſt ſtate of the church was feruent: for the Chriſtians in that golden world, were inflamed with an ardent loue and feruent charitie to ſhedd their blood for Chriſt, and in this ſtate, Chriſte was deliuered vnto thoſe faithfull chriſtians vnder both kindes, that drincking the blood of our Lorde, they ſhould moſt cheerfully ſhedd their blood for him, as S. Cyprian teacheth in his Epiſtle to Cornelius, and his Epiſtle to the Thybaritans. Neither did he altogether wiſh it ſhould be giuen to euerie one of the laytie, but in time of perſecution to ſhedd their blood for Chriſt. In the ſecond ſtate, the church was zealous, though not ſoe feruente, and ſoe Chriſt

*Salmeron tractatu 34.*

*S. Cypri. epiſt. ad Cornel.*

Christ was giuen vnto the christians vnder one kinde, that is to say of bread, which was dipped in blood as may be gathered out of manny fathers and councells. In the third state the church was colde and luke warme, and so was Christ giuen vnto the laytie vnder one kinde without dipping it into the blood. This the church hath done for good cause, beinge taught herein by the holly ghoaste, which euer followeth the churche, whose authoritie is of the same force nowe as it was then.

8. You vrge the wordes of Christ saying. *Matt. 26.* *Bibite ex hoc omnes*, drinke yee all of this. I aunswere that these words were spoken and directed to the disciples that were present, and vnto the priestes their successors when they shoulde celebrate; vnto whome also was said, doe this in remembrance of me; and therfore that glorious Martyr said; *quotiescunque &c.* whēsoeuer yee shall drinke *Roffensis.* thereof &c. because that the precepte of drinckinge is not soe absolute as the precepte of eatinge his bodie, vnto which noe condition is added, therfore it is a precepte deliuered vnto them with condition as, when they will drinke of the Chalice, they shoulde doe it and offer it in remembrance of him: for the wordes of the imparatiue moode doe not alwayes include in them an intente of bindinge as vnder paine of sinne, for by them wee pray: *Miserere mei Deus*, haue

haue mercy on vs. *Patientiam habe in me*, haue patience with me; Sell all that thow haste and giue it to the poore, yett wee are not bounde to perfourme this precepte; Euen soe in these wordes: *Drincke yee all of this &c.* wee are not bounde to perfourme it, but such as are priestes when they cōsecrate, and therfore the three Euangelists doe declare, that our Lord did sit with the twelue Apostles, and not with other disciples, and therfore none excepte the Apostles, and such as lawfullie doe succeede them, haue power to blesse or to consecrate the Eucharište, as Clemens, Chrysostome, Ambrose, & S. Bernarde, doe affirme.

9. Likewise, when he gaue power to remitte sinne Iohn 20. only the Apostles were assembled: for as it is not the charge of euerie one to preach, to baptise, or to feede, so it is not the office of euerie one to forgiue sinnes, or to consecrate the Eucharište, which only belonges to lawful priests, vnto whom by those wordes he gaue power to consecrate, offer & dispense the Eucharist; For the laytie by those wordes; *doe this in remembrance of me*, haue no other authoritie, then that from the priests they shoulde receaue godlie and deuoutlie the Eucharište, after whatsoeuer forme it should please the churche to giue them, eyther vnder one kinde, or two kindes. Doe this whensoeuer yow shall drincke in my remembrance, by which

which words, it is not absolutly commaunded to drinke, but whensoeuer yow drinke, that it should be done in his remembrance, as it was done in times paste. In eatinge of the lambe, it was simplie commaunded that euerie one should eate thereof, but to drincke wine, euerie one was not bounde in the supper of the lambe. Otherwise the abstainer which did abstaine altogether frõ wine should grieuouslie sinne, and should not be so highlie commended of God for abstaininge from wine. And in like manner the Nazarits, should alsoe offend for abstaininge from wine as they did. For although man can liue without wine, yet he cannot liue without bread, euen soe without the chalice a man may liue spiritually, but without the blessed bread he cannot liue spiritually, and soe wee say alwayes in the *Pater noster, panem nostrum quotidianum*, giue vs this daye our daylie bread. *Hier. 35.*

10. Adrianus the 4. did dispense with those of Norwaye to consecrate vnder one kinde, by reason of the scarcitie of wyne in that countrie, for soe they should performe the obligation of receauing this blessed Sacramente. This is also confirmed vnto vs by the three famous and generall councells and assemblies of the flower of all the best and learnedst men in the worlde, videlicet the councell of Constance, Basill, and Trente with in the harte of Germanie, where this article *Conc. Cõst. sess. 13. Basil. ss. 30 Trid. ss. 21*

article of receauinge vnder one kinde of the laitie was defined and decreede, and the sentence of Anathema was pronounced against all those, that should hould the contrarie. And whosoeuer will not obey these generall councells assembled together by the vertue of the holie ghoast, whose asistance was promised vnto the church in such occasions, doth iniurie not onlie to the church but also vnto that holy spirite: of these kind of people is said, *vos duræ ceruices spiritui sancto resistitis*, you stiffnecked people, yow resist the holy ghoaste. Therfore the Emperor Marcianus after the definition and ordinaunces of the councell of Chalcedon, said he is a wicked and sacrilegious person that would oppose his owne priuate opinion against the authoritie of the whole churche in such a generall assemblie, and this is the cause that S. Aug. defended S. Cyprian from heresie, for that it was not decreede by any generall councell, that such as were baptized by heretiques, should be rebaptized againe as the said S. Cyprian helde, and because the Donatistes did persiste in this doctrine, after the definition of the generall councell, they were condemned of the churche for heretiques, as S. Aug. doth testifie; and therfore those dogmatistes of our time, because they defende not onlie this doctrine, but also many other peruerse and damnable opinions not onlie against the defini-

*None ought to prefer his priuat opinion before the generall definition of a generall councell.*

finition of these generall councells, but also against godes ordinances, ought to be reputed for heretiques.

11. S. Thomas doth saie, that it was the custome of the churche, for danger of sheddinge, that the priest at the alter should receaue vnder both kindes, the laytie vnder one kinde, for this said he is not against Christs institution, for whosoeuer receaues the bodie, receaues the blood alsoe, because that Christe is vnder both kindes, aswell in respecte of his bodie, as his bloode. For all sacrifices did appertaine vnto the priestes, the Manna, the paschall lambe was eaten of the people which were figures of this Sacramente, and they were not comaunded to drincke after it. And although you vrge that Melchisedec did offer bread and wyne in token of this Sacrament, I aunswere that he was a prieste, for so the scripture saith. *Erat enim sacerdos Dei altissimi*, for he was a priest of the highe God. In our Lordes prayer wee aske our dailie bread without wyne, which petition many holy doctors doe interprete to be mente of the Eucharist, and when our Lord had fedd soe many thowsands, there is noe mention made, either of water or of wine, that feedinge beinge a figure or token of the holy bread of the alter, by which the faithfull Christians are releeued. For our Lord makes mention of the Chalice but thrice, of the eatinge of the bread

*D. Thom. in 6. Iohn. lect. 7.*

*Exod. 16. Genes. 14.*

*Tertul. in orat. Dom. Cypr. in orat. Dom. Ambr. l. 5 de sacra Hier. c. 6. Matt. homil 9. Aug. l. 50.*

bread he makes mention fifteene tymes, ſoe as wee may perceaue that the churche may vſe both the kindes ſeuerallie. *Qui manducat hunc panem viuet in æternum.*

*Theophil. in eadem verba. Aug. li. de consensu Euangeli c. 25. & ser. in feria 2. illius diei. Beda lib Comment in Lucam. Petr. Damianus Card. lib. de diuinis officijs.*

12. Chriſt allſo goinge to Emaus, ſittinge at the table, did feede only the twoe diſciples with breade alone, and being perceaued in the breakinge of the bread, did vaniſh awaye, by which fraction or breakinge, many holy fathers did vnderſtande the Euchariſte: wherby wee may gather, that the Euchariſte, was giuen vnto the laytie vnder one kinde vppon eaſter daye, that is to ſay to Cleophas and to Lucke, as many ſaie. And although they were the diſciples of Chriſte, yet they were not prieſtes. For at his laſt ſupper he did not ſaie to others then to the twelue Apoſtles theſe wordes; *Doe this in remembrance of me*, and vnto thoſe diſciples that went to Emaus, he gaue onlie the bread without wine, & ſo vaniſhed awaye.

*Epiſtola Ephesios.*

13. S. Ignatius made mention but of one kinde to be giuen to the laytie. *Eruditi à paracleto &c.* Yow beinge inſtructed of the holly ghoaſt, remaininge in true obedience to the Biſhops & prieſts which breake the bread vnto yow with due reſpecte and perfect deuotiõ, which is the medicine of mortalitie, the onelie preſeruatiue of life againſt death by Ieſus Chriſt; The bleſſed Sainte did not ſpeake any thinge of the Chalice, when

when the Pope goeth in any pilgrimadge or iourney, he carries with him the blessed Sacramente but vnder one kinde. S. Hierom doth reporte, that it was the custome of the faithfull at Rome, to haue our Lordes body at home in their houses, because they did not presume to goe to the church beinge letted by coniugall societie, which saith he, I doe not commend or discommend. S. Ambrose also doth reporte, that his brother carried with him this dreadfull hoaste to sea, and hauing suffred shipwreacke, did by vertue of this blessed Sacrament escape drowninge, the blood he did not carry, beinge not soe conueniente for carriadge. The Christians did in tyme past vse to carrie with them the Sacrament vnder one kinde, least in their greatest danger of death, they should not be releued of their greatest liuely hoode. S. Ambrose in the houre of his death, did receaue the blessed Sacramente of the Bishopp of Vercell vnder one kinde, as Paulinus doth reporte. The like is also reported of S. Patronilla, S. Hierome, S. Martyn, S. Benedict, S. Lucia, & S. Francis of whome the histories make mention, that in the time of their death they did communicate vnder one kinde. Amphilogius wrote, that when S. Basill did celebrate in the church, a Iewe went to gaze and to behoulde the christians as they receaued the blessed hoast, he ioyning himselfe with them, sawe an infante

*Hier. in Apolog. pro libris contra Iouinianũ*

*Ambr in orat. funebrii de obitu fratris sui Satyr.*

*Paulinus in vita eius.*

*In vita S. Basil.*

infante diuidinge the hoast in the handes of S. Basill, and soe came to all the communicantes, as also to the said Iewe, which whē he receaued, the blessed bread was forthwith tourned into fleash, and beinge astonished at this miracle, he himselfe with his wife and children, were made Christians.

14. Euagrius a greeke historiographer, and Nichephorus doe deliuer vnto vs, that it was the auncïente custome in the church of Constantinople, to giue vnto children such as went to schoole, the relickes and fragments of the blessed hoaste, if any were left after the comunicantes, but it were great absurditie to giue the relickes of the chalice vnto them, their tender age and weake disposition being not capable thereof: soe it should be a great indecencie to keepe the same, being in a short time subiect to corruption. With these children vpō a certaine daie, went a boy the sonne of a glass-maker, who beinge asked of his father, what he did with the children of the christians, he toulde him that he receaued the christian foode, his father being enraged and enflamed with extreame furie, cast the childe into a burninge furnace, where he was accustomed to make his glasses, wherein he continued 3. daies, his mother searchinge him in all places, and at lenght shee cominge towardes the fornace, and callinge the childe aloud by his name, the childe aunswered, and openinge the

the mouthe of the ouen, founde him in the middeſt of the fire, hauinge receaued noe harme from the flame therof: and askinge the childe how he was preſerued harmleſſe, he anſwered that a woman cloathed with purple, came often to him, and did often powre water vppon him, and did extinguiſh the coales, and gaue vnto him meate, which beinge tould vnto Iuſtinian the Emperor, he put the Father of the childe to death, as beinge conuinced of the murther of the childe: this hiſtorie is related amoungeſt the latynes by Gregorie Turonenſis.

*Gregor. in opere plurimorum mart edito de miraculis beatæ Mariæ.*

15. Gulielmus Abbas doth relate, that a certaine ſtubborne, and diſobedient Moncke once receauing the bleſſed hoaſte at the handes of S. Bernard, could neuer lett it downe, and conſideringe with him ſelfe that he was wilfull and not obedient to S. Bernarde, he went vnto him, and tould him what had happened, and beinge abſolued and penitente of his contimacie, preſentlie he ſwallowed the bleſſed hoaſte. Alexander Hallenſis did obſerue how certaine religious peſones demaundinge that both kindes ſhould be giuen vnto them, the prieſt ſayinge Maſſe at the breakinge of the hoaſte, he ſawe the patene all ẽbrewed with blood. None that is acquainted with the liues and monumentes of Sainctes can be ignorante, but that oftentimes this myſticall Sacramẽt of the bodie and blood of Chriſte hath, both

*Guliel. in vita S. Bernardi.*

*Hallenſ. in 4. part. ſummæ.*

to resolue the doubtfull, and to strenghten our loue and deuotion in Christe, appeared in a visible forme of a lambe, or a childe, yea and in the collour of fleshe and blood, that it which was inuisible by mysterie, should be visible and made manifest by miracle. The sixt generall councell did describe the manner of communicatinge to the laytie which with their handes did receaue the Eucharisste from the priest, afterwardes in the tyme of Balsamon Archbishopp of Antioch, which did coment vpon those cannons, that were prohibited.

*Serm. 42. de tempore hom 10.*

16. S. Augustine also willed the men, whē they came to receaue, that they should washe their handes and that women should bringe white and cleene lynnen with them that they may receaue the bodie of Christe, and euen as men should washe their handes, soe they should wash their consciences with Almesdeedes, and as women should prepare fine white lynnen cloth when they receaue Christs bodie, soe they should prepare also a chast bodie, cleane thoughtes, and a contrite harte, that with a good conscience they may receaue the Sacraments of Christe: thus farr S. Augustine, who shewes that in this time weomē receaued the blessed hoaste in fine lynnen cloathe. Againe the said sixt councell did institute, that the piestes in lente only should celebrate vpon Saterdaie, and Sundaie, and the Anunciation of the blessed

blessed Virgin, on other dayes they shoulde vse hoastes alreadie consecrated, as it is don in the latine church euerie good fridaie, which Rabanus affirmeth to haue bene the custome more then seauen hundred yeares agone, for that saith he, to consecrate is more befittinge tymes of solemnitie, ioye and gladnes, then in tyme of sorrowe and sadnesse as the lente is. And when the Gretiãs did vse the hoasts alreadie consecrated, and that wyne coulde not be soe much reserued without it were sower or corrupted, it is a signe they did receaue then vnder one kinde, as the latine priestes doe vpon good fridaie without any reprehension therein: Rodolphus the Abbott of S. Trudon who did florishe in the tyme of Henry the 4. Emperor, and a most religious Father as Trithemius wittnesseth, doth yeald reason wherfore the laytie ought not to receaue vnder both kindes by these wordes. *Trith. lib. de eccles. histor.*

*Hic & ibi cautela fiat nè præsbiter ægris*
*Aut sanis tribuat laicis de sanguine Christi,*
*Nam fundi posset leuiter, simplexque putaret,*
*Quod non sub specie sit IESVS totus vtraque.*

The priest ought to be warie that he giue not of the blood of Christ, either to the sicke or sounde laitie, for it may vpon light occasion be shedd, or the simple may thinck that Christe is not vnder ether of both kindes a parte.

17. But yow will aske, when was it

first instituted in the Churche that the laytie should receaue vnder one kinde. I aunswere wee can finde noe beginning thereof, nor any constitution, but the councell of Constance and Basil doe condemne all such as finde faulte with this manner of receauinge or should change that custome, and doe also decree that this was an ould custome of the Church: and when wee can shew noe beginninge hereof out of Ecclesiasticall histories, it is a great signe (accordinge to the rule of S. Augustine) that it was allowed of Christ and his Apostles, and that Christe lefte power to his church to dispose of this matter, according as she should thincke it moste fitt for places and tymes, being induced by many sundrie reasons to communicat the laytie vnder one kinde, as I haue said alreadye, and nowe I alleadge others. For first if it were not soe, manny trulie were depriued of this benefitt, for that many Northeren countries haue noe wine and although the rich may haue it, yet euerie poore cannot haue it, yea many there are, that did neuer drinke wine, and if they should drincke thereof, they should vomitte: therfore sith the yoke of our Saviour is sweete, wee must not thincke that he will compell any to that which he cannot performe. The second reason is, for besides Christ which is aswell vnder one as vnder both, there is not in the other

*Aug. epist. 218. cap. 6 tom. 2.*

other kinde but an accident without a subiect, as is apparente by the councel of Constance and Basil. The third reason is, that it was lawfull for the prieste aswell in the greeke church that did receaue in lente vnder one kinde, as the sixt councell doth manifest, as also in the latine church, for the priest that receaues it vnder one kinde vpon good fridaie. The 4. reason that Christe is aswell vnder one kinde as vnder both kindes, and he that receaues it in that manner, receaueth as much fruite, as if he had receaued vnder both.

*6. Conc. cano. 52.*

18. Yow vrge against this custome of the church, Vnlesse yow eate his fleash and drincke his blood wee shall haue noe life in you. I answere that the coniunction, &c, is taken disiunctiuely, as if Christ had said vnlesse yee eate my fleash or drincke my blood &c. and soe S. Paule saith these wordes, *quicunque &c.* whosoeuer will eate the bread, or drincke the Chalice of our Lorde vnworthilie, did vse the wordes disiunctiuelie not copulatiuelie, in which place S. Ambrose did read, *aut*, that is to saie, or, in the Greeke, H. which is a disiunctiue particle, and a disiunctiue commaundement is fulfilled, if one parte be perfourmed as it is said in Exodus, he that killeth his father & mother let him die the deathe, for the sense is, he that killeth his father or mother shall die, because the one was sufficient. Also in

*1. Cor. 11.*

*Exod. 15.*

Cap. 3. the actes, S. Peter beinge demaunded almes, answered that he had not siluer and goulde, that is not siluer nor goulde, else he had not answered sufficiently, siluer onlie suffisinge to giue almes. And although we should grãt that Christ did giue a precepte to the laytie to receaue Christ vnder both kindes, yet the laytie doe aswell receaue both vnder one kinde, as vnder two, for he receaueth flesh and blood in the one and in the other. For although by effecte and force of the wordes and sacramentall forme, *hoc est corpus meum*, this is my bodie, Christs bodie is there, yet his blood, soule, and diuinitie are also there, by due consequence and concomitance, all these beinge inseparable since his resurrection vnited in Christs person: and soe vnder the forme of bread, the laytie receaue Christes blood with the bodie, though not in forme of drincke, or drinckinge, but eatinge, for which cause S. Cyprian called it, eatinge of Christes blood.

*Cypr. ser de cæna Dom. & epist. 3.*

19. This is also proued *à posteriori*, by the maruelous effect and euente of receauinge vnder one kinde in the combustion and miserable troubles of the last warres in Fraunce, procured by Caluine and Beza, and other firebrandes their followers, that rushed out of hell for destruction of their countrie. Caluine sendinge a Minister of his called North vnto Rochell, who hauinge corrupted with his poisoned heresie

reſie the Mayor of that towne, with many of the cheefeſt, did ſurprize it, and his laſt attempte was to ſeaze vpon the poore catholique cleargie, which beinge gathered together into a church, and expectinge nothinge elſe then to fall into the cruell handes of this diuiliſh miniſter; the Abbott of S. Bartholomew which was the cheefeſt and the learnedſt of that clergie beinge in number 24. tooke a loafe of bread and did vſe the woordes of conſecration applyinge it to the bread (for he durſt not haue the bleſſed Sacramente in the pixe accordinge to the cuſtome of the church, leaſt thoſe damned and impious crewe ſhould caſt it to their dogges, as they hade done in other churches in Fraunce) and euerie one of that heauie clergie did receaue. *Domini viaticum*, which before the receauinge thereof, were both fraile in faith, and fearfull of death, and readie to make ſhippwreacke of their profeſsion and religion, as I was tould by men of good creditt in that towne, but after the conſumation thereof, they were ſoe firme and ſoe conſtante, that euerie one of thoſe 24. except one, did endure a moſt cruell and vilde death, which is knowen to all both catholiques and heretiques at Rochell, to wit, that euerie one of them with a ſtone about his necke, was caſt downe headlonge oute of the higheſt pinnacle of the highe tower in the entrie of the

the keaye of Rochell into the ſea, with men in Boates readie to knocke them downe into the bottome of the ſea, if perhappes anie of them ſhoulde ſwimme vpon the water.

20. The vertuous Queene both of Frãce and Scotlande Marie Steward the Kinges mother, had the bleſſed Sacramente reſerued in a little pixe, which ſhee her ſelfe receaued a little before her execution, by which noe doubte ſhee conſtantlie and moſt patientlie did endure ſuch a violente death, as is knowen to the worlde. Wee knowe that the vſe of the Chalice did ſucceede ill vnto all thoſe kingdomes and regions that obſerued the ſame, for in the eaſt, beſides that they were infected with ſundrie errors, and hereſies, they are plunged into the yoke of the miſerableſt captiuitie that euer was, vnder that damnable tyrant the enemie both of God and man. In the countries of the weaſt alſoe, they which doe and did obſerue that cuſtome, are not onlie now ouerwhelmed and ingulfed in all pernitious and blaſphemous hereſies, but alſoe intoxicated with hatred, itched with ambition, confounded with tumultuous in ſurrections, and turbulent rebellions, wearied with bloodie and cruell warres and defiled with all impudicitie of beaſtly concupiſcence, and corrupted with all exerciſe of extortion & iniuſtice: and beſides, their labours are without

*The wofull lott of ſectaries.*

without fruite, their ſoules without conſcience, their liues without honeſtie, and their conuerſation without ſhame, they are become plaine Athiſtes, worſe then either Iewe, Turcke, or Gentile.

21. And in all thoſe countries of the eaſt and weaſt, where nowe this wicked hereſie infecteth, worſe then ether the poiſon of vipers, or the corrupte aire of Baſilisks, the people, eſpecially the nobilitie were diuided into factions and hatred, euerie one emploing his beſt time and his greateſt skill to be reuenged vpon his competitors, and therfore did embrace this hereſie, not for godes ſake, but for a reuenge wherby he might ſatisfie his vnlawfull ambition, and filthie deſires, for as the wiſe-man ſaith. *Anima callida quaſi ignis ardens non extinguetur, donec aliquid deglutiat.* A turbulent minde is like a burninge flame of fire, which ſhall hardly be extinguiſhed vntill he ſhall deuoure & conſume ſomwhat. And the Princes that fauoure theſe hereſies, are ſoe miſcarried, & miſled with this vnſatiable thirſt both of ambition leacherie, and couetouſnes although they pretend religion herein, that they ſhall neuer be ſatisfied, nor their thirſt ſhalbe extinguiſhed, thoughe all the Chalices in the world had ben giuen vnto them. It was graunted by the counceil of Baſil, the vſe of the chalice to the kingdome of Bohemia, and the ſame permitted vnto them

them by Paulus 3. and by his 3. Legates, that he did send to Germanie, as also by Charles the fifte, this graunt did them no good, but rather did much harme, for in a little tyme there grewe foure sectes of heresies in that kingdome, as the Thaborites, Adamites, Howelites, and Orphans, soe as Pius the 2. was fayne to reuoke the graunt that was giuen them by the councell, and trulie wee must not expecte great fruite nowe if it were graunted, for our cleargie men are noe better then those that went before, neither seculer Princes more vertuous or more iuste then their predecessors, neither are heretiques more humble or more honest for hauinge the vse of it.

*Theoph in cap. prioris ad Corinth.*

22. Yow vrge against vs out of *Theophilactus in cap. prioris; Tremendus hic calix cunctis pari ratione est traditus,* this dreadfull chalice is giuen to all after one fashion. I answeare that his meaninge was to tell, howe it was all a like to the twelue Apostles, yea to Iudas himselfe, yea it may be giuen also to others, but Christ did not forbidd those to whome he comitted the gouernment of his church to denie it also to other some, as it is said in the scripture, that God hath giuen all cattle and beastes to the vse of man, yet by that graunte or donation, he hath not forbidden the superiors for disciplines sake to forbid their subiects in certaine tymes, the vse of certaine meattes, as God in his lawe by

*Genes. 9.*

by ſpeciall commaundemente did forbidd the children of Iſraell all vncleane beaſtes, and ſuch that were ſtrangled, which neuertheleſſe the church nowe doth teach and preach, not that herein ſhee doth againſt Gods lawe or his precepte, but that beinge taught by the holy ghoaſt, ſhee doth interprete godes meaninge in the lawe; For the poſitiue lawe of the church, is nothing elſe then a certaine preſcription of godes lawe, and a certaine determination of that which is giuen in common. God almightie commaunded vs in generall to praie, to doe pennaunce to receaue the Euchariſt, but the church according to her wiſdome and diſcretion, reſpectinge rather the intente of the lawe-giuer, then the lawe it ſelfe, did preſcribe both the tyme & manner wherein and by which, wee ought both to receaue the bleſſed Sacrament, and to doe pennance and praie, for the vulgar ſorte yea, and men of great learninge and ſcience, vnleſſe they had bene endued with great charitie, without theſe particuler determinations, and comaundements of the Church, would not keepe theſe generall comaundements. Luther ſaith, that the had noe other cauſe or any ſufficient motiue to giue the Chalice to the laytie, but that the church and the fathers did comaund the contrarie. And in another place he diſſuaded Chriſtians from confeſsion, and from the Euchariſte in time of

*Luth. in lib. de formula miſſa lib. de Cõfeſsione parte 3. para. 14.*

of easter, because that the Pope commaunded it. I will not obey his commaundemente, saith he, I will doe it, saith he, another tyme, accordinge to myne owne pleasure, but not accordinge to his precepte. But Luther and all his malitious and turbulent followers, ought to embrace the counsell that the Angell gaue to Agar, the woman Genes. 16. seruante. *Reuertere ad domum tuam & humiliare sub manu illius*: retourne to thy house, and humble thie selfe vnder her power. This was spoken litterallie of Agar, that shee should obey Sara and returne to her house: which is allegorically spoken of the church, vnderstoode by Sara, and of the congregation of heretiques meante by Agar, as S. Augustine doth teach vs.

*Whether the Catholicke Church doth add to this Sacramente, in makinge it both a sacrifice, and a Sacramente.*

## CHAPTER II.

1. I Answere, that the Catholique church doth add nothinge, nor inuente any sacrifice, but that which Christe instituted for a Sacramente, which is our spirituall foode, and may be said to be our daylie bread, as allso the great sacrifice of the newe testamente, and soe Christ is said to be offered for vs two manner

*Cypr. epist. 66. Chrysost. hom. 11. Damasc. serm. de cæna.*

ner of wayes videlicet bloodilie, and vnbloodilie. In the firſt manner, he offered himſelfe for vs *in ara crucis*, vpon the alter of the croſſe, which oblation the paſchall lãbe without ſpott, which was offered by the Iewes, did ſignifie. In the ſecond, he offred himſelfe in his laſt ſupper, and nowe his prieſts doe offer him vpon the alter for the quicke and for the dead; that accordinge to S. Cyrill the oblation of Melchiſedech, who did offer bread and wyne, ſhould be accompliſhed, and that he ſhould remayne a true prieſt accordinge the order of Melchiſedech, and that his prieſt hoode which is according to his humanitie, and not accordinge to his diuinitie, might endure for euer. Soe as the Euchariſt amongeſt other Sacraments of the old teſtamente, hath this priuiledge, and prerogatiue, that it is a Sacramente, when it is receaued by the faithfull; and a ſacrifice in aſmuch as it is dailie offred for our offences to the eternall father. And although euerie ſacrifice be a Sacrament, becauſe it is a ſacred thinge religiouſly inſtituted, to ſanctifie our ſoules, notwithſtãdinge euerie Sacrament is not a ſacrifice, becauſe it is not offred vnto God vnto whome ſacrifice is offred, and a Sacramente is ordained for men. Soe as the Euchariſt is of greater value and vertue as it is a ſacrifice, then as it is a Sacramente, as Ioannes Roffenſis ſaith, in his articles againſt Luther, and vpon this place

*Cyrill. ad Hebr. 9. Hier. cap. 9. ad Titum.*

*How the Euchariſt is a ſacrifice and a Sacramẽt.*

*Salmer. tracta. 16. in Ioannē* place related by Alfonso Salmeron. That the Eucharist is a sacrifice of the newe lawe, it is proued most aboūdantlie both by scriptures, fathers, and by councells.

2. The first is by Malachias the prophett, who did prophesie of this sacrifice after this manner. *Non est mihi voluntas in vobis &c.* I haue noe likinge of yow, and I will not receaue a gifte from your hand, *ab ortu solis vsque ad occasum &c.* from the risinge of the sunne vnto the goinge downe thereof; *magnum est nomen meum in gentibus, & in omni loco sacrificatur & offertur nomini meo oblatio mūda: quia magnum est nomen meum in gentibus*: my name is great amoungest the gentiles, and in all places they doe sacrifice and offer vnto my name; a cleane oblation. This said the Lorde of hoasts, he said that his name should be great amoungest the gentiles, of whome this oblation should be offred, for before the ghospell of Christe was preached vnto them, noe oblation of theirs was lawfull, neither the oblatiō of the Iewes was cleane it selfe, but accordinge to the faith and deuotion of him that did offer the same: besides they could not offer but at Hierusalem onlie, and consequentlie, it was not in all places of the worlde, as it is mente heere from the easte to the weaste. Neither can it be meant of a spirituall sacrifice, either of prayers, faith, mercie, or a contrite harte, which in scriptures are called sacrifice,

*Mal. c. 1. Psal. 112.*

ſice, as the Auguſtane Apologie doth interprete, for manie reaſons, becauſe that all theſe be not one ſacrifice, but many ſacrifices, as alſo becauſe they doe not ſcceede the old ſacrifices, for in the old teſtament, there was vſe of thoſe kinde of ſacrifices as with vs, and moreouer becauſe they were not properlie called ſacrifices, but metaphoricallie, neither are they offred in all places, becauſe they be ſpirituall thinges, which needes noe place. And much leſſe are they vnderſtoode of the preachinge of the ghoſpell, as Bucerus writinge to Latonius doth interprete, becauſe preachinge is not properly called a ſacrifice, neither ſucceedeth it the olde ſacrifices. Neither the conuerſion of the gentiles, by the preachinge of the ghoſpell is this ſacrifice, as Æcolampadius doth expounde vnto the Senate of Baſil, for this is called an improper ſacrifice, neither one ſacrifice, but many accordinge to ſoe many nations conuerted: wheras this ſacrifice ought to be one onlie ſacrifice in number and not in forme. Neither ſhall it be allwayes, but for a tyme, for when the nations ſhalbe conuerted: *Omnis Iſrael ſaluus fiet.* All Iſraell ſhalbe ſaued, as the Apoſtle doth witneſſe. Neither laſt of all was it ſpoken of Chriſte on the Croſſe, a Kemnitius would haue it, for that was not allwayes, it remaining but the ſpace of an houre, neither in all places, but in Mounte Caluarie,

neither was it offred properlie of the genti-
*Psal. 75.* les. *Quia notus erat in iudea Dominus*, because God was knowen in Iudea, and in Israell his name was great.

3 Wee must therfore vnderstand, that this prophesie is vnderstoode of the oblatiō of Christe in the Eucharist, and that it shalbe alwayes celebrated in the church of Christe, from the easte to the weaste, as it is (God be thancked) in despite of the diuill and all his instruments. This is proued by the litterall sense of the texte of Malachias his prophesie, and by the tradition of the fathers, which is the certaine key of the vnderstandinge of the scriptures. For soe *Clement. Martialis. Iustinus Martyr. Ireneus. Tertul. lib. in Iudeos c. 16. Euseb. lib. 1. de demonstratione Euangelica cap. 10. Cyrillus lib. 1. de adoratione in spiritu & veritate. Damascenus lib. 4. c. 14. Aug. lib. 18. de Ciuitate Dei cap. 20. & 35. Hieronymus. Theodoret. Remigius Haymon*; Rupertus & Lyranus in their Comment. vppon Malach. & Concil. Trid. sess. 22. interpret: We must consider, that the worde sacrifice in the Hebrewe tonge as Salmeron doth set downe, is called *zebeach*; which is properlie called a bloodie sacrifice, and in the place of an oblation is putt in the hebrewe tounge *mincha*, which was properly meate, or a guift vnbloody. Therfore for all the sacrifices of the old lawe, whether they be bloodie or vnbloodie, our Lord by his pro-

*Clement. l. 7. Const. Apost. D. Martial. epist. ad Burdigalensis. Iust. Martyr. Dialogo in tripho. Iren. lib. 3 cap. 23. Tract. 27.*

prophett said. *Corpus autem aptasti mihi*, thow haste made my bodie befittinge all of them. This vnbloodie hoaste is soe cleane and pure in it selfe and soe acceptable vnto God, as by the wicked life of him that doth administer the same, it cannot be defiled. And although in the prophesie it is said in the present tense, yet for the certitude and vndoubtfullnesse of the prophesie, the time present is vsed for the time to come. *Offeretur & sacrificabitur, it is sacrificed,* for it shalbe sacrificed, *ab ortu solis vsque ad occasum &c.* from sunne risinge vnto sunne sett, my name shalbe great amoungest the Gentiles.

4. By this worde therfore wee must note and marcke, the amplitude and largnes of the church, against the narrowe streight of the Iewes, and the smale corners of the heretiques, which by their offences and heresies are vtterlie depriued of this hoast, and sacrifice. The catholique church doth celebrate and solemnize the sacred praises of God, in which this prophesie is accomplished, by the benefitt shee daylie receaueth by this sacrifice, by which shee is daily fedd, and by which shee offers herselfe withall her forces, vnto this liuinge God, singinge praysses vnto him. Yealdinge and consecratinge herselfe in all humilitie of spirite, in all perfect deuotion of faith hope and charitie, to the glorie of the great God, vnto whome, and to none els, this great sacrifice

is offred, for which Sacrifice, Churches, Alters, Chapples and Conuents were builded, Priestes, Deacons, and Leuites, and so many blessed orders of cleargie men were instituted, for which causes soe many benefices, personages, vicariadges, Cannonries, Prebendes, Tithes, profittes, stipendes, reuenewes, landes and liuinges, for the honest maintenaunce of such as should offer this sacrifice, were lawfully and charitably bestowed, by the godlie and deuoute christians.

5. But yow saie that the papists herein did robbe both this great God of his honnor, by comittinge idolatrie againste his maiestie, and also the christians of their landes and goodes, inuentinge this sacrifice, as yow saie, against God, for to deceaue the godlie people of their goodes. I desire yow if the Papists did deceaue the people herein, why should not yow make restitution to the right owners of those landes? for if yow take anie thinge from a theefe, by all lawes both ciuill and cannon, yow ought to restore it againe to the true owner, and as yow saie yow restore to God his owne honor by takinge awaie this Sacramẽt, why should not yow restore also vnto the christians their tithes and liuinges giuen in tymes paste for priestes, principally to offer this sacrifice, by which the name of God hath bene most glorious amoungest the nations?

But

But as God is not the more glorified by your doinges, ſoe your neighbor is not the more edified by your examples, and vntill yow reſtore to God his ſacrifice, yow will neuer reſtore or make anie reſtitution to the Chriſtians of their goodes. But you follow Gnatho and Philoxenus who beinge ſlaues of their bellies, to haue all the bankett and feaſte to themſelues, were wont to ſpitt & blowe their noſes into the diſhes, that others ſhould not eate thereof: ſoe yow ſpit vppon the Maſſe for the which thoſe church liuinges principallie were giuen, and therfore yow charge prieſts with couetouſnes, and other enormities, that yow your ſelues may poſſeſſe freely their ſpoiles and goodes, and abuſe them as yow doe with exceſsiue riotouſnes: you bark alſo againſt the faſt of the Church and the continente life of cleargie men, that you may miſpend thoſe liuinges by ſatisfying your filthie appetites, which cannot be ſatisfied. Yow knowe, or at leaſt you ſhould knowe, that thoſe who will not ſerue at the alter, ought not to liue by the alter, and if yow refuſe this office, in thinckinge it to be impious and idolatrous, yow ſhould alſoe refuſe the reward and promotion of idolatrie and impietie, as thoſe liuinges which were conſecrated to the alter, by the laſt teſtament of the teſtators; for Beneuolus, for that he would not conforme himſelfe to Iuſtina the Empreſſe, *Plutar.*

against S. Ambrosebeinge defiled with the Arrian impietie, restored vnto her all the
*Lib. 7. cap. 13.* ensignes and titles of honnor he had of her, as Zozomenus writeth.

6. The second place to proue the trueth of this Sacrament, is taken out of the Psal-
*Psal. 109.* me. *Iurauit Dominus & non penitebit eum, tu es sacerdos in æternum secundum ordinem Melchisedech.* Our Lord hath sworne, and he will not repent himselfe thereof; thou art a priest for euer, accordinge to the order of Melchisedech; for that this priest-hoode shall neuer be taken from him. For not onlie in his last supper did he offer himselfe, but also on the Crosse, and also by his priestes by whome he shalbe offered vnto the worldes ende, as
*Æcumen. cap. 5. Cyp. epist. ad Cæci. Damasc. in 4. lib. de fide orthodoxa.* *Aecumenus, D. Cyprianus, Clemens Alexandrinus, Athanasius, Eusebius, Epiphanius, Arnobius, Hieronymus, Ambrosius, Augustinus, Theodoretus, Theophilactus, Damascenus*: and others affirme. For Christ offeringe himselfe vnto his Father nowe in heauen, & before vpon the Crosse, cannot be saide, that he is a prieste according the order of Melchisedec, but rather accordinge to that of Arron. as S. Thomas teacheth when he did offer himself in a bloody fashion vpon the Crosse, whose oblation was but once, and not foreuer as S. Paule saieth: for besides that Christ instituted a churche, and ordained sacramentes, he offered two sacrifices, the one on the crosse, the other at his last supper, both of

them

them but one sacrifice in substance, yet differ in forme and manner: by that of the crosse, Christe was a priest, but not an eternall priest, nor accordinge to Melchisedech, because that was once only offered, and being bloodie, resembleth not the vnbloodie sacrifice of Melchisedech: but by that he offered at his last supper, for he by his priestes offeringe still that sacrifice in the Masse, is a priest accordinge to Melchisedech, whose sacrifice consisted of bread and wine. And therfore euen as accordinge to S. Paule, Melchisedech was a figure of Christe accordinge to his priest-hoode, so was he a figure accordinge to his sacrifice, for sacrifice and priest-hoode haue a speciall connexion and relation one with an other, but his order can not be said to be in a bloodie manner. For wee doe not read that euer Melchisedech did offer any bloodie sacrifice, therfore this order must needes consist in an oblation of an vnbloodlie sacrifice. And although wee shoulde graunt that he offred himselfe accordinge to both, the oblation accordinge the order of Melchisedech, and the oblation of the crosse, yet the sense of the oblation of the crosse, ought not to take awaie the sense of the oblation of the other.

7. The third place to proue that it is a sacrifice, is by the institution of the Eucharíste: for when he made an ende of the supper of the lambe, that was to be sacrifi-

ced, it is ſaid our Lord tooke bread (for this was the manner that the prieſt did vſe in ſacrifice) and hauinge lifted vpp his eies, as if he woulde offer vpp to his father that holie breade, into which as Hierem. ſaith, the Iewes did caſt their wodde: and as the Maſſe or Liturgie of the Greekes hath. *Accipiens panem in ſanctas immaculatas manus &c.* Takinge the breade into his holie, vnſpotted, innocente, immortall handes, liftinge vpp his eies, and ſhewinge vnto yow God the Father &c. And in the Maſſe, both of the Latines and Greekes it is ſaid. *Gratias agens*, giuinge thanks for the redemption of the worlde, offeringe therfore vnto his father a ſacrifice of thanks giuinge *benedixit*, he bleſſed, neither did he ſooner offer, then he cõſecrated, and conſecratinge he offered himſelfe willinge to be ſacrificed. He ſaid alſo, *accipite &c.* Take and eate, this is my bodie, wherto S. Luke doth add. *Quod pro vobis datur*, which is giuen for yow, or which is broken for yow, as S. Paule hath. *Quod pro vobis offertur*, as S. Auguſtine doth interprete; and alſo it is ſaid of the bloode in the preſent tenſe of the four Euangeliſtes. *Funditur*, not becauſe that preſentlie out of hande he ſhould be offered vpon the croſſe takinge the tyme preſent, for the tyme to come, but at this inſtante he offered himſelfe in that heauenlie miſterie vnto his father, for *dare, frangere, tradere, fundere* and *facere*, are wordes

*Hier. 2.*

*Liturg. græcor. in miſſa D. Iacobi.*

*Matt. 26. Luc. 22. 1. Cor. 11.*

des belonginge vnto a ſacrifice, for it is ſaid, that God loued the worlde that he ſhould giue his only begotten ſonne, vid. in ſacrifice for vs, he did not ſpare his only ſonne, *ſed tradidit*, but he deliuered him for vs. Moreouer he was a prieſte accordinge to the order of Melchiſedech, therfore he was to offer in bread and wine as he did. *Iohn. 3.* *Rom. 8.*

8. Againe he ſaid, I deſire to eate this Paſche with yow, for Paſche is a ſacrifice: and as euerie man is a liuinge creature, ſo euerie Paſche is a ſacrifice, which is confirmed, in the 6 of S. Iohn: the bread that I ſhall giue, is my fleaſh for the life of the worlde, therfore the bread giuen in the ſupper, doth conteine the fleaſh giuen for the life of the worlde vppon the croſſe for ſacrifice, ſo that neither in the ſupper, nor vppon the croſſe, was it a ſacrifice, or els in both it was a ſacrifice, for the worde *giuen*, was repeted twiſe. And although it ſhould be once repeted, yet it hath the force of a ſacrifice. *Panis quem ego dabo caro mea eſt pro mundi vita*, the bread that I ſhall giue is my fleaſh, for the life of the worlde. For the Euchariſt in aſmuch as it is a Sacrament, profiteth onlie him that receaues it, but foraſmuch as it is a ſacrifice, it is the ſoule of the church, and the life of the worlde, therfore the bread giuen by Chriſte and containinge his fleaſhe, neceſſarily was immolated and ſacrificed, and alſo offered vnto *Argumentū à ſpecie ad genus affirmatiuum valet.* *Iohn. 6.*

his

his Father. Moreouer our Lord saied when he deliuered this bread. *Do this in remembrance of me*, by which wordes he shewed the nature of a sacrifice saying, as it were: hitherto yow haue offered the figuratiue, and Paschall lambe, nowe I doe not take away the oblation of a sacrifice, but I doe transfer and change the same vnto a more worthie oblation of offeringe my bodie and bloode. Therfore Pope Leo saieth, lett the shadowe giue place to the bodie, let Images giue place to the trewe patterne. *Antiqua obseruatio nouo tollitur Sacramento:* lett the old custome giue place to the newe sacrament, *hostia in hostiam transit, sanguis sanguinem excludit, & legalis festiuitas vt mutatur, expletur.* Lett one hoaste passe vnto another, one blood doth expell another, the accomplishinge of the legall festiuitie, doth importe a change thereof.

*Rupert. D. Thom: Luc. 22. 1. Cor. 11.*

9. This is the cause that Christ that nighte did offer thrise: first in a pure figure: secondlie he offered his bodie and blood vnder both kindes of bread and wyne, which was both the thinge it selfe and a figure; last of all he offered himselfe (beinge the thinge it selfe) vnto death when he went vnto the place where he was taken. This is declared in the forme of the cannon of the Masse which S. Ambr. vsed in the church of Millā vid. *Qui sacrificij perennis formam instituens, primus omnium hostiam Deo obtulit, & primus omnium*

*S. Ambr. Masse.*

*omnium illam docuit offerri*, who institutinge the forme of the euerlastinge sacrifice, as the first of all that offred an hoste vnto God, & the first that taughte the same to offered. The Church of Æthiopia hath these wordes in the Canon of the Masse related here by Salmeron which he hath seene in printe. *Hoc facite in meam commemorationem. Nunc autem recordamur mortis tuæ, & resurrectionis tuæ, tibique gratias quod per hoc sacrificium dignos nos fecisti standi in conspectu tuo.* Doe this in remembrance of me, now wee being mindfull of thy death, and of thy resurrection, wee giue thee thancks for that thow voutsafest that wee stand in thie presence. The constitution of the Apostles hath these wordes. *Primus igitur natura pontifex est vnigenitus Christus, qui non sibi honorem arripuit, sed constitutus à patre &c.* The first Bishopp by nature, is the only begotten Christe, which did not arrogate vnto him selfe honor or renowme, but beinge appointed of the Father, which for our sakes became man, and offeringe vnto God a spirituall sacrifice, and vnto his Father, before his passion he commaundeth vs onlie to doe this.

*The masse of Æthiopia.*

*Salmeron tract. 27.*

*Clement. Romanus l. 8. const. cap. vlt. Hebr. 5.*

10. Moreouer our Lord by the worde (*facite*) doe this, comaũded that they should consecrate and offer, take, receaue, and dispense to others &c. For in the holie scripture, the word *facere*, is taken for *sacrificare* vid.

*Exod. 13. Leuit. 15.*

vid. to ſacrifice as, *facietis & hircum pro peccato*, yow ſhall ſacrifice a goate for ſinne, alſo Numer.6. *facietque ſacerdos vnum pro peccato*, and the prieſt ſhall offer one for ſinne: for not without cauſe did our Sauiour vſe the ſpecificall worde of offringe, conſecratinge, receauinge, or diſtributinge, for he did vſe the generall worde comprehending vnder it ſelfe all theſe ſpecificall. S. Iames the Apoſtle in his Maſſe hath theſe words. *Offerrimus tibi Domine hoc ſacrificium verendum & incruentum, orantes ne ſecundum peccata noſtra nobiſcum agas, neque ſecundum iniquitates noſtras retribuas nobis &c.* We offer vnto thee ô Lorde, this fearfull & vnbloodie ſacrifice, neither deale with vs accordinge to our ſinnes, neither giue vnto vs accordinge to our iniquities. The Maſſe or Liturgie of S. Baſil. hath theſe wordes. *Suſcipe nos Domine appropinquantes ſancto altari tuo &c.* Receaue vs ô Lord approachinge vnto thy holie alter accordinge to the multitude of thy mercie, that wee may be worthie to offer vnto thee, that reaſonable ſacrifice without bloode for our offences, and the ignorance of the people, and to the intent that this ſacrifice may be acceptable vnto thy holie ſupper celeſtiall, and intelligible alter in odor of ſweetnes, caſt forthe vppon vs the grace and fauour of the holie ghoaſt. The Maſſe of S. Iohn Chriſoſtome hath theſe words. *Pontifex noſtrum extitiſti, & miſteriæ huius ac incruentis hoſtiæ*

*S. Iames his Maſſe.*

*S. Baſil his Maſſe.*

*S. Iohn. his Maſſe.*

*hostia sacramentum, nobis tradidisti.* Thou beinge our Bishopp thou hast deliuered vnto vs the Sacramente of this misticall and vnbloodie hoaste. S. Paule also doth argue that priest-hoode beinge translated, it is necessarie that a translation of the lawe be also made, because that the lawe and priest-hood were ordeined together, and whosoeuer will take awaie the one, taketh away the other; for priest-hoode hath greater connexion and relation to the sacrifice, then to the lawe, because that priest-hoode is ordained for to offer sacrifice, and sacrifice can not be offered but of a lawfull priest. *Hebr. 7.*

11. Againe the olde priest-hoode was externall and was instituted to offer externall sacrifice, neither is it properly translated into a spirituall priest-hoode, for any thinge that was either in the lawe of Moyses, or of nature, written or sett downe, was comon to offer it spiritually, as to offer spirituall hosts of praises and praiers, and such like: therfore it was translated into the externall sacrifice of the Eucharistе, for the oblation for the which priestes were instituted and ordeined, for to offer anie spirituall oblatiō whatsoeuer, the laytie were as fitt as the Priests: & as the priest-hoode of the old law was translated into the priest-hoode of the lawe of grace, so their sensible sacrifice into the sensible sacrifice of the Eucharist, which only doth fulfill and accomplish all the prophesies

phesies and figures of the old lawe, and doth succeede the same. And euen as the paschall lambe beinge offered euerie yeare, did not take awaie the sacrifice of lambes that was offered euerie morninge and eueninge commaunded in Exodus, so neither Christ being bloody offered vpon the crosse takes nott awaie the vnbloodie and quotidian sacrifice of the masse. And although that Christ is said to be offered from the beginninge of the worlde, yet that takes not awaye the externall sacrifice of the lawe of nature, or of Moyses, but they rather haue their vertue and force from Christe his sacrifice, as they are said to smell sweetlie in gods presence. Much lesse taketh it away the externall and sensible sacrifice of the newe testament, which is a certaine sensible representation of Christes bloodie sacrifice. Otherwise the church in the newe testamét is in a worse case, then the church either in the lawe of Moyses, or in the lawe of nature, in which by their externall sacrifice they could represente Christs death and passion, which the church in the lawe of grace cannot doe, if yow take awaie frō her this only sacrifice left with her. Moreouer she had bene depriued of that dignity & excellécy of offering external sacrifice, which the church in those two states had & consequentlie the priests in the lawe of grace had been more obscure and of lesse dignitie in the power of priest-hoode, then those of Leuie.

12. But you will peraduenture answere, that the office of priest-hoode is to offer sacrifice in spiritt and trueth. Wherto I replie, that the olde fathers alsoe in the lawe of nature, and Moyses coulde soe doe, and likewise euerie other person. If you take awaie this sacrifice, it is not true that Christe vpon the crosse is a priest accordinge the order of Melchisedec, but accordinge to the order of Aaron, whose hoasts and sacrifices were bloody, as that of Melchisedec was vnbloody in bread and wine. Againe, if yow will haue noe other priest, but Christ vpon the crosse, to be the onlie priest, of the newe testamente, and that there is noe other priest or sacrifice, then Isaias is a lyar, and his prophesie is false, for in the ende of his prophesie he said there should be new priests and Leuites, for he did not speake of the priests of the olde lawe, and in vaine should he speake of the newe priests if they should offer noe sacrifice. Did not S. Paul saie. For this cause I left thee in Crete, that thou shouldest reforme the thinges that are wanting & shouldest ordeine priests in the cities; Also he saith vnto Timothy, doe not neglect the grace which is in thee, and which is giuen vnto thee by prophesie with the imposition of the hands of priest-hoode. S. Iames wished the sicke person to send for the priests,

*Obiection*
*Answer.*
*Priests proued.*
*Ad Titum. 1.*
*1. Tim. 4.*
*Iacob. 5.*

priests, which should annoile him and praie for him, & those that S. Paule called Priests, afterward he called Bishoppes, but it is manifest that none can be a Bishopp without he were a Prieste, a Bishopp beinge a degree aboue priest-hoode, if therfore in the newe testament, there be Priests selected from the people, they ought to sacrifice and offer.

*Hebr. 5.* S. Paule saith, euerie high priest taken from amonge men, is appointed for men in those things that pertaine to God, that he maie offer giftes and sacrifices for sinnes. Therfore besides the bloodie sacrifice of Christe vpon the crosse, there must be a sensible and a common sacrifice instituted of God, and that soe noble as euerie one cannott offer the same.

*Clemens lib. 1. cōst. apost. c. 1* 13. Clemens saith. *Post assumptionē Christi nos oblato secundum eius ordinationem sacrificio puro, & incruento constituimns Episcopos, presbiteros, & diaconos numero septem:* wee after the assumption of Christe, accordinge to his institution, haue appointed Bishopps, Priests, & Deacons, in nomber seuen for this pure and vnbloodie sacrifice. S. Hierom saith if it be commaunded to the laie people to abstaine from their wyues for prayer, how *Hier. resp. ad Titum.* shoulde wee thincke of the Bishoppe which is ordained to offer this vnspotted sacrifice, aswell for his owne sinnes as for the people? S. Cyrill of Hierusalem calleth the Masse, a spirituall sacrifice, by reason of the bodie of Christe

Christe which is spiritualized by the diuinitie, and is spirituall in deede though not in substance, yet in qualitie and manner of existence. Anacletus commaundeth Bisshoppes and priests not to sacrifice, without wittnesse to assist them. Sother Pope commaundeth two at leaste to be present, because the Prieste saith. *Dominus vobiscum, & orate pro me.* Euaristus willeth, that the places wherin Masses should be said, be consecrated, and that alters should be sacred by chrisme. Pius the first, telleth how that Eutropia hauinge giuen her howse to the poore, he celebrated Masse with the said poore Christians. Clemens the first Ep. 3. forbiddeth to saie Masse, but where the Bisshopp will assigne. S. Gregorie did write vnto the Bisshopp of Syracusa and Isidorus, that S. Peter did institute the order of the Masse, and it seemeth saith Origines, to pertaine to him onlie to offer continuall sacrifice, who deuoted himselfe to continuall chastitie *orig. lib. 1. contra celsum.* And in the 8. booke of the constitutiōs of the Apostles as S. Clement dothe affirme, Euodius was made Bisshoppe of Antioche by S. Peter, and afterward Ignatius by S. Paule.

*Cyrill. ca. 4. myst.*
*Anacletus ep c. 2.*
*Sother de consecr. dist.*
*Gregor l. 7. regist. epist. 63. toui. 2.*
*Isid. lib. 1. de offijs cap. 15.*
*Clement. const. 8.*

14. This sacrifice, as it hathe many names in holy scripture, soe it is expressed of the old fathers with many significant tearmes; Dauid called it, the sacrifice of praise, the sacrifice of iustice, a waie to see the saluation

*Psal. 49.*
*Psal. 4.*

uation of God: of Daniell it is called *Iuge*
*Malach.* 1 *sacrificium*, the daylie and continuall sacrifice,
*Luc.* 1. a pure oblation: of Malachias, the sacrifice
*Matt.* 5. of Iuda and Hierusalem: the bloody lambe
*Iud lib.* 4. of S. Luke: of S. Mathewe the oblation that
*cap.* 34. should be offered at the altar: of the Apostle,
1. *cap.* 5. it is tearmed our pasche, & the table of our
1. *Cor.* 10 Lorde: of S. Luc, the fraction or breakinge
*Heb.* 10. of the bread: and also in a liturgie of S. An-
*Act.* 2. drewe it is called, a lambe sayinge; I offer
*Cle. Const.* daylie a lambe vnto God which when it
*Apost l.* 8. shalbe eaten, it shall remayne whole and
*cap. vlt.* sounde. The councell of Nice calles it, the
*Dionys.* lambe that takes awaie the sinnes of the
*Areop.* worlde. S. Clement calls it the pure and
*cap.* 3. *de* vnbloodie sacrifice. S. Dionysius the obla-
*cæleft.* tion of the liuely hoaste. S. Martialis, a sa-
*Hier.* crifice and a cleane oblation. Ireneus the newe oblation of the newe testament. S. Cyprian a trew & perfecte sacrifice. S. Athasius, an vnbloodie immolation: Eusebius Cesar. and S. Chrysostome, a dreadfull, terrible and euerlastinge sacrifice most honnorable: others call it a singuler sacrifice, excellinge all the sacrifices that euer were. Others a true, vnbloodie, vnspotted, perfect hoast, our daylie sacrifice, our Lorde his lambe: S. Aug. the sacrifice of our price and redemption, the sacrifice of our mediator: S. Gregorie calls it the healthsome hoaste, the hoast of oblation: others call it the sacrifice of christians &c. with many such epi-

pithetons, and last of all S. Paule calles it: *Consummatio Sacramentorum*, the accomplishinge of the Sacramentes.

15. Besides traditions of the Apostles, decrees of all generall councells, authoritie of all the fathers and holie doctors, and the common and vniuersall practise both of the greeke and latine churche, many irrefragable and approued reasons there are to confirme the infallible trueth of this blessed sacrifice. For Christ is a Prieste for euer, and by his death deserued to haue the order of euerlastinge priest-hoode, and therfore an euerlastinge sacrifice; for this sacrifice cannot be euerlastinge, either for the oblation once offered vpon the crosse, or for the oblation once offered at his last supper, but it is eternall and euerlastinge by the sacrifice which daylie in all the worlde he offereth by his Priests and ministers euen vnto the daie of judgmente. And soe Oecumenus saith that Christe is a Prieste for euer, not for his passion, but in respecte of this presente sacrifice, by which that great Priest doth offer sacrifice. *Theophilact. Eusebius Cæsar. in lib. de demonstratione Euangelica, & Haimo in epistola ad Heb.* and many other fathers say, that Christ is the high prieste, or the great priest, accordinge to S. Paule, or the greatest bisshoppe accordinge to all, and not Metaphorically but properly, therfore he oughte to haue inferior Priests vnder him that shoulde

*Oecum. in Cathena. Psal. 109.*

alſo offer, otherwiſe he ſhoulde not be called the greateſte, for a ſupreame order or
power hath a relation to an inferior. The
perfecte prieſt-hoode of Chriſte ought to
take away the impefect prieſt-hoode of the
old lawe, and as he inſtituted a newe lawe,
ſo he ought alſo to inſtitute a newe prieſt-
hoode, for euerie lawe oughte to haue his
Prieſthood which ſhould interprete the law,
as it is ſaid by Malachias, aske the lawe of
*Malac. 7.* the Prieſte, the lippes of the Prieſts ſhall
*Deut. 9.* keepe wiſdome: and as it is ſaid in Deut. if
there be any harde or doubtfull queſtion
betwixte ſtocke and ſtocke &c. goe your
waies to the Prieſts and whatſoeuer they
ſhall comaunde yow to doe, doe it; and as
he tooke awaie the olde lawe, ſo he tooke
alſo the olde Prieſthoode, and as two lawes
cannot conſiſt, ſoe two prieſt-hoodes cannot remaine. *Radix peccati*; the of-ſpringe
*Libr. 1. Mac. c. 1* of miſcheefe Antiochus, that he might take
awaie both lawe and Prieſthoode from Ie-
ruſalem, and from the children of Iſraell,
he tooke awaie both ſacrifice and oblations
from the temple.

*Daniel. 12* 16. Daniell propheſied that when Antechriſte ſhall come. *Ablatum fuerit iuge ſacrificium,* that he ſhall take awaie the daylie ſacrifice, as by that meanes to take awaie both the lawe and memorie of Chriſte that inſtituted this ſacrifice: vpon this place; S. Hypolitus that noble Martyr hath theſe wordes.

des. *Ecclesiarum ædes sacræ tigurij instar erunt, pretiosum corpus Christi & sanguis non extabit, liturgia extingetur, psalmorum decantatio cessabit, scripturarum recitatio non audietur?* In the time of Antechriste, saith he, sacred howses of the church shalbe like a cottage, the pretious bodie and blood of Christe shall not stande, the Masse shalbe extinguished &c. If this holie Martire had bene in these wicked daies and should see how these heretiques bringes churches and Monasteries to ruyne, and oppose themselues against this blessed sacrifice, he vndoubtely would saie they are the harbingers of Antechriste. Eusebius saieth that Licinus the Tyrante, and Competitor of Constantine the greate, in all his dominions did forbidd the christians to exercise this Sacramente and sacrifice. *Quid infandos loquar apostatos Licinium & Iulianum &c.* what speake I of the wicked apostates, Iulian & Licinius saying, that for noe other cause Christe was put to death by the Iewes, but for that he broughte a newe sacrifice vnto the worlde: for by these mens gouernment our sacrifice was taken awaie, euen as wee may reade in the life of those Martires Iouentinus and Maximus: with S. Chris. the holie boord, saith he, is defiled, the holie vessells polluted, and taken away, in which sacrifice was offered to the sonne of Marie. Heresie and sacriledge were euer soe ioyned one to another, that the heresie

*Ex lib. Hypoli. qui extat. Hiero. in Daniell. citat.*

*Euseb. lib. 10. c. 3.*

was firste detected by the sacriledge; so Elias did crie out vppon the heretiques for
3. Reg. 19 their sacriledge: *Domine altaria tua destruxerunt*. Lord they haue cast downe thyne altars. In the heresie of the Arrians, S. Basill
*Basil. ep. 70. & 71 Naz. ora de Arrianis.* and S. Nazian did deplore that the altars were destroied, that this blessed sacrifice was polluted. Optatus Milleuitanus in all his sixt booke, speaks of this sacriledge exercised by the Donatists.
*Optat. lib 6. in Permenan.* *Quid tam nefarium, quã altaria Dei in quibus & vos aliquando obtulistis pangere, radere, remouere, in quibus vita populi & membra Christi portata sunt:* what is more wicked, thẽ to breake, surprise, ouerthrowe and remoue the altares of God, in which somtimes yow haue offered your selues, on which the life of the people, and the members of Christ are layed? S. Leo Pope spake
*Leo 1. ep. 75.* in like manner of the Eutichian hereticks at Alexandria, *per crudelissimam &c.* they (saith he) cast foorth their most cruell hands, and with al raginge madnes they extinguish the lighte of the celestiall Sacraments, the oblation of the sacrifice is interrupted, and the sanctification of the chrisme is intercepted, and with their bloodie murtheringe hands, they haue taken awaie all misteries. Finally,
*Lib. 20. cap. 13. contra Faustum.* S. Augustine doth reproue Faustus Manacheus, for accusinge the christiãs of Idolatry, in sayinge, that in honoringe this blessed sacrifice, they honnor and reuerence therein Bachus and Ceres.

17. Yf the Gentiles themselues were soe curious and soe respectiue in offeringe sacrifice vnto their false godes, and their lawes and edictes were in nothinge soe seuere and soe extreame, as vppon such as shoulde prophane the same, and all the persecution that they inuented against the christians was because they did not offer sacrifice vnto their strange godes, and as Suetonius relates, the Emperor August. Cæsar did ordeine, that all the Senate of Rome before they should sitt in their rancke, should euerie one of them first offer incense before the altar of that God, in whose church they were, for they could not all meete together but in churches. How much more ought we christians to be curious, and religious in seruinge of the true liuinge God, by our sacrifices and oblatiōs, which are the cheefest actes by which wee honor & reuerence him? S. Aug. saies against Faust. aleadginge that of the prophett. *Sacrificium laudis glorificabit me &c.* The sacrifice of praise shall glorifie me, and this is the way by which I shall shewe him my sauior, this is the sacrifice of the flesh and blood of Christe which was promised before his cominge by similitude and likenesse of oblations, which was perfourmed in the pasion of Christe by the trueth it selfe which was celebrated in his memorie after his ascension, and in that place he said. *Sicut autem non ideo contem-*

*Sueto. in oct. c. 35.*

*Aug. cōt. Faust. lib. 20 c 21.*

*Aug. ibi.*

*nenda &c.* Euen as the virginitie of Nunnes ought not to be despised or detested, because the vestales amoungest the Romanes were Virgines, soe the sacrifice of the fathers ought not to be despised, because the gentiles haue also their sacrifice, *quia diuinus honor est sacrificium,* for the diuine honnor must be acknowyledged by a sacrifice, & this honor as S. Aug. saith is latria, which is a dewe seruice to the diuinitie, and vnto this due seruice pertaines the oblation of a sacrifice; for to offer, or to sacrifice vnto God, is a morall precepte pertaininge to the lawe of nature, which Christe in his ghospell hath not taken awaie, but confirmed the same, which is ingraffed in euerie reasonable creature vid. that sacrifice ought to be offered vnto God, and that the best is to be offered vnto him; soe Abell did offer vnto God of the best cattel he had. Therfore in offeringe sacrifice vnto God wee err not. *Sacrificium significat actionem misticam aliquam rem externam applicatione ad Dei cultum & oblatione sacrantem*: for to sacrifice doth signifie as S. Augustine saieth and S. Thomas, a certaine misticall action, hollowinge and thinge externall, that is applied and offered to the worshipp of God, and this sacrifice is not offered to any other creature but to God.

*Aug. de ciuit. lib. 4 cap 10. ante finẽ.*

*Aug. ibid.*

*Aug epist. 46 q 3. tomo 5.*

18. And although saieth S. Augustine the christian people doe vse a religious solemnitie in remembringe the Martyres both to

*Aug cont. Faustum l. 20. c. 21.*

to kindell in themselfes a desire to imitate them, as also to be partakers of their merittes and to be relieued by their praiers, yet wee doe not offer sacrifice vnto anie Martyr, but vnto the God of Martyres, although wee establish alters for their remembrance. For what Bishoppe or Priest at the sepulchers of these holie bodies beinge at the alter doth saie these wordes. *Offerrimus tibi Petre & Paule aut Cipriane? sed quod offertur, offertur Deo qui martires coronauit &c.* Wee offer vnto thee Peter, or Paule, or Cyprian, but that which is offered is offered vnto God, which crowned the Martyres, thus farr S. Augustine. Wherunto Innocentius agreeth, saying that wee must honnor God with churches, alters, sacrifices, priesthoode with vertuous and with the internall worship of latria, and soe he saide that there are two kindes of seruices; the one which is due to the creator; the other which is due to the creature, neither churches, alters, priesthoode are offered vnto Sainctes in the honnor of God, but rather vnto God, they are consecrated in the honor of the Saincts. Wherfore in all lawes, and in all states of the worlde, were offered vnto God of the fruictes of the earth, and Melchisedec did offer bread and wyne, Abraham did offer Isaacke, in the lawe of Moyses also there was a sacrifice offered as the bread of proposition and fine flower sprinkled with oile and franckensence

*Leui.* 26. 9
10 11.12.
*Psal* 21. 1
*Eley* 58.
*Gen.* 14.

ſence &c. with manie other thinges. Euen ſoe in the lawe of grace there muſt be a ſacrifice which is the onlie ſacrifice of the law both nowe and for euer as S. Cyprian ſaith. *Nec ſacerdos eius penituit Deum.* God was not not diſpleaſed at that prieſthoode, for the ſacrifice which he offered vpõ the croſſe was ſoe acceptable to God, and of that perpetuall vertue, that it is of no leſſe force and efficacie this daie, then that day when the freſhe blood and water iſſued out of his bleſſed ſide, and the ſcarres yet lefte in his bleſſed bodie doth challenge and exacte the iuſt price of the redemption of mankinde: ſoe that it is the ſelfe ſame hoaſt and oblation, which is nowe offered by the Prieſtes in the lawe of grace, and that which himſelfe did offer vpon the croſſe, which was ſignified and repreſented by all the former ſacrifices of the lawe of nature, and of the lawe of Moiſes, and much more repreſented and expoſed to the viewe of the chriſtians in the lawe of grace, & therfore S. Iohn calles him. *Agnus qui occiſus eſt ab origine mundi,* the lambe that was killed from the beginninge of the worlde, I meane in all the ſacrifices that euer was, by whome all ſacrifice had and ſhall haue their value, force and vertue, ſoe as it doth comprehende both the bloodie and vnbloodie ſacrifice, for in both of them that lambe is offered which taketh awaie the ſinnes of the worlde, and that vnbloodie ſacrifice

*Cypr. ſer. de bapt.*

crifice which the church doth offer, is of the ſame force, with that which Chriſte himſelfe did offer at his laſt ſupper. And euen as the baptiſme giuen by Chriſte is not of greater force then that which is adminiſtred by a ſimple prieſte, although, *ex opere operantis*, vid. by the meritts of him that giues the baptiſme, he may conferr greater fruicte to thoſe that he himſelfe doth baptiſe, or for whome he offers this bleſſed ſacrifice, thẽ the baptiſme or ſacrifice don by a prieſt: and as the malice of the Prieſte cannot hinder the fruicte of the ſacrifice, *ex opere operato* in nature of the Sacramente, ſoe the hollines of him cannot increaſe the grace thereof, although he that adminiſters it by ſpeciall praiers, may profitt him in ſome ſorte, for whome he offers the ſame. And as S. Nazianzenus ſaid, lett there be two Ringes, one of golde and the other of Iron, and both of them engrauen with the Image of the kinge, in ſealinge of lettres or puttinge their impreſsion to anie waxe, both of them haue equall force and value, for noe man by the impreſsion or ſealinge of them can diſcerne, which was the goldẽ ringe, or the iron ringe, becauſe it was but one charecter, although the matter and ſubſtance were ſundrie: euen ſoe it is, the ſame baptiſme, the ſame abſolution, and the ſame ſacrifice, that is offered of good prieſts and which is offred of badd, although the church haue comaunded wicked

*Naz. in oratione in ſanct. lan.*

ked and irreguler Priests to abstaine from the alter, and from the Sacraments, and also that the christians should refraine from them, if they perceaue them intangled or detected with any enormous publick offence: for it is the same word of God whether it proceede from the good, or from the badd.

19. As touchinge an ordinarie obiection that euerie sacrifice ought to be bloodie, and to be slaine, and soe consequentlie Christe beinge not slaine at the Masse cannot be a sacrifice. I aunswere with S. Thomas, that S. Paules meaninge was, that the sacrifice which the highe priest offered, when he wente into *Sancta Sanctorum*, which was but once a yeare was bloodie, but the generall and vniuersall nature of a sacrifice requireth not it should be bloodie; & as the philosopher saith. *Non omne quod conuenit speciei, conuenit etiam generi*, vid. although man be a liuinge reasonable creature, yet it pertaines not to the nature of euerie liuinge creature to be a reasonable creature. Was not the sacrifice of Abell, Caine, Melchisedec who offered bread and wine in token of this sacrifice without blood? was not the goate of the Iewes without bloode? yet it was a sacrifice and did carrie vppon his backe all the sinnes of the people of Israell. Abraham also did sacrifice his sonne Isaacke, yet he was reserued afterwardes aliue, soe Christe as Rupertus saith: *Iterum immolatur & tamen impas-*

*D.Tho. in Hebr. 9.*

*impaſsibilis permanet & viuus,* is a ſacrificed againe, yet he is impaſsible and liuinge. Luther himſelfe ſaieth, that the trewe ſacrifice of the newe teſtamente be praiers, almeſdeeds, faſtinge and watchinge, as S. Paule ſaieth, I beſech yow bretherent hat yow offer your bodies as a liuely hoaſte which is a ſacrifice, moſt pleaſinge before God. Therfore it is not neceſſarie that euerie ſacrifice ſhould be bloodie, and trulie Chriſte doth offer himſelfe nowe in heauen vnto his father for vs as he did when he was in this life, ſoe as Chriſte is ſaid to be offered for vs two manner of waies vid. bloodily and vnbloodily. And as Chriſte died but once, nor neuer ſhall die againe, ſoe he in that violẽt painefull and bloodie ſorte, can neuer be offered againe, neuertheleſſe as Chriſte died and was offered after a ſorte in all the ſacrifices that euer were from the beginning of the world al of them being figures of that one oblation vpon the croſſe, ſoe is he much more offered in the Sacramẽt of the alter of the newe teſtament more diuinely and truly expreſsinge his death, his body crucified, his bloode ſhedd though in hidden, ſacramẽtall miſticall, and vnbloodie manner, as all the holy doctors doe ſaie, which did call this *incruentum ſacrificium,* an vnbloodie ſacrifice in reſpect of the carnall ſacrifice of the Iewes, which as S. Aug. ſaieth, was the prefiguring of the fleaſh of Chriſt which he was to offer for ſinnes.

*Aug. de fide ad Petr. c.*

Whether

*Whether the Catholicke Church commit any offence in leaninge to the litterall sense of Christs wordes, in the blessed Sacramente of the Altar.*

## CHAPTER III.

1. IF yow beleeue the omnipotent power of Christe, as also if you consider his moste incomprehensible and wonderfull loue towardes his churche, for which he yealded himselfe vnto death for her clensinge, soe he gaue himselfe vnto her for her feedinge, & that shee & he maie be made one ioyned together, as it were a bodie ioyned vnto the heade. And to shewe vnto yow the trewe, plaine and euidente demonstration of those words to be ment litterally, accordinge to the tenor and significant tearmes of the woords (for as the philosopher saith: *voces sunt signa cōceptuum*, our wordes and voices doe signifie what inwardly we intend) I will beginne with the sixt Chapter of S. Iohn, that yow may more plainlie conceiue of what force that place is to proue the reall presence of Christs flesh and bloode in the blessed Sacramente. Yow shall first therfore vnderstand, that the Iewes of Capharnaum, which therof are comonlie called Capharnites, after they had bene miraculously fedd

*Ephe. 7.*

*Arist li. 1. de interp. cap. 1. & 2*

fedd of Chriſte with fiue Barlie loaues, and two fiſhes , beinge themſelues in number aboute fiue thowſand , retourned vnto Chriſte againe for ſome other like banquet, and to prouoke him the more as they thought, they beganne to bragge how their fore-fathers did eate Manna in the deſert; giuing him to vnderſtand therby, that if he would gett creditt amoungeſt them , he ſhould in like ſorte feede them , wherupon our Sauiour tooke occaſion to declare vnto them before hand, that miraculous & heauenlie foode whichhe minded afterward to ordaine in his laſt ſupper, and which ſhould not onlie equalize their Manna, but ſoe farr ſurpaſſe the ſame , as a trewe bodie ſurpaſſeth a ſhadowe, and therfore he ſaid vnto them. The bread which I ſhall giue is my fleſhe: and that he ment by thoſe wordes, to leaue his trewe fleſhe indeede to be eaten in ſteede of their Manna, it appeareth by thatwhich followeth moſt euidentlie . For whereas the Capharnite Iewes, grudged ſtreight way ſayinge.how can this man giue vs his fleaſh to eate? conceauinge ſuch a carnall and groſſe eatinge of Chriſtes fleaſh as of other common fleſh, yet he did not take away that ſcruple as our proteſtants do now a dayes, with ſaying that it ſhould be a bare figure only , or that they ſhould eate bread onlie and not fleſhe,and feede on him onely ſpiritually by faith , no he ſaid none of all

theſe

these thinges, but cleane contrarie, to confound their murmuringe infidelitie and to confirme his former woordes, he added therunto other woordes of more vehemēce, saying. *Verilie, verilie, I saie vnto yow, if yow eate not the flesh of the sonne of man, and drincke his bloode, yee shall not haue life in yow*: with many more of like perspicuitie and plainenes, for if he should, haue answered them accordinge as the protestants expounde that place, to be figuratiuely ment, he should haue soone appeased their anger, grudginges, and faithlesse conceite of those wordes, by occasion whereof they quite forsooke him sayinge. This is a hard speech who can beare it? Whereas if he had ment of a bare signe or figure, by tellinge the trueth only, he might haue kepte them continually in his companie. In truth it could not stand with the intralls of Christs charitie, beinge sent principally to conuerte the Iewes from their infidelitie, and beinge cheeflie ordained to saue the lost sheepe of Israell, that he should
*Matt.* 15. vse those woordes figuratiuely, and not declare the same plainly vnto them, beinge a matter of the greatest importance, and consequence, that euer was, for takinge away their repininge misbeleeue, the truth wherof he confirmed with his accustomed oath. *Verilie, verilie* &c. *vnlesse they should eate his flesh* &c. *they should not haue life*, yea he vsed these wordes imediatlie after their grudging.

2. S.

2. S. Chrisostome vpon those stubborne woordes of the Iewes. This is a hard speech who can beare it, saith it is the parte of a scholler, not to inquire curiously of that his maister affirmeth, but to heare, and beleeue and to expecte in due season a resolution of his doubts: and as for those people by the former miracle don by him in feedinge their hungrie stomacks beinge soe many in number, they might beleeue, that whatsoeuer he said, he could doe, or whatsoeuer he promised he could performe. For when he declared his loue towardes vs, he mingled himselfe by meanes of his body together with vs, that the body and the head should be vnited together; and to wittnesse his singuler affection towardes vs, he permittted himselfe not to be seene of such as are desirous, but to be touched and eaten and their teeth to be fastened in his flesh and all men to be filled and satisfied with the desire of him. *Tanquā leones igitur ignem spirantes ab illa mensa recedamus, facti diabolo terribiles &c.* Let vs rise therfore from the table as it were lyons breathinge out fire, makinge the diuill himselfe a feard. This misticall bloode chaseth away deuils farr off frō vs, and draweth the angells neere vnto vs, for the diuills when they see within vs the blood of our Lord, are putt to flighte, and the Angells make haste to assist vs, thus farr S. Chrisostome, whose doctrine herein is noe lesse

*Chrys. ho. 45. in Ioannem.*

*Chrys. ho. 61. ad populum Antioch.*

*Homilia prædict.*

irckſome and repugnant to the ſacramentarie Proteſtants, then to thoſe lumpliſhe Iewes, becauſe accordinge to that holy doctor, none oughte to be curious in askinge howe or by what meanes that which Chriſt affirmeth is brought to paſſe, for as the Iewes were ouermuch curious in murmuringe amoungeſt themſelues and ſayinge. *How can he giue vs his flesh to eate?* How ſhall our ſtomacke awaywith it? what a hard kind of ſpeech is this? Is it not againſt nature that one man ſhould be nouriſhed with an other mans fleaſhe? Doe not our mouthes and ſtomacks, abhorr the ſame? Soe this ſacramentarie proteſtantes haue noe other thing in their mouthes, then howe can Chriſts fleaſh, blood, and bones be conteined in ſoe little a roome? how can his body be at one tyme in heauen and on the alter? how can it be in a thowſand places at once? with many other ſuch Iewis interrogatiōs which doe daylie proceede out of their giddy braines voide of grace, not willing, *captiuare intellectum in obſequium fidei,* as S. Paule ſaith, becauſe they would not reſigne their wilfull opinions, and their blinde vnderſtāding vnto the trewe direction and obedience of faith, for if they beleued that God were able by his word to bringe all this to paſſe, they would neuer reaſon after ſuch a ſorte, for otherwiſe they may by like interrogations diſcreditt the whole chriſtian faith, and

and aske how God made the worlde of nothinge? how a Virgin could bringe foorth a sonne? how God came downe into the world to be incarnate, and yet remaine still in heauen? with many such strange interrogations, which wee knowe rather by diuine faith supernaturallie infused vnto vs, then by any naturall reason conceiued by our grosse vnderstandinge: which according to Aristotle in his metaphisickes, is as ignorante of naturall knowledge in respecte of thinges naturall, as the owle is, of the sunne in the middell of the daie. So as this holie doctor, impugneth these interrogations as arguments of incredulitie and lacke of faith, which are interrogations of the Iewes and protestãts, both which as they agree by two sundrie extreames in this infidelitie of discreditinge Gods omnipotencie: soe if yow compare both those extreamities together, you shall finde also that these mens extreame madnes, deserueth more blame and farr exceedeth that of the Iewes.

3. But the catholique church vseth a meane betweene both, for it vseth none of those incredulous questions which Saincte Chrisostome cõdemneth, but simply beleeueth that to be trewe which Christe affirmeth; shee holdeth not with the capharnits, whoe thought because he said his fleash was meate indeede, they should eate him visibly; nor yet with the sacramẽtaries, who thincke

because he said it is the spiritt that giueth life, therfore this fleash is to be eaten by faith onlye. But contrarie to them both, and in the righte meane, and trewe meaninge betweene both, ioyninge all Christs woordes together, it concludeth, that vnder the forme of bread, Christes trewe flesh is realy and substantially receaued: by sayinge vnder the forme of bread, it taketh away the Capharnits grosse and carnall imagination: by affirming trewe flesh realy and substantially to be presente, it condemneth the protestants spirituall and faithlesse figuratiue intention: in all which, the Catholique church is sufficientlie grounded and instructed, by the plaine authoritie of Christs owne words, touchinge the truth of their pretended difficultie. For in the 6. chapter of S. Iohn are thies woordes. *I am the liuely bread which came downe from heauen, if any man eate of this bread, he shall liue for euer. And the bread which I shall giue is my fleshe, which I shall giue for the life of the world.* And where the Iewes fell at variance amoungest themselues, saying. How can this man giue vs his flesh to eate? Iesus said vnto them. *Verilie, verilie I say vnto yow, vnles yow eate the flesh of the sonne of man and drincke his blood, yow shall not haue life in yow: he that eateth my flesh and drincketh my blood, hathe life euerlastinge, and I shall raise him vpp at the latter day, for my flesh is verilie meate, and my bloode is verilie drinke,*

*drinke, he that eateth my flesh, and drinketh my blood, dwelleth in me and I in him &c.*

4. This comunication our Lord had with the Iewes teachinge in the sinagoge at Capharnaum, and a twelmoneth after at his last supper, when he instituted the same blessed Sacramente and performed his foresaid promise as they were at supper, as the Euangelist saith. *Iesus tooke bread gaue thancks and blessed and brake it, and gaue it to his disciples sayinge. Take and eate this is my bodie which is giuen for yow, this doe in the remembrance of me, likewise takinge the challice after he had supped, he gaue thanckes and gaue it them sayinge. Take and diuide it amounge yow, and drinke all of this, this is my blood of the newe testamente?* S. Paule writeth thus much to the Corinthians saying. *For I haue receaued of our Lord that which I haue deliuered vnto yow, for our Lord Iesus the same nighte he was betrayed, tooke bread and giuinge thancks brake and said, take and eate, this is my body which shalbe deliuered for yow, doe this in remembrãce of me, likewise the chalice also after he had supped sayinge. This chalice is the newe testament in my blood, doe this soe often as yee shall drinke in the remembrance of me, for soe often as yow shall eate this bread and drinke this chalice, yee shal shewe forth our Lords death vntill he come, wherfore whosoeuer shall eate the bread and drincke of the challice of our Lord vnworthilie, shalbe guiltie of the bodie and blood of our Lord.*

*Mat. 26. Marc. 14. Luc. 22.*

*But lett a man examine himselfe and soe let him eate of the bread and drinke of the chalice, for he that eateth and drinketh vnworthilie, eateth and drinketh his owne iudgmente, not discerning the body of our Lord.* Yow see plainlie the beleefe of the catholique church to be noe forged beleefe, but moste firmelie builded vppon Christs plaine wordes as the 4. Euangelists and S. Paule doe wittnesse, by which the vndoubted doctrine of this highe misterie of the blessed Sacramente of the alter, is substancially and most certainly confirmed.

*Chrys. in Math. ho. 83.* 5. But to confirme the same by the testimonies of the fathers, S. Chrisostome saith. *Sicut in veteri &c.* Euen as in the olde testamente, soe likewise in the newe, Christe hath for our benefitt lefte behinde him and gathered together the memorie of his misteries, bridlinge therby the mouthes of heretiques: for when they aske how it is proued that Christe was sacrificed and put to death, besides many other thinges to musell and shutt vpp their mouthes with all, wee shewe thē these misteries, for if Christ died not, whereof is this sacrifice a pledge and token? Thus yow see how diligente Christe was and desirous that wee should haue continually his death in remembrance. For whereas these heretiques, Marcion, Valentinus, Manicheus, and their disciples did denie this dispensation and worke of God in flesh, Christe by this misterie soe bringeth

bringeth vs allwayes in minde of his passion, that no man vnlesse he be madde, can be seduced. By which woordes of S. Chrisostome, the certeintie of Christs bodie in the Sacrament is proued, for by the truthe thereof beleeued therein, Marcion a foresaid and Valentinus, and other like heretiques were confounded, who said Christe had noe true bodie, in which he mighte suffer on the crosse: but if the church should haue holden, in the tyme of S. Chrisostome that Christe was presente only in the Sacramente by a figure, nothinge could haue bene concluded against those heretiques, for they denied not but it was figuratiuely also present one the crosse. Wee must also vnderstand, that this Sacrament is a pleadge or token, not as the sacramentaries would wreaste it, vid. a pleadge or token of his passion which is liuelie there represented and brought to remembrance by the trewe presence of that selfe same body that suffred. And therfore Christe at the institution of this Sacrament after he had said, take, eate, this is my body, adioyned therunto those other woordes. *Doe this in the remembrance of me*, which woordes Sainct Paule expoundeth verie plainly, sayinge. *Soe often as yow shall eate this bread and drinke of this chalice, yee shall shewe forth our Lordes death vntill he come.*

6. The said S. Chrisostome, in the fore-

said homilie vppon this texte, *hoc est corpus meum*, saith lett vs haue noe doubte but beleeue, and behold with the eyes of our vnderstanding, for noe sensible thinge was deliuered vs of Christe, but vnder thinges sensible. But as for those thinges which he deliuered, they are all out of the reache of our senses. Soe in baptisme is that excellẽt guifte that is giuen by water which water is a sensible thinge. But that which therin is wroughte I meane the spirituall generation, that is to be conceaued by the vnderstandinge: for if thow hadest bene without a bodie, he would haue deliuered these guiftes simply also without bodies. But for as much as thy soule is coupled and ioyned to a body, therfore they are deliuered vnto thee, vnder bodilie and sensible thinges, that they may be the better vnderstood. *O quot modo dicunt vellem formam & speciem eius, vellem vestimenta ipsa, vellem calceamenta videre: hunc ipsum vides: ipsum tangis: ipsum comedis.* O how many doe say now a dayes, I woold faine see his forme & phisiognomie, behold thou seeste himselfe, thow dost touch himselfe, thow dost eate him, thow desirest to see his garments, but he deliuereth himselfe vnto thee, not that thow shouldest see him only, but touch him, and haue him within thee. Lett noe mam therfore come neere, whose stomacke wambleth or riseth against it, nor anny that is

*S. Chrys. hom. 24.*

cold

cold of deuotion, but lett all ſuch that approach herunto, be ſturred vpp and feruentlie inflamed, for if the Iewes did eate their Paſchale lambe with haſte, ſtandinge on their feete, with their ſhoes on, and holding their ſtaues in their hands, how much more muſte we watch and be diligent? for they were takinge their iourney from Egipte to Palleſtine, and therfore they had on wayfaringe and pilgrimes apparell, but thow art goinge vpp from earth to heauen, wherfore thow muſte watch and take good heede. Yf a Duke (ſaith he in that homilie) if the coũcell it ſelfe, yea if he that wereth the crowne: come herunto vnworthilie, forbid him, keepe him backe, thie autoritie is greater then his. If ſoe be that a fountaine of moſt pure water were comitted to thie chardge to be kept cleane for thie flock, when thow ſhouldeſt ſee moſt ſtinckinge and filthie ſwine drawe nere, thow wouldeſt not ſuffer them. And now whereas a moſt holie fountaine, not of water but of blood and ſpiritt, is comitted vnto thee, if thow ſhalt ſee thoſe men drawe neere which are moſt defiled with ſinne, wilt thow not take indignation and forbid them? Thus farr S. Chriſoſtome, who moſt plainlie declareth Chriſts reall preſence, not only in this homilie, but vpon the firſt Epiſtle of S. Paule to the Corinthians. And alſo moſte euidentlie in his ſecond homilie to the people of Antioch

*Chryſoſt. hom 24. 1. Cor. 1.*

Antioch saying. What will yow say then if I shewe yow, that soe manny of vs as be pertakers of the holie misteries doe receiue a thinge farr greater then that which Elias gaue, for Elias left vnto his disciple his Cloake, but the sonne of God ascendinge into heauen, lefte with vs his flesh. And againe Elias wēt himselfe without his cloak, but Christe both lefte his flesh with vs, and ascendeth hauinge with him the selfe same fleshe &c. By which the sacramentaries can not possible mantaine the blessed Sacramente to be a remembrance only of Christs flesh, if they will admitt this holy and learned doctors testimonie. For Elias lefte a remēbrance of himselfe alsoe, when he lefte his cloake behind him. But herein standeth the force of this comparison, that Christ farr passeth Elias: & therfore saith S. Chrisostome, he did not only leaue a farr more excellent thinge vid. his owne flesh, but allso tooke the same with him into heauen, which he lefte behind him.

*Cyrill. li. 4. c. 13. in Iohn.* 7. S. Cyrill that famous Bishoppe of Alexandria in Egipt, who for his great sanctitie and science was appointed president of the generall councell of Ephesus against Eutiches and Dioscorus *anno Domini 434.* doth agree with S. Chrisostome, who vpon S. Iohns ghospell in his 6. chapper hath these woordes. Then the Iewes fell at variance amoungest themselues sayinge. *Quomodo*

*modo potest hic nobis carnem suam dare ad manducandum?* How can this man giue vs his flesh to eate? The malitious and wicked minde whatsoeuer he vnderstandeth not, he reiecteth vpon pride, as vaine and false, nether will he giue place to anny other, or thincke any thinge true which is aboue his owne capacitie, and such wee shall finde the Iewes in this place: for whereas they hauinge nowe perceiued by those miraculous signes Christs diuine power, they should of right haue allowed that which he said, they cleene cōtrariwise saie; *how can this man giue vs his flesh?* They crie out blasphemouslie vpō God, not callinge to minde that with him nothinge is impossible: for beinge as S. Paule saith, sensuall, and carnall, they could not vnderstand spirituall thinges, but this great misterie seemeth vnto thē peeuishnes and folly. But let vs I beseeche yow take greate profitt of other mens sinnes, and beleeuinge stedfastlie those misteries, let vs neuer vtter with our mouthes, or soe much as thincke with our harte, that same (how) for it is a Iewish word, and deserueth extreame punishmente. And Nicodemus therfore whē he saied, how may these thinges be brought to passe, was aunswered accordinglie, arte thou a maister in Israell, and ignorant hereof? A little after in that place he saith. How was Moyses rodd turned into a serpente? how was his hand stroken with a leprosie,

*1. Cor. 2.*

*Exod. 4.*
*Exod. 7.*

leprosie, in a momente restored againe to his
*Exo. 14.* former state? how the waters were turned
*Exo. 15.* into blood? how did their fore fathers esca-
*Exo. 17.* pe through the middst of the sea, as though
they had walked vpon the drie land? howe
*Iosue. 3.* were the bitter waters changed sweete by
*Iosue. 6.* the tree? howe fountaines of water did
flowe oute of the stone? howe the running
riuer of Iordan stoode still? There are innumerable thinges in which if thou aske how,
thow must needes ouerthrowe the scripture, sett at naught the doctrine of the prophetts, and Moyses owne writinges, wherfore yee Iewes should haue beleeued Christ
rather then like dronken folke cry out, how
can this man giue vs his flesh: Thus farr S.
*Cap. 14. in Ioh.* Cyrill, and more at lardge in his 4. booke,
alleadginge that of Isaias, for if yow be-
leeue not saith he, yow shall not vnderstād,
First therfore they should haue fastned the
rootes of faith in their minde, and afterwardes aske those questions meete for men
to aske.

*Cyrill. lib. 4. c. 13.* 8. And the said S. Cyrill in another
place saith. Yee doe not vnwisely denie,
that the flesh hath altogether power to
quicken and giue life, for if yow aske the
fleash alone by it selfe, it can nothinge at
all quicken, as lacking that which should
quicken it. But if yow will search the misterie of the Incarnation and will knowe
him that dwelleth in flesh, although seshe

by it

by it selfe be able to doe nothinge, yet then yow will beleeue that it is made able and powerfull to quicken, vnlesse yow will contend alsoe that the holy ghoaste hath noe power to quicken. For whereas flesh was ioyned with that word which quickneth and giueth life therby, yt was made alsoe of power to quicken and giue life; and although therfore the nature of flesh as it is flesh, cannot quicken or giue life, yett it worketh that nowe, because it hath receiued the whole operation of the woord: for this bodie is not the bodie of S. Peter, nor S. Paule, nor of any such like, but the bodie of life it selfe, and of our Sauiour Iesus Christ, in whome the fullnesse of the God head corporallie dwelleth and is able to doe this; for if honny whereas it is naturally sweete, maketh those thinges sweete, with which it is mingled, shall it not be verie foolish to thinke that the liuelie and quickinge nature of the woord, did not giue vnto that man in whome it dwelleth, power also to quicken and giue life? for which causes the flesh trulie of all other men doth not auaile or proffit in deede any thinge, but the flesh of Christe alone is able to giue lyfe and quicken, because the onlie Sonne of God dwelleth in it: But he calleth himselfe spiritt, because God is a spiritt: thus farre S. Cyrill. *Coloss. 2.*

9. By this yow may perceiue the false *2. Cor. 3.*

inter-

interpreration of the proteſtants vpon theſe woords. *The ſpiritt is that which quickneth the flesh auaileth nothinge*, by which woordes they ſaie that the reall preſence of Chriſts fleſh in the Sacrament can nothinge proffitt vs, and that the ſpirituall eatinge thereof by faith only, ſhould be ſufficient; for S. Cyrill teacheth plainly that by this woord he meant the God head which was vnited in one perſon with that fleſh of his, & which gaue vnto it that power to quicken and giue life, which noe other mans fleſh euer hadd. And the comon Schoole of all diuines doe affirme, that when; *Verbum caro factum eſt*: when the woord was become fleſh, & when fleſh was vnited vnto the woord: the fleſh by the woord doth quicken, and giue life: and as S. Nazianzenus ſaith, that as Iron beinge putt to the fire doth burne, and performeth the operation and action of fire: ſoe the fleſh beinge vnited vnto the woord, doth quicken, giue life, and worketh by the influence thereof; And as S. Thomas ſaith. *Quo intimius eſt aliquid cum principio influente, eo magis participat de eius influxu.* The more intimate and neerer a thinge is to its firſt influent cauſe, the more it receaues the influence & operation therof. So the bleſſed fleſh of Chriſt noe doubt, beinge ioyned and vnited vnto the principall cauſe of all cauſes, receaueth a moſte liuely operation from the ſame.

10. S.Hillarie also that famous Bishop of Poetiers, in his 8. booke of the Trinitie against the Arrians, hath these woordes. *De veritate carnis & sanguinis non est relictus ambigendi locus, &c.* There is noe place lefte to doubte of the veritie of Christs flesh and blood, for by the confession of our Lord, and by our faith, it is verilie flesh, and verilie blood; and beinge eaten and dronke by vs, it bringeth to passe that wee are in Christe, and Christe in vs. Ys not this trewe? it seemeth verilie, not to be trew to these incredulous people which deny Christe to be trewe God. S. Hillaries argument, was against the Arrian heretiques, who held that God the sonne was not one with God the father in substance, but only in will: to disproue which assertion, he alleadgeth a texte of scripture where Christe prayeth that wee all may be one with him, as he and his father are one, but wee (saith Sainct Hillarie) by receauinge of Christs trewe bodie and blood in the blessed Sacrament, are not vnited vnto him in will only, but also to his fleash and substance: wherfore it mustes needs followe, that Christ is vnited to his father by nature and substance of his God headd, and not by will only. which argument of his doth plainly declare, that the trueth of the reall presēce of Christ in the Eucharist, was then approued and receaued of all men, for otherwise he would *Ioh. 17.*

neuer

neuer haue conuinced them by that argument; and vnlesse yow denie Christ to be God, yow can not denie him to be trulie & really in the blessed Sacrament. And he proceedeth further in that booke and saith, If the woord was truly made flesh, and if wee truly receaue the woord (beinge made flesh) in the meate of our Lorde, how shall he be thoughte not to abide naturally in vs, who both beinge borne man, tooke vnto him the nature of our flesh to the nature of eternitie vnder the Sacramēt of flesh, which is to be communicated of vs? for soe wee all are one, because both the father is in Christe, and Christe is in vs, for himselfe saith. *My flesh is verilie meate and my blood is verilie drinke, he that eateth my flesh and drinketh my blood, abideth in me and I in him.* In another place he saith expoundinge those wordes of S. Paule. *Accipite & bibite hic est sanguis meus &c.* Take and drincke, this is my blood, this is my body, who shall dare hereafter to doubte of the trueth therof, sith he did certeinly saie, this is my blood? who euer will affirme the contrarie or saie, it is not his blood? *nam specie panis dat nobis corpus, & in specie vini dat nobis sanguinem &c.* for vnder the likenesse of bread he giues vnto vs his bodie, and in the likenesse of wyne he giues vs his blood, that when yow take it yow shall taste the bodie and blood of Christe beinge made pertaker of the

*Sermone Cathechesi mystag. 4. 1. Cor. 11.*

the ſelfe ſame body & blood, ſoe wee beare and carry with vs Chriſte in our bodies when wee receaue his bodie and blood into our intralls, and accordinge to Sainct Peter, are made pertakers of the diuine nature. And a little after he ſaith. *Quamobrem non ſic hæc attendas velim tanquam ſit nudus & ſimplex panis, nudũ & ſimplex vinum. Corpus enim ſunt & ſanguis Chriſti:* whertore I would not haue yow to thinke of theſe thinges as they were naked and ſimple bread, naked and ſimple wyne, for they are the body & blood of Chriſte, and though your ſenſes do tell you the contrarie, your faith ſhall confirme and ſtrenghten you, doe not iudge by thie taſte, when thie ſure faith ſhall guide thee from all doubte.

11. S. Auguſtine vppon theſe woordes. *Adorate ſcabellum pedum eius*, adore and worſhipp his footeſtoole, becauſe it is holie, *quia in ipſa carne hic ambulauit &c.* Becauſe he walked here on earth in that verie ſame fleſh, and gaue vs the verie ſame fleaſh to eate, for our ſaluation: and noe man eateth that fleſh vnleſſe firſt he adore and worſhipp it, it is found oute how ſuch a footeſtoole of our Lord ſhould be adored and worſhipped, and that wee doe not only not ſinne in adoringe and worſhipping it, but wee ſinne in not adoringe and not worſhippinge the ſame. Therfore when thow doſt bowe downe and proſtrate thie ſelfe vnto any ſuch *Aug. in Pſal. 98.*

earth, doe not behould it as earth, but behould that holie one whose footestoole that is which thou doest adore and worshipp, because for his sake thow dost adore & worshipp it.

*Aug. cont. Iul. Pela. lib. 1.*

*Amb. de ijs qui misteriis initiantur cap. vlt.*

12. S. Ambrose that blessed Bishopp of Millane, of whome Sainct Augustine saith. *Veneror vt patrem in Christo &c.* I reuerence him as a father, for he through the ghospell in Christe Iesu begott me, doth plainly confirme this truethe, saying. *Ipse clamat Dominus Iesus. Hoc est corpus meum &c.* Our Lord Iesus himselfe crieth. This is my body, before the benediction of those heauenly woordes another kinde of nature is named: after consecration the bodie is signified or mentioned: he himselfe called it his blood, before consecration, it is named an other thinge after consecration, it is called blood. And thow saidst therunto Amen, that is to say it is trewe, let thie inward minde confesse that which thie mouth speaketh, and let thie affection thincke, that which thy speech soundeth. And in that chapter he saith. But perchaunce yow will saie, I see an other thinge with myne eyes, how then doe yow tell me that I receaue the bodie of Christe? this then remaineth yet by vs to be proued, how many examples therfore doe wee vse to shewe that this is not that which nature formed, but that which benediction consecrated. And that the power of bene-

benediction is greater then the power of nature, for so much as nature it selfe is changed. Moises held in his hand a rodd, he cast the same foorthe and it was made a serpent. againe, he tooke vpp the serpent by the taile, and the same retourned to the nature of the rodde: yow see then by the grace giuen to that prophett, that nature both in the rodd and serpent was twice changed; the riuers of Egipt rann with pure and cleane water, blood sodainlie brake out from the springes, and fountaines, there was drinke to be hadd out of the riuers, and at the prophetts prayers the blood of the riuers ceased, the nature of the water retourned. All the rest of the holie fathers and doctors that liued before these, and such as came after, doe confirme with one vniforme consent this sacred doctrine.

13. S. Andrewe the apostle, as Aloysius Lipomanes a moste graue and learned aucthor doth gather out of the approued aucthors, when he was to be crucified said these wordes. *Ego omnipotenti Deo &c.* I doe daylie sacrifice to the omnipotent God the vnspotted lambe, who beinge trulie sacrificed and his fleash allso eaten of the people, remaineth both sounde and aliue. S. Ignatius which was disciple vnto S. Iohn the Euangeliste, writing against the heretiques Symonianus and Menandrianus who as they denied the Incarnation of Christe, soe

*Ignat. ep. ad Smyrnenses.*

they did alsoe denie the misterie of this blessed Sacrament. *Sic, ait, Eucharistias & oblationes non admittunt, quod non confiteantur Eucharistiam esse carnem saluatoris &c.* Soe they doe not admitt eucharistes, and oblations, because they doe not confesse the Euchariste to be the flesh of our Sauiour, which flesh did suffer for our offences, which the Father accordinge to his benignitie hath raised vpp: this place is cited by Theodoretus. Tertulian also reprehending wicked priests exclaymeth against them, sayinge. *Semel Iudei Christo manus intulerunt & vos &c.* The Iewes did offer violence vnto Christe, but so yow doe also violatt and handle his bodye moste irreuerentlie, such irreuerent handes should be cutt of &c. And how should he saie these wordes, if he should thincke that in the Eucharist should be only the figure of Christs bodie? So *Orig. homil. 13. in Exod.* expoundinge the 25. of that booke, *homil. 7. libr. numeri in caput Math. 26. Math. vbi sic legimus homil. 7. Leuit. homil. 9. in Leuit. concita. in cap. 15. Matth.* So Cyp. who suffred death *Anno Domini 259. sermone de lapsis.* So Athanas. who is citted of *Theodoretus, Cyrillus, Hieroso. initio Cathechesis. 4. mistagogice, & in tota fere Cathechesi. Greg. Nyss. in lib. de vita Moysis.* So S. Optatus Milleuitanus which did florish in sanctitie and learninge in one tyme with S. Ambrose. *Quid enim est tam sacrilegum?* what is more

*Theo. dialog. 3.*

*Tertull. lib. 2. ad vxorem & in libro de Idolatria.*

*Theod. 2. Dialog.*

more deteſtable then to deſtroie and defile the alter on which ſomtimes yow haue offred your ſelues, in which the deſires of the people and the members of Chriſte are carried? and a little after, what is the alter but the ſeat of the bodie and blood of Chriſte? S. Naz. liuinge alſo in the ſame tyme, *abſque confuſione & dubio &c.* without confuſion and doubt we eate his bodie and drincke his bloode. *Nazianz. oratione de Paſcha.*

14. S. Ephrem the familiar frinde of S. Baſill & of that authoritie that in the church after the ſcriptures his woorks were read as S. Hero. doth wittneſſe, ſaith. *Quid ſcrutaris &c.* whie ſhould yow ſearch the inſcrutable thinges of God? if you curiouſly ſearch them, yow ought not to be accompted a faithfull chriſtian, but a curious companion, be faithfull and innocent, be pertaker of the vnſpotted body of oure Lord, and aſſured with a ſounde faith that yow eate whole the lambe himſelfe. S Epiphanius which was a familier frinde of S. Athanaſius, doth compare the heretiques that denie Chriſts bodie to be in the Sacramente, with Æſops dogge, who hauinge a peece of fleſh in his Iawes, paſsinge ouer a riuer and behoulding the ſhadowe thereof in the water, did let goe the trewe fleſh, ſtriuinge by duckinge vnder the water to gett only the ſhadowe, and ſoe he had neither the one nor the other: ſoe the heretiques letts goe the trewe fleſh *S. Hieron. in cathalogo ſcrip.*

of Christe, only for a figure, and soe they haue neither benefitt by the one, nor by the other. Sainct Gregorie, as Ioannes Diaconus doth write, did proue by a miracle that was don, that the bread was turned into Christs fleshe. Damascen which liued in the tyme of Leo the Imadge breaker, in the yeare of our Lord God 740. saith. *Panis vinumque &c.* Bread wyne and water by the inuocation of the holy ghoste, are supernaturally turned into the bodie and blood of Christe, and they are not two, but one and the selfe same thinge; bread and wyne are not the figure of the bodie and blood of Christe, God forbid, but it is the selfe same bodie of our Lord deified. Vnto this agreeth Theophilactus who liued in the yeare of our Lord 800. saying. *hoc est corpus meum &c.* this is my bodie; he sheweth that the selfe same bodie is bread which is sanctified vpon the alter, and not answering a figure, for he did not saie this is a figure, but this is my body.

*Io. Diaco. lib 2. vitæ sanctit. q.*

*Theophil. in cap. Math. 26.*

15. In the life of most sacred diuines, I I cannot forgett the worthie and holye Saincte one of the best preachers that was in the worlde since the Apostles tyme, I meane Sainct Vincent Ferrer. who thus writeth. *Deus à principio mundi voluit adorari sub aliqua forma.* God from the beginninge of the world would be adored vnder some forme or visible figure, because God accordinge to his substance or essence, cannot be percei-

*Vincent. sermone de institutione Sacrament. Eucharist.*

perceiued or beholden of any. And ſoe the Patriarches as Adam, Abraham, and others, did behould him vnder an other forme, which was not God, and ſoe they adored not the forme, or figure, but God in the forme or figure. Afterwardes in the tyme of the prophetts amoungeſt whome Moyſes was the firſt vnto whome God appeared in the forme of fire, in a burninge flame, and Moyſes did not adore neither the fire nor the flame, but God in that figure. In *Exod. 19.*
Exodus God gaue the lawe in Mont Sinai, and God diſcended there in the forme of fire, and Moyſes and the people did adore God, and not the fire, but in the forme of the fire. In another place he comaunded *Exod. 29.*
Moyſes to make the Arck both within and without gilded with gould, and ſoe all the Iewes did adore not the woode thereof or the gould, but God which would be adored vnder that forme: and ſoe (ſaith this Father) the Iewes doe ſcorne vs becauſe wee adore God in the forme of bread. Soe in the booke of kinges when by gods comaundement Salomon made the Temple and the *3. Reg 8.*
Arch ſoe ſecreetly kepte in *Sancta Sanctorum* as none could behold it, God would be adored vnder the forme of a cloude: ſoe Salamon and all the people did adore not the cloude, but God vnder the cloude. Afterwardes God came vnder the ſhape of a man, vnder which ſhape he was alſo adored of

the faithfull, and so when he was to passe out of this world, he ordayned an other shape vnder which he should be adored, which is not the terrible fire, neither the Arck, or the cloude: but the bread which is better then all these formes, or figures, which giues life, because that the life of man principally consisteth in bread, and soe wee doe not adore the bread, neither that whitenesse which representeth the diuine puritie, neither the roundnes thereof which representeth the diuine eternitie, which hath neither beginninge nor ende, but God vnder the forme of bread, as he was honored of the faithfull before his pasion, as of the Magi, of the Leper, of the Chananean, of the Hemorissa, of the blinde borne, and of many others, and after his pasion beinge risen from death, he was honnored of the Apostles and of the deuoute women, according to Sainct Mathewe. And now beinge glorified in heauen wee behoulde him also in the Eucharist, and although he discendes daylie therin, yett he forsakes not heauen, euen as the son giuing light to al the world forsakes not his owne spheare, and the voice although it resoundeth in the eares of manny, yett it remaines with vs. And if the corruptible or transitorie word, or the created lighte, can doe this, much more the eternall word which was from the beginninge, the sunne of Iustice which is is Christe Iesus can doe more beinge nowe made flesh, and sufferinge for flesh, & came to feede flesh. And as Ioseph was adored in all Egipt because he preuented dearth by prouidinge corne: whie should not Christe be adored of the Church in this blessed Sacrament which gaue bread from heauen vnto vs in great aboundance? thus he. *Genes. 41.*

16. Let vs therfore awake out of sleepe, I meane out of the drowsie and slumbering sleepe of sinne and heresie, & with Elias, to eate as the prophet Dauid saith of the bread *3. Reg. 19.* of Angells, for wee haue a longe iourney in this persecution of the church, where already the dreadfull proclamations doe soūd the alarum in all the corners of poore Irelād, wee ought therfore euerie one to awake and gett vpp oute of the quaikmeere and pit of our former misdeamenors, and to prepare our selues with a cleane harte against the thundringe threatnings of this bloody battaile. This is the counsell of S. Cyprian *Serm. de Euchar.* in the persecution of the faithfull, that euery one prepare and dispose himselfe to receiue this blessed Sacrament. This was done in our dayes by the constant priests at Rochell, in those tragicall garboiles of the Hugonitts, the cheese of them beinge called the Abott of S. Bartholomew, and the towne beinge surprised by the instigation of one Northe, a minister sent thither by Caluine, for that purpose. And the poore Abbot

Abbot to fortifie the poore priests did vse vppon the sudden the woordes of consecration vpon comon bread, for that he durst not celebrate or reserue the holy hoasts, *in sacrario*, for feare they should be cast vnto the doggs, or otherwise be irreuerentlie handled, as those Hugonotts were accustomed to doe in other places of France, and gaue it vnto those constant Martirs to the number of 24. and euerie one of thē beinge resolued rather to suffer any death, then to make shippwracke of their faith, were cast headlonge with a great stone about their neckes from the highe steeple that standeth ouer the keye. The kinges mother also, that constant Martyr, receiued this blessed Sacrament before her execution, which shee reserued in a sacred pix beinge secreatly sent vnto her. Soe as euerie constant Martyr ought to applie to himselfe in his greatest extremitie, this soueraigne medicine, which is of greater force to animate and fortifie weake fainted harts, then all the amber greece in the world, and euerie vertuous Christian ought to saie with the Apostle.
*Galat. 2.* *In fide viuo filij Dei*, I liue in the faith of the sonne of God, which loued me and yelded
*Ephes. 5.* himselfe for me, and soe the same Apostle said in ā other place, which loued his church and yealded himselfe for her, and for whose clensinge and purifienge from sinne, and sāctifienge hir with grace as the said Apostle saith,

ſaith, *Factus eſt nobis iuſtitia ſanctificatio & redemptio*, he is ſanctification and redemption leuinge vnto vs continually a bleſſed Iewell which is his ſacred fleſh, to worke thoſe wonderfull effects, which noe other fleſh could euer bringe to paſſe, for God doth make an inſtrument of thoſe thinges for our ſaluation by his grace, which otherwiſe were moſte offenſiue and hurtfull vnto vs. By the tree wee were made ſlaues, by the noble tree of the croſſe wee are made free. By the vniuerſall diluge of water the whole world was ouerthrowen, by the water of baptiſme, the ſame was reſtored. By a dreame, Ioſeph was made a ſlaue and abuſed, by a dreame he was ſett free and aduaunced to the higheſt dignitie of Egipt. By a woman the whole ſtock of Adam fell, by a wooman the ſame was raiſed vpp againe. By meat the whole world ſuffred death as it is written. *In quacunque die comederis ex ea &c.* Whatſoeuer houre you ſhall eat thereof you ſhall die the death, by meate the ſame obteined life, himſelfe pronouncinge the ſame, *qui manducat hunc panem viuet in æternum*, whoſoeuer ſhal eate this bread (which he plainly affirmeth to be his fleſhe) ſhall liue for euer: which fleſhe is the only remedie vnto Virgins, againſt the frailtie and raginge concupiſcence of fleſhly deſires, although matrimony after the fall of Adam was ſecondarily ordained againſt the furious paſsions therof

1. Cor. 1.

beinge

beinge a ſecondarie effecte of the ſame, yet in the lawe of grace, when a ſacred Virgin brought foorth a Virgin withoute the carnall operation of voluptuous ſenſualitie: this virginall, immaculate, and vnſpotted fleaſh brings foorth ſoe many millions of Virgins, which haue bene and ſhalbe in his church vnto the worldes ende, and becauſe you taſt not of this fleaſh makinge it but a bare figure, yow cannot liue either chaſte or continent, much leſſe Virgins, for it is a cheefe paradox in your doctrine, that noe man can liue chaſte.

17. Laſtly, this is proued by the infallible trueth of Chriſts promiſe, who performed whatſoeuer he promiſed, but he promiſed plainlie and euidentlie to giue his trewe fleſh truely, therfore he did performe the ſame. The maior is knowen, vnleſſe yow will charge Chriſte with a lie; The minor is proued in the 6. chapter of S. Iohn. *The bread that I shall giue is my fleshe for the life of the World:* and ſoe he performed it when he ſaid. *Hoc eſt corpus meum*. And in that place he ſaith. *Caro mea verè eſt cibus & ſanguis meus verè eſt potus*, and alſo he ſaith vnto the Iewes, vnleſſe yow eate of the fleaſh of the ſonn of man, yow ſhall not haue life in yow. And when he ſaid trulie, he did exclude figuratiuely, for the one taketh awaie the force of the other. But here perhaps an heretique will obiect, that if wee adore the Eucha-

*Iohn 6.*

Euchariſte for beinge the bodie of Chriſte, the people adoringe the ſame beinge not conſecrated, by the iniquitie of the prieſte ſhould comitt idolatrie? Wherto I aunſwere, that as Laban cauſinge Lia to lie with Iacob inſteede of Rachell, was not any imputation to the ſaide Iacob, he beinge ignorant thereof for that he thoughte her to be his proper wyfe: ſoe it ſhould not be idolatrie for the people ignorantly adoringe Chriſte in an hoaſte not conſecrated: euen as it is not an offence before God, if one ſhould reuerence a falſe brother, for a ſuppoſed or pretended vertue, though otherwiſe he were a diſſembler, for he doth not honnor the impietie of hypocriſie of the ſaid diſſembler, but the religion and ſanctitie that is thought to be in him. Or as if a blinde man ſhould ſaie vnto S. Peter, *Ieſu the ſonne of Dauid haue mercie vpon me*, thincking him to be Chriſt, ſhould not comitt Idolatrie. Euen ſoe the Church ſhould not be deceiued or be conuinced of Idolatrie, if a wicked prieſt would not conſecrate through his malicious intent, for the catholique faith holdeth it for an aſſured beleefe, that Chriſte is not in anny hoaſte, but in that which is rightlie conſecrated: nor euerie one lawfully regenerated or with God reconſiled, that is not lawfully baptiſed, and orderlie and rightlie reconſiled.

*That*

*That there is a purgatorie, which is proued aswell by Scriptures, and auncient Fathers, as also euen by the testimonies of Protestant thẽselues.*

## CHAPTER I.

1. THis is proued by reason, for if you grant that God is merciful and iust, as indeed he is, yow must alsoe proue purgatorie. For if a man doe liue most wickedlie all his life without any remorse of conscience, or any other pennaunce, and at his death doth aske for mercy, I thinck yow will not saye he shalbe condemned vnto the euerlastingepaines of hell, because he sought for godes mercie, nor yet shall he enioye presentlie euerlastinge blisse, for that God is iust in punishinge the sinnes of wicked people, for as S. Gregorie sayes, as the shadowe doth followe the bodie, soe pennaltie and paines doth followe sinne: but he shall not haue euerlastinge paines; therfore he must be lyable to a temporall which was not inflicted vppon him in this life tyme, therfore in some other place, which is purgatorie.

2. Although God dothremitt sinne, *quantum ad reatum culpæ*, which is the guilt of sinne,

sinne, yet he doth not remitt temporall paines, as may appeare by Dauid, who although his sinnes were remitted vnto him, yet he suffred temporall punishment, as likewise Ezechias, the Niniuites, and others, who notwithstandinge their sinnes were forgiuen them, yet they suffred temporall paines and pennalties in this life, as the Israelits whose pennance was that they should not enter into the lande of promise. *S. August. tract. c. 24. in Iohn.* saith *productior est pœna quam culpa*: and therfore the church imposed pennaunce after the absolution as wee may see *in Conc. Nyce. cap. 12. Laodic. c. 1. Dionys. Areop. de eccl. Hier. ca. 5. Tertull. lib. de pœna qua nihil prodest de pœnitentia d. 3. Hieron. epist. ad Ocea. Amb. lib. 5. ca. 10. Orig. homil. 15. in Leuit. August. epist. 54.* Bullenger a great protestant doth acknowledge the old doctors of the Church to haue prayed for the dead. I knowe saith he that the great Doctors of the Churche S. Augustine as allso S. Chrysostome, and other great and eminent doctors haue written of this matter; I knowe, saith he, that the fathers doe say that to pray for the dead is an apostolique tradition, alsoe that S. Aug. did say that to offer sacrifice for the dead, was obserued in the vniuersall Church. And Aerius was condemed for reprouinge prayers for the dead, thus farre Bullenger. This Aerius for beinge refused of a Bishopricke, as S. Augustine

*Bulleng. decad. 4. serm. 10.*

*Aug. ser. 32. de verbis Apostoli.*

Aug to.6. de hæresibus ad quod vult Deum hæres. 53. Musc.cap. de orat. pag. 515. Zuing. to. 1. Epicheresis caminusæ. Caluini st. li 3. ca. 2. tomo 5. Conr. in Tobiã c.4 Vrba in Baruch. 3. Brent. in apol.conf. VVittẽb. cap. 5. de bapt. 1. parte.

gustine said, fell to Arianisme and reproued prayers for the dead. Musculus also another Protestant, doth testifie the same. Zuinglius said, that the Apostles did vse the same. Caluine saith, that this was vsed in the church aboue 1300. yeares a goe: Also Conradus Pellicanus the cheefe protestant at Tigur, did alleadge, that Tobias did allowe the auncient custome to sacrifice for the dead. Vrbanus Regius another great protestant saith, that Baruch the prophett did praye for the dead. Brentius saith, that the Christians would not haue praied for the dead, if they had not bene instructed by the preceptes of Christ and his Apostles. The said Vrbanus which was the cheefe instrument with Luther to sowe Lutheranisme in Sueth-land and in the Dukedome of Lumburge, *à parte operum in formula cautè loquendi,* when the Apostle reproued the Thessalonians for howlinge and cryinge after the manner of Gẽtiles for their dead, he tooke not awaye, the care or memorie for the dead, but confirmed the same. The same Vrbanus affirmeth that Luther was of this opinion sayinge, that it belongeth to Christian pietie, that wee should commend vnto Christe by deuout prayers, our Christian bretheren as it hath bene the custome of the church allwayes, withall the doctors and holie fathers thereof. The same Vrbanus further affirmeth in the place aboue cited

De locis communibus c. 19.

cited, that wee ought not to depart from the practise and beleefe of the fathers herein, vnlesse wee will contradict the word of God.

3. This Protestant citeth many fathers also to confirme his doctrine as S. Nazianzenus in the funerall oration vnto Cesarius his brother, concerninge his mother, and Gregorie Nissenus, Chrysost. homil. 69. S. Ambrose of the death of Theodosius Emperor, the councell of Affricke *cap. 8. S. Aug. confess. lib. 19.* which praid for his mother, and in the booke *de ciuitate Dei: cap. 9. & in libro, de cura pro mortuis agenda cap. 4. vid.* in the booke which he did write for the care wee should haue for the dead: *& in lib. de hæresibus hæresis 53. & in lib. de cura pro mortuis habenda cap. 1.* he writes that a certaine heretique did giue out that wee ought not to praie for the dead. *Damascenus in sermone de ijs,* which departed this life in faith saith, that the Apostles and disciples of our sauiour admonished vs, that in the dreadfull and liuinge Sacrament, wee should haue a speciall remembrance of the faithfull departed this life, and saith that this is the receaued and generall decree of the catholique church, and the obseruation and old custome of all christians, for the which are cited the bookes of the Machabees, *Dionysius Areopagita cap. vltimo ecclesiasticæ hierarchiæ.* S. Nazian. z S. Chrisostome S. Gregorie Nissen S. Athana:

*Idem locis communibus cap. 18 de purgator.*

*Idem prima parte.*

and S. Basill. The said Vrbanus allso verie earnestlie proued that the Apostles of Christ tanght the same, out of Tertulian, S. Athanasius and S. Ambrose. He declared allso that Asia, and Muscouia doe praie for the dead.

4. It is allso manifest that the Greekes doe praie for the dead, by the confession of the Greekes sent to the Lutherans of Germanie, by Hieremie Patriarch of Constantinople, *anno Domini 1579*. Did not Christ praie his father for Lazarus that was dead? Did not the widdowe of Naim praie vnto Christ for her child that was dead, although shee prayed for restoringe him vnto life, yet much more, for remission of his sinnes? doth not S. Iohn say. There is a sinne vnto deathe, there is another sinne allso not vnto death? of these as Oecumenus saith vppon that place. they which die in deadlie sinne, for them I say lett noe man praie. S. Augustine sayes, that the soule departes from our bodies in one of these three degrees. The first degree, is of those that departe perfect and good. The second of those that are imperfect and impenitent, the third of those that are in a meane betwixt both, neither altogether good, nor altogether badd. For the first wee neede not to praye, of whome it is said. *Cum dederit dilectis suis somnum ecce hæreditas Domini &c*. when it shall please God to giue the elect, reste and quiettnes, behold they possesse their inheritance

*Purgatory.*

*Io. 1. cap. vlt.*

*Aug. lib. de cura pro mortuis agēda*

ritance &c. I meane ſuch as are hollie in deede, either holye by their deathe as Martyres, or ſuch as otherwiſe in their liues ſhewe both to God and man extraordinarye holines and compleatt perfection, of them there are fewe in reſpect of thoſe; *Qui ducunt in bonis dies ſuos, & in puncto ad infernum deſcendunt*, that made themſelues ſlaues vnto the apparent, but falſe ſhewe of worldlie, and tranſitorie goodes, and in a moment they doe goe downe into euerlaſtinge damnation. For the ioy of an Hypocritt is meaſured by an inſtant, for which people wee may not praie: for our ſauiour ſaid they receaued their rewarde in this miſerable life with the richman. But for the other in the third rancke wee praie as S. Dioniſ. Areopag. ſaies. *Diuinus ſacerdos pro mortuis orans, &c.* the diuine prieſt prayinge for the dead, he praied for ſuch as liued holie, yet they hauing contracted ſome blemiſh by reaſon of their humaine infirmitie, are detained in purgatorie, and as S. Auguſtine ſayes, our ſuffrages proffitts them that are in a meane betwixt good and badd, of which kinde of people S. Paule ſaith, *ſaluus tamen fiet, ſed tamen per ignem*, he ſhalbe ſaued, but yet through fire. Accordinge to which S. Cyprian ſaith. *Aliud eſt miſſum non exire inde &c.* It is not all one beinge ſent to priſon neuer to depart thence vntill the laſt fardinge be

*Dyoniſius Areop. c. 7. eccleſ. hierar.*

*Aug. Euc. ca. 110. tom. 3.*

*1. Cor. 3. 15.*

*Cypr. Ep. 52.*

praied, and to receaue presentlie the reward of faith and vertue: it is not all one to be purged and clensed by the torments of a longe fire, and to haue all his sinnes whatsoeuer already refined & purged by sufferãce. And because wee doe not knowe certainlie the state of euerie one that departs this life, S. Augustine saith. *Pro mortuis siue altaris, siue orationum sacrificijs solemniter supplicamus, quamuis non pro quibus fiunt omnibus prosint.* For the dead wee make our supplications, aswell by the sacrifice of the alter, as by our prayers, althoughe euerie one receaues not proffitt thereby, but such as when they liued merited the same: but because wee doe not discerne what they be for whome wee ought to offer the same, none such as are regenerated, may be omitted, vnto whome this benefitt may or ought to be due: for it is better it should be superfluous vnto them, that receaues noe proffitt or harme therby, then it should be wanting vnto thẽ which may reape benefit by it.

*Aug. lib. de cura pro mortuis habenda.*

5. But let vs further see what other holie fathers say. S. Cyrill saith, let vs pray for all that departed amoungest vs. S. Iames saith. *Dominum oremus*, lett vs make our prayers to our Lord, that our parents and brethren which departed before vs, may rest in peace. Allso S. Clement of Rome saith, that the Deacon at Masse did praie for the dead. S. Athanasius saith. If the soules departed

*Cyrill Cathe mist 5. I. S Iacobi liturgia.*

*Clemens Romanus lib. 6 cõst. apost cap. 30.*

parted receaued noe benefitt of the ſacrifice of the bodie of Chriſt, it ſhould not be vſed for the commemoration of the dead, *de varijs quæſtionibus q. 39.* Tertulian allſo ſaith. *Oblationes pro defunctis, pro natalitÿs annua die facimus.* Wee make oblations for the dead and, doe obſerue their anniuerſarie dayes. S. Iohn Damaſcen hath theſe woordes: the diſciples and diuine Apoſtles of our Sauiour haue ordained, that in the pure and tremblinge miſteries which giue life, there ſhould be memorie of the faithfull departed, which the Catholique Churche euer obſerued and will obſerue vnto the end of the world. Paulinus affirmeth the ſame *epiſt. 31. lib. 3. cap. 34. Gregor. Nyſſ. oratione Cathecheſi. c. 8. Hier. Ioh. cap. vlt. in fine. Idem in Oſee. cap. 14. Hier. in Matth. ca. 3. Amb. in Pſal. 118. ſer. 3. ſer. 20. in fine, id. in Luc. cap. 12. Aug. in Enchi. cap. 67. Aug. de ciuitate lib. 21. cap. 13. & ſequentibus de Geneſ.* againſt the Manichees *lib. 21. cap. 20. lib. 8. quæſt. q. 1. Homil. 16.* and in other places. *S. Cyprian. li. 1. epiſt. 4. Euſeb. lib. 4. de vita Conſtantini cap. 71. Nicephorus lib. 8. cap. 26. Plat. in vita Sixti, S. Aug. ſer. 34. de verbis Apoſtol.* who boldly affirmed that it is not to be doubted, but that the dead are holpen by the prayers of the holie churche by the healthfull ſacrifice and almes that are giuen for the ſoules of the dead. And in another place he ſaith, wee ought not to omitt our ſuffrages, and prayers

*Tert. de Corona*

*Ioh Damaſ de fide oratione.*

*Paulinus.*

*Aug. lib. de cura pro mortuis.*

prayers for the dead.

*Purgatory.* 6. Laſtly the councell of Carthage doth cōfirme this trueth whoſe wordes be theſe. *Pœnitentes qui attentè leges pœnitentiæ exequuntur*: ſuch as are penitent for their ſinnes and performe the pennaunce that was enioyned vnto them; if by chance they dye either by ſea or land, when as otherwiſe wee cannot helpe them, lett vs remember them in our prayers, and ſacrifices. S. Auguſtine praid for his Mother, ſayinge: *Pro peccatis matris meæ deprecor te exaudi me &c.* I beſeech thee to pardon the ſinnes of my Mother by the cure of thy bleſſed woundes, which hanged vppon the Croſſe, & ſittinge at the right hand of God that thou make interceſsion for vs. *Aug. Confeß.* This is proued by Scripture. *Iſa. 4. Malach. 3. Math. 12. 1. Corinth. 3. Machab. 12. Pſal. 76. Luc. 11. Daniel. 4. Philip. 4. Eccle. 4. 6. 2 Reg 28. Pſal. 118. Marc. 12. Apoc. 5. Math. 5. 1. Ioh. 5. Apoc. 5. 3. 13.* This is allſo proued by ſoe manny apparitions of the dead, made vnto thoſe that were liuinge in this world, deſiringe them to praye for them, of which S. Gregorie makes mention in the 4. bookes of his Dialoges, and venerable Bede in his 5. booke cap. 13. cap. 14. and 15. allſo in his fourth booke. cap. 25.

*Eccleſiaſt. hiſt. gentis Anglor.*

Tou-

## *Touchinge the Popes Authoritie, in releasinge of soules out of purgatorie.*

## CHAPTER II.

1. THe learned deuines doe teache, that the Pope dothe, and lawfully may applie, vnto the soules departed by his keies, some parte of the churches treasure which consisteth of Christes satisfaction, and the satisfactions of other of his saincts, by which they that are departed, as they haue neede, may receaue benefitt: For the due vnderstāding whereof, there are two things; The one is, a sentence of absolution definitiue, pronounced vpon the person penitent; The second is, the recompence of the dept of sinne, remitted by the said absolution, through the application of the churches treasure, by the power of the officers keies: none of these two ioyntlie can euer be exercised vpon any person not subiect, though the one may. For absolution cannot properlie be giuen nor be fruitfully receaued by any man, not subiect to the geuers regiment. But the application of the treasure, may by the keies procure mercie for them, that be in neede (*per modum suffragij*) so that, the Popes doe not absolue any man departed absolutly, but only offeringe in the person *Indulgence.*

phecies and figures of the old lawe, and doth succeede the same. And euen as the paschall lambe beinge offered euerie yeare, did not take awaie the sacrifice of lambes that was offered euerie morninge and euenninge commaunded in Exodus, so neither Christ being bloody offered vpon the crosse takes not awaie the vnbloodie, continuall [illegible] sacrifice of the masse. And although that Christ is said to be offered from the beginninge of the worlde, [illegible] waye the externall act [illegible] nature, or of Moyses, but the passions of Christ [illegible] their vertue and force [illegible] bodie which is his [illegible] crifice, as they are said [illegible] gods presence. Much lesse taketh it away the externall and sensible [illegible] newe testament, which is a certaine sensible representation of Christes torments that the [illegible] Otherwise the church [illegible] should be is in a worse case, then [illegible] the lawe of Moyses, [illegible] to encreaase, ture, in which by [illegible] of the church, to they could represent Christs death and passion, which the church in the lawe of grace cannot doe, if yow take awaie from her this only sacrifice [illegible] the had bene depriued of that dignitie & excellecy of offering [illegible] the church in those two lawes were figured by quentlie [illegible] been more obscure [illegible] vpon that place.

Rof. con. Luth.

Col. 1.

Genes. 25.

plainly [illegible] who institutinge the forme of the euerlastinge sacrifice, as the first of all that offred an hoste vnto God, & the first that taught the same to be offered. The Church of Æthiopia hath these wordes in the Canon of the Masse related here by Salmeron (which he hath seene in printe) [illegible] *in tuam commemorationem. Nunc* [illegible] *mortis tue, & resurrectionis tue,* [illegible] *quod per hoc sacrificium* [illegible] *fecisti* [illegible] *standi in conspectu tuo.* Doe this in remembrance of me; now wee being mindfull of thy death, and of thy resurrection, [illegible] giue thee thancks for that thou [illegible] that wee stand in thie presence. The constitution of the Apostles haue these wordes. *Primus igitur natura pontifex* [illegible] *Christus, qui non sibi honorem arripuit, sed constitutus à patre &c.* The first Bishop by nature, is the only begotten Christe, which did not arrogate vnto him selfe the honour [illegible] but beinge appointed of the Father, which for our sakes became man, and offeringe vnto God a spirituall sacrifice, and vnto his Father, before his passion he commaundeth vs onlie to doe this.

30 A Moreouer our Lord by the worde (*facere*) doe [illegible] charged that they should consecrate and offer, take, receaue and dispense [illegible] God &c. For in the holie scripture, the worde [illegible] is taken for *sacrificare* [illegible]

*vide.*

*The masse of Æthiopia.*

*Salmeron in Canon.* [illegible]

*Clement. Romanus l. 8. const. cap. vlt. Hebr. 5.*

*Exod. 13. Leuit. 15.*

ſerue at the Alter accordinge to the ſcripture, muſt liue by the alter. S. Thomas ſaith that indulgence may proffit one two manner of wayes. Firſt principally and directly it proffits him that receaues the indulgence vid. when he doth that, for the which indulgences are graunted: as when he viſitts the ſepulcher of ſome Saincts. Secondarilie and indirectly the indulgences doe proffitt one, when for his ſake one performed that which was the cauſe of grauntinge the indulgence. But if the forme of the indulgēce be ſuch as whoſoeuer that will perfourme this or that, he that accompliſheth the ſame ſhall haue thē indulgence, he cannot transfer the fruit of the indulgence vnto another, becauſe he cannot applie the vniuerſall intention of the church by which all comon and vniuerſall ſuffrages are comunicated, and applied, but if the indulgence be of that fourme, that whoſoeuer doth this or that, he, for his father, or any other that he thinckes good, that is detained in purgatorie, ſhall haue ſo much indulgence, ſuch an indulgence is not onlie available for the liuinge, but alſo for the dead, for the church hath aſmuch power to conferr and beſtowe, the fruict of her comon ſuffrage vnto which, the indulgence doth relie, vppon the dead as vpō the liuing. thus far S. Thomas as aforſaid And ſoe ſaint Auguſtine ſaith, that the ſuffrages doe proffit thoſe that are in a meane

*D. Thom. Supple. 3. p. q. 61. artic. 10. ſcip. q ar. 1. q. 16. ar. 3.*

betwixt

betwixt good,& badd, but such as S. Thom. saith are in purgatorie: for the paines of purgatorie are to supplie the satisfaction which was not fully accomplished in this life, and soe the worke of one may satissie for another, whether he be dead or aliue, for as S. Gregorie saith, God doth change his sentence, but not his councell as may appeare of the Niniuites, Achab, and Ezechias, against whome Godes sentence beinge giuen, was changed and reuoked by his mercie.

*Greg. lib. moralium c. 23.*

*Whether it be against the lawe of God, to forbid Priestes to marrie: and whether vowes and votaries are rather the inuention of men, then the ordinance of God.*

## CHAPTER III.

IOuinian aboue 1000. yeares a goe, alleadged S. Paule, as protestants doe now saying, that time should come, when men erringe in faith, should prohibit marriadge: by which doctrine many Nunnes at Rome (as S. Hierom against Iouinian and S. Aug. in his booke affirmeth) were mislead and brake their vowes, and rann headlonge vnto all turpitude of sensualitie. But this text of holie scripture, is expounded alwell by those fathers, as by others, that he meant of such as should say, that mariadge in his owne nature should be euill

*1. Tim. 4.*

*Aug. lib. de hæresib.*

*Tertul. li. Præscrip. Chrys. 12. in 1. Tim. Irene. lib.*

Aug. heres. 40. — Hiero. contra Iouini. — Ele. 1. ep. 17. — Ber. serm. 60. in cãt. — 1. Cor. 7. — S. Ambr.

[illegible] Tatian, Mar- [illegible] with their disciples, Eu- [illegible] Priscillianists, [illegible] doth reuerence [illegible] the 7. Sacramẽts, [illegible] for they make noe [illegible] doth only for- [illegible] violatinge of [illegible] my bodie and bloode [illegible] alleadge against [illegible] let the [illegible] give place to the [illegible] it is better [illegible] but this is spoken of such as are free persons, and not of pro- [illegible] as all writers doe expound. Saint Gregorie saith: if they cannot [illegible] tenta- [illegible] their saluation, [illegible] the state of mar- riage, for it is written. *Melius est nubere quam vri,* it is better to marry then to burne. S. Ambrose vpon this place hath these woor- des: [illegible]

[illegible]

[illegible] ... Christ saith ... a Priest ... Melchisedech ... [illegible] ... therefore ... his sacred ... to forsake and leaue of what they haue solemnly promised, [illegible] priesthoode, so was he a figure [illegible]. But S. Mathewe saith, that the Apostles forsooke all and folowed Christ, yet our newe ghospellers forsoke Christ and tooke the worde onely vpon these wordes. *Melius est nubere quam vri*, better it is to marie then to burne. I would they would vse S. Paule his medecine against their burninge concupiscence. *Castigo corpus meum &c.* I chastice my bodie and I reduce my flesh in the seruitude of the spirite, least that preachinge pennaunce vnto others, I should become reprobate my selfe. Dauid also did vse the same, when he said: *Operui in ieiunio animam meum, & posui vestimentum meum cilicium.* I couered my soule with fastinge and my bodie with a heare cloathe: doe you but so, and yow shall haue godes grace to resiste all the occasions of the worlde, temptacions

1. Cor. 9.

Psal. 68.

of the deuill, and aluremented of the flesh as S. Paule had, vnto whome God said.
2.Cor. 12. *Sufficit tibi gratia mea*, it sufficeth to haue my grace, God is faithfull who will not suffer vs to be tempted aboue our strenght, for as Christ saith, the kingdome of heauen suffereth violence, and none can gett it, but by force: *nemo coronabitur &c.* none shalbe crowned vnlesse he shall fight lawfully; Therfore S. Gregorie saith. *Fortitudo iustorum est carnem vincere &c.* The fortitude of the iust, is to master his fleshe, to resiste the appetites of his proper will, to extinguish and despise the delightes of this life. I would they had taken example by the serpent, who to cast off her old skin fasteth three dayes, and then doth wreast her bodie through a narrowe hoale, and soe doth cast away the old rugged and withered skinne, and a newe presentlie doth growe, and so S. Paule bids vs to doe the like when he saith. *Induite nouum hominem*; put on the new man which was created accodinge to Godes Image in iustice and sanctitie of life; for he said in another place that our sanctification is the will of God, that we should abstaine from fornication, and that by the narrowe way of pennaunce wee must enter into life. And then might you saie with the said Apostle. *Omnia possum in eo qui me confortat.* I can doe all thinges in him that doth strenghten me; whosoeuer destroieth the temple

temple of our Lord, God will destroie him.
Moises spake vnto the Leuiticall priests, be
you holy, because your Lord God is holy;
be you cleane that carrie the vessells of our
Lorde.

4. Now the continencie of priestes is
plainlie proued by the lawe of God. *Qui* *Cor. 7.*
*sine vxore est sollicitus quomodo placeat Deo*, he
that hath a wife is carefull how to please her, and soe he is deuided. S. Paule saith,
It is good for a man not to touch a woman.
Our Sauiour saith, there are Eunuches
which gelde themselues for the kingdome *1. Cor. 8.*
of heauen. Wherfore it is good to be sole and
single wherby one may with greater libertie
pray vnto God, administer the Sacraments,
and be more liberall to the poore. For S. *1. Cor. 7.*
Paule willeth a Priest to keepe hospitalitie,
but his wife and children would not suffer
him that is weded to performe the same. S. *1. Timoth.*
Paule biddeth Timothy to keepe himselfe *4.*
chast, but the wife will saie. *Redde debitum*,
render coniugall debt. Saint Paule forbiddeth widdowes to marrie, that haue *1. Cor. 7.*
vowed chastitie. *Vouete & reddite*, vowe *Psal. 75.*
vnto God, and performe the same saith the
prophett. The priestes of the old lawe notwithstandinge that for speciall causes they
might marrie, for that priesthoode went *1. Para.*
then by succesion, and not by election, as *24.*
ours doth, yet duringe the tyme of their office in the temple, they were separated both
from

*Luc. 1.* [illegible]
*Exod. 11.* [illegible] lawfull for the [illegible]
*3. Reg. 19* [illegible] the Pascall lambe, vnlesse they [illegible]
[illegible]
*1. Reg. 21* [illegible] S. Basil
*Basil. ep.* [illegible]
*70. & 71* [illegible]
*Naz. ora* [illegible]
*de Arria* [illegible]
*nis.* [illegible]
*Optat. lib* [illegible] S. Hierom [illegible]
*6. in Per-* Chapter of saint Paule to Titus [illegible] alleadges
*menan.* that place saying [illegible] There
is so much difference betwene the [illegible]
*Aug. ser.* [illegible] Christ [illegible]
*37 ad fra-* [illegible] the body [illegible]. Which
*tres.* [illegible] S. Paule counseled [illegible]
[illegible]
[illegible] Corinth [illegible]
*Leo 1. ep.* riadge a certaine tyme for prayer sake [illegible]
*75.* [illegible] priests should alwayes abstaine,
because they are bound alwayes to praie
for the people, as S. Ambrose saith. And S.
Hierome saith, [illegible]
vnlesse she abstaine [illegible]
locke, [illegible] alwayes,
offer [illegible] alwayes,
[illegible] And S. Basil saith, that he
*Lib. 20.* [illegible] Melse-
*cap. 13.* chedus, [illegible] Apostates [illegible]
*contra* [illegible]
*Faustum.* [illegible] S. Paules wordes, saying [illegible]
Bishop must be the husband of one wife.

Whereof

[illegible] and saint Clement [illegible]

Hier. ad Ioui.

So Hieron. in epistola.

Psal. 109.

Hier. contra Ioui. lib. 1 c. 19

Conc. Cart. 2. cap. 2.

Italie, Fance, Spaine Greece & Asia in Egipt, & in al the east as may appeare by *Concilium. Eliberti: ca. 33. Epiph. in canpen. & in heres. 59. contra Catharos Hiero. contra vigil. cap. 1. Bibliander in pref. Epistolarũ Zuingl. & Oecolamp.*
*Cal. lib. 4. instit. c. 13* Caluine allso hath these woordes. *Fateor ab vltima memoria hoc fuisse obseruatum*, I confesse that was obserued from the beginninge, that they tied themselues by a vowe of continẽcie, who dedicated themselues to godes seruice, and this was obserued in the old tyme. *Martyr de votis pag. 490.* Peter martyr, another protestãt saith, that in the tyme of S. Clement of Alexandria, which was next vnto the tymes of the Apostles, that people professed chastitie and vowed continencie. *Magdeb. hist. Cent. 5 cap. 4.* Madeburgenses and Beza, *in prefatione noui testamenti principi codensi*, do wittnesse thus much.

6. Lastlie, the only cause why the protestantes would haue priests to marry is, because they thincke that it is impossible for them to liue chaste, and that wedlocke should be a remedie against luste, but filthie raginge concupiscence is not taken awaie or anny thinge abated, by the operation and execution thereof, but rather by his contrarie vertue, as may appeare, by a certaine apostate Priest, who fallinge vnto Lutheranisme obtained the encombencie of a parish church in Germanie and married a wyfe, whom within a litle after he murthered, for that his filthie luste was not satisfied therby, and

and that soe he might be more free to purchase another: but the murther being knowē and beinge demaunded what was the reason that he comitted such a wicked acte, he answered that the disordered appetites of luste amoungest the ghospellers, are not restrained by one wooman as yow may see by experience, that one vice is not taken away or restrained by another vice, but rather by his contrarie vertue. I would these ministers had vsed those meanes to bridle their filthie luste and ouercome the furious passion of fleashly pleasures as S. Paule and other holy Saincts did sayinge. *Castigo corpus meum & in seruitutem redigo carnem meam*; I chastice my bodie and I reduce my flesh into the seruitude of the spirite, or as Christe coūselled to geilde themselues for the kingdome of heauen, but forasmuch as they imbrace the wicked doctrine of Caluine, that it is a sinne for a man not to sinne, and in another place, that to restraine any desire that comes vnto a man, is to resist God and to sinne, for that God is the efficient cause of all euill woorks, this mortification and punishinge of the fleash cannot sounde well in their eares, whose doctrine & life is repugnant to mortification, religion, discipline, & all woorks of pennaunce.

*Surius.*

*Cal. lib. 1. instit. cap. 18.*

uation of God: of Daniell it is called *Iuge sacrificium*, the daylie and continuall sacrifice, a pure oblation: of Malachias, the sacrifice of Iuda and Hierusalem: the bloody lambe of S. Luke: of S. Mathewe, the oblation that should be offered at the altar: of the Apostle, it is tearmed our pasche, & the table of our Lorde: of S. Luc, the fraction or breakinge of the bread: and also in a liturgie of S. Andrewe it is called a lambe sayinge: I offer dayly a lambe vnto God which when it hath be eaten, it shall remayne whole and sounde. The councell of Nice calles it, the lambe that takes awaie the sinnes of the worlde. S. Clement calls it the pure and vnbloodie sacrifice. S. Dionysius the oblation of the liuely hoaste. S. Martialis, a sacrifice and a cleane oblation. Ireneus the newe oblation of the newe testament. S. Cyprian a trew & perfecte sacrifice. S. Athanasius, an vnbloodie immolation. Eusebius Cesar and S. Chrysostome, a dreadfull, terrible and euerlastinge sacrifice most honorable: others call it a singuler sacrifice, excellinge all the sacrifices that euer were. Others a true, vnbloodie vnspotted, perfect hoaste, our daylie sacrifice, our Lorde his lambe: S. Aug. the sacrifice of our price and redemption, the sacrifice of our mediator. S. Gregorie calls it the healthsome hoaste, the hoast of oblation: others call it the sacrifice of christians &c. with many such

*Malach. 1. Luc. 1. Matt. 5. Iud lib. 4. cap. 34. 1. cap. 5. 1. Cor. 10. Heb. 10. Act. 2. Cle. Const. Apost l. 8. cap. vlt. Dionys. Areop. cap. 3. de cælest. Hier. lib. 52. c. 56. in Ioan.*

epi

the power of priest-hoode, then those of Leuits. But you will peraduenture answere, that the office of priest-hoode is to offer sacrifice in spirit and truth. Whereto I replie, that the olde fathers also in the lawe of nature, and Moyses coulde so doe, and likewise euerie other person. If you take awaie this sacrifice, it is not true that Christ vpon the crosse is a priest according to the order of Melchisedec, but according to the order of Aaron, whose beastes and sacrifices were bloody, as that of Melchisedec was vnbloody in bread and wine. Againe, if you will haue no other priest, but Christ vpon the crosse, to be the onlie priest of the newe testament, and that there is no other priest or sacrifice, then Isaias is a lyar, and his prophesie is false, for in the ende of his prophesie he saide there should be new priests and Leuites, for he did not speake of the priests of the olde lawe, and in vaine should he speake of the newe priests if they should offer noe sacrifice. Did not S. Paul saie: For this cause I left thee in Crete, that thou shouldest reforme the thinges that are wanting & shouldest ordaine priests in the cities; Also he saith vnto Timothy, doe not neglect the grace which is in thee, which is giuen vnto thee by prophesie with the imposition of the handes of priest-hoode. S. Iames wisheth the sicke person to send for the priests,

*Obiection* *Answer.*

*Ioh. 11.* *Cyril li 7 cap. vlt.* *Aug. trac. 49. in Ioannem.* *Luc 17.* *Aug. de vera & falsa pœnit c. 19. & ser. 8. de verbis Domini.*

[illegible]

*Ad Titum. 1.*

*1. Tim. 4.*

*Iacob. 5.*

church to absolue all sinners which trulie repent and beleue in him, of his great mercie forgiue thee thine offences , and by his authoritie comitted vnto me, I absolue thee from all thy sinnes In the name of the father the sonne and the holy Ghost. S. Aug. saith. Some thinckes that it is enough for them to confesse their sinnes only vnto God which knowes the secreattes of euerie ones harte, because either for shame or for some other cause, they would not vnfould their offẽces vnto the priestes , vnto whome God haue giuen sufficient authoritie to discerne betwixt leper and leper, but I would not haue yow be deceaued or confounded, for confessinge thy sinnes before the viccar of our Lord. The same he confirmed further saying. Let no man say I confesse before God secreatlie, God knowes my harte, who will pardone me, if that be soe, saith he, in vaine it is said: whose sinnes soeuer yow forgiue they shalbe forgiuen, in vaine also the keies of the kingdome of heauen are giuen to the churche. S. Ambrose also refellinge the heresie of the Nouatians, which taught that God neuer gaue power to any to remit sinnes saith. God bid vs to obey his ministers, and by doinge soe wee honour God &c.

*Aug. lib. 2. de visitatione infirmorũ cap. 4. & lib. 1. c. 2*

*Aug. lib. 50. homil 49.*

*Amb. li. 1. de pœna cap. 2.*

3. This is also proued by S. Chrisostome who said that trewe pennaunce doth cause a poore sinner to suffer all thinges willinglie: in his harte, perfect contrition,

*Chrysost. homil 29. ad populum.*

in

in his mouthe confession, in his workes all humanitie: for, saith he, this is a most fruictfull pennaunce, for by what meanes wee haue offended God, by that meanes also wee should be reconsiled vnto him vid. by our harte by contrition, by our mouthe by confession, by our acte throughe satisfaction. Holy councells also as the councell of Florence, haue determined this truth, and all the fathers of the church as, *S. Cyprian Epistola 10. Epistola 15. Epistola 1. 62. cap. 52. Hugo aduersus luciferanos Cyp. lib. de lapsis 15. Orig. in leuit homil. 2. & psal. 32 Aug. Epistola 54. Socrates lib. 5. cap. 19. Zozo. lib. 7.*

4. Againe, by takinge away from the christians the only bridle (which is this sacramentall confession) that should curbe and restraine them from their wickednes, they giue occasiō that they runn headlong to all dissolution & wanton exercise; which the protestantes of Germanie perceauing by experience to be true, they requested the Emperor Charles the 5. being then at Norimberge, that by his imperiall authoritie he *in 4. d. 18.*
would cause cōfession againe to be brought *q. 1. ar. 1.*
in: wherat Sotus a learned diuine beinge with the Emperor, did aunswere laughing, and said: if by the lawe of God, men are not bound to vnfould their sinnes to a prieste, nor by that lawe the priest can absolue, as they said, how can they be compelled therunto by the precept of man, for by hu-

maine precept noe man will reueale his secreat ſinnes to any man?

5. Pacianus anſwereth the heretiques that ſay God only remitteth ſinnes. *Sed & quod per ſacerdotes ſuos facit, ipſius poteſtas eſt:* and a little after he ſaith, that as not only the Apoſtles doe baptize but alſo their ſucceſſors, ſoe not only they remitt ſinnes but alſo their ſucceſſors. *Paulinus in vita Ambro.* S. Ambroſe hearinge confeſsions, wept as the penitentes confeſſed their ſinnes, and by weepinge moued them to contrition. Tertulian tells, how the chriſtians in his time kneeled to the prieſts for remiſsion. *S. Hieronimus epiſt. ad Heliodorum.* God forbid that that I ſhould ſpeake ill of prieſts who ſucceedinge to the Apoſtles, by their holy mouth, doe make the body of Chriſte, by whome wee alſo are chriſtians, who hauing the keies of the kingdome of heauen, doe in ſome ſorte iudge vs before the day of iudgment. Vict. 2. perſ. Vand. recounteth how whē the prieſts were baniſhed by the Arriās the catholique people cried out moſte lamentably, to whome doe yow leaue vs miſerable, whiles you goe to your crownes? who ſhall baptiſe theſe little ones, with the fountaines of euerlaſtinge water? who ſhall giue vs the guift of pennaunce and free vs from the baundes of ſinne by the indulgence of reconſiliation? becauſe to yow it is ſaid. Whatſoeuer yow ſhall looſe vpon earth

ſhall

ſhall be looſed in heauen. Our Sauiour gaue to his Apoſtles & conſequentlie to S. Peter power to remitte ſinnes, whoſe ſinnes yow forgiue &c. and ſeinge the Pope is the law-full ſucceſſor of S. Peter, it followeth that he ſucceded to him in his authoritie. And although the heretiques doe aunſwere that this power was giuen them by baptiſme and preachinge, yet it ſufficeth not, becauſe this pouer was giuen them in diſtinct places from the place alleadged, to witt in the laſt place of S. Mathewe, and S. Marcke, his ghoſpell: and although by baptiſme & preachinge the Prieſte in ſome ſorte remitteth ſinnes, yet he cannot remitt the ſinnes comitted after baptiſme, which cannot be reiterated, and neither by baptiſme or preachinge can he be ſaid to retaine ſinnes.

*Whether faſtinge from one ſorte of meate, more then from another, or for to vſe any obſeruation therin, be ſuperſtitious accordinge as proteſtants doe affirme.*

## CHAPTER V.

1. AErius the heretique, as S. Auguſtine and S. Epipha. ſay, defended this doctrine againſt the catholique churche, as Luther and his followers doe now a daies, for that, ſay they, they would not ſubmitt themſelues

*Aug lib. de heres. cap. 33. Epiph. heres.*

ues to any thinge that the churche comaunded. They alleadge scriptures for themselues, as the wordes of our Sauiour, not that which entreth into the mouth defileth a man &c. Aso they alleadge for themselues for breakinge of fasts the 14 chapter of S. Paule: alsо S. Paule to Timothy. In the last tymes men shall departe from the faith, attendinge to spiritts of error and doctrine of deuills, speakinge lies in hipocrisie, forbiddinge to marrie and abstaine from meates which God created &c. To all which I aunswere with S. Augustine, that catholiques doe not abstaine from certaine meates, for that they esteeme any meat vncleane, either by creation, or by iudaicall obseruation, but they abstaine for chastisinge of their concupiscence. It is sinne only which properly defileth man, and meates of themselues or of their owne nature doe not defile, but by accident they make a man to sinne, as the disobedience of Gods comaundements, or of our superiors who forbidd some meates for certaine times and causes, is a sinne: as the apple which our first parents did eate, though of it selfe it did not defile them, yet beinge eaten against the precepte, it did defile, for neither flesh nor fish of it selfe doth defile, but the breach of the churches precept is it which defileth. And as for S. Paule, he speaketh as S. Chrsostome said, of the Manichees, Eucratites

*Matt. 15. Mar. 7.*

*Aug. lib. de morib. Ecc. Cath. cap. 33.*

*Genes. 3. Chrys. homil 12. in 1. Timoth.*

tites and Marcionistes, and S. Ambrose addeth vppon this place the Patritians: also S. Epiphanius, S. Hierom S. Augustine and generally all antiquitie affirme the same, both of them, and also of the heretiques called Apostolici, Ebiointes and the like, whose heresie about marriadge was, that to vse the act of matrimonie was of Sathan.

*Epiph. here 45. 26. 61. Hier. contra Iouin cap. Aug heres. 25.*

2. Touching the prohibition of meates, or vse of certaine creatures, made to be eaten, there were many opinions, the first was of Philosophers, Pithagoras, Empedocles, Apollinaris, Porphirius and others, who condemned the vse of meates, as of beastes, for that they thought that al beastes had reasonable soules, and that they passed from bodie to bodie. The second was of heretiques which condemned the vse of these meates, for that they said they were created of the diuill, and not of God, as Marcion, Tatian, and Manichees: against whome S. Paule his meaninge is to be construed in the said place of Timothy, as it is declared in the Canons of the Apostles, and in the councells of Ancira, Gangrensis, the first of Toledo, and Braga, as also by Epipha. The third opinion touchinge prohibition of meates was, of certaine christians in the beginninge of the churche, and after the publishinge of the ghospell, who thought that christians were bound to abstaine from such meates as were prohibited by the old lawe,

*1. Tim. 4.*

*Epiph. heres. 42. 47.*

lawe, of which opinion S. Paule ſpeakes in the 14. chapter to the Romaines, which he diſproues aſwell there, as in the Actes of the Apoſtles. Soe that by theſe places of ſcripture miſaplied, they goe about to aboliſh all faſtinge, which our Sauiour and all holie people as many as euer were in this world did obſerue, and begon and finiſhed their heroicall workes withall: for our Sauiour faſted 40. dayes, S. Iohn did abſtaine from all delicate meates and drinckes, the Recabites and Nazaretts are comended in holy ſcripture for their faſtinge, alſo the Niniuites for their faſtinge were pardoned, S. Iohns diſciples faſted, and Chriſt ſaid to his diſciples, that they ſhould obſerue the ſame after his departure from them.

*Act.* 10. 15. *Matt.* 4. *Mat.* 3. 11 *Mar.* 1. *Num* 6. *Iere.* 35. 14. *Iona* 3. *Mat.* 9. 14

3. Now the difference of the faſt of the churche of God, and of heretiques, Saint Auguſtine declareth and Theodoretus, alſo S. Bernard, *ſupra Cant. ſer. 66. Epipha. in lib. de compend. doctrinæ catholicæ*, for he ſaith that in the church there was great difference of faſtinge, accordinge either to the vowe or mortification of euerie one: ſome faſted frō all kinde of fleaſh, ſome faſted from eggs and all white meates, ſome from any thing that ſhould be ſodd and from all kinde of fruictes, for before the flood noe wine was droncken, noe fleaſh was eaten. And all the poore people either in the old lawe or in the lawe of grace, did obſerue this faſte. Moiſes

*Aug. li.* 5. *contra Fauſtum cap.* 5. *Theod. in Epito. diuinorum decretorū c. de abſt.*

and

and Elias fasted 40. dayes ether of them. Samuell was comaunded he should drincke noe wine. All the priestes that were imploied in the misteries of the church, were forbidden to drinke any wine, or any thinge else that should distemper them. Iudith, Hester, Daniell, and the Machabees, by their fastinge haue archeeued and perfourmed those worthie exploites which are registred in holie scriptures. Againe wee are bid by Ioell to turne to God by fastinge. *Ioel. 1.* David said that he couered his soule with *Psal. 68.* fastinge. The iustification of a christian in this life as S. Augustine saith, is fastinge, *Aug. in* prayers and almesdeedes: and therfore the *Psal. 4.2.* catholique church, as she ordained certaine times of prayers, soe shee ordained certaine dayes and certaine tymes of fastinge, not without significant misteries correspondent to euerie time.

4. Also she hath made a prohibition of certaine meates to tame the wantones and exorbitāt luste of our fleashly inclinations, disposinge and impellinge the spiritt to yeld vnto her consent, aswell by the suggestion of Sathan, as her owne delectation, and so to make our poore soule which otherwise ought to be the harbenger to intertaine the inspiration of the holy ghost, to receaue the suggestion of the diuil, & her filthy delectation, she I say hath prohibited certaine meates, therby to deliuer the spiritt from the stinge

ſtinge of the filthie motions of concupiſcence and ſenſualitie, and to humble the ſame vnto the lawe of God and rule of reaſon. S. Auguſtine ſaith, the church doth with great reaſon abſtaine from certaine meates certaine tymes, as Dauid, *cum mihi moleſti eſſent &c.* when thoſe carnall motions did vexe me, I did weare haire cloathe and did humble my ſoule with faſtinge. S. Paule when he was attatched with theſe carnall motions, he praied vnto God three tymes, he chaſtiſed his bodie, and yet he was the elected veſſell of God. And in another place he ſaid; let vs exhibit our ſelues as the miniſters of God in watchinges, faſtinges and chaſticements, for ſuch ſaith he as are the members of Chriſt, they crucifie the fleſh with the vices and concupiſcence thereof: our Sauiour alſo ſaid, that notwithſtanding the Apoſtles ſhould be repleniſhed with the holie ghoaſte, yet they ſhould faſt. He ſaid alſo that certaine diuills are ſo terrible to offend, and ſoe dreadfull to tempte vs, that they cannot be ouercome but by faſtinge and praier, and therfore the Angell ſaid vnto Tobias, that praier with faſtinge is good, and Daniell by faſtinge did propheſie ſoe many things to come of the militant churche.

*Aug. cont. Fauſt. Manich.* — *Pſal. 34.* — *2. Cor. 6.* — *Gal. 5.* — *Matt. 9.* — *Luc 5.* — *Act. 13.* — *Matt. 7.* — *Daniel. 9*

5. He is a bad patiēt that doth not abſtaine from certaine meates certaine times, accordinge to the rule and preſcripte order of his

his corporall phisition, concerninge, his bodilie disease: and is not he a bad christian that doth not obey the comaundemēt of the church & his ghostlie phisition touchinge the spirituall sicknesse of the soule? and yet such is the protestant who is soe fleashlie giuen, that he would not abstaine his carnall appetites from fleash vpon good friday. A certaine Irishman beinge sent ouer by the Lord deputie of Ireland, to a great noble man in England with grehounds, the said noble man hauinge asked of him what meate those grehounds were wont to eate, and the man hauing told him certaine distinctions of meate, the noble man said, that by that obseruarion of diett, they were papists doggs; the Irishman said, they were as good protestants doggs as any were in all Ingland, for said he, they will not refraine from any flesh vppon good fridaie. Wherein these heretiques imitate Aerius, who would not haue the christians to obserue any time of fastinge, as S. Epiphanus said, and therfore by him and others condemned for an heretique, as also Iouinian for that occasion, was condemned for an heretique by S. Hierome.

*Amb. lib. de Helici & ieiun. Cyp. de ieiun. & tentat. Hier. li. 1.*

6. But wee ought not to transgresse the the bondes and decrees of our auncestors and elders, therfore wee ought not to followe Luther, who said he would not faste because as he said the Pope biddeth the same.

But,

*Hieron. Epist. de consecrat. dub. 5. Can. 68. 19. Mogunt. cap. 35. Tollet. 8. cap. 9.*

But it is the discipline and custome of the vniuersall church to fast the lent, the aduents, the eues of the Apostles, and fridaies and Saterdaies, and this from the begining. So the Canons of the Apostles doe teach, and holie councells as Gangrenie, Mogunt. and the councell of Tollet, which excommunicated all such as would despise the ecclesiasticall constitutions touchinge fasting, or that without ineuitable necessitie should eate flesh in lent time: the prophett confirminge the same, *solemnize and institute a faste,* wherin the christians ought to obey & beleue the church according to the saying of S. Athanasius, who hath thies wordes.

*Ioel. 2.*

*S. Athan. lib. ad Virgines post initiū.*

If anny will come and say vnto yow, doe not fast often, least yow should be more feble and weake, doe not beleeue them nor harcken vnto them, for the enemie of mankinde doth make an instrument of them to whisper and suggest thies thinges, remēber that which is written, when the 3. children, Daniell and other were brought in captiuity by Nabuchodonosor kinge of Babilon, it was comaunded that they should eate of the meate that was prepared for the kinges bord, and that they should drincke of his wyne, Daniell and the other 3. boies, would not be polluted or defiled with the kinges table: but they said vnto the euenuche who had charge of them, giue vnto vs of the rootes of the earth: vnto whome the euenuch said,

ſaid, I feare the king, which ordained and appointed meate for yow, leaſt that your countenãce ſhould appeare and ſeeme more leane and pale then that of the other boies, which are fedd at the kings boord, and ſoe ſhould puniſh me, vnto whome they did ſaie, trie your ſeruants tenn dayes and giue vnto vs of the rootes of the earth, and he gaue vnto them pulſe to eate, and water to drinke, and brought them before the kinge, and they ſeemed more beautifull then the other boyes which were nouriſhed by that kings royall meate. Doe yow ſee what faſtinge doth? it heales diſeaſes, and drieth diſtillations of the bodie, it chaſeth awaie diuills, expelleth wicked thoughts, makes the mind clearer, it purifies the hart, it ſanctifies the bodie, it bringes a man into the throne of God; and leaſt that yow ſhould thincke that this is raſhlie ſpoken, you haue teſtimonies of this in the ghoſpell pronounced by our Sauiour, when the diſciples did aske how vncleane ſpiritts ſhould be caſt forth, our Lord did anſwere, this kind is not caſt forth but by praiers and faſting therfore faſting is the food of Angells, and whoſoeuer vſeth the ſame, he is thought to be of an angelicall order: thus farr S. Athanaſius.

*Whether the Protestant assertion be true, which affirmeth that generall councells can erre.*

## CHAPTER I.

1. WHen anie controuersie either of state or the publike weale doth rise in any comō welth, the princes with all the state thereof assemble together, and whatsoeuer is ennacted and decreede by them, the rest of the subiectes must obserue and obey the same. Soe in any controuersie of religion, when the cheefe pastors and prelates of the church who haue more power, and authoritie of God then all the princes of other common wealthes, beinge assisted by his blessed spiritt, whatsoeuer they haue decreede for the good of the churche and the weale publike of Christendome, their subiectes (if they be of Christe his flocke) ought to submitt themselues to their definition and determination. Soe in the actes where the first christian councell was held, and afterwardes in euerie age as occasion serued, the councell of Chalcedon, and the six generall councells, and S. Celestine the Pope auerreth, that generall councells are by manifest declaratiō shewed by Christ in these wordes Math: 15. *Whensoeuer two or three*

*Acto 15. Chal. in epist. ad Leonē & 6. Synodus act. 17. Celest. papa epist ad Conc. Eph. Tolet. 3.*

*three shalbe gathered together in my name, there I shalbe in the middest of them*. The Apostles which were replenished with the holy ghoaste, did celebrate the first councell by the inspiration thereof, when they said. *It seemeth good vnto the holie ghoaste and to vs.* *Acto.15.*

2. There are four sortes of councells, some whereof be generall, some nationall, some prouinciall, and some diocesiall. Of the three formest S. Augustine makes mention, of the laste the councell of Tollet. The generall councells are such as when all the Bishopps and prelates of the whole world, vnlesse they be lawfully letted, doe assemble, and the Pope or his legate ought to be President. Nationall, is when the Prelates of one kingdome and the Primate and Patriarche of that kingdome doth assemble together. Prouinciall is of one Prouince. Diocesiall, is of one Diocesse. General councells approued are reckned 18. in number. The firste is of Nyce, which was celebrated from the yeare of our Lord 328. vnto the yeare of our Lord 330. which was the 15. of Siluester the Pope, and the 20. of Constantine the Emperor, in which there were 318. Bishopps. The second councell of Constantinople, which was celebrated against Macedonius that denied the deitie of the holie ghoaste. S. Damasus beinge Pope and Theodosius the great Emperor. There were 105. Bishopps and 4. Patriarches, Nectarius of Constan- *Aug. li. 2. de bapt.* *Prosper in chronico.*

Constantinople, Timotheus of Alexandria, Miletius of Alexandria and Cyrillus of Hierusalem. Anno Domini 383. The 3. of Ephesus, Celestinus beinge Pope and Theodosius the yonger Emperor, Bishopps 200. Patriarches. 3.vid.S. Cyrill. of Alexandria that was the Pope his Attourney, Iohn of Antioche, Iuuenall of Hierusalem, against Nestorius Bishopp of Constantinople Anno 434. The 4. of Calcedon against Eutiches, Leo the first beinge Pope and Matianus Emperor 454. accordinge the computation of Mathewe Palmer, Bishopps there were 630. The 5. of Constantinople Vigilius being Pope and Iustinian Emperor. The 6. of Constantinople Agatha beinge Pope, Constantine the 4. Emperor Anno 681. against those that held one nature only in Christe. The 7. of Nice. Adrian beinge Pope against Imadge breakers: *Anno Domini 781.* in which there were Bishopps 360. The 8. of Constantinople Adrian the 2. beinge Pope and Basilius Emperor: *Anno Domini 87.* The 9. of Lateran Celestine the 2. being Pope and Harrie the 5. Emperor, wherin there were 900. Bishopps Anno 1123. for the recouering of the holy land. The 10. Lotherius 2. wherin there were a thowsand Bishopps Anno 1237. Innocentius beinge Pope and Lotherius the Emperor. The 11. of Lateran Alexander the 3. Pope and Fredericke the first Emperor for the reformation of the church against

*Prosper in Chron. Socrates lib. 7.*

*Paulus Diaconus in vita eiusdem.*

*Ibid. lib. Rom. rer.*

against Waldenses Anno 1558. The 12. of Lateran against many heresies, Innocentius the 3. being Pope, and Fredericke the 2. Emperor for the recoueringe of the holie land. The 13. of Lyons against the Emperor Fredericke the 2. Innocentius the 4. beinge Pope, and for the recoueringe of the holie lande. The 14. of Lyons wherin there were a thowsand fathers amoungest which there were 500. Bisshopps *Anno Domini 1274.* against the errors of the Greekes, Gregorie 5. beinge Pope and Rodolph Emperor. The 15. of Viena Clement the 5. Pope and Henry the 7. Emperor against many heresies. Bisshopps there were 300. Anno 1311. The 16. of Florence against the errors of Greece Eugenius the 4. & Albert Emperor 1489. The 17. of Lateran against scisme in the time of Iulius 2. Leo 10. & Maximilian Emperor. The 18. of Trentt which was begon Anno 1545. ended 1563. against the heresies of Luther, Caluine, and others in the time of Paulinus 3. Iulius 3. and Pius the 4. Charles the 5. and Ferdinand Emperors. There were present 6. Cardinales 4. Legates 3. Patriarches 32. Archbisshopps 208. Bisshopps; But all heretiques refuse generall councells as the Protestants doe, and as the councell of Trent saith, noe otherwise then wicked theeues refuse the triall of indifferent iurie.

3. But we say that the holy councells of Gods church, lawfully assembled by S.

Peters successors not only by their personall presence, but allso by their legates and substitutes in the definition of faith or good manners cannot erre. For when our Sauiour said, whensoeuer two or three shalbe assembled together in my name, there I wilbe in the middest of them, he added afterwardes, of a man that is incorrigible tell the church thereof, and if he will not heare the church, let him be as an ethincke or publican I meane without faith and without grace. He added moreouer in that chapter, whatsoeuer yow shall binde in earth shalbe bound in heauen, and if two or three being lawfullie assembled together in Christs name, Christ be in the middest of them (vid.) to assist them by his councell and light of vnderstandinge, in those things that are necessarie for them: how much more all Bishopps and Prelates which God hath appointed to gouerne and rule his churche shall obtaine of God knowledge and vnderstandinge for that function? This argument the councell of Calcedō did vse in an Epistle to Leo the Pope, saying. Our Sauiour did promise to send the holie ghoast that should teach the Apostles all trueth, and that he meant allso the same to the successors of the Apostles he said, that the holie spirite shall remaine in his churche for euer, but the holie ghoast doth not teach the Bishopps in priuate or disioyned, therfore when they

*Matt.* 18

*Concil. Chalc. act.* 6 *con act* 17. *Io.* 16. *Io.* 14.

be

be gathered together: and therfore they say it pleaseth the holie ghoaste and vs, which holie ghoaste, is noe lesse necessarie for the conseruation of the churche nowe, then in the begininge for the fondation thereof, and therfore our Sauiour saith. I wilbe with yow vnto the consumation of the world, and the gates of hell shall not preuaile against the church, which as S. Paule saith, is the firmament and piller of truethe.

*Mat. vlt.*

*1. Tim. 3.*

4. The generall councell representeth the vniuersall church, as the assemblie that was made by Salomon in the Temple, represented the whole church of Ierusalem, but the vniuersall church cannot erre, therfore the generall councells cannot erre. For Atha. S. Epipha; Euseb. S. August. doe call the generall councells the congregation of the whole world, and the consent of the vniuersall churche. All such places of scripture as doe proue that the Pope cannot err in the definition of faith, proues also that the generall or nationall councell assembled by his authority cannot erre. Also such places of scripture as proues, and teaches that wee ought to reuerence Bishopps, as Pastors, to heare them as maisters, followe them as captaines, he that heareth yow heareth me &c. obey your rulers, be subiect vnto them, and imbrace their doctrine, with many such places; all which doe argue that they cannot deceaue vs, or if they doe, wee

*3. Reg. c. 8. Athan. in epist. de Synodis Arimin. & Seuleuciæ & ep. ad Episcopos Affricanos. Epiph. in fine Ancorat. Euseb. lib. 3. de vit. Const. Aug. li. 3. cont. Donatist. c. 18 Ephes. 4. Act. 20. Luc. 10. Hebr. 13. 1. Tim. 3. Tit.*

may attribut the blame to our Sauiour that bids vs to obey them, and imbrace their doctrine.

*Atha. epi. Epist. Epiph. heres. 77. Aug. 162. Nemo ca. de summa trinit. & fide catho. Gela. ep. ad Episc. Sardinia.*

5. This same is proued by the fathers, that the difinition of a generall councell is the last iudgment of the church, from which there is noe appellation, as Athana. and Epiphanius and others with S. Augustine doe affirme, and soe Leo the Pope requested the Emperor Martianus, saying that the definition of the generall councell should neuer be brought in question, which the said Martianus established by lawe. The same also Gelasius the Pope decreed in the councell of Ephesus *circa finem*, and in the councell of Calchedon *Act 5. Canone vlt.* Moreouer the fathers and all councells doe teach, that they are excomunicated, and ought to be countted heretiques, that doe not rest themselues vpon generall councells, and therfore all generall councells doe pronoũce Anathema, I meane the sore censure of excommunication against such as doe contradict the finall decree of generall councells as Athanasius doth wittnesse of the coũcell of Nice, and soe it is in all other councells. Grego. Nazianz. doth write when the Apolinaristes denied that they were not heretiques, and that they were receaued in a catholique councell, said let them shewe this and wee wilbe contented. S. Leo writinge to the emperor Leon said, they ought not to be

*Athan in epist. ad Episcopos Afri æ. S. Gregor. Nazianz. in epistola priori ad Clidoniũ. Leo epist. ad Anatolium.*

be accounted catholique that doe resiste the councell of Calcedon. And soe he writes the like to Anatolius: and S. Basil writes that they ought to be suspected of heresie, that doe cal in question the determination of the councell of Nice. S. Augustine did excuse S. Cyprian of heresie, because noe generall councell defined any thinge to the contrary towchinge the baptisme of heretiques. Also S. Gregorie pronounced excommmunicatiõ against all that would not receaue the decree of generall councells. Constantine the great in his epistle to the churches, called the decree of the councell of Nice, celestiall preceptes. Athanasius also said that the decree of the church was the diuine precept which should remaine for euer. S. Cyrill calles it the diuine, iuste, and holie oracle. S. Leo saith that the Canons thereof, were ordained by the holie ghoast, and that the councell of Calcedon was assembled by the holy spiritt. S. Gregorie also saith that he reuerenceth the first 4. generall councells, as the 4. Euangelistes. Nicholaus the first also saith, that the decrees of generall councells are inspired by the holy ghoast. S. Ambrose doth affirme that wee should rather die, than wee should departe from the definitions of generall councells. I will, saith he, followe the decree of the councell of Nice from the which neither death nor sword shall separat me. S. Hillarie suffred banishment for the faith

*Basil. ep. 78.*

*Aug. li. 1. de bap. ca. 18.*

*Greg. li. 1. epist. 24.*

*Apud Euseb. l. 3. de vit. Const.*

*Atha. ep. ad Episc. Africanos.*

*Cyrill. l. 1. de trinit.*

*Leo epist. 53. ad Anatoliũ & 54 ad Martianũ & ep. 37. ad Leonẽ.*

*Aug. Gre. lib. 1. ep. 24 Nice. epist. ad Michaelẽ.*

*Ambros. epist. 32.*

*Hilar. in fine lib de Synod. Victor. in libris trib. de persec Vandalic Hier. lib. cont. Luciferanos.*

faith of the councell of Nice. Victor Africanus describeth many worthy martires which suffred for the decree and definition of the faith sett downe and explicated in the councell of Nice. S. Hierom also speakinge of Athanasius and S. Hillarie and other holy confessors saie. How could they doe any thinge against the councell of Nice, for the which they suffred banishment.

6. This is proued by reason, for first if the generall coũcells should err, ther should be noe certaine or setled iudgment in the church, by which controuersie should be determined and descided, and by which the vnitie and concord of the church should be preserued, for which generall councells were ordained. Secondly, if there were not an infallible iudgment of these generall councells, then the Arians had not bene condemned for heretiques for sayinge the councell of Nice did erre, nor Macedonius for an heretique for sayinge the councell of Chalcedon did err, nor Nestorius for an heretick for sayinge the councell of Ephesus did err, nor Eutiches for sayinge the councell of Chalcedon did erre. Thirdly, wee should haue noe certaintie of many bookes of the holie scriptures, as of S. Paule to the Hebrewes, the 2. epistle of S. Peter, the third of S. Iohn S. Iames his epistle, S. Iude and the Apocalipes, they beinge called in question vntill the trueth of them was made knowen

knowen by generall councells.

*That the catolique church, in those thing shee doth propound to the christians to beleeue, whether they be contained in the Scriptures or not, cannot erre.*

## CHAPTER II.

THis is proued by scripture, for that the church of Christe is the firmament and piller of truethe, the spouse of Christe, the holly cittie, a fruitfull vineyarde, a highe mountaine, a direct way, the only doue, the kingdome of heauen, the bodie of Christe, and multitude vnto whome the holie ghoaste is promised, is gouerned of Christe beinge her head, and of the holy ghoast beinge her soule, as it is sett downe by S. Paule, saying. *He gaue him as a head aboue euerie church which is his bodie.* And in another place he said, *one head and one spirite*, and he said as the husbād is the head of the wife, soe allso Christ is the head of his church, for if the church had bene impeached of error, that imputation should be laide on Christe and the holie ghoaste, therfore Christ did instruct her by his said holie spirite, sayinge the spirite of trueth shall teach yow all trueth. Againe wee are bounde vnder paine of excommunication to beleue the church in all things, as may appeare

*Ad Tim. 3*
*Ephes. 5.*
*Apoca. 21*
*Psal. 79.*
*Isa. 2.*
*Matt. 13.*
*1. Cor 12.*
*Ephe. 1.*
*Ephe. 4.*
*Ioh. 16.*

*Matt. 18.* appeare by S. Math. *If he will not heare the church, let him be vnto you as an ethnick and a publican.* Further more wee say, that the church is holie, both in her profession and in the assertion of her faith, therfore christian profession ought to containe nothinge but that which is trewe and holie touching faith. Lastlie, the fathers in all their doubtes and controuersies towching faith and religion, did submitt themselues to the arbitrement of the church which they would not doe if they thought the church did err, for S. Augustine saith, it is an insolent madnesse to dispute against any thinge that the vniuersall church decreede. And in another place he saith. Wee haue the trueth of holy scriptures when wee doe that which pleaseth the vniuersall churche. And our Sauiour saith, whosoeuer heareth yow heareth me &c. whatsoeuer they comaund yow doe it &c.

*Aug. epi. 118. & l. 1. contra Crescentiũ cap. 33.*

*Luc. 10.*
*Matt. 23.*

*Whether Catoliques are to be charged with arrogancie, for thinkinge that their church cannot faile.*

## CHAPTER III.

1. WEe ought not to be cõuinced of arrogancie to affirme that Christe did not lie when he said, that the gates of hell should not preuaile against his churche. Heauen

*Matt. 16.*

Heauen and earth ſhall paſſe, but his wordes ſhall not paſſe, what woorde but that which is vniuerſally preached by the catholique churche, when he ſaith behold I am with yow to the worldes ende. The ſpiritt of trueth faileth not for euer, Chriſt praieth that the faith of Peter ſhould neuer faile, ſhe is his ſpouſe, and the kingdome of heauen, wherfore ſhould ſhee then faile beinge the piller of truethe? ſhee cannot faile ſhee beinge his wife, his doue, his kingdome, his portion, his vineyarde, his inheritance, his dwellinge howſe, for the which he ſuffred his paſsion, he died and ſhed his pretious blood ſhee cannot faile.

*Matt. 24. Matt. 28. Ioh. 14. Ephes. 5. 1. Tim. 1.*

2. This was a cheefe argument by which S. Chriſoſtome did proue againſt the Gentiles, that Chriſt was God, by reaſon of his power in ſettinge foorth his church by poore and ſimple people, and the continuance thereof in full force and authoritie, notwithſtandinge all the power and plotts of Sathan, and all the might and ſtrenght of earthlie potentates, with the imploimēt of all their malice and ſtrange pollices which were combined and conioined together for her direction. If S. Chriſoſtome did proue the diuinitie of Chriſte by the continuance of his church 400. yeares, how much more *a minori ad maius*, ſhould we proue the diuinitie and power of Chriſte, not againſt gentiles as S. Chriſoſtome did, but againſt

*Contra Gent.*

wors

worst infidels, as caluinistes and other heretiques, who with greate malice, and more cunninge deuises, seeke to ouerthrowe the church of God, then all the enemies thereof as Iewes, Goathes, Hunnes, Gaules, Vandals, Sarasins, Longobards, Bolgares, Turcks and all other infidels, and yet she is preserued now these 1620. yeares, and shall allwaies continewe in full force & authoritie to the worldes ende.

*Psal.* 87. 3. The continewance of godes church, is sett downe by the prophett. *Disposui testamentum electis meis*, what testament saith S. Aug. in enarrat ibid. but the newe testament. I haue sworne vnto my seruant Dauid: what is this that God bindeth with an oath, that the seede of Abraham shall con-

*Ad Gal.* 3 tinewe for euer euer? And soe saint Paule saith. If yow be of Christ, yow are the seed of Abraham inheritors of that promise, this is the church saith saint Augustine not that fleash of Christ taken of the blessed Virgin, but all wee that beleue in Christe. And in another psalme he saith. I will dwell in thy tabernacle: wherfore S. Augustine saith, that his church shall not be for a time, but shall continewe for euer, vnto the ende of the worlde. And in the 14. our Lord hath bene mindfull of his testament and of the

*Psal.* 14. word that he comaunded to a thowsand generations, and giuen to Abraham that which he did also sweare vnto Isaac, and apointed

apointed for a lawe. He said his word should neuer passe away, what word, but that which did not only continewe duringe the Apostles time, but that word and sacrifice which shall continewe to the worldes end, our Sauiour plainlie declaringe the same, I wilbe with yow vnto the worldes ende, as S. Leo the first and Leo the second writes. Also when S. Paule Ephes. 4. makes mention of soe manny dignities of ecclesiasticall order in Christ his churche, as Apostles, Prophetts, Euangelists, Pastors and Doctors, he saith that they should continewe to the worldes end, as the Prophett saith. *Deus fundauit eam in eternum.* God founded the same for euer. I meane his church as S. Augustine expoundeth, and this is proued by the 91. chapter of Isay, which chapter is vnderstoode of the churche of the newe testament, as our Sauiour taughte.

*Matt. 24.* *Matt. 28.* *S. Leo prius epi. 3. ad Pulcher. Aug. Leo 2. epist. ad Constan.* *August.* *Psal. 47.* *Luc 4.*

4. The same is also proued by the psalme 88. His throne shalbe like the sunne in my presence, and like a perfect Moone for euer, and I will put his seate and his throne as the day of heauen. Daniell also doth manifest the same saying. In the dayes of these kingdomes God shall raise vpp the kingdome of heauen, which shall neuer be dispersed, and his kingdome shall not be giuen to another nation. And accordinge to saint Luke, of his kingdome there shalbe noe end. Moreouer that psalme doth say if her children

*Psal. 88.* *Daniel. 2.*

dren will offend, and ſhall not keepe my lawes and comaundements &c. yet I will viſitt in a rodd their iniquitie and their ſinnes in ſcourges, I will not for all that put away my mercie from the ſame, which place ſaint Cyprian aſwell in this pſalme as alſo in the 2. of Daniell doth expound to be mēt of the afflictions and tribulations of the churche. S. Bernard alſo, *in illud tenui eum nec dimittam.* I held him, and I will not let him goe &c. neither then, nor after the chriſtian ſtocke ſhall not faile, neither faith from the worlde, neither charitie from the churche. Lett all the raginge fire, all the tēpeſtuous waues inſult & freate againſt her, they ſhall not caſte her downe becauſe ſhe is builded vpon a firme rocke, and the rocke is Chriſte, which neither by the pratinge of Philoſophers, or the cauillation of heretiques, or by the ſworde of perſecutors, can or ſhalbe ſeperated.

*In Cant. ſerm. 79.*

5. Illiricus a proteſtant writer ſaith, that the trewe church in the middeſt of all perſecutions, deſtructions of citties, comon wealthes and people, is preſerued miraculouſly by godes ſpeciall protection and aſsiſtance. This is alſo proued by Oecolāpadius vppon Iſay cap. 2. by Melancthone, *in locis communibus cap. de eccleſia editione 1561.* by Brentius vppon *S. Luc cap. 17. homil. 19. Luth. tomo. 4. in Iſa. cap. 9.* by Bullenger *in Apocali. Canc. 72.* For the fall and deſtruction of the church cannot

*Illir. Gloſ. in Math. cap 2.*

cannot be denied, without the deniall of all the articles of our faithe, and fondation of christian religion, the trinitie of God, the incarnation of Christ, his preachinge, his death, his passion, his eternall kingdome and priesthoode, and all other misteries of catholique religion. For what ende was his cominge to take fleash by his incarnation, but to ioyne vnto himselfe in an indissoluble knott of mariadge, his churche from which he would neuer be diuorced or seperated? To what end was his preaching, but to erect and establish the same, his passion was to sanctifie it and to leaue her an euerlastinge remedie to blott out her sinnes and offences. And I pray yow who is an euerlastinge king that hath not an euerlasting people, obeying him and obseruinge his lawes? how can he be an euerlastinge priest, whose priesthoode and sacrifice for soe manny yeares was applied to none, and availed for none? To what purpose was the holie ghoast sent but to remaine with his churche for euer, and to instruct her in all trueth? wherfore to affirme that this church hath failed, is to affirme that Christs prophetts and Apostles are all liers, and all that is written both in the old and newe testament to be fabulous.

*Osee. 2.*
*Ephes. 5.*
*Ioh. 17.*

### *That this Church which shall neuer be hid, but remaine visible, is manifest by the parable of Christe our Lord.*

## CHAPTER IV.

1. THe church of God is called a Barne, in which there is corne and chaffe, a nett in which there is good and badd fishes, a field in which there is cockle and wheate, a banquett at which there are good and badd, a flocke in which there are sheepe and goates, all which doth signifie a visible church, but the inuisible church hath but only the good accordinge to the opinion of the protestants, which is contrarie aswell to the said parables, as to our Sauiours owne wor-
*Matt. 13.* des saying *He will make cleane his barne, the wheate he will gather into his garner, but he will burne the chaffe, with an inexstinguible fire,*
*Matt. 3.* which shall not be vntill the day of iudgmēt. Our Sauiour saith, suffer both of them (I meane the wheate and the cockle) to grow vntill the haruest, which will not be vntill the day of iudgment. For a kingdome must be meant of people that are knowen in the kingdome, but the churche, as before is alleadged, is the kingdome of God, therfore the dwellers thereof must be knowen. S. Augustine doth proue the same lardglie against

against the Donatistes, who said the church perished. O wicked and impudent voice that the church should perish, this they say because they be not in her &c. Our Sauiour did referr vs to the church when he said. *Dic ecclesiæ*, tell the church, now which way should wee tell the church thereof, without the churche be to be seene? and therfore our Sauiour tooke away all doubt and said, it is a cittie placed vppon a hill, which shall giue light to the world. *Aug. in Psal 101. concio. 2.*

2. This is proued by reason, for none can be saued vnlesse he enter into the church, of which the arcke of Noe was a figure, & as all perished that did not enter into the arcke, soe they perish also that enter not into the church, but none can enter into the church which he knoweth not, therfore all must perish because they cannot see this churche. The profession of a christian ought to be visible not hidden, therfore the church in which this profession is made, ought to be soe, for it is said, *Whosoeuer shall denie me before men, I will denie him before my father who is in heauen.* *Roman. 10 Matt. 10.*

3. The comparison brought for the forsakinge the sinagoge of the Iewes, is not a like, for shee was but a figure and a shadow of the holie catholique church, the oracles of the holie prophetts, all the mornefull cries of the blessed Patriarches, all the sacrifices of the Leuitts, all the oblations of the

Iewes, signified or represented nothinge else then the cominge of the Messias, at whose cominge all the other rites and oblations of the sinagoge should haue an end,
Genes. 94. as it was prophesied: *Quando venerit qui mittendus est, cessabit vnctio vestra*, vid. when the Messias shall come, your vnction, & your sacrifice shall cease, which also was prophesied and foretould by the Patriarch Iacob when he was dyinge, who hauinge all his childrē about him, said these wordes. *Non auferetur sceptrum de Iuda, nec dux de fæmore eius, donec veniat qui mittendus est, & ipse erit expectatio gentium vid. the scepter shall not be taken from the tribe of Iuda, nor a captaine from her loines, vntill he come which is to be sent, and he shalbe the expectation of nations.* Soe as after the cominge of Christe, aswell the seate royall of the kingdome, as also the legall obseruations of the Iewes, withall their sacrifices and oblations, were accomplished in the death of Christe when he said, *consumatum est*, it is accomplished, and soe instituted a newe lawe, and founded his church, which was the seate of Dauid, that was giuen vnto him, of whome it was said, *he shall raigne*
Luc. 1. *in the howse of Iacob for euer, and of his king-*
Damas. 4 57. *dome there shalbe noe ende:* and that all the
Esa. 6. 5. world should imbrace the God of Abrahā,
Osee. 2. as it is said by the prophett Esay. The Princes of people shalbe gathered together with the God of Abraham, soe as wee see not only

only the Christiās, but allso Turcks and Mores to imbrace the God of Abraham as the trewe God, of whome it is said allso. *I haue giuen yow a light vnto the nations that yow may be my saftie vnto the vtter most parte of the world.*

4. Wherfore he hath instituted a newe sacrifice by which his honnor should be vphoulden, and by which his name should be glorified, which accordinge to the prophesie of Malachias, should be the trewe oblation that should be offred vnto him for euer and in all places of the world: this was not meant of the sacrifice of the old lawe, for that could not be offred but at Ierusalem as the holie scriptures wittnesse, and therfore it is meant of the blessed sacrifice of the Masse, which shalbe offred for euer in the churche of God, for the which Christ hath instituted and ordained priestes which shall offer sacrifice vnto the eternall father, accordinge to the institution of Christe and prophesie of Malachias, and therfore S. Augustine, *lib. de vnit. ecclesiæ cap. 12. 13. de ciuit. lib. 20. cap.* 8. *& Psal. 85. ad illud tu solus Deus magnus. Psal. 70.* affirmeth thē to denie Christ and to robb him of his glorie and inheritance bought with his blood, which teach that his church may faile or perish, and S. Ierom refuteth the same wicked heresie in the Luciferans, prouinge against them that they make God subiect to the diuill, a poore miserable Christ, that imagine that the church

*Malac. 1.*

*Dialog. ad Lucif. c. 6.*

church may either perish or be driuen to any corner of the worlde.

4. And although the Sacraments, ceremonies, and the legall obseruations of the Iewes did faile, because it is said, the lawe, and the prophetts were vnto Iohn, yet notwithstandinge the church of Christ did not faile, which was collected and composed of both the nations, I meane Iewes and Gentiles, as S.Paule doth wittnesse in many places, that the first fruictes of the holie ghoaste, and the first christians were the Apostles which were Iewes, therfore the churche of the Iewes did not faile so as that none of them did remaine therin as the said Apostle proues. *Hath God (saith he) reiected his people? God forbid for I am an Israelite and of the seede of Abraham and of the tribe Beniamine, for God did not cast of his people.* The glosse vpon this place saith, that the Iewes are not infidels altogether, and soe God did repell thē in parte, but not in whole, because he hath not reiected me and others that are predestinated, thus farr the glosse. For he reiected the howse of Saule, but not of Dauid, vnto whome in reward of the ardent desire and feruent deuotion that he had to builde a temple for godes glorie, he promised that he would build for Dauid an euerlasting kingdome, and a perpetuall howse from whome he should neuer take away his mercie, for which he made the 88. psalme wherin he confirmed

*Matt.* 11.

*Rom.* 11.

confirmed this promise.

---

*Whether that papistes doe amisse, in hauinge their churches and monasteries soe sumptuous, their alters and ornamentes soe riche, and ecclesiasticall possessions soe great, the poore wanting the same.*

## CHAPTER I.

1. WHatsoeuer is giuen to Christs church, is giuen in his honor that suffred for the said church, beinge his spouse, his portion &c. for as our Sauiour saith. *Beatius est dare quam accipere*; It is better to giue then to take, and noe maruaile that christians should giue vnto God some parte of his owne, as the prophett saith: what shall I giue vnto him that giues vnto me all thinges? I pray you tell me, whether it be a greater offence to robb and ouerthrowe the kinges howse, and to spoile his subiects of their goodes, depriue them of their liues and to comitt all other outragious facts vpõ them, then to build the same, maintaine and enriche the same, to bestowe lardgl e vpon his seruaunts, to defend and protect them &c? Tell me I praie you whether Salomon that built the temple of Ierusalem soe sumptuously, and which by the riches thereof

was most famous through out the world, was more offensiue vnto God for soe doing, then Nabuchodonosor kinge of Babilon, and Antiochus Epiphanes, which were not contented to ransacke and spoile that worthie temple, cast downe the pillers, take away the golden alter and candlesticks, and all other sacred vessells or religious ornamentes, but allso defiled the same and prohibited any oblatiō or sacrifice to be offered therin? For this cause these two tirants doe represent the diuill, and Salomon is a figure of Christe. And if Salomon was soe comended in holie scriptures for buildinge the said Temple for the sinagoge, how much more christiā princes for buildinge churches for Iesus Christe.

2. I praie you tell me allso, whether Constantine the great, merited more before God & the world, for buildinge so many churches vppon his owne charges, and for augmentinge and enrichinge the patrimony of Christe, then kinge Henrie the 8. that did cast and pull downe soe many churches, monasteries and chapples, and did disolue soe manny Religious howses, robbed them of all their sacred ornaments, and by soe doinge, spoyled God of his patrimonie? Yow saie that whatsoeuer kinge Henrie the 8. did, was donn for the reliefe of the poore and the ease of his subiects to be freed from subsidies and impositions, as was related in that

that verie parleamēt, wherin monasteries & churches were surprised, and religion prophaned. And therfore it was added in the said parleament, that the truly poore of the kingdome perished, and that Abbey Lubbers (for soe they called religious persons) did possesse their liuinges. To this effect there was a supplicatiō exhibited to the kinge against Bishoppes, Abottes, Priores, Deacons, Archdeacons, suffragans & priestes in forme following &c. What tyrāt euer oppressed the people like this cruel & vēgeable generation? Before these came there were but fewe theues, yea thefte was at that tyme soe rare, that Cæsar was not compelled to make penaltie of death vpon felonie as your grace may wel perceaue in his institutes: ther was also at that time but fewe poore people, and yet they did not begge, but there was giuē them enoughe vnasked. Wherfore if your grace will build a sure hospitall that neuer shall faile to reliue vs all your poore beads men, take from them al these thinges, set these sturdy boubies abroad in the world to get thē wiues of their owne, to get their liuinge with their labour in the swette of their browes accordinge to Gene. 1. Tie all idle theues to the cartes to be whipped naked about euerie markett towne, that they by their importunat begginge take not away the allmesse that the good christian people do giue, then shall aswell the number of

our

our foresaid mounsterous sorte, as of the baudes, hoores, theeues and idle people decrease, then shal these great yearly exactions ceate, then shall all your people encrease in wealthe &c. these are sett downe in Iohn Fox, his Chronicles. Iudas in like manner (when the deuout wooman Marie Magdalē anointed Christs feete with a moste pretious ointment) did saie, *vt quid perditio hæc*, what destruction is this, had it not bene better, said he, that this had bene sold and giuen vnto the poore? our Sauiour aunswered, let her alone, and added moreouer, that in what place so euer of the world his gospell should be read, her deuotion should be comended. And as Iudas herin did not care for the poore, as the scripture reporteth, but hopinge it should retourne to himselfe: soe perleament protestants did not care for the poore, but all their drifte was to haue the liuinges and treasures of the churches themselues, as itt fell out.

3. I praie you tell me, whether the poore were better and more reliued, or the subiects more eased of subsidies and impositiōs before the suppresion of the church, or after? Doctor Sanders writes, that England was neuer troubled with greater impositiōs & subsidies then it was in the later daies of kinge Henry the 8. nor any kinge in england had lesse treasure in his cofers then he at his deathe. And as for the poore people

it is

it is manifest, that they haue lesse releefe now then euer they had. I am sure there are not 300. persons relieued by all the churche liuinges of England, and Ireland beinge in those mens handes which haue as little charitie towardes God, and pittie towardes the poore, as they haue remorse of conscience to keepe them, or morall honestie to bestowe them. And as for other ecclesiasticall dignities and spirituall benefices out of which the greatest liuely hoode should be deducted, they saie. *Non sufficit nobis & vobis*: wee haue not inoughe our selues, much lesse will wee imparte any thinge vnto others, hauinge such a diluge of chitts and childrē, with which the countries of this ghospell doe abou͂d, that S. Paule should not bragge nor glorie more for begettinge children, *per euangelium*, by the gospell of Christe, then they by their voluptuous gospell. And soe eche of them maie saie. *Genui vos per euangelium*. I haue begotten yow by the gospel, but I would to God they had gotten them spiritually as S. Paule did, and not carnallie as they doe, whose voluptuous gospell is. *Crescere, & multiplicare ex sanguinibus, aut ex voluntate carnis, sed non ex Deo nati sunt*. By filthie concupiscence accordinge to the will of the fleash, but are not borne of God, whose vnhappy and wofull offspringe, did robb Christ of his patrimony, and did not onlie destroie the ecclesiasticall state of his church,

church, but alſo haue almoſt brought to ruine the ciuill, and temporall ſtate: hauing made their inundation (with which all England and Irelād are ſo ouerwhelmed) into their neighbours poſſeſsions and territories, that the boundes and banckes of theſe countries are not able to reſiſte their violent irruptions, neither yet a meane continent is not able to conteine the confuſed and diſordered multitude of their iſſue; ſoe as if England either by conqueſt, or ſome other courſe doe not appoint their habitation, and dwellinge place in ſome other countrie, as Virginia or Guiana, or elce where, the kingdome of great Brittanie and poore Ireland, ſhall feele the ſmarte, and eſpecially the nobilitie and cheefeſt, into whome they prie daylie, ſeekinge by all diſhoneſt courſes to intrude into their landes and liuinges, as they haue donn alreadie by ſuppreſsinge them in all thoſe countries where this goſpel tooke footing, for I dare ſay and boldely affirme, that theſe goſpellers haue putt downe and ſurpriſed as many howſes of noble men and gentlemen, as monaſteries and churches, but it is the iuſt iudgment of God that theſe potentats, and great people ſhould feele their greateſt ſmarte, by whom they were ſollicited, defended, and protected in this their newe goſpell. And that for two cauſes vid. libertie to liue diſſolutelie without controllment of their ſpirituall paſtors,

paſtors, and couetouſnes with greedie deſire to poſſeſſe and enioye the churche liuinges, which ſorte of people, for that they contemne all ſpirituall power or iuriſdiction, which the church ought to haue ouer them, as the ſpiritt ouer the fleaſh, did eaſilie yeald to any heretique impugninge and reſiſtinge this ſpirituall power, and takinge away all eccleſiaſticall diſcipline, and ſpirituall correction, and ſoe they gaue them full ſcope to all abhominable riotouſnes, and wanton diſſolution.

4. But to retourne to my purpoſe, that God is not diſpleaſed nor good Chriſtians offended for buildinge churches and monaſteries, or other religious howſes for his ſeruice, nor the poore hindered of their releefe for anny charitable oblations, or donations that the deuout chriſtians doe beſtow on the church, but rather God much pleaſed therby and the poore releeued. Firſt, Da- *2 Reg. 7.*
uid for hauinge a deſire to build a temple *Geneſ.*
for Godes honor, was rewarded with and euerlaſtinge howſe and a perpetuall kingdome. Iacob but only for conſecrating a ſtone to godes glorie, it was ſaid vnto him, I will cauſe thee to encreaſe and multiplie. The engliſhmen vppon their firſt cominge to Irelande vnder kinge henrie the 2. dedicated to the ſeruice of God, the firſt land they tooke which was in the countie of Wexford, and made two famous monaſteries,

teries, as Donbrody and Tentarom of the order of S. Bernard, and haue endued thē with great and ample possessions, as also many churches in that countie, and in euery place where they came, which was noe smale cause, they had such good successe in their enterprise. Henry the 5. before he tooke the warres of Fraunce in hand, builded two famous monasteries by Richmounde, one of the order of Carthusians, and the other of Sion Nunes, of the order of S. Bride, eche monasterie standes one againste the other, and the riuer of Themes betwixt them, which he dedicated to the seruice of God, whom they praised with celestiall alleluias as diuine praises which were neuer omitted either by day or by night, soe that when thone would make an end, the other would beginn, the bells giuinge them notice therof. Therfore God did prosper him soe well in those warres, that he brought almost all France to his subiection, and his sonne kinge Henry the 6. was crowned kinge of Fraunce at Paris, beinge but xi. yeares of age. Yea I could recken more then a thowsand examples of the like subiecte.

5. And, for the releefe of the poore, as the pretious ointment that Marie Magdalen bought for our Sauiours feete, was not a hinderance for the poore: soe whatsoeuer is giuen to further his seruice, doth rather further then hinder them. Is there anie coun-

countrie in Europe more charitable to the poore, and more liberall to godes seruants, and all other ecclesiasticall persons then Spaine, and yet noe countrie more sumptuous and costlie in their churches, and more deuoute and lesse sparing of any thinge they haue for the settinge foorth of godes glorie, for adorninge churches and monasteries with all ornaments, and implements pertaininge thereunto? Is there anie country in the world that can shewe such hospitales in all citties, townes, villadges, and hamletts for the cure of the sicke, and for the releefe of pilgrimes and strangers, such colledges for poore virgins that be depriued of parents and frindes, where they be kept and brought vpp in all honest and godly education, befittinge gentle women vntill they be married vppon the cost and chardges of the colledge, in euerie cittie or great towne in Spaine such confraternities being erected for all workes of mercie, by which meanes all sortes of distressed persõs are relived: soe many hospitalities for cast children, for whome they haue nurses to giue them sucke vpon the hospitalles charges, which also giues releefe vnto them vntill they be able to helpe themselues. Soe manny colledges for orphanes, soe manny vniuersities for schollers, as noe countrie can shewe soe manny, hauinge 24. vniuersities, and so manny howses of mercie, that I dare

dare saye that the howse of mercy of Lisborne, doth more workes of charitie, and sustaines more poore people, and marryes more virgins for godes sake, then all the protestante countries in Europe.

6. To conclude, England and Ireland cannot denie, but there was better prouision for the poore, before the church was destroyed then after, and that the most parte of all colleges and hospitalles were builded by church men themselues. Did not the faithfull bringe all their goodes vnto the Apostles, to be disposed accordinge to their charitie? S. Paule likewise did receaue the offringes of the faithfull. I require, saith he, the fruite of your deuotion, for whatsoeuer is bestowed vppon the church, the poore are againe releeued therby. And as S. Hierom saith: *Quod clericorum est, totum illud pauperum est.*

*Act. c. 5.*

*Of the vnhappie endes and other punishments, by which God doth chastice those that presume to robb Churches, or otherwise to prophane and abuse sacred things.*

## CHAPTER II.

*Ioseph antiq lib. 15. cap. 8. & 12.*

Osephus doth regifter the modest behauiour of Gn. Pompey, towardes the church of Hierusalem, and also the couetousnes of Marcus Crassus,

Crassus, by which he robbed the same, who was punished by God, he beinge slaine, and all his great armye ouerthrowen by the Parthians, and that most miserably. And although thorough necessitie kinge Herod did open the sepulcher of kinge Dauid, thinking therby to haue great treasures, the said Ioseph saith that he was attached with great calamities for his presumption. In the holie scriptures wee read, that Nabuchodonosor kinge of the Assirians did robb the temple of God, and afterwardes was transformed into a beaste, and his sonne Balthazar for prophaninge the holie vessels that his Father brought from the temple of Hierusalem, was slaine by his enemies, and the kingdome taken and possessed by them. Kinge Antiochus was eaten by wormes for doinge the like. The treasure and goulden vessels brought by Titus out of Hierusalẽ, and by Gensericus kinge of the Vandalles, brought oute of Rome vnto Affrique amoungest other spoyles, and beinge tost to and fro through the handes of manny kinges, aswell Romaines as Vandalls, none that euer possessed them escaped an ominus end, neyther the wrathe of God surceased, vntill the kingdome of the Vandalls beinge vtterly destroyed by Belisarius (who tooke in a most bloody battle the last kinge of them called Gibnier) by the comaundement of the Emperor Iustinian, they were

*Daniel c.1*

*Daniel.5.*

ſent backe againe to Hieruſalem, hauinge giuen a ſore blowe to all ſuch as polluted their handes withall.

Act. 5. 2. In the actes of the Apoſtles wee read, the miſerable death of Ananias and Saphira, not for robbinge the goodes which others had giuen to the churche, but for keepinge with themſelues parte of that which once they offered vnto God, wherfore (ſaid S. Peter vnto them) did Sathan tempt yow, to lie againſt the holie ghoaſte, and to deceaue vs of parte of the land you ſould? was it not in your powre not to ſell it, for herin you haue not deceaued men but God? and loe both man and wife fell downe dead at his feete. To giue vs to vnderſtand, what accompt wee muſt giue vnto God of anny thinge that is once conſecrated vnto him. And therfore Alaricus kinge of the Goathes, when he tooke Rome, comaunded vnder great penalties, that none of his ſoldiors ſhould robbe any church, neither touch any thinge that was in them ſayinge, that his quarell was againſt man and not againſt God, neither againſt his Saincts. Alſo A certaine gentleman of the Goathes tooke a virgine that was conſecrated vnto God, in the church of S. Peter, and vſinge great force and violence to gett of her the golden veſſells and churche ſtuffe that was conſecrated to Gods ſeruice, ſhe ſaid that thoſe were the goodes of the Apoſtle S. Peter, and as for

for her parte shee was not able to defend them. The said Goath beinge astonished at the virgins resolute behauiour, did forbeare to lay violent handes, either vpon the virgine, or vpon those consecrated vessells: for the said kinge comaunded, as Paulus Orosius writeth, that his souldiors should carrie vppon their owne backs those holie vessels with all other thinges pertayninge to the church, and as manny Christians as should followe them, should not be touched. *Paulus Orosius.*

3. The ecclesiasticall histories are full of the like examples, yea the verie gentiles did containe themselues from spoilinge religious people or robbinge churches, not so much for any deuotion, but for verie feare of the wrath of God, whose greeuous punishmentes was by them experienced vppon others for attemptinge the like sacrilege. Iulian the vncle of Iulian Emperor the Apostate, did committ a wicked robberye vpon the church of Antioch, and did mingle the holly vessels with the plate of his Nephewes, & was therfore chastised by God publikely for the same, for his entralles putrified his body was tormented with such horrible vlcers, and filthie botches, out of which there came, vglie wormes which gnawed and consumed his carcasse, by which he was exhausted and eaten, and soe ended most miserablie. Fælix Iulians threasurer and companion in the robberie

aforesaid , died vomittinge all his blood out of his mouthe . Mauricius Cartularius did persuade Isacius, who was the Exarcke of Italie for the Emperor Heraclius, that he should robbe the church of Rome, which he did, & not longe after the said Mauricius was emprisoned by the said Exarcke where he died most miserably: & the said Isacius died vppon the suddaine within a little after, as Carolus Sigonius doth write. Leo the 4. Emperor of Constantinople, tooke away a Crowne of gould verie riche which the Emperor Mauritius did offer vnto the church of Sainte Sophia, in which crowne there was amoungst other pretious stones, a carbuncle of inestimable valoure ; and puttinge the same vpon his head, presentlie there grewe vpon him an in apostume of which he died, which was called the carbuncle.

*Lib. 2. de regno Ital. Zozo. to. 3 & baptist. Aegnat. in vita Leonit. Blond. lib. 1. deca. 2. Nicephor. hist li 18. cap. 4. 2. Nice. in chronico ducis Bauariæ.*

4. S. Gregorie Turonensis writeth in his historie, that certeine soldiors who did robbe the church of S. Vincent of the cittie of Agence, were soe chastised of God , that one of them had his hand burned : into the other the diuill did enter, by which he was torne in peeces cryinge vnto the Sainct: the other did kill himselfe by his owne proper handes. Trithemius doth declare , that it was reuealed vnto him, that Dagobert king of Fraunce, for vsurpinge the goodes of the church, was accused before the throne of God, and that Charles Martell a captaine of

of great vallor, father of kinge Pepine, and vncle vnto Charles the great, was alſo condemned for the ſame, and that S. Eucherius Biſhopp of Orleans did comaund, that his ſepulcher ſhould be opened, and that nothinge was found in it, but a moſt vgly ſerpent of ſtrange bignes. Peter the 4. king of Aragon, died within 4. dayes after he had abuſed the picture of holie Tecla. Vraca the Queene of Spaine had her belly burſte, and ſo came to a badd end for robbinge of churches. Aſtialpus kinge of the Longobardes, and Fredericke the Emperor, came likewiſe to a bad end, for robbinge of churches. Francis Tarafa writeth, that when Gundericus tooke Siuill and intended alſo to ſpoile the churches thereof, that the diuill did poſſeſſe him, and ſo he died miſerably. S. Iſidor writeth, that Agila kinge of the Goathes, did prophane the temple of S. Aciſclo martyr, where his bodie was, and that he made of the church a ſtable for his horſſes, wherupon his armie was ouerthrowen by thoſe of Cordima, and that he fled himſelfe to Merida, and was ſlaine by his owne ſeruauntes. In the life of the S. Aſtregiſill Biſhopp of Burgis in Fraunce, wee read ſtrange puniſhmentes vpon thoſe that robbed godes churche, and prophaned his monaſterie.

*Paul. Aemil. l. 2.*

*Zurita tomo annal. cap. 39.*

*De regib. Hiſpaniæ in Hono.*

*Ambr. de Onorales p. 1 lib. 10. cap. 23.*

*Surius tomo 3.*

5. When Philipp kinge of Fraunce in his warres againſte Peter kinge of Aragon

*Zurita annali: l. 4. c. 69.*

tooke the cittie of Giron, and his soldiors prophaned the churches thereof, and robbed the sepulcher of S. Narciscus patrone of that cittie: out of that sepulcher there did issue such swarmes of flees and froggs of wonderfull greatnes, which so flew vppon the souldiors and vppon their horsses, that that there died within fewe dayes after 40000. French men and more. And the said kinge Peter in a letter written to Sanchius kinge of Castile, did certifie that there died 40000. horsses, and the kinge himselfe died shortlie after in Perpinian: soe as the
18. *Mart.* prouerbe grewe in that countrie, *of the flies of S. Narcisus* as Cæsar Baronius notes vpon the Martiriologe of Rome.

6. In the yeare of our Lord 1414. when the French armie tooke the cittie of Suesson, which belonged vnto Iohn Duke of Burgundie and earle of Flanders, and prophaned the church of S. Chrispine and Chrispinian, whose bodies are reuerenced in that cittie, the next yeare after beinge the verie daie of those Sainctes, the selfe same armie which was both puisant and great, in which all the nobilitie of Fraunce were, was vanquished, torne and altogether destroied by the english armie, which was but as it were a handfull in respect of the great multitude of the French, which the daie before refused to graunt any reasonable composition vnto the said english, and this was the iuste iudge-

iudgment of God, inflicted vpon them by the intercesſion of thoſe bleſſed Martyres, whoſe church they had defiled.

7. The Earle of Tirons ſoldiors, did robbe and ſpoile the monaſterie of Timnlage, and Kilcrea, and prophaned other churches cominge to releeue the Spaniardes, that were compaſſed about (they being within Kinſale) by the engliſh armie, conſiſtinge for the moſte parte of Iriſh catholique ſouldiors, the engliſh beinge altogether (ſauinge a verie fewe) conſumed through famine and cold, beinge not able to indure the toile and labour of ſo vnſeaſonable a winter campe. Yet Tirons cōpany exceeding the other in multitude of people, and euer before that time terrible to the engliſh, by reaſon of ſoe many great ouerthrowes giuen vnto them, were brocken and put to flight, by a fewe horſſmen that iſſued out of the engliſhe campe: beinge therunto ſollicited and procured by the earle of Clenricard an Iriſhe earle then in the engliſh campe. Wherfore the ſaid earle of Tiron retourninge from that ouerthrowe ſaid, that it was the vengeance of the mightie hand of God, and his moſt iuſt iudgment, which ought to be executed vppon ſuch wicked and ſacrilegious ſoldiors, that perpetrated and comitted ſuch outrage vpon ſacred places.

8. Doctor Owen Hegan, that permitted

or rather willed certaine soldiors of the Clencarties ( beinge then in open hostilitie in the weaste parte of Mounster against Queene Elizabeth ) to robbe a certaine Church, into which the poore people of the counteie sent their goodes, hopinge to find a safe sanctuarie therin, and within a seanight afterwardes, his owne brother, who was one of the Queenes subiects, was slaine by the verie same people vnto whome he gaue leaue to spoile the said Church, and alsoe within one moneth himselfe was slaine, and another priest with him, not by the English, but by Irish subiectes: soe as there is noe acception of persons with God, who beinge an indiffrent and iust iudge, doth giue to euerie one according to his workes, whether they be good or badd, let noe man therfore say he is a priest, or a catholique, to collour and cloake therby his scandalous actions, who of all men ought to shunn scandall, and the occasion thereof. Truly I haue found by certaine relation, that the Irishmen neuer spared noe church, monasterie, or anny sanctuarie in their last commotions and insurrections, and that therfore such as haue bene noted to defile and spoile such places, did not escape a miserable end, shorthly after the sacrilegious acts was comitted.

9. Wee knowe that spirituall benefices and other ecclesiasticall dignities were not bestowed

bestowed vpõ the worthieste for learning, or more vertuous of life, but vpon those that were vpholden and defended by the strongest faction of the nobilitie there, soe as fewe came in at the right doore like trewe pastors, but like theeues in at the backe doore, soe as that kingdome was subiect to this abuse & confusion in S. Malachias his time, as S. Bernard sayes, who beinge made Bishopp of Downe & Conor in Vlster by the sea apostolique, beinge soe holie, and learned as the said S. Bernard was, sayes he was banished from Vlster by the Neales, to haue that dignitie for one of their owne familie, and who did entermiddle more in this busines, then the Geraldines of Mounster? who by the sword defended and vsurped the ecclesiasticall supremacie, noe otherwise then kinge Henry the 8. did, and two of his children, although they haue not don it by parleament as the other did yet by the sword, they haue done it: soe as the ouerthrowe of that howse, & of other great howses may be ascribed vnto the couetous desire they had of the liuinges of the Church, and the little regard they had to churchmen, and churches, or any other place, though neuer soe sacred. Yea sometymes they would not spare their competitors at the verie alter, which in manny places they polluted with their blood.

10. The

*Geneb. in Chro. Anno 988. Anno iuris.*

10. The french histories doe write, that this was the cause also, that tooke away the crowne of Fraunce from the linage of Clodoueus, which was the firste Christian king of Fraunce, beinge conuerted vnto the faith of Christe, by the praiers and deuotion of his most vertuous Queene Clothilda which was passed ouer vnto Charles the great, and also after the line of Charles the great, were careles of their dutie to God and his church, God tooke the crowne from them also, & gaue it vnto Hue Cape, and to those of his howse.

*A prosecution of the last Chapter.*

## CHAPTER III.

*De mirabilibus 2. cap. 1.*

1. WEe should neuer make an end if wee should register soe manny examples as doe daily occurre in this matter. Petrus Cluniacensis, who ~~liued~~ liued in the same time with S. Bernard, a most holie man, and therfore called in his life time Peter the venerable, said that there was a certaine Earle in Macon a cittie in Fraunce not far from Leon, who vsurped the liuinges of the churches, and persecuted church men. This man beinge feastinge one time with his frindes in his pallace, there started vp a gentleman of that maiesticall contenance

nance that he put all the gueſtes, in great feare that were with him, and with a terrible voice and dreadfull aſpect, comaunded the earle to followe him, and that with ſuch maieſtie that he could not otherwiſe chooſe. Comming to the gate, there was a mightie horſſe prepared for him, and he was compelled to mounte vpp a horſſbacke, and preſently the horſſe did fly vpp into the skies, and the miſerable earle cryinge moſt pittifullie, vaniſhed away with the horſſe. Thoſe that were within the pallace, durſt not to goe foorth, but ſhutt the gates out of which the miſerable earle was carried away by the diuill.

2. Paulus Emilius a diligent hiſtoriographer of the matters of Fraunce, doth note the like accident of a certaine Earle called Willian, a great perſecutor of the church, who beinge alſo at a great feaſt, accompanied with other great earles, was comaunded by one that was at the gate to goe foorth, and ſoe riſinge from the table went foorth to knowe what he was, where he met with one a horſſbacke which tooke him away, and did neuer appeare any more. He added moreouer, that in the very ſame place the Earle of Niuers, a great perſecutor of the immunities of the church, was ſerued in the like maner. The kinge of Aragon called Sanchius through extreame neceſsity was forced to make vſe of the church liuinges

uinges of his kingdome in his warres against the Moores, and although it was for the defense of Catholique Religion, yet he made restitution of all that he had so tooken from the Church. Many good authors doe note and obserue, that the church liuinges neuer profittes any, and that they doe not only succede bad with them that take them, but also consume and destroye their temporall possessions withall; for like as the mothes, the rust, or the canker, consumes the wood, the cloath, the iron, and the fleashe that ingenders them, and euen as the feathers of the Eagle beinge ioyned with the feathers of any other, consumes and spills them; soe church liuinges wrongfully detayned, or violently taken from the church, consumes and ouerthrowes the temporal estate vnto which they are vnlawfullye ioyned and annexed.

3. This England, France, and Ireland may testifie, for France enioyed but smale quietnes since Clement the 7. annexed vnto the crowne of France by the procuremẽt of Francis the firste (when the said Clement married his Neece called Catherina de Medicis vnto Henry the 2. Daulphine of France at Marcells) all the promotions and donations of church liuinges vnder the crowne of France; And as for him that sought it, or by what meanes it was giuen, I leaue that to the French historiographers; yet wee knowe

knowe that he and all his issue, liued and ended most miserably, their kingdome and state was most pittifully broken with soe manny bloody garboiles, all the nobilitie consumed and exhausted with soe mannie cruell battles & ouerthrowes, so many rich townes and citties ransaked, soe many coũtries and prouinces vtterly destroied, soe many churches and monasteries dissolued, and cast downe, soe many religious people murthered, and soe many sacred virgins deflowred and rauished: soe as France through heresie (which by this donation crept into it) was a spectacle of all miserie, famine, pestilence, warres, vprores, & cōbustions to all other nations. And although the said Henry the 2. had 6. sonnes whereof 3. of thē were kinges, yet all died without yssue, and not one of that race is left aliue: and soe, the lyne of the howse of Valois, in whome the crowne of France continewed the space of 260. yeares, is altogether extinguished, and the crowne came to the howse of Burbon, their auncient and implacable enemies, and nowe succedinge them in the crowne and kingdome. Henry the 8. not by any grant or indulgence of the Pope, but by force and feare of violent lawes, made and deuised by him (leacherie and couetousnes intisinge him therunto) tooke vnto himself a spiritual iurisdiction, and besides suppressed & cast downe all the monasteries; who, although

although he had six wiues, and left behinde him, one sonne, and 2. daughters yet now there is none liuinge nor any of their lyne or race, man or woman now extant.

4. And as for the nobilitie of England, and Irelande, which were instruments more ready to serue the kinges humour, then to please God, they be all for the most parte extinguished of whose discent or race one amoungest 20. is not to be seene this daie to possesse their ancestors liuinges, vnto whose patrimonie others crept in and succeeded, some perhappes being their mortall enemies. The Duke of Norfolque, and the earle of Arundell were the cheefest instruments that Queene Elizabeth had in the first parleament shee assembled, to putt downe the church, and to drawe all spirituall iurisdiction vnto her selfe, hopinge that by this seruice the one should be contracted with her in mariage, the other should be in extraordinarie fauor with her, I would they had taken S. Paules aduise. *Oportet obedire Deo magis quam hominibus.* Wee ought to obey God more then men, or the prophet his caueat, *maledictus qui confidit in homine*, cursed is he that trusteth in man. This Duke (as a certaine graue matrone prophesied and tould him to his face cominge from the parleament, that he should lose his head by her, whome to please he did displease God, and made ship-

*Scisma Angliæ.*

wreaque

wreaque of his religion ) was condemned and put to death for highe treason against the Queene at Tower hill in London, and his eldest sonne the earle of Arundell after beinge condemned and arrayned, after much mourninge and longe imprisonment, died in the Tower of London. And the other Earle of Arundell died without yssue male of his bodie, and it is thought if he had liued any longe time, he should haue tasted of the same cuppe with the other.

5. The Earle of Ormond, which was the onlie instrument for Queene Elizabeth in Ireland to strenghten the voices of the parleament, for her spirituall supremacie, as yet liuinge, is depriued of his sight, and of his only sonne, and the only ioy and felicitie he had in this world: and of his end wee knowe not, but wee knowe he hath church liuinges, and wee are certaine that who hath them vnlawfully shall neuer thriue the better. And therfore Charles the 7. kinge of France beinge in great wāt of mony through the warres he had with the English about the dukedome of Normandie, of which the quiett state of his kingdome depended, would not make vse of the tithes of his kingdome, beinge therunto moued by a great prelate, for that he knewe they would not succeede well with him. Osforius in the historie of the kinge of Portingall Emanuell, writeth, that the Pope dispensed with him

him for the tithes of his country towardes his warres in Affricke, and hauinge perceaued that he had not soe good successe as before the takinge of them into his handes, he determined with himselfe, not to make any more vse of them. God would not haue thinges dedicated to his honor to be transferred to any prophane vse, vppon anny pretence whatsoeuer. And for that Nicephorus Phocas Emperor, made a lawe, by which he reuoked and called backe all lawes that were made in fauor of churchmē, for that they had such ample patrimonie, and that the poore, as he alleadged was not releeued, nor the soldiors had wherwith to eate. The Emperor Basilius did repeale that statute, by another lawe by these wordes. Vnderstandinge that the lawe of Nicephorus made (after that he vsurped the empire) against the church and church liuinges, was the only cause and offspringe of all our mischeefe and present callamities, for that lawe was not only don in preiudice of the church, but also it was plainly against the honnor of God, and seinge wee finde by experience to our great greefe, that nothing succeeded well with vs, neither did wee want continuall callamities after the makinge thereof, therfore wee comaunde that it shall cease, and be of noe force, nor anny other lawe against the church.

*Lib. 1. in in Constit. 69 orient.*

6. In like manner Alexis Comnenus Empe-

Emperor of Constaninople, besides that he made streight lawes against those that vsurped anny thinge consecrated vnto God, to declare his greater deuotion, he in the golden bull added these wordes. If euer hereafter (ô Lord God) anny shalbe soe maliparte or soe presumptuous, as to take anny thinge that is alreadie consecrated to God, or hereafter shalbe dedicated to his holie church, let such an one neuer enioye the cleere lighte of thy vision, neither the light of the sonne that giues lighte in the morninge, neither thy aide or protexion, but euermore let him be dispised and forsaken of thee. The same malediction in substance, the Queene Theodolenda did giue vnto all those, that would vsurpe the goodes and landes which shee did giue and bestow vppon the church of S. Iohn Baptiste in the cittie of Moucia, as Paulus Diaconus doth write. The like malediction other Princes haue cast foorth vppon those that would frustrate their godly endeuours, for that they feared that one time or another, the greedy desire and couetuousnes of wicked people, would breake all bondes of godes lawes and religion.

*Lib. 4. c. 7. de gest. Longobardorum.*

7. Allas how manny maledictions were cast vppon the protestants, for comittinge sacriledge and for robbinge of churches? as that of Corronell Randale, and 500. English soldiors, withall their munition and vic-

tualls, which were blowen vpp into the ayre by their owne pouder by an extraordinarie accident of a Woulfe who rann with a firie taile into the church of Derrie in Vulster, which by the said Randall was polluted, all which in a moment did perishe with a shipp that was at anker by the said church *Anno Domini 1565.* Also of one Sentleger beinge master of the mint that was at Rosse in Ireland, in the monasterie of S. Francis in kinge Edwardes dayes, who for that the workmen told him that they were beaten by S. Francis euerie night, went himselfe of meere presumption vnto the said monasterie to lodge: the verie first night he went thither, he was soe assaulted, that he rann madd, and rann headlounge that verie nighte into the riuer and drowned himselfe, and his carcase was found dead vppon the sand that morninge. In the warres of Garret Earle of Desmond the English garrisō that was at Yonghull, a porttowne in the prouince of Mounster, in their sally foorth vppon the enemies, went to a certaine monasterie called Melanie, which is scituated in an Iland, and in the riuer of that towne called the broade water, one captaine Peers, beinge the leader of that garrison, caused a fire to be made, and one of his companie called Bluett an Irishman and natiue of Yonghull making fire of the image of that Sainct called Melanye, vppon the

suddaine

ſuddaine fell madd, and died within 3. dayes after. And the ſaid captaine for that he comaunded him ſoe to doe, was depriued of the vſe of his limmes, and falling into a dead palſie, was neuer ſounde vntil he died, and his companie were all killed by the ſaid Earle his Senſciall; this happened 1580.

8. Allſoe one Poet an Engliſhman, breakinge downe a monaſterie of S. Dominiques in the North part of Yonghull, fell dead downe from the toppe of the church, all his limmes beinge broken. Anno Domini 1587. Allſo three ſouldiors of that towne, which did caſt downe and burne the holye roode of that monaſterie, died within one ſeanight after they hade done it; The firſte *An.* 1580 fell madd, and died within 3. dayes after; The ſecond was eaten with liſe, and died within 5. daies; And the third was kild by the ſaid Earles Senſciall within 7. daies after; all which manny of that towne now liuinge can wittneſſe. The Lord Crowmell *An.* 1608 that caſt downe the ſteeple of S. Patriques Church in Vlſter, dyed within one ſeanight after, ſome ſaid he fell madd, and died therof. Allſo an Engliſh carpenter, that went vp vpon the veſterie of S. Patriques church of Dublin, fell downe, his bones were brokē, and died frantique within 2. dayes after. An Engliſh captaine that pulled downe the *An.* 1609 holie roode of Cahir, rann madd and caſt himſelfe from the toppe of the caſtle of the

ſaid Cahir, headlonge into the riuer, and drowned himſelfe.

9. Garrett Earle of Deſmounde, after beinge proclaimed traitour, accompanied with his brother Sr. Iohn of Deſmound and 800. more in their company, for their firſt exploite, inuaded the towne of Yonghull, which they ſpoyled, ranſacked, burnt, and deſtroyed the howſes, tooke away all the poore inhabitants goodes, ſtript them moſt cruelly of all their cloathes, and left them both man and wooman naked, not permittinge them to hide or couer their ſecreat pertes which nature it ſelfe would faine couer, rauiſhinge married woomen, with manny other wicked actes which they perpetrated, not ſparinge church or ſanctuarie, nor any thinge whatſoeuer that was ſacred, which they polluted & defiled, and brought euery thinge to vtter confuſion and deſolation, makinge hauocke aſwell of ſacred veſtimentes and chalices, as of any other chattle. Certaine Spaniardes which were with them at that wicked exploite, perceauinge by the furniture and ornamentes of the churches, that the townes men were all catholiques and containinge their handes from ſpoiling, were reproued by ſome of that wicked companie, for that they tooke not parte of the ſpoile as others did; but they aunſwered, that they ought not to robbe or ſpoile better chriſtians then themſelues. And one of the ſaid

ſaid Spaniardes cut his cloake as S. Martine did in fiue partes, and diſtributed the ſame vppon fiue children which were ſtript of their cloathes and lefte naked by ſome of the kearnes. But very fewe or none of them eſcaped a miſerable end; For the Earle himſelfe was beheaded by a poore souldior, beinge found in a woode with a verie ſmale companie, and not one ſlaine but he: whoſe head was carried into england, and ſtandes diſgracefullie vppon London bridge for a traitors head. His brother Sr. Iohn was found vppon the highe way by Sr. Iohn Souch, and hauinge notice that the engliſhmen were marchinge towardes him, he was not able hauinge a principall good horſſe to moue hand or foote, vntill the engliſh souldiors came vppon him, and kild him. This is the iuſte iudgment of God, executed vppon them that made the world beleue their quarrell was for religion, and yet their firſt exploite and crueleſt acte was putt in execution vppon poore catholicks churches, ſanctuaries, conſecrated veſſells which they polluted & prophaned. Nothinge doth diſpleaſe God more then hipocriſie, for as a holy man ſaith. *Simulata ſanctitas, eſt duplex iniquitas:* fained holines is double iniquitie, for noe vice is more often reprehended of our Sauiour, then this vice and wickednes, and although he pardoned all manner of *Matt. 23.* ſinnes, yet vnto hipocrites he cried out woe,

 and

and courſe and that many times.

10. Sr. Iohn Norrice in his Portingall voiage with the baſtard don Antony going to take Lisbone and to make him kinge thereof, of his great armie (which conſiſted of 18. thowſand able men) he brought not men enough to bringe home his ſhippes: the firſt enterprice that he attempted, was vppon a monaſterie by the Grine, which his ſoldiors deſtroied and caſt downe. The Earle of Eſex that was the only Phenix of England, the cheefe fauoritt of the Queene, and the only man that all the contrie flatterd and followed, and all the Engliſh nation applauded, was arraigned and condemned of high treaſon, and beheaded in the tower of London, who when he tooke Cales in Spaine (an exploite both terrible to the Spaniardes, & ioyfull and honnorable vnto England) the churches and ſanctuaries of that cittie felt the greateſt ſmarte, which he prophaned, burned, and caſt downe whoſe ſacred veſſells his ſouldiors tooke away and turned them into prophane and filthy vſes; for the which fewe or none that aſsiſted in that exploite, eſcaped an ominous and fatall end, as manny doe obſerue and note. In the Machabees, Heliodorus doth teſtifie thus much who counſelled his kinge if he had an enemie, that he ſhould ſend him to robb the Temple of Hieruſalem, and he ſhould find the ſmarte thereof, becauſe there is in that

*Macha. 2. Cap. 3.*

that place the power of God, which doth destroie and confound such as come to annoy that place.

11. S. Ambrose speakinge with Valentine the yonger vsed these wordes; If you haue noe right to doe anny iniurie to any mans priuate howse, much lesse, can you take away from Gods howse, which neuer suffred sacrilegious persons vnpunished and robbers of churches and sacred thinges, as by the precedent examples appeares: as also by the griuous punishment of Cardinall Wolsy is euident, who for erectinge his new college at Oxford and at Ipswiche (as Stow writteth) obtayned licence of Clement the seauenth to dissolue to the number of fortie monasteries of good fame, and bountifull hospitalitie, wherin the kinge bearinge with all his doinges, none durst controll him. In the executinge of which busines, fiue persons were his cheefe instruments, which were sore punished by God, two of them fel at discord amoungest themselues, and the one slue the other, and the surminor was hanged for his labour, the 3. drowned himselfe in a well, the 4. being wealthie enoughe before, begged his bread to his dyinge day, and the 5. was Doctor Allen. The cheefe instrument amoungest them was murthered by Thomas fitz-Gerrald. The Cardinall fallinge afterwards into the kings greuous displeasure, was deposed, and died *Epist.* 33.

miserably, and the colleges which he meant to haue made soe glorious a buildinge, came neuer to good effecte. For this irreligious robberie was done of noe conscience, but to patch vpp pride, which priuate wealth could not furnishe.

*Whether the kinge may take away church liuinges at his pleasure; And whether as he is absolute kinge of the temporall goodes of his subiectes, he be so also of the Church, and of Churche liuinges.*

## CHAPTER IV.

1. THe only argument Protestants vse to proue this doctrine, is that of the Prophett Samuell, who said to the children of Israell, that if they would needes haue a kinge, he would take away their vineyardes their landes and liuinges, and would bestowe them vppon his seruants &c. The holie doctors doe expound this place to be ment of Tyrannicall kinges, who followinge their passion or proper will, and not lawe or reason, would performe this towardes those stiffnecked people. And soe to diuert and disswade them from the vehement desire they had to gett them a kinge he vsed those wordes, not that of right or iustice a good kinge ought soe to doe. And soe S. Gre-

*Testado in lib. Reg. cap. 19.*

Gregorie doth expound the same sayinge, that Tyrantes and not good kinges will doe this, for ( saith he ) in that historie of kinges wee read, that God was highly displeased with Achab for takinge away the vineyarde from Naboth, for which the said Achab with his Queene Iezabell, was sore punished by God for the same, therfore S. Gregorie saith this was not godes comaundement; And therfore Dauid beinge sollicited at the request of Orna Iebuseus to take a platt of grounde for to edifie an alter for our Lord, he would neuer take or accept it vntill he made payment thereof. Soe as whatsoeuer is sett downe by the prophett Samuell, is to giue warninge to good kinges what they should obserue, and what they should forbeare to doe, thus farr S. Gregorie.

*Lib 4.c 2. & in Reg. cap. 8.*

2. S. Iohn Chrisostome did reprehend the empresse Eudoxia the wife of Arcadius the Emperor, for takinge away from a certaine widdowe her vineyarde, and seinge that he could doe nothinge with her by faire meanes, he caused the church gates to be shutt against her. For Emperors and kinges are not absolut Lordes of the landes, and goodes of their subiectes, neither can they take them away accordinge to their pleasures, vnles it be for great offences, although many protestant courtiers, doe say the contrarie only to flatter their Princes: for

for if Kinges,and Princes had the proprietie and dominion of their ſubiectes goodes, then there ſhould be noe neede of anny parleament, or courtes to treate with the ſubiects for the kinges neceſsitie, but they may take from the ſubiects all they haue at theire owne pleaſure. But the kinge for beinge head and Lord of the kingdome, and for his paines taken in the gouernment thereof hath his owne patrimonie, rents and ſeruices with ſuch like: or if this be not ſufficient for the defenſe of the weale publique & chriſtiã religiõ, the ſubiects ought to ſupplie his wãts, rather by requeſt then by violence. But theſe newe goſpellers ſay with the matchevillians, that kinges by their prerogatiues, may take all their ſubiects goods to their pleaſure: as a flatterer ſaid to the kinge Antigonus, that all thinges are lawfull for the kinge to doe, vnto whome the ſaid Antigonus made aunſwere. Vnto tirannicall and barbarous Princes ſuch thinges are lawfull, but vnto vs, nothinge is lawfull but that which is honeſte.

*Plutar. in Apo.*

3. This is the difference betwixt the good kinge and the tyrant, for the one is ſubiect to the lawes of God and nature: the other is ſubiect to noe lawe, but to his will and his paſsion, hauinge noe reſpect to lawe, conſcience, faith or iuſtice. The one doth reſpect cheefly the good of the weale publique: the other his owne priuate comoditie:

moditie: the one doth enriche his ſubiects by all the beſt meanes he can, the other doth impoueriſh them with all extorſion and impoſition. The one doth reuenge the iniurie don vnto God & the comon wealth, and pardones his owne proper iniurie: the Tyrant doth the contrarie, and doth reuenge his owne quarell, and forgiue the iniurie done vnto God. The one endeuours to preſerue loue and amitie amoungeſt his ſubiects, the other doth ſowe diſſentions and factions amoungeſt them to deſtroy them, and by their deſtruction to enriche himſelfe with the confiſcation of their goodes. The one makes great accompt of the loue of his ſubiects, the other euer groundes himſelfe in the hatred of his ſubiectes; The one doth ſearch the beſt and the moſt vertuous to beſtowe offices and promotions on them: the other doth beſtowe them vppon the wickeddeſt people he can gett. The one is a paſtour to feede his ſubiectes, the other is a woulfe to deſtroy them.

4. But to come to my purpoſe, that it is not lawſull for kinges to doe what it pleaſeth them, the verie heathens haue obſerued the conrrarie. Traian the Emperor when he gaue the ſword to the Pretor of Rome, ſaid theſe wordes. If I ſhall comaund anny thinge that is lawfull or iuſte, vſe this ſword for me, if otherwiſe I ſhall bid or comaund anny thinge againſt iuſtice, vſe it

*Zonarus tomo 2. in Traiano.*

againſt

against me. The kinges of Aegipt did cause their magistrates to sweare, not to obey them, but in thinges lawfull, the same did Phillipp the beautifull kinge of France: and Antigonus the 3. who comaunded his presidentes and magistrates, that they should not execute his comaundement, though it were signed with his owne hande, vnles it were iust, & lawfull. It is an ould prouerbe: *Melius est imperium in quo nihil licet, quam imperium in quo mihi liceat.* It is better to be vnder his gouernment where the lawe giues noe scope, then vnder his where all thinges are lawfull without any restrainte.

5. And for their spiritual comaunde, S. Gregorie Nazian. doth admonishe thē, you (saith he) that are sheepe aske not to feede your pastors, neither intermidle in things that pertaines not vnto your charge, doe not iudge your iudges, nor prescribe lawes to your law giuers, if yow will haue me to be plaine with yow, for the lawe of Christe hath made you my subiectes, and referred you to my tribunall, and that yow are sheepe of my flocke. And therfore S. Chisostome willed kinges to containe themselues within their limittes, for the boundes of priest-hoode is distinguished from the boundes, & limittes of kinges, for that of priest hoode is more, then that of kinges, for the kinges power exceedes not temporall thinges, but the power of priest-hoode came from heauen: the

*Orat. 17. ad Ciues timore percussos.*

*Chrysost. de verbis Isa. Homil. 40*

the kinge hath the charge of our bodyes, but the priest hath to deale with our soules. Luciferius Bishop of Caler saith these wordes. What power haue you (speakinge of Princes) of Bishopps which if you shall not obey by the sentence of God alreadie giuen, you shalbe condemned? S.Iohn Damascen saith, that Princes haue nothinge to doe in Church matters, for that their office is not to gouerne ecclesiasticall state, and therfore S.Paule saith. *Nescitis quod Angelos iudicabimus, multo magis secularia?* Doe you not know that wee shall iudge Angells, much more seculer thinges?

6. The inconuenience of this is declared by two examples, of a politicke courtier, and a religious christian. Ecebolus Sophist, was maister to Iulian the Apostate, and much esteemed of him, this polititian in the gouernment of Constantius, did frame himselfe a christian, to conforme himselfe to the Emperors humour: & when the said Constantius became an Arian heretique, the said Sophiste tourned his çoat also. Againe when Iulian the Apostate, was Emperor, & denied his faith & became an infidle, the said Ecebolus became also an infidle: afterwards when Iulian died and Iouinian also & that a most deuout and godly Catholique succeeded Iulian, Ecebolus like the Cameleon did conforme himselfe to the newe Emperor, & cast him selfe at the Church doore, crauing

pardon

*Lib.3.c.11* pardon of the Christians, as Socrates saith. A liuely representation of the polititians of this time, of whome Iouinian the Emperor *Socrat. li. 3. 21.* said, that they worshipp not God, but the Prince.

7. The other example is of Cesarius, who as his brother S. Gregorie Nazianzen saith, beinge honoured with great offices, and promotions of the said Iulian, and for that he would not forgoe his religion beinge a Catholique, he was disfauoured of the said Iulian, and forsakinge the worlde and the fauor of the Emperor, did set little by all wordly promotion and credit of the Emperor, in respect of the Catholique religion. This example of Cesarius, doth represent vnto vs a fine Catholique, and the other of Ecebolus a fine Polititian of these our dayes. Wherefore if wee endeuour to followe the Princes Religion, as often the kinge doth change the same, soe often wee must alsoe change ours, and soe wee make of the Prince a God, and forsake the liuinge God.

*That*

*That the protestant religion, whose principall foundation and groundes are these articles aforesaid, is nothinge else then a denyinge of all Religion and pietie, and a renewinge of all heresies.*

## CHAPTER I.

1. CAluine in his institutions saith, that S. Augustine of all antiquitie is the best & faithfullest wittnes, but he enrolled your Patrons amoungest old heretiques, as Iouinian, Vigilantius, Aerius, Aquarios, Armenians, Nouatians, Pepusians, Pheudapostles, Euuomians, Pelagians, and Donatistes. Iouinian the Moncke saith, that fastinge or abstinence are of noe worthe. He destroied also the virginitie of the blessed Virgin, affirming that shee lost her virginitie when shee was deliuered of Iesus, and said that continencie in Virgins and religious people, was noe better then matrimonie: and soe certaine Virgins beinge at Rome vpon this heresie did marrie, by which (saith S. Augustine) was comitted a prodigious thinge, and was extinguished so represently that it did not gett footinge amoungest other priestes.

*Inst. li. 4. 14. 7. 15.*

*Aug. to. 6. ab hæresibus 82.*

2. S. Ierom exclaimed against Vigilantius

tius vsinge these wordes. It is a sacrilege to heare what the filthie fellowe calls vs, ashmoungers and idolaters, for that wee reuerence dead meanes bones, which he ment by the reliques of the holie Sainctes. And the said S. Ierom writes, that he denyed the sepulchers of sainctes to be reuerenced, and worshipped, and said moreouer, that the praiers of the holy martyrs profitts nothinge after this life: imitatinge herin wicked Porphiry and Eunomius by callinge them the sorcerie of diuills: therfore S. Augustine did condemne Vigilātius. Aerius did barcke against prayers, and suffrages of the dead: and maketh noe difference betwixt priestes and Bishopps. The Peputians would haue women to be priestes, vnto whome they haue attributed all principalitie August. de hæres. 27. as the Protestantes haue done to Queene Elizabeth Anno 1. Parl. c. 1. Of the same heresie also were condemned, Eunomius, as the said *S. August. de heresi heres. 54. de hæres. & ad Luther*. Nouatus was condemned for an heretique by saint Augustine and saint Ambrose, for denyinge poure of absoluinge sinnes vnto the priests, and confirmation to Bishopps, as saint Cyprian doth wittnes *lib. 4. epist. 2. Theodoret. lib. 3. de hæreticis*. The Pelagians denyed original sinne in infantes: and taught that baptisme is not necessarie for them as saint Augustine writeth.

*Aug de ecclesiasticis dogmatibus c. 73.*

*Luther. tomo 2 li de capti uit. Baby. Aug. Homil 50 de Socrat. hist. l. 4. Cap 23. Ambr de penit. li. 1. cap. 2.*

*Aug. heres.* 88.

3. S. Au-

3. S. Augustine and saint Optatus doe putt the Donatistes in the rancke of heretiques, for sayinge that the churche fayled in the whole world, and that it remayned amoungest themselues in Affrique: the like Caluine saith of the Catholique churche. Those Donatistes did cast the blessed Sacrament vnto doggs, burne churches, and breake alters, tooke away all church ornamentes as you doe, they abolished the sacrifice of the Masse as you doe, of which kinde of people Ignatius sayeth, there hath bene some that would not away with sacrifices and oblations, because they confessed not the Eucharisle to be the flesh of our Sauiour Iesu Christe. Arrius, Nestorius, Dioscorus & Eutiches, as saint Augustine and saint Athanasius saye, and as it is alleadged in the 7. generall councell, act. 1. denied all traditions and the wittnesses of the fathers, they said alsoe they would allowe nothinge but the scriptures sayinge; What scripture doth proue that the sonne is consubstantiall or coessentiall with the Father? the same alsoe did Simon Magus saye.

*Aug. de heres. 69. de vnitate eccle. & lib. cont. litteras Petul. Opta. lib. 2. Cal. inst. l. 4. cap. 15. Optat l. 2. Theod. Dra. 5.*

*S. Aug. lib. contra Maximũ. Atha. p. 488. Exemplũ Synodale,*

4. With Symon Magus, Valentinus, and Manicheus, you denie free will. With Flornius and with Symon Magus, you affirme God to be author of all euill, as S. Augustine, Clemens Alexandrinus & Tertulian saye of the said Symon Magus. With Constantius, you saye that euerie Ciuill

*Aug. heres. 4. 6. Clemens, Alexandrinus li. 3 recognitionum. Tertul. de præscript.*

Prince ought to be head of the churche accordinge to Euſeb.lib. 3. Wherfore S.Athanaſius called him antechriſt, and the abhomination of deſolation, of whome allſoe S. Hillarie ſaith theſe woordes ; I tell you when I ſhall ſpeake vnto you, that I ſpeake to Nero & that Decius & Maximianus ſhal heare me, you fight againſt God,you thunder againſt the church , you perſecute the Saincts , you take awaye the Religion of Chriſte , you are not onlye the Tyrant of men, but of God , you doe preuent antechriſt,and worcke his miſteries , you coyne faith, liuing without faith, thou of all men the moſt wicked : this he ſpoake to him in his life time.

*Atha. epi. ad ſolitariam vitã degentes. Hilar. lib ad Conſtãtium ex li. qui incipit tempus eſt loquendi.*

5. With Marcius and Manicheus , and other heretiques you condemne manny bookes of the ſcriptures,which would not receaue the ſcriptures : *Niſi cum adiectionibus & detractionibus factis*, but with cuttinge & mãglinge of them. You take away Chriſme with Nouatus, who denied the holye ghoaſte. With Iouinian , as S. Auguſtine ſaith of him, you take away pennaunce from the church : who ſaid allo that all ſinnes were equall. Allſo with Pelagius yow take away the Sacrament of orders and prieſt-hoode, with Petrus Abalardus, Wicleffe , and Hus all vocall prayers . And with the Armenians you ſay that matrimonie is noe Sacrament . You take away generall councells with

with the Arians, that would not obey the councell of Nice. With Nestorius that would not obey the councell of Ephesus, with Eutiches and Dioscorus, that would not obey the councell of Chalcedon. With Iouinianus (as saint Augustine wittnesseth) you eate all meates euerie daye without any obseruation of dayes or difference of meate, you doe the like obseruinge noe faste. Caluine tooke away singinge from the church with the heretique Hillarus, as saint Augustine and saint Ambrose say, when Christe is praysed the Arrians are madd. With Iouinian you say, that all which be in heauen are equall in glorie, because all iuste persons are equall in this life in merittes, and all sinners are equall in sinnes. With the Catharies you denie all sacraments; With the heretiques called Lamprini, you take away vowes and votaries. With the Eustachians yow take away churches and alters dedicated to martirs.

*Aug lib. de hæresibus.*

*Aug. li. 1 retract.*

*Ambr. in quadam orat. cont. Maxentiũ de Basilicis tradẽdis quæ ponitur in lib 5. sententiarũ.*

6. Againe, with the Eutichian heretiques, yow take away oblations, sacrifice, and chrisme, as Leo the Pope complained by his letters to Martianus the Emperor epist. 75. where he saith. *Intercepta est sacrificij oblatio, defecit chrismatis sanctificatio.* The oblation of the sacrifice is intercepted, and hallowinge of the chrisme faileth. And as in the time of Antechriste (as that auncient holy father and constant Martyr Hipolitus,

*Epist. 75.*

that liued in the yeare of our Lord 220. saith. *Ecclesiarum ædes sacra tigurij instar erint: pratiosum corpus & sanguis Christi in diebus illis non extabit &c*, the church shall be like cottadges, the blessed body and blood of Christ shall not be seene, the Masse shalbe vtterly defaced, soe as yow seeme to be the precursours of this beast. For with the Donatists (as Optatus writeth) yow giue the blessed Sacrament to dogges, the chrismatorie with the sacred chrisme, yow violentlie cast vpon the grounde, with them also yow breake alters, with them also and with the Arrians of Affricke (as Victor saith) yow ouerthrowe churches, monasteries and chappels, and as they made shirtes and briches of the vestimentes and alter cloathes, burned bookes, spoiled churches of their ornamentes, as appeared in an epistle by the bishoppes of Egipte to Marcus the Pope, and as Nazianzenus saith, *misteria verterunt in commedias*, the misteries of our religiō they turned to playes and comedies, euen soe doe you the like.

*Optat. l. 6. contra Donatist. Optat. l. 2. contra Donatist. Victor de persecut. Vanda. l. 1. cap. 3. Vict. li. 3.*

7. Againe, you refuse with these heretiques, to come to the generall councells, to giue an accompte of your doinges, as saint Augustine saith of them; With Nabuchodonozer the kinge of Babilon, and Antiochus Epiphanes, and Iulian the apostate (which represente the diuill against Christe his spouse) yow spoile his church, yow robbe

*Aug. li. 3. cap. 45. contra Crescen. 4. Reg. 25. 1. Mach.*

robbe her of her treasure, yow violently inuade all sacred places and sanctuaries, yow take away alters, pattens, challices, candlesticks, and all other ornamentes dedicated to the seruice of God: yow defile, abuse and staine all sacred thinges, and as they prohibited sacrifice and oblations, soe yow doe the like. With the said Iulian (which of a vertuous and catholique Prince, became suddainlie a tirannicall persecutor of Christe and his members) yow banishe priestes and religious people, but exceedinge his tiranny herein, yow put them to the cruelest death that the diuill can inuente: yow contemne the crosse of Christe and called them wretched men (as saint Cyrill saith of him) for doinge reuerence to the said sacred crosse, as for making the signe of the crosse in their fore heads, for planting it ouer their doores, for keepinge it in their howses, he did also reproue them for visittinge their sepulchers, for worshippinge reliques of Martyres, for prayinge vnto them at their graues, and called them dead men. And as he ouerthrewe the Image and picture of Christe, the arke and shrine wherin were religiously kept the bones of S. Iohn Baptiste, brake them open, burned them and dispersed abrode the ashes, so yow doe the like. And as the Iewes crucified the Image of Christe as S. Athanasius saith, as their fathers crucified Christe himselfe, soe you doe the like.

*Cyrill. l. 6. contra Iulianum.*

*Cyril. l. 16 contra Iulianum.*

*Zozo. l. 5. cap. 12. Theod. l. 3 cap. 6.*

And as the ethinckes brake the Image of Christe, yow doe the like. Yow followe Aerius, who refused to obserue prescript and appointed fastinge dayes, alleadginge for himselfe that he should not be vnder the Iudaicall yoke of bondage, as our Iuell and other protestantes said, therby claiminge the libertie of their newe gospell.

*Lib. de passione imagini Christi. Zozo. lib. 5. c. 12. Aug. lib. de hære. cap. 33. Epiphan. hæres. 7. 5.*

8. The Manichees and Eustachians, did fast vppon sundayes, for that they would not seeme to reioyce for the resurrection of Christ, as S. Ambrose epist. 83 and saint Augustine epist. 86. doe declare: as also saint Epiph. Heres. 75. Also the Priscilians did fast vpon sondayes and vppon the natiuitie of our Lord, least they should seeme to alow of the humanitie of Christe, as S. Leo in his epistles dooth sett downe. All these you followe, doinge all thinges in despite of the church as Luther did. *Ecce (inquit) quando homo præcipit (Scil. papa) ob id ipsum non faciã, & si non præcepisset vellem facere*, when man comaundes (vid. the Pope) I will not obey him, for that he comaunded, and if he had not comaunded, I would haue don it, I will doe it when I shall thincke good; as the said Aerius saide, that he would not obey the churche in his fastinge, and yet did not God comaũd vs to obey his church and the rulers thereof in manny places sayinge, whosoeuer despiseth you despiseth me? &c.

*Luth. de conf. part. 3. parag. 14.*

*Matt. 16.*

9. The

9. The Donatistes taughte (as S. Augustine saith) that the churche of God consisted only of the good, and that the visible church manny yeares agoe did perishe, and that it did consiste only of their owne secte and congregation, as you hold the same to be in your owne secte onlie. If wee must become protestants, wee muste embrace all these foresaid heresies condemned by all the holie doctors, generall councells of Christendome, and the vniuersall Catholique churche in all ages: wee must also mantaine newe heresies farr worse then the former, and inuent more of them. As that the Trinitie of God, the deitie of Christ, his passion, death and resurrection, are but papisticall inuentions, and that they oughte, as breers as brambles to be cast out of the vineyard of the Lord, these be the wordes of one of the familie of loue, in the articles printed at London.

*Aug. lib. de vnitate eccles. c. 12.*

*An. 1579.*

10. Did not the Protestantes of Hungarie putt vpp conclusions at Albaiulia, that it is Idolatrie to adore Christe, which also they haue defended through all Germanie? Did not Whitakers say, that the image of Christe is as verie an Idoll, as the image of Venus or Iupiter? That Christe is not gotten of the substance of his Father. That S. Peter was neuer at Rome. That the succession of Popes is antechriste, that the vniuersal church is antechriste? They say moreouer

*VVitak. cont. Sander. pag. 150.*

*VVhitak. 4. cap. pag. 154.*

that the blood of Christe auailes nothinge for our saluation, and that it did putrifie more then 1500. yeares agoe. Conradus a protestant writer doth charge Caluine with this doctrine and other protestants, that we be not iustified by the meritts of Christe, with manny such blasphemies vide sup. *Ex Caluino Turcismi lib. 4. cap. 22.* that wee cannot obserue godes lawes. Buny in his christian exercise dedicated to the Archbishopp of Yorke did saie of the blessed virgin, when shee stoode at the crosse in the time of Christe his death, that shee violated the first comaundement, as also the 5. 6. and 9. comaundement.

*Conrad. in Theologia Caluin. l. 1 artic. 6. fol. 26. Curius in spongia fol. 250.*

11. Moreouer, Beza saith, that Christe was borne as other children are borne, and that Marie brought him forth naturallie. The same also Peter martyr, and Caluine holde. The said Caluine saith, that Christ was borne as Constantinus Copronimus was borne, which all Greeke writers call the mounster of Affricke, and the sincke of all impietie, and mischeefe. Which wicked doctrine is against the catholique Faithe which saieth in our creede, that Christe was cōceaued of the blessed Virgin. So Archiball Hamelton shewes, that they make the vildest wooman in the world, equall vnto the blessed Virgine. Caluine attributed ignorance vnto Christe, & saith that he obtained godes fauour by faithe. That Lutherans denie

*In præf. noui testamenti Peter Martyr dialogo corporis Christi. Calu Harmo. Mat. 2 Constant. Manaßes in Analib. pag. 114 Hamelton Calu. confus. de monst l. 2 Calu. in Ca. 24.*

denie Christe his assension into heauen. That Caluine denies Christe his descension into hell: others of them denies the true passion of Christe vppon the crosse. Luther saith, that if wee haue faith, wee are equall in dignitie with saint Peter, and saint Paule, with the blessed Virgin and all the sainctes, and that God is as fauorable vnto such as haue his faith, as to Christ himselfe, and that wee haue noe lesse righte vnto life euerlastinge, then he: and that wee be noe lesse deliuered from eternall death then he.

*Cal. Matt. 27. Smidl. in vita Bullenger. Calu. inst. l. 2. Carlil. impress. Londini 1582. Luth. to. 5 in enarratione in Petr. c. 1.*

12. Others said, that whosoeuer hath this faith, God is bound to giue vnto him the kingdome of heauen, and that through our faith though neuer soe little (notwithstandinge anie wickednes) wee should be secure of heauen, & that there is no sinne before God, but incredulitie. That the tenn comaundements pertaine not to Christiãs. That accordinge to Caluine it is impossible to the Sainctes to obserue the comaundements; Also that there is noe paines of damnation for man, but to thincke that God is aduersarie to him. Petrus Rycherus said, (who was it were the Idoll of Beza, and who was sente by Caluine vnto the weaste Indies) that Christe should not be prayde vnto. Wherfore he tooke *Gloria Patri & Filio &c.* out of the Psalmes of Dauid.

*Beza in confess fidei. Gene. c. 4. Luth. de lib. Christ. Luth. ser. de Moyse. & lib. de Capt. Bab. Calui. 2. inst. cap. 7. Calu. lib. 3 cap. 25.*

13. Did not Cartwrith say. I cannot be persuaded that saint Peter and saint Paule were

*Cart. in 2. repl. pa. 191.*

were soe foolish, as to thincke, that a poore miserable man, which they saw with their eyes, was their God. Beza alsoe holdes the same, and many others of that stampe, yea some of them, that were burnt in Queene Maries dayes, and related by Fox for Martyrs, houlde. That Christ was in desperation when he was vppon the crosse, accordinge to Caluine. That God is the author and cause of sinne, the procurer, and intiser, comaunder and worker, and that the adulterie of Dauid, and the treason of Iudas, was as well the worke of God, as the conuersion of saint Paule. And that man hath noe free will: with manny such horrible blasphemies to tedious for me to repeate, and irksome for anny Christian to heare. Soe as by these wicked paradoxes, it must followe, that God is turned to be a diuill, and that he is most vniuste to condemne men for the offenses which they cannot shunne, hauinge noe free will to auoide them, nor noe force to resiste God, the worker, counceller, and intiser to sinne.

*Beza in respō. ad arg. Brētij Epist. 6. Fox. in hist. Carelessi pag. 1534. Calu. in Hermo. in Euange. Calu. insti. l. 1. c. 18. Peter martyr in 1. Sam. 2. Melancthon in c. Rom. 8. Calu. li. de eterna Dei præ-dest. pag. 101. Zuinglius li. de prouidentia.*

*That*

*That noe iott or ſillable of Chriſtian religion, ought to be counted a thinge indifferent or of ſmale moment, and that whoſoeuer doth not agree with the Catholique Church in all pointes of beleefe, cannot be ſaued.*

## CHAPTER III.

1. S. Thomas ſaith, that whoſoeuer doth err in one article, he hath noe faith of the reſt: for as ſaint Vincentius Ferar. ſaith, vertue hath noe more fondations then one, and the ſame is indiuiſible, which is the diuine trueth, which cannot be deceaued, nor deceaue: and ſoe whoſoeuer doubteth in one, hath noe foundation of the reſte For if a rocke ſhould fall, vppon which there ſhould be 12. chambers, all thoſe chambers would fall alſo: euen ſoe the proteſtants in the beginninge fell from the church, which is the rocke vppon which Chriſte builded theſe 12. chambers, I meane the twelue articles of our beleefe, ſoe once they fallinge from the church, they fell from theſe 12. articles; and came vnto vs, *in ſpiritu erroris & mendacij*, in the ſpirite of error and lienge. This Martin Luther ſaid of the Zuinglians. In vaine (ſaith he) they beleeue in God, the father, the ſonne, and the holie ghoaſt, and all the reſt, becauſe they denie this one article

*S. Thom. 2. 2. q. 5. 3.*

*Luth. dialog. 6. c. 11*

article. *Hoc est corpus meum:* this is my bodie.

2. For this cause Iconoclasters or Image-breakers are auncient heretiques, because they denie that article of the catholique church of the reuerencinge of sacred images. How many of al estates, prelates, nobles and common people, suffred eyther death or banishmente in the time of the Emperors that were image breakers? for they considered that whosoeuer obserueth all the lawe, and offendeth in one, is guilty of all the reste. The trewe mother of the child would haue noe diuision thereof. *Nonne isti* (saith saint Augustine) *quos vocatis hæretici*, doe not these which you call heretiques, confesse the same trinitie, beleue also in Christe, and yet they were called auncient heretiques, whose heresies were knowen and nowe altogether extin-
*Aug. lib. 2 de trinit. cap. 17.* guished through their absurdities. *Hoc qui credunt* (saith he) *lib. 2. nec tu in catholica fide, sed in schismate aliquo aut hæresi credunt*, whosoeuer beleeueth all articles of the creede and otherwise remaininge in any scisme and heresie, cannot be in the catholique faith.
*Zozo. li. 3. cap. 17. Theod. l. 2 cap. 18. & 21.* The Arrians denied but one letter in the creede, and yet saint Ierom saith, that if the church had not resisted the Emperor Valens which did fauour the Arrians, touchinge that letter which was *Omusion*, in steed of *Omision*, Christendome (saith he) would haue bene in great danger.

3. When

3. When the prefect of the Arrian Emperor Valens, dealt with saint Basil that he should not be soe obstinate or wilfull in his opinions, but that he should conforme himselfe to the Emperor and liue in his fauour, he answered; that such as are fedd with the daintie feastes of holy scriptures, they would suffer all kinde of tormentes rather then any iott, sillable or letter should be chaunged. And as for the Emperors frindshipp, he did esteeme it well, soe that it were not against pietie and religion. S. Chrisostome vppon that place of saint Paule. *Hauinge peace with euerie bodie.* Wee ought not to preferr (saith he) peace before godes trueth, when the same is in danger, but rather to offer our liues for the defence thereof. Soe as yow see that the Arrians were condemned for heretiques for one letter, beinge in all other pointes catholiques, but the protestantes haue raised from hell all the heresies that euer were, for noe heretiques almoste that euer were, but kept ecclesiastical seruice and ceremonies like the catholiques, but the protestants haue taken away all: therfore they should not bragge that their religion is agreable to the word of God, or the Romish church, or that the Romish church, or anny member thereof, should ioyne with them therein.

*In vit. Basil. Naz. orat 20. in laudem Basilij.*

*Rom. 12.*

*That*

*That the newe Religion, for that it takes away all religion, is worse then that of the Turckes and Gentiles.*

## CHAPTER IV.

*Stur. de rat. concordiæ ineundæ.*

1. STurmius a protestant wryter sayeth, that Lutherans and Caluinistes do destroye and take away the cheefeste articles of Christian religion, and the fondation of our faith. Which thus is proued to be true; That religion is beste, which thinckes of God most reuerentlie, and of their neighbours most charitably: but the Turcks and Gentiles doe farr excel the new religion in worshippinge God and helpinge their neighbors: therfore it must needes be better, then the new. Cicero sayeth, that God is a certaine excellent and eternall nature, and that the order of ecclesiasticall thinges, is the beawtie of the world: who although they did speake of manny godes, yet they affirme Iupiter to be the father of all the reste, and saie that they did worshipp but one God, and the reste of the godes as the ministers of one God, as Iustinus martyr said, and Plato saith. *Deus qui bonus est, malorum causa non est*; God which is good, is not the cause of euills: and in another place he saith, God is not vniust, but most iust. But the new religion doth say (in

*Cicero lib. 2. de diuinitate.*

*Instit. de monarchia Dei lib. 3. cap. 1.*

*Plato de repub. dialogo 2. in fine.*

(in the chapter aboue recited) that God is the cauſe of all miſcheefe and wickednes: by which wicked aſſertion they make him a deuill.

2. All philoſophers did referre all the inferior motions, to a certaine ſupreame motiue, by the conſideration whereof, they found a certaine ſupreame mouer, and a certaine euerlaſtinge cauſe, which is the center of bediningе, and principle of all thinges, vnto whome all thinges are ſubordinated. The Turcks ſaie, that God is immutable, mercifull, pittifull, one onlie, who giues euerie man according to his worckes, reward to the good, and tormentes to the badde, and ſoe they call God, *la, Ila, Mahomet reſulã* God, God aboue, and Mahomet his prophet. But the new religion doth ſay he giues noe reward to the good, nor tormentes to the badd, ſoe that he hath any iott of faith with him, and the more wicked a man is, *Lutherus.* the neerer he is to Gods fauour. The Turcks doe beleue that it is poſsible to keepe godes lawes, but the newe religion doth ſay it is impoſsible, and that heauen is giuen to thoſe that haue any faith, without anny reſpect to works or mans endeuour. The Turcks alſo affirme, that Chriſte aſcended vnto heauen in his fleaſhe, and ſitteth in the preſence of God. The Turckes Alcoran ſaies, that Ieſus Chriſte was the ſonne of the Virgin Marie, was inſpired by God, that

that he was the worde, the ſpiritte, the wiſdome, and the minde of God the father, and that he was the Meſsias, and the Prince
*Thent.l 6. cap. 4. Alcoran. Azoar. 2. 20. Azoar. 31.* that was promiſed vnto the Iewes. Alſo they ſay, that the ſpiritt of God did enter into Marie, and that Ieſus was begotten of her, ſhee beinge a moſte pure Virgine. That God did indue her ſoule, with greater grace and vertue, then the ſoule of anny that was, and that of all men and women ſhee was the beſt, the pureſt, and the godlieſt, and that of all the children of Adam, none was vnſpotted and vndefiled by Sathan but Marie and her child. Azoar. 3. 76. The new religion beleeues of her noe ſuch matter, and compares her with their owne mothers and ſome of them calle her, a ſaffron bagg.

3. Vnder the dominion of the Turcks, the chriſtians are permitted without anny reſtraint, to exerciſe all the rites and exerciſes of chriſtian religion: not ſoe vnder princes of the new religion, who are greater perſecutors of the catholique chriſtian religion, then anny Turcks, Iewes, Gentiles or pagans that euer were. In Conſtantinople there are many monaſteries ſtanding, and repleniſhed with religious people, in Grecia and other of the Turcks Dominions, are at this day many degrees, orders, and eccleſiaſticall dignities of the church, and chriſtian paſtors, as Patriarches, Metropilitans, Archbiſhoppes, Biſhopps, and Prieſts,

Priests, vnto all which it is lawfull to consecrate, to say Masse, and Mouncks, Deacons and Subdeacons, doe minister at the Alter. There are all also other officers which they call Agnests, which doe read vppon sondayes the epistles. There are also *Archimandritæ*, that is to say, the Fathers of Moncks. These Patriarches are chosen by Metropolitans, Archbishopps and Bishopps, and are confirmed by the cheefe Bassa the kinges viccar: the next vnto these, are the Metropolitans, the cheefest of them, is the Metropolitan of Thessalonica, which hath vnder him 10. Bishopps, the Metropolitan of Athens, hath vnder him 6. Bishopps. In that cittie of Athens, were seene in a publique profession together 250. priests, there is a Metropolitan of Mitelin, but he hath no Bishopps vnder him. The Metropolitan of Chalcedon hath vnder him 60. priests. There is a Metropolitan of Nyce, but he hath noe Bishoppe; The Metropolitan of Ephesus, hath hnder him 50. churches. The Metropolitan of Philipen, hath 150. Antioch 40. Churches, Smyrnensis 150. and Corinth, with other Metropolitans 6.

4. All doe agree with the Catholique religion in euerie pointe, exceptinge 3. or 4. errors of the Greeks. This is knowen by the censure that Ieremie the Patriarche hath giuen of the protestant religion, which was sent by him thẽ into Germanie, who sought

an vnion betwixt them and the Greeke church, seeinge they forsooke the Latine church, or rather God, and the Latine haue forsaken them; but the said Patriarche did abhor, and refuse an vnion with them, and said there was asmuch difference betwixt them, as betwixt heauen and hell. You may read more of this matter in Michell ab Iselt Anno 1580. Also the Patriarch of Philadelpha called Gabriell, did write vnto Martinus Crusius a Lutheran of this matter, requestinge him neuer to trouble him, touchinge either, vnion or confirmation of his doctrine.

*Surius hist. ibid.*

5. To cōclud this matter, if Turkes, Iewes, and Gentiles, thincke more reuerently of God the Father, of Christ Iesus his sonne, and of his blessed mother, yea and do shew more fauor to christians, then those of the new religion doe, I must thincke and conceaue a better opinion of Turckes then of these new vpstarts, for S. Thomas saith, that heresie is a greater sinne, thē paganisme and Iudaisme: for althoughe infidels denye more articles of faith then heretiques, yet because heretiques do persecute the church with greater malice then the other, and the greater malice argueth the greater sinne, therfore heretiques are the greater sinners. For as saint Paule saith, an hereticall man is damned by his owne proper iudgment: therfore I leaue the conclusion to the consideration of the reader.

*D. Tho. 2. 2. q. 10. art. 6.*
*Tit. 4.*

An

*An answer vnto Protestants, barkinge against the religious institutions of holy Orders, saying that religious vocations were not instituted by our Sauiour.*

## CHAPTER I.

1. IF humane nature had continued in that blessed perfection of originall integrity, in which it was created, there would not be required (that grace excepted which in the beginning was infused and superadded vnto it) so many other graces and helpes, preueniēt & subsequent, exciting her slacknes and brackwardnes, and expelling her corrupt inclination and propension to sensuality, to corruptible, base, and vile creatures. Wherfore the creator and protector of man whose nature is goodnes, whose proper worke is mercy (as S. Leo saith) doth neuer cease or desiste from giuinge of all helpes and meanes to repaire and redresse this humane imbecillitie, by proposing and intimating all such sufficient motiues to worke our saluation withall, conuincing our negligence and vnprouident carelesnes, if wee will imbrace and put the same in due execution: so as for curing and healing the contagious maladies and restles diseases

contracted and engendred by originall and capitall sinne, he instituted the Sacramente of Baptisme, and also for cleansinge and purginge vs from actuall and personall comitted after Baptisme, he hath ordained and deuised other Sacramentes, either to be supported by them that wee should not fall, or to be raised vp againe and releiued, if wee were fallen.

2. Amongst all conuenient meanes ordeined, either for reforming our said vicious inclination, or increasing our perfectiō, noné are so certaine, or so secure as the religious state, the assured sanctuary and common support of all Christians, and specially of such as are plunged and perplexed, with the continuall fluxe and reflux of humane frailtie, and Adams agony; For besides so many euident testimonies of Gods particular fauour and spirituall consolation that he doth bestowe on it, to take away the occasion of sinne, who euer liued more vertuously or more religiously then those that were retired & sequestred from the daungerous occasions thereof, & the alluring inducementes of the vanities of this world? *Elongaui fugiens & mansi in solitudine*, I fled retiring my selfe, and remained alone vid. from such as by their importunate and alluring conuersation of filthy concupiscence, sought to bringe me to confusion.

3. It is said in the person of a religious man

man exempted and freed from all seculer designementes. *Audiuimus eum in Euphrata,* I haue heard him at the pleasant riuer of Euphrata, that springeth out of paradise, I haue founde him in the fertile feildes amids the woods. Not in the pallace of King Pharao, but in the wildernes, the Angells appeared vnto Moises, wherefore in the desert he receaued the deuine lawes with many other spirituall consolations. S. Iohn Baptist, least his blessed conuersation should be defiled and prophaned, with the idle and loose cõmunication of his kinsmen, fled into the wildernes. When God through speciall fauour appeared vnto Abraham, and would recapitulate certaine great and hidden misteries vnto him, he said these wordes. Departe from your natiue country, and your carnall freindes, and goe a farr off. It is said vnto the spouse of Christe. *Obliuiscere populum tuum, & domum patris tui.* Take no care of thine owne kindred, and remember not thy fathers house. The Apostle after he became the seruant of Christe. *Non acquieuit carni & sanguini,* did bid adieu to flesh and bloud. Elias and Mary Magdalen in the wildernes, were dreadfull vnto the deuills, gratefull vnto the Angells, acceptable vnto God, and famous to the world. *Gen. 12.*

4. Did not Elias resemble the state of a religious person, who was without wife, without children, without family, allwaies

liuinge chaste and continente, being in that pouerty, as he is described with hairy skinnes, and as it were begging his bread of a
*4. Reg. 1.* poore widdow, somtimes receiuing it from a crowe? Did not Elizeus, giuing ouer his
*3. King. 17* *3. Reg. 19* landes and chattells, & forsaking parentes, house and home, giue good example of a religious state, followe that perfection, and accomplishe that votary life. Wherefore S.
*Hier. ep. 4* *Epist. 15.* Hierom calls them monckes of the ould testament; in which number he reckoneth himselfe, saying. Our prince Elias, or leader Elizeus, our captaines, the children of the prophets also in the said ould law were the
*Num. 6.* Nazarites, dedicated to the seruice of God, so as saint Basill, calleth the religious people
*Nazianz. oratione in laudem Basilij.* of the ould testament Nazarites, which by solemne vowe consecrated themselues wholy to this religious profession: they refrained from wine, and from any thinge that might distemper their mindes, that so wee likewise should not only abstaine from sinne, but also from all the prouocations and inducementes of the same; neither from man, or by man did it come, but from
*VValdēs. de sacrament tit. 9 cap. 33. Clito. l. 3. cap. 9. Greg. 2. dial. cap. 8* the sonne of God, in which are all the treasures of wisedome and knowledge, as all holy fathers doe witnes, and especially Thomas Waldensis against Iohn Wickliffe, Clitoueus against Luther and other heretiques of his time. S. Gregory against Florineus, which most sharpely persecuted S. Benedict

and

and his holy order.

5. What more euident proofe or conuincing reasons can we haue, then our sauiours owne wordes? for the religious state consisteth of three vowes, I meane perpetuall chastity, voluntarie, pouertie, and constant and perfect obediēce, which Christ ordayned against the three maladies of our soule, which is concupiscēce of the eye, concupiscence of the flesh and pride of life; touchinge the first, he saith, there are Eunuches which haue gelded themselues from the beginning from the kingdome of heauen, meaning therby that such people by their solemne vowe of religious chastitie, and of inuincible and vowed continencie, did cutt away all liberty and occasion of wedlocke, and vnchaste desires of fleshly allurementes. Of pouerty he said in plaine tearmes; vnlesse one will renounce all that he possesseth, he cannot be my disciple. In another place he forbiddeth the Apostles to carry either goulde or siluer, scrippe or purse. Of obedience he saith. He that listeth to come to follow after me, let him deny himselfe, take vp his crosse and follow me. By this abnegation and deniall of himselfe, the holy doctors haue euer vnderstood the vow of obedience, as may appeare plainly by the counsell of Zenon; all which three vowes our Sauiour counselled, which are called euangelicall councells, and so they are

*Matt. 19.* *Luc. 14.* *Luc. 10.* *Luc. 9.* *Conc. zen. decre.*

*Matt.* 19. recorded by the Euangelistes, as may ap-
*Mar.* 10. peare by the younge man that sought our
*Luc.* 18. Sauiours counsell for the purchasing of life euerlasting, who neuerthelesse from his childehood kept the commaundementes, yet he counselled him, if he would be perfecte, to goe and sell all that he had, to giue the same to the poore, and to follow him, and he should haue greate treasure in hea-
*Matt.* 19. uen. For by selling all his goods, he should make himselfe incapable to demaunde them againe: & by following of him doth plainly signifie other euangelicall counsailes, especially that of obedience, which counsell, being vnaduisedly reiected of the young man, was embraced of the Apostles, for S. Peter in the name of them all saith, wee forsooke all thinges; by which wordes saint
*Iere, lib.* 1. Hierome prooued against Iouinian, that the
*in Iouin.* Apostles being after admitted to the Apo-
*S. Tho.* 2, 2 stolique dignitie, were continente and
*opus.* 88. chaste without exercising coniugall society;
*ar.* 4. *ad* 3. so saint Thomas and sainct Augustine saie,
*Aug.* 17. that the Apostles obliged themselues by
*de ciuit.* 4. vowe, to follow this estate of perfection, when by forsakinge all thinges they followed Christe.

*That*

*That the Apoſtles and their followers in the primatiue church, followed this eſtate of perfection.*

## CHAPTER II.

1. WEe reade in the actes, that all thinges amongſt the Chriſtiãs were comon, & whatſoeuer lãds, houſes, chattels, or mooueables they had, all was ſould and the price thereof brought before the Apoſtles. And this they did as they were obliged by vowe, and as votaries they accompliſhed the ſame as ſaint Hierome expoundeth (related by Platus, *de bono ſtatu religioſi*) vpon that place of the Actes, where Ananias with Saphira was ſtroken dead by S. Peter for reſeruing to himſelfe parte of his goodes which he had gotten for the land he ſould. For you (ſaid he) did not lye to man but to God: but had not he promiſed the ſame, he ſhould not haue bin taxed with that imputation of a ly againſt the holy ghoſte, nor ſo ſore a puniſhment would haue bin inflicted vpon him, had it not bin in his free choiſe to bringe the valew and price of all his goodes vnto the Apoſtles; And S. Hierom ſaith, that the ſtate of the Chriſtians in the beginninge, was like vnto that of the Monks in his owne tyme, in ſuch ſorte that none had

*Act. 5.* *Act. 2. v. 44.* *Act. 5.* *Act. 2.*

had any propriety of goods, none rich or poore amoungst them, theire patrimonie was equally distributed, euerie man receiuinge an equall portion: they imployed their study and their tyme in prayers, psalmes, reading and other religious exercises, as S. Luke and Phylo doe reporte.

*In descriptione Ecclesiæ apud Philonem.*
*Act. 2.*

2. Cassianus testifieth that this religious discipline of monasteries and conuentes, was not only begunne by the Apostles, but also was much increased and augmented by them, and much more by their immediate and next successors, men and weomen were disioined and sequestred one from another, absteining from wedlocke, communication of flesh and bloud, and from all idle and friuolous conuersation of worldly vanities. And therefore for solitarines they were called Monkes; and for communitie of all thinges amongst themselues, they were called Cenobitę. This religiouse discipline and strict profession, was first practised by saint Marke the Euangeliste, as S. Hierom & Cassianus doe auouch, for not only at Hierusalem and Alexandria this order was established, but in other partes of the world, as in Ethiopia the daughter of the Kinge there, was consecrated vnto God by saint Mathew the Apostle, holy Thecla by saint Paul in Grecia, Domitilla by saint Clement at Rome, in Fraunce saint Martha the good hostesse of our Sauiour erected a monaste-

*Cass. 2. lib. cap. 5. & col. 18. c. 5*

*Hier. in vita Mar.*

monasterie by Marcells in a place very remote, where she with other religious weomen liued most vertuously.

3. Dionysius Areopagita saint Paules disciple, declareth at large, not only their increase in his owne time, but also of their profession, ceremonies, and honour they had in the world. Philo the Iew, which spake with saint Peter at Rome, did write a booke in the commendacion of the professors of this religious profession, thereby to extoll his owne nation for that they were so vertuously addicted: Eusebius allso alleadgeth Philo, and largely setteth downe his wordes to this purpose. Tertullian wrote a booke of the vailing or mourninge of Virgins. So wee read a decree of Pius the first Pope of that name, being set foorth Anno 147. of the order in consecrating of virgins, which order or ceremonies, saint Ambrose and saint Eusebius sett downe. Also Iustinus martyr Apologetico 2. *pro christianis*, *Clemens Alexandrinus ad Stromatum 2.* Ignatius disciple to saint Iohn the Euangelist ad Tarsenses. *S. Cipr. lib. 1. epist. 11.* and *Origenes Homil. 17.* S. in Luke, doe write of the order and consecration of Virgins. Ruffinus and Theodoretus doe write when S. Helena went to Hierusalem to finde out the crosse of Christe, that then she founde virgins there dedicated to God; and all auncient writers that euer wrote were not forget-

*Dionys. de Eccles. Hier. c. 10 in descrip. Eccles. in vita Mar.*

*Euseb. 1. Eccl. hist. cap. 17. Tert. de veland. virg. 10. q. 1. ca. virginis.*

*Lib. de inst virg c. 17. Euse. c 4.*

*Ruff. l. 10. hist. Theod. l. 1 cap. 18.*

forgettfull of virgins, vowes, and votaries, with which the Churche of Chriſt floriſhed in all ages.

*Of the increaſe of religious orders, and how the ſame continued from time to time vntill our dayes.*

## CHAPTER III.

1. THe church of Chriſte hauing no intermiſsion or time of breathinge from the cruell and terrible ſtormes of bloody perſecuting tirantes for the ſpace of 300. yeares, when all the princes of this world complotted, all deuiſed pollicies, extended their force, exercifed theire bloody imbruementes to deſtroy her, no prince or monarche being a chriſtian vntill Conſtantine the greate, about the yeare of our Lord 305. became a chriſtian, at which tyme the church floriſhed in great peace and proſperity. This religiouſe inſtitution of Virgins, increaſed alſo by the great ſaint Antony the Moncke of Egipt, commonly ſo called for his great ſanctity, auſterity of life, contempt of the world, mortification of his carcaſe, hatred of himſelfe, and inflamed charity towardes God; and althoughe wee reade there were religious places wherein this religiouſe profeſsion was exercifed, yet as ſaint Athanaſius

*Athan in vita Anthonij.*

sius writeth, he was the first that reduced and trained them to the order of monasticall rules and discipline, instructing them with the rudimentes of this spirituall warfare, and that vnder the gouernment and leading of others, from whome like the industrious Bee, he collected certaine spirituall honie, as well for his owne education, as for the instruction of others, his resplendent sanctity being a shining light in the whole world: by his blessed examples all the desertes of Armenia, Scithia, Nitia, and both Thebaidas were replenished with monasteries, all which were directed by the prouident care and wisdome of the said S. Antony, being as it were their father generall, whome others imitated and followed, as S. Hillarion who was another S. Antony, who founded first monasteries in Palestine as S. Hierom saith. Our Lord Iesus hath old S. Antony in Egipt, he hath younge Hilarion in Palestine, and so others followed his steps, and many monasteries learned from his, the precepts of a celestiall life,

2. In the same tyme also S. Basill the great (so called also for his great learninge and sanctity) instituted in Greece monasticall order and discipline, who in a certaine epistle writeth thus; Wee are accused (saith hee) that we cause men to exercise piety, to forsake the world and all temporall cares, which

which our Lord compared to thornes which hinder the fertility of Gods worde, for such people doe carry the mortification of Iesus in their bodies, and carringe their crosse, they followe Christe. I heare (saith he) that in Egipt there be some that doe imbrace this vertue, and perhaps in Palestine there be some that follow this euangelicall life. I heare also that in Mesopotania there are blessed and perfect people, but wee are boyes in cōparison of such as be perfect: so that S. Basill both augmented and directed this reguler life, according to order and rules; for first of all he established most holy lawes, that should confirme this holy institution, he also determined a tyme of triall, which being expired, euery one was bound to accomplish his vowe. Of whom Naziazē saith, he was the first, not only for his owne good, but for the good and spirituall consolation of other that founded monasteries, and reduced the old obseruation and ceremonies of the old monkes, into a certaine forme and order more agreable to religion.

3. S. Augustine writeth, that he saw at Millan a monastery mainteined by S. Ambrose; and saint Augustine himselfe as Posidonius declareth, founded monasteries for men and weomen in Africke: the same also writeth S. Antoninus, that before saint Augustine was annointed Bishop, he erected a monastery in a wood neere Hippo, which

*August 8. conf. cap. 6*

*Antonin. 3. tit. 24. c. 14.*

as

as well in his life tyme, as allso after his death was much increased, by whose blessed propagation and budding offspringe out of the conterminat citties, others retired themselues vnto that deuout and safe sanctuary, but certaine yeares after saint Augustines death, by the irruption of the Barbarians, they were cast downe and dispersed, some came to Italy, some to other places, which before liued in the wildernes as Ermits, and were reduced afterwardes to liue in monasteries and conuentes in citties by Innocentius the 4. Pope of that name 1243. that by their religious examples their neighbours might be edified and instructed.

4. S. Benedict who flying the world and liuing in the wildernes instituted his ordre in Moũt Cassin anno 520. in a short tyme made 12. monasteries, and brought colonies into France by Maurus, into Cicilia by Placidus, into other places by others: more of him is related by saint Gregory the great. Frõ this religious order many other families sprõge, the first was that of Cluny, which about anno 923. tooke his name of Odõ Abot of Clunie, who being a moste learned & religious man, reformed this order, & being through antiquity and other causes slackned, was by him reduced to his former sanctity, whose religiouse example, was imbraced and followed by other Abotes in Italy, Spaine, Germany, and England, euery one casting

*Greg. 2. dia. cap. 3. & 36.*

casting and laying downe a certaine proiect for this reformation, and vsing all possible meanes, crauing herein the authority of the Popes, which they obteined for the renuinge and obseruinge the said auncient discipline.

5. Next him followed Romualdus, who laboured and accomplished this reformation in the yeare of our Lord God 1000. whose family are called those of Camulduensis, which florished in all examples of sanctity and perfection of life, and so mooued all places of the world where they were to follow their blessed and rare institution.

6. Next him succeded those of Valle Vmbrosia by one Gualbertus, this man was so infestuous and offensiue to a certaine person for murthering his brother, that he neuer omitted the pursute of him, vntill he tooke him, who neuertheles for that he prostrated himselfe at his feete, and asked pardon and mercy of him for the passion of Christe (whose feast at that very season was solemnized by the christians) did remitt vnto him that trespas, and did him no harme, in so much that former malice and rancor was turned to loue and charity. Whereupon the said Gualbertus, went to the next church and praied before the Image of the crucifixe, which bowed its head vnto him, as if the said Image would imbrace him; after which tyme he was so inflamed and enkindled

led with the loue of that religious and contemplatiue life, that in that very place of the Vale of Vmbrosia, he determined to put his religious purpose in due execution, which afterwardes increased by many that followed him.

7. And What family in the world more famous for the like sanctity, then those of Cister? which in the yeare of our Lord 1098 had their beginninge and offpringe, in the tyme of Henry the 4. Emperor, and Philip the first king of France, by one Robert which was prefect of the abbie of Mollissmē, who for that he saw the Monckes through great riches, and other worldly allurementes degenerate from their first rule and institution, departed with twentie one of such as were more perfect then the rest into Burgundy, where in a certaine desert called Cister he fixed his aboad, and so sequestred, he liued most religiously; but the Monkes being mooued with pennaunce, requested his returning againe vnto them, & promised vnto him to be reformed, and reclaimed; he therefore hauing placed in his rome one Stephen, returned to his former monastery. But Cisters was 15. yeres afterwardes confirmed in sanctity and increased with monasteries by saint Bernard, who entred into the same with 30. fellowes and 3. of his brethren, who increased in estimation, & credit both with God & men, wherupon

in a ſhorte time was builded for him 160. monaſteries, and all this familie ſprunge out of the inſtitution of S. Benedict.

8. About that time alſo, being 16. yeares before the inſtitution of ſaint Bernard, begāne the order of the Carthuſiās through the ſtrange and dolefull example of a great doctor of Parris, who being by the common opinion of all men, counted a verie good and honeſt man, yet after his death at his exequie and funerall, in the open aſſemblie he ſaid the firſt time, that he was accuſed; the ſecond time he ſaid, he was iudged; and laſte of all that he was condemned: at which dreadfull voice one Bruno, an eminent and learned Doctor of Parris being preſent, was ſo amazed and terrified, that turning himſelfe to ſome that were with him, he ſaid, who can be ſaued vnles he doe forſake the whole world? Wherfore he fled preſently into the deſertes neere to the cittie of Gratianople in Fraunce, and there liued ſolitarie. And that his ſaid purpoſe was acceptable vnto God, it was reuealed in ſleepe to one Hugo Biſhoppe of that dioceſe, that God deſcended into thoſe deſertes, that he made a worthy pallace to himſelfe, that 7. ſtarres lifted vpp themſelues being of wonderfull ſplendor like a crowne aboue the earth, the one different from the other.

9. After this the order of Carmelites

was

was reuiued by Albert Patriarche of Hierusalem, which as Thomas Waldensis writeth beganne in Mount Carmelé, in the first church that was dedicated to the blessed Virgin Mary in the Apostles tyme, but discontinued by the inuasion of the Sarazins into Palestine, wher before their comming, this order florished with multitude of saintes and holy people. After this time followed the holie orders of saint Fræuncis, saint Dominique, and saint Celestine, the former, I meane saint Frauncis, was confirmed by Innocentius the 3. 1202. S. Dominique who was first a cannon regular in the churche of Oxman in Biscaia, hauing imployed his learning and his trauelles for the space of 20. yeares at Tolosa in Fraunce against the heretiques, by the consent of certaine of his fellow laborers instituted his order, stiled the order of preachers, which was approued and allowed by the said Innocentius the 3. in the time of the generall councell of Lateran, and afterwardes confirmed by Honorius the 3. 1206. *VVald. de sacrament. tit. 9. c. 84*

10. The order of saint Celestine, beganne by one Petrus Moromus, who liued in the wildernes with great example of holines of life and multitude of miracles, which was approued by saint Gregory the 10. in the generall counsell of Lions 1274. And it is called the order of Celestine, for that the said Peter beng the author ther-

of, was made Pope afterwardes, and called by the name of Celestine the 5

11. The order of Obseruants beganne in the time of Fredericke the 2. Emperor, who was a great enemie to the Pope and church, and spoiled all the territories thereof, they dedicated themselues to the seruice of the blessed Virgin, and being in number 7. verie noble and welthy men, went into the wildernesse, and there liued remoued from all the enticementes and inducementes of mischeife, which was the occasion that others also forsooke the vanities of the world. Many other godly people in all ages and countries, haue bene by a speciall fauor of God, raised vp to knocke the hammers of pennance at our slumbring and lumpish hartes, oppressed with dead sleepe and Lethargie, to sounde the trumpet of Gods wrath in his church, to awake rechles and forgettfull soules out of the slumbring dreames of fleshly concupiscence, crying & repeating to the carelesse children of Adam our sauiours heauie and dreadfull voice, vnles yee repent, you shall euerie one perish.

*That preestes in the primatiue church, euen from the Apostles time, were religiouse and obserued religious order of life.*

## CHAPTER IV.

1. BEing that religion consisteth of the foresaid three vowes, obedience, chastity and pouerty, and that the Apostles and their successors haue accomplished and performed them, they were religious and obserued a religious life: for when the preistes receaued holy orders, they promised perpetuall chastity, and if any of them had wiues, by the example of the Apostles, they willingly of their owne accorde refrained from the vse of wedlocke. They obliged themselues also to cannonicall obedience, as Sulpitius writeth of saint Martin, whome saint Hillary sollicited that he should be made preiste by himselfe, and whome for his great vertue he loued, for that in receauing holy orders of him, he would be obliged to stay with him and render to him obedience. S. Gregory also declareth, that it *4. Epi.74*
was the custome of Rome, that no preist could deaparte from thence that receaued ther holy orders. Cōcerning pouerty, which is the third, the preistes in old tyme imbraced the same, in so much as when they

were made priestes they made a resignation of all they had, whether it was patrimony, or anny other worldly substance, which S. Hierome declared saying, that this was the cause why the preistes were shauen, that it should signifie a cuting off and forsaking of all temporall wealth. Prosper confirmeth the same, saying it is expedient and meete for the acquiring of perfection, to despise his proper goodes, and to be contented with the goods of the church, for the goods thereof are not proper but common; and so he brought examples of saint Paulinus and S.Hillarius, who when they were made preistes and Bishops, they sould their patrimony, and gaue the price thereof to the poore, and were diligent administrators of the patrimony of the church, distributing to each one proportionably according to his degree and necessity. S. Clement writeth that the common life was requisite and to be followed of those that addicted and yeelded themselues wholy to the seruice of God and to the imitation of the Apostles: the like obseruation of life saint Gregory the greate wished saint Augustine to institute, amongst the cleargy of england. The same is allso confirmed by the decree of Eugenius the 2. and Vrban Pope, in his epistle to all the cleargy.

*Lib. de vita contẽplatiua cap. 9.*

*Epist. ad clerum Hierosolimitanum.*

2. Of this grew the Canons regulars, which life began in the Apostles days, and after-

afterwardes was renewed and restored by by saint Augustine, as Posidonius writeth, that he had a monasterie within the church, in the which nothing was propre, but all was common; But after that saint Augustine was deade, and Hippo of which he was Bishoppe being destroyed and ransacked by the Vandales, Gelasius a holy man of that institution, with some others came into Italy, & being made Pope, the rest that were with him liued most regulary in a monestary that was founded by them nere to the church of Lateran, which continued 800. yeares, vntill afterwardes thinges that were common were made proper, euery one hauing a portion assigned vnto him. Of this order of Canon regulars, was saint Patricke the Apostle of Ireland, and also saint Dominicke, before he instituted his order. In the primatiue church all preistes obserued this religious community, and especially such as dwelling in citties and great townes had any charge in them, as wee may read in saint Augustine, but such as were ordeined to be incumbentes in the country, in respect of seuerall parish churches, and seuerall distinct incumbencies, were permitted to haue seuerall prouisions and distinct benefices, and as the christians encreased, so their pastors and preistes increased also: the spirituall want of the christians, the maiestie of God, and the dignity of the church

*Possid. in vita D. Aug.*

*Aug. ser. 1 refertur. 12. q. 1.*

requiring and exacting many seruantes to serue the one, and many pastors and preistes to serue the other, in the multitude whereof, it were very hard to preserue and continew the splendor and sincerity of the former feruor and charity of that heroicall age, which had as it were the florishinge springe, and the first fruictes of the holy Ghost, and therefore the prime and the cheefest season of holines and religion: Of whose blessed vigor of piety, the lesse wee sauor by tract of tyme, the more our owne proper loue increaseth, and the loue of God decreaseth.

3. But in all ages God sendeth some to reforme the auncient discipline, and to reuiue the languished vigor therof, not only in themselues but in others, especially in this so generall a corruption, not only of nature, but also of manners, of religion and lawes, of ciuill honesty and religious pietie, as Ignatius Loiola 1540. began his reformation of the clergy, and by the institution of his order confirmed by Paule the 3. Pope, renued the old discipline by reducing his order and institution therunto. It is also a matter of no lesse consideration then the former, that in one night he was borne in the house of Loyola nere the towne of Bergara in Ipulcha a prouince betwixt Biscaie, and the kingdome of Nauarre, and Luther was borne in Saxony in a towne nere Wittenberge called Ilesby 1483. vpon S. Mar-

*The founder of the order of the Societie of Iesus.*

*Surius.*

S. Martins daye. Both of them employed theire wittes at one time, the one to bring all religion and ecclesiasticall order to vtter confusion and miserable desolation: the other to restore the same to the auntient perfection thereof; the one of a religious man became an Apostate, of a continent became lecherous, of a saint became a diuell: the other of a seculer became religious, of a souldier became a saint, of a man became an Angell. And as at one time and in one night, S. Augustine was borne in Africke, and Pelagius the heretique was borne in Englande, and as Pelagius intended to ouerthrow the church with his peruerse heresie, and S. Augustine laboured to restore the same by his sounde doctrine; so the blessed Ignatius with his religious & blessed family, labored to destroy the darnell and cockell of heresy, which Luther, Caluin and all their most wicked and blasphemous sectaries, haue sowen in the feild of our Lord which is the Catholique Church.

4. Others after him were made instrumentes to reforme the slacknes and desolation of the clergy, as Phillip Nereias, and other godly people at Rome and els where in our owne dayes, and haue also cast their beames into other kingdomes, especially Italy, Fraunce and Spaine. Seing that God can neuer be glorified in this world but by his church, nor his church can neuer be manteyned

teyned but by ſacrifice and ſacramentes,nor ſacraments can be offered or done but by priſtes, for the which they are ordeyned and inſtituted cheifly and principally. And whoſoeuer goeth about to take away preiſthood, taketh away both ſacrifice, ſacraments,religion, church, and conſequently robs God of his honour, ſpoiles him of his glory,and depriues Chriſtians of theire knowledge & loue of him.

5. This preiſt-hoode is deuided into two orders,the one ſpeculatiue, and the other practicall; and as Chriſte was interteyned by two deuout ſiſters, Mary & Martha, ſo he is alſo continually ſerued in his church by two religious orders, which Mary repreſented. I. meane the ſpeculatiue, and the order of the cleargy which Martha ſignified; This ſaint Ambroſe declareth ſaying. *Ambroſ. epiſt. 25.* Who can be ignorant that in the church of God there are two excellencies, the one is the office of the Clergy,the other the inſtitution of Monkes, the one to be exerciſed and practiſed amongſt men, the other to be trained vp and accuſtomed to abſtinence & patience, the one to be repreſented on the theater, the other to be hidden in a corner, the one to be a ſpectacle to the world, the other to be kept in ſecret. And therefore that worthy champion of our Lord ſaith, *ſpectaculum facti ſumus Deo, angelis & hominibus.* Wee are become a ſpectacle to God,

to

to Angells,and to men: the one fighteth againſt the confuſion of the world, the other againſt the allurementes of the fleſh, the one more profitable for his neighbor, the other more perfect for himſelfe, both of them denie themſelues, that they may ſerue Chriſte perfectly, becauſe to men of perfection it is ſaid, *Whoſoeuer will come after me, let him deny himſelfe and follow me*; the one doth ſtrugle wiih the world, the other wreſtleth with the deuill: the one ouercometh the baites of the world, the other flies from them,vnto whome the world is crucified, and he vnto the world: the one hath greater tentation and greater victory, the other leſſe daunger and greater ſecury: thus farre ſaint Ambroſe, by which you may perceiue the ſtate of thoſe that liue in Cloiſters and Monaſteries and Monkes Friers, and ſuch as liue abroade in the world, in continuall feare and manifeſt daungers, in which many are fallen, and many others are vpholden.

*Of the multitude of religious perſons.*

## CHAPTER V.

1. NOthing is ſoe irckſome vnto our corrupt nature and carnall diſpoſition, altogether corrupted with the too much alluring humors of ſenſuality,

ſuality, intoxicated with the blinde affection thereof, as to caſte the yoake thereof away from vs, by taking vp Chriſtes croſſe, by denyinge our ſelues to follow Chriſte, whereof in ſo doing wee may apply to our ſelues that verſe of the prophett. *Derupuiſti Domine vincula mea, tibi ſacrificabo hoſtiam laudis.* O Lord thou haſt broken my fetters, I will ſacrifice vnto thee a ſacrifice of praiſe. Which euer was obſerued in all ages of the goſpell, by vtterly renouncinge the world with all the pompes thereof, which was put in execution by the perfection of religious vocation.

2. How many thouſandes, or rather millions, by the examples of ſaint Paule the Hermitt and ſaint Antony, haue caſte off this yoake, abandoned or rather abiured the world; retired themſelues to the deſertes, there with greater liberty of ſpirite, better ſecurity for their ſaluation, and les daunger of tentation, to ſerue God all the dayes of their liues? Of the ſaid ſaint Antony it is written by a moſte holy ſainte, that in the mountaine there were monaſteries as if they were tabenacles full of deuine quires, of ſuch as ſonge pſalmes and praied, which ſeemed to inhabite a certaine infinite region ſeperated from all conuerſation: amongſt whome (ſaith he) there was peace and concord, there none hated another, either by word or frowninge: wherefore that of the ſcripture

*Athan. in vita eius.*

ſcripture may be verified thereof, *quam bona domus tuæ Iacob*, how good are the houſes of Iacob, the tabernacle of Iſraell, they are like woodes that doe ſhaddowe, like a paradiſe vpon riuers, like tabernacles which are pitched of our Lord, and like Cedars of Libannus about the waters. *Num. 23.*

3. The like teſtimony ſaint Hjerom giueth of ſaint Hilarion, who about that time founded many monaſteries in Paleſtine, wherein alſo Macharius the diſciple of ſaint Anthony and Cariton, founded many monaſteries, in one of which as Iſodorus recordeth, were a thouſand Monkes. It is ſaid alſo that one Apollonius, had 5000. Monkes vnder his gouernment. In the mountaine of Mitria which is 40. miles, from Alexandria, were 5000. monkes in 50. monaſteries which were all gouerned and directed by one Superiour. Syria and Ægipt did alſo abound with ſuch ſwarmes of holy monkes, that the wicked Emperour, Iulian the Apoſtate and Valens, compelled them by force and violence to goe as ſouldiers to the warres, but quickly afterwardes God puniſhed both the one and the other for their labour; ſaint Hierome wrote the life of thoſe Monkes. *Hieron. in vita Hilarion.*

4. Palladius Biſhop of Cappadocia, went in pilgrimage barefooted, being accompanied with 7. to viſite the Monkes of Ægipt, they came vnto a certaine citty by

Thebes

Thebes called Oxirnicum, in which they found ſuch religion and ſanctity, as they by word could not expreſſe, in which there was no heretique nor gentile, and wee ſaw more monaſteries and religious houſes there (ſaid he) then prophane houſes, ſo that euery ſtreete and corner thereof were repleniſhed with deuine praiſes and celeſtiall Alleluias, the whole citty being as it were but one only church, inhabited and poſſeſſed of the ſeruantes of God, the Biſhopp of that citty tould them, there were 20. thouſand Virgins, and 10. thouſand Monkes: wee are not able (ſaith he) to expreſſe with what entire affection, honour, and feruour of charity, they enterteined vs. He ſaw alſo at Babilon and Memphis, an inumerable multitude of Monkes, which were endewed and adorned with ſundry giftes of the holy ghoſte, this is the place where the Patriarche Ioſephe kept in ſtore prouiſion of wheate for ſeuen yeares ſcarcity. He maketh mention of Amonius the father of 3000. Monkes, dwellinge neere Thebes, and Paconius which liued 400. yeares after Chriſte which had 7000. Monckes diſioined the one from the other in diuers houſes. Alſo Serapion which had 10000. vnder his gouermente, whoſe liues were ſo famous for their ſanctity, and eminent vertues, that many went in pilgramage to the deſart to ſee them, amongſt whome was

that

that holy woman Paula, as saint Hierom reporteth. Who beinge astonished with their admirable vertues, & forgettinge her owne sex, wished to dwell amongst so many thousand Monkes, who neuer went to any of their cells, but she prostrated her selfe vpon her knees, before each of them, beleeuing she saw Christe in euerie one of them. *Epitaph. epist. 27.*

5. Many thousand virgins imbraced this religious perfection as the ecclesiasticall histories recorde, especiallie Theodorus who writeth, that there were an infinite number of Monasteries and conuents of Virgins in moste partes of the easte, as in Palestine, Ægipt, Asia, Pontus, Siluia, Siria and Europe, from the time that Christ was borne of a Virgin, the swarmes of Virgins were multiplied, in all which multitude both of men and weomen, no irreguler or disordered confusion was practised, none was impeached with any imputation of shameles or irreligious misdeameanour, the cheefest consideration of theire rules and institutions (as saint Hierom saith) was to obay their superiours in all thinges, except (saith he) the time of publique exercise of prayers, and meditations. The Monkes of Ægipt liued altogether by their owne labours, and what euerie one could gett by his toile, and industrious acquisition, sauing a small portion, which he reserued for his owne sustentation and liuelie-hood, they brought *Religiosa histor.*

brought it to their father generall to be distributed vpon the poore, & so they were wonte to send ships loden with corne and prouision vnto Alexandria for the releife of the poore prisoners, and other needy distressed persons; for in Egipt were not such number of poore people which could consume the Almes and bountifullnes of these saintes.

6. But let no man carpe or take occasion of detractinge of the religiouse persons of this time, for that they doe not so labour: for those Monkes of Egipt and Palestine had no other purpose or imployment, but to serue God and to labour for their owne proper perfection, not respecting their neighbours, and so for the moste parte they liued in remote places, and it was also prouided by their institution to labour with their bodies: but the Monkes and religious orders of our tymes, they are bound by the institution of their order, not only to helpe themselues spiritually, but allso their neighbours, and so they are bounde to preach and teach and heare confessions. For the accomplishing of which worke, to doe it well, they must needes study, and labour very much, which cannot be accomplished or well done, if they should bestow their tymes in any seruile worke.

7. Europe allso is bewtified and famous with these religious orders and obseruations

tions of Italy, as saint Gregory the great, maketh mention in his 4. dialogues, which he composed for the moste parte of the liues and miracles of many religious sainctes of that country. Trithemius doth write; that in his owne tyme which was about anno 1470. there were of the order of S. Benedict in the prouince of Moguntia 124. abies besides 10. that were seperated from the rest, and added that there were in other places 5000. compleat abies, besides many small monasteries. Other authors doe write as Cæsararius, Bruto, and the author of the beginning of the order of Cisters Montaluo, and *Arnoldus Abion in ligno vitæ*, that there were 37000. monasteries of the order of S. Benedict in the world, 14000. Priories, Nunries 15000. that there were canonized of that order 55000. that there were popes 46. Cardinalls, 300. Parriarches and Archbishops 1600. Bishops 4000. Emperours 25. Empresses 29. Kinges 54. Queenes 53. sonnes and daughters of Emperours 54. sonnes of Kinges 49. daughters of Kinges 72. doctors that wrote bookes 15000. Martirs 5270. For the space of 300. yeares, all the Popes were of that order: for the space of 600, yeares all the vniuersities were gouerned and directed by that order: and 33. kingdomes were conuerted by that order vnto the christian religion. Tertullus father to Placido the Monke, bestowed vpon saint Benedict

28. prouinces, 98, cities and villages, all the kinges of theſe partes of the world for the moſte parte were buried in the monaſteries of the ſaid order: the Kinges of France in the monaſtery of ſaintes Denis, the kinges of Englande at Weſtminſter, the kinges of Naples at S. Seuerine, the kinges of Cicily at Palermo, the kinges of Arragon at Poblete, the kinges of Nauarre at S. Saluador, the kinges of Portugall at Alcobaco, the Emperours in the Monaſtery of Fuldenſe. The Abbay of Floriacenſe with the monaſteries therunto belonginge, is worth a million by the yeare.

*Bernard in vita S. Malachiæ*

8. S. Bernard writeth that in Ireland there was a monaſtery that brought forth many thouſand Monkes, & was the head of many monaſteries, a place (ſaith he) truly holy, fertile of ſainctes, and moſte aboundantly fructifyinge vnto God, ſo as one of the children of that moſt holy place called Luanus, was the founder of an hundred monaſteries. Ireland (ſaith the ſame ſaint Bernard) being ſo inriched by theſe bleſſed people, may ioifully ſinge the verſe of Dauid. *Viſitaſti terram & inebriaſti eam, multiplicaſti locupletare eius*. Thou haſt viſited the earth, and thou haſt ouerflowen and abundantly inriched the ſame with the ſwarmes of theſe holy people, who made their excurſions and caſt forth their beames into other places, out of which came holy Columbauns into

*Plati. de bono ſtatu religioſi lib. 2. c. 24*

into Fraunce, and builded the famous monastery of Luxouia, where heauenly and deuine Alleluias, surceased not any instant or moment by night or by day, whose blessed quire is incessantlie supplied by religious Monkes: thus farre Saint Bernard.

*Of many great and eminent men, who forsooke and contemned the World, to become religious.*

## CHAPTER VI.

1. BEing to speake of many great and eminent persons who contemned the world to become religious, and were the flower and ornament of the catholique church (the number whereof, are almost inumerable) I wil endeuour to exẽplifie them, first in the grecians, and next in the latines. Of these in the first ranke I may put Serapion, who in the yeare 193. beinge a younge man, imbraced a monasticall life, and was made the 8. Patriarche of Antioch after saint Peter, none in his time being soe learned, or soe eloquent as he, who wrote manny learned bookes. After him succeeded Pamphilus anno 240. being the learnedest of his time, of whose great librarie saint Hierome made mention: he was put to death by Maximianus. About that time allso was Lucianns

*Hier. de script. Eccles.*

 which

which as Suidus saith, kept schoole at Antioch, who also was famished to death by the said Maximianus. After him florished saint Iohn Climachus, the ornament of his tyme, who liued in the monasterie of Moũt Sinay; Not inferior vnto him was holie Ephrem, whose writinges next after the scriptures, were read in many churches of the East, as S. Hierom recordeth.

*Hier. ibid.*

2. Others were most famous both for their incomparable learninge and sanctitie, as saint Basil and saint Gregory Nazianzen, both of which professed monasticall life. For the said Nazianzen, trauailing by sea vnto Athens and being affrithed with great tempest, made a vowe to serue God in monastical profession, if he did ariue safe, which vowe when he had ended his studies he accomplished. S. Epiphanius also a man verie memorable, beinge the light of his age, by the helpe of one Lucius Mounke, retired himselfe to religious sanctuarie. What shall I say of S. Iohn Chrisostome Archbishoppe of Constantinople, who liued anno 400? and of saint Iohn Damascen, who liued anno 730. haue they not also applied themselues to serue God in this euangelicall discipline? I ought not to forgett Nilus, Isacius, Euthimius, Anastasius, & Besarion, the last wherof was the anchor in the general councell of Florence for the reconsiliation & vniõ, of the Greekes, vnto the latine, church,

who

who for his great learning and hollines, was created Cardinall by Eugenius the 4. thus farr of the Greekes, besides others thowsandes which were to tedious to recite.

3. Amoungest the Latines wee will put in the first rancke, the two pillers of the church, saint Hierome and saint Augustine, both which consecrated themselues to the seruice of God in monasticall profession. As for saint Hierom, from his childhoode he was trained vpp therein, and soe addicted therunto, that he refused to take holie orders at the handes of Paulinus Bishoppe, of whome he was soe earnestlie sollicited, therunto, yet he would neuer take it vpon him but conditionallie, that he should neuer leaue off monasticall professiō, of which writinge to Pamacius, he said he would not leaue of, that for the which he forsooke the worlde: and when he was stricken in yeares, he retourned vnto Hierusalem, and at the cribe of our Lord he by ioyninge his helpe with saint Paule, erected two monasteries, one for men, another for women; and amplified, and enlaidged them at his owne proper charges, and as he himselfe witnesseth, did send Paulinus to sell all his patrimonie for the entertaininge, and reliuing of all such Mounks, as out of all places of the world came to see him. *Epist. 61.*

4. As for saint Augustine, although it be

manifest by other authors, and specially by Posſidonius, that he obſerued this institution, yet his owne, wordes can best declare the ſame. I (ſaieth he) the writer hereof haue most intierlie loued the perfection of which our Sauiour ſpeaketh ſaying; *Goe, and*
*Aug ep. 4.* *ſell all that thou haſt, and giue it to the poore, and come and follovve me:* neither by my owne force haue I don ſoe, but by his grace helpinge me, and none knoweth how much I proffited by this way of perfection but my ſelfe, and to this purpoſe I exhorted others aſmuch as I coulde, and in the name of our Lord I haue many conſorts, who are perſwaded by my meanes. In another place he ſaith. Petilianus with his curſed tounge
*Contra Petil. c. 4.* did not forbeare to ſlaunder, and find fault with Monaſteries, and Mounckes, reprouing me that this kinde of life was instituted by me, which order being ſpred through the whole world, he ſaith he knoweth not, or at leaſt he faineth ignorance therein: thus farr ſaint Auguſtine.

*Hier epiſt. 13.* 5. In their times was that charitable Prelate, Paulinus, Biſhopp of Nola, who was a Mouncke as ſaint Hierome recordeth, his bookes doe teſtifie his great learninge his workes of mercie doe witnes his great charitie: for when Nola was ranſaked of the Vādals in Affrick, he would needes put himſelfe into captiuitie for the redemption of a poore Widdowes onlie ſonne. I ought not here

here to neglect the worthie Prelate S. Martin Bishopp of Toures, who builded 3. monasteries; the first at Millain, out of which he was driuen violentlie by Auxentius the Arrian. The second at Poiters. The third at Toures, where though he was a Bishopp, he obserued reguler discipline with 8. Mounckes vntill he died, as Sulpitius writeth. About that time alsoe florished Iohn Cassianus, a Scythian by nation, being first disciple to saint Iohn Chrisostome, who erected a monasterie at Marsells. Next vnto him was Eucherius Bishopp of Lyons, and monck, brought vp in the conuent of Lyrinensis, and Prosper Bishopp of Rhegē, who was a mouncke, and secretarie to Leo the great.

6. How famous was Fulgentius in Affrique and in all partes of the world for his great learning, in writinge so much against heretiques, who being a Bishopp, obserued monasticall life? Immediatly after him, followed that worthie man Cassiodorus, who being Senator of the cittie Danenan, and chauncelor to Theodoricus king of the Romanes, whome (for that the said kinge killed Boetius) he forsooke together with the worlde, and became a mouncke of the order of S. Bennet Anno 550. After him succeded Gregorie the great, soe called for his great learning, and sanctitie, who of a mouncke of the said order, was made

Pope. What ſhall I ſay of S. Gregorie of Toures, who was taken out of the monaſterie to gouerne that Sea? of ſaint Eutropius Biſhopp of Valentia, he being alſo a mõcke? Of Iſidorus who was taken out of his monaſterie to be Biſhopp of Ciuill? Of Alfonſus who from the conuent was aſſumpted to be Archbiſhopp of Tolledo in Spaine, whoſe learned bookes doe edifie the world; How glorious is France by ſoe learned mounckes, and religious people as S. Bernard. S. Ceſarius Biſhopp of Orlians, and Anſelmus with many others? Italy by S. Benedict, ſaint Bonauentura, ſaint Thomas of Aquinus, ſaint Frauncis &c. England by ſaint Beda, ſaint Bonifacius &c. Irland by ſaint Patrick, ſaint Malachias, ſaint Columbanus, ſaint Columba, ſaint Brandan with infinitt others.

*Of Emperors Kinges and Princes who forſooke the World to become religious.*

## CHAPTER VII.

1. ALthough our ſoules in the ſight of God who made them, are equall by nature, yet he maketh choice rather of the poore, then of the powerfull and riche: of the humblieſt and baſeſt, then of the proude and
1. Cor. 1. loftieſt; For as the Apoſtle ſaith, there are not

not many noble nor wise accordinge to the fleshe, for God maketh of the poore his scelected people to confound the rich, the foolish of this world he prefers before the wise thereof, he deposeth the mightest from their throane, and exalteth the humble and meeke: the more that a man is intangled with the worlde, and allured by the vncertaine and deceitfull promisses, and promotions thereof, the greater difficultie hath he to forgoe it, and the lesse feelinge, hath he to preuenent the dangerous ruyne, and dismall lott of the same, and a man once being ingulfed in the filthie puddle of beastlie concupiscence, which euer doth insult ouer the spiritt, the lesse feeling hath he of godes inspiration, and the lesse swaie beareth the interior man, which in carnall and beastlie people is altogether restrained from his operation, by their insatiable and inextingible appetites of their fleshlie inclination, and disposition, to these vilde and corruptible thinges.

2. When the greatest and mightiest Monarches and Potentates of this world are in this case, especially if they be wantonlie trained vpp in voluptuousnes, and enticed with lasciuous and wanton exercises, they forgett and forgoe all spirituall motions, to make themselues as it were dull and insensible to all celestiall influence and illustrations, forgetfull of God, obliuious of his

comaun-

comaundementes, negligent of their charge, carlesse and vnprouident of the end, and marke for the which they are exalted, and aduaunced to the regall scepter, which is the peace and tranquillitie of the comon wealth. But they not respectinge either comon good, or the peaceable estate of their kingdomes, abusing their powerfull force, and dignitie with wanton lusts, and other execrable vices, and wickednes, of whome
Psal. 134. it is spoken by the holy ghoast. *Gaudium hipocritæ instar puncti*, their ioye, and allacritie shall quickly be ended, and they likewise eyther themselues or their posteritie shalbe plunged an perplexed with the vsual troubles, continuall calamities, and fatall reuolutions, which commonly are incident vnto such princes, of whome it is said; *Virum iniustum mala capient in interitu*. The euils and mischeefe of an vniust and wicked man shall intrappe and compasse him, euen vnto his destruction and vtter decaye; They may for a smale tyme raigne ouer wicked natiõs, for whose dreadfull and abhominable trespasses and wickednes, God suffreth or rather stirreth vpp Tyrants, to vexe, punish and ouercharg their miserable subiects with grieuous and intollerable oppresions, tyrannicall extortions, impositions and irreparable callamities, who euer maketh choice of wicked officers and ministers, which frame and conforme themselues to please

please their wicked humors, and are skilful architects to putt in execution their detestable plottes and purposes, slaues of their bellies, enemies of Christs crosse, captiues, and seruants of the diuill, whose chiefest reward and promotion for performing their dreadfull and bloudie tragedies, is the gouernment of such prouinces and citties, to whome they haue comitted them.

3. And although Ferdinande King of Castile and Arragon, father to the good Queene Katherin of England, was as vertuous and iust a prince as liued in all Europe in his daies, yet whē he was dienge, he gaue a mournefull sigh, and said, he had rather then all the kingdomes in the worlde, that he were a poore lay brother in some religious order, seruing in a monasterie, then (said he) my cōscience shoulde be disburdened of the heauie, and dreadfull terror of my dangerous accomptes, for the heauie burden, of soe manny kingdomes, states, & Prouinces for the which I miserable wretch must aunswere, being scarse able to satisfie or yelde accompt for my owne secrett and peculiar offenses, much lesse for the gouernmente of all those regions committed by God, to my charge and ouersighr. After that the Empire Anno 800. was translated by Leo the 3. Pope into the West, and Charles the great King of Fraunce being made Emperor some of the Emperors that succeeded him, forsa-

*Zonarus tomo 3.*

forsaking the Empire, became religious, as Lotharius, who beinge fifteene yeares Emperor, and liued a most vertuous Christian, remembringe the speech that his father Lodouicke vsed in the time of his death of the vanitie of the worlde, and of the miserable estate of such as are the slaues therof, became a Mounck anno 865.

4. Hugo. the Emperor, after many victories that he had against his enemies, became a Mouncke. Rachisius kinge of Italie resigninge his kingdome to his Brother Astulpus became religious in the Monasterie of Mount Cassius, of the which he was as it is thought, Abott anno 741. Pipine kinge also of the Romanes and eldest sonne of Charles the great, followed that blessed example, who became a mouncke in a monasterie that he builded himselfe at Verona anno 805. In Spaine Bamba very prosperous, and fortunate both at home and a broade, amoungest his other victorious exploites, defeated and discomfited 200. shippes of Moores that were Pyratts, tooke also Paule kinge of Fraunce prisoner that came to inuade Spayne, at lenght beinge moued by diuine inspiration became a mouncke anno 674. whose blessed example, Verenundus kinge of Castile followed. Ramiris kinge of Arragon first became a mouncke in his fathers life time, who beinge dead without yssue of other Children, was compelled to returne

returne to the worlde and marrie, and hauinge yssue which was a daughter, returned to his monasterie againe.

5. But of all kingdomes of the world, England was most famous for the number and sanctitie of their religous kinges, as Sigibertus kinge of Nothumberland, who forsakinge the worlde, tooke a religious habitt vpon him Anno 640. Ethelred kinge of the Merceans anno 704. who gouerning his kingdome with great pietie and religion, resigned the same ouer to his sonne beinge but a childe, and erected a monasterie of which he was made Abott. But when the childe came to riper yeares, he followed his fathers steppes, went to Rome, and receaued the habitt of Constantine the first then Pope, and spent there the remainder of his dayes, with great sanctitie and hollines, his name was Chenredus, in whose companie went Offa kinge of the East Saxons, who in the prime of his youth, settinge at naught the vanities of all worldlie prosperitie, contemninge his opulent, and rich kingdome, tooke vpon him a voluntary death, which was, to betake himselfe to a perpetual silence, banishing from his vowed and inuincible chastitie, all fleshlie enticementes and prouocations; Not longe after him Inas kings of the said Saxons, a man of of an incomparable pietie and deuotion, made his whole kingdome tributaire to the

sea

sea Apostolique went to Rome forsakinge his kingdome, and became religious; The same Geolfus did, vnto whome Venerable Beda dedicated his historie, who beinge kinge of Northumberland and considering the dangerous estate of kinges, fled vnto a monasterie, there to serue God, with greater securitie of his saluation, and resigned his kingdome to Egebert his Vncle, who after that he had raigned 20. yeares, followed also his Nephewe to the monasterie, and died therin in that religious vocation.

6. In Germanie the example of Charlemaine was famous beinge sonne to Charles Martell, and beinge kinge of Austria and and Suethland came to Rome in a poore mans attire and vnknowen to any, where he receaued holie orders of Zacharias the Pope, and afterwards entred the monasterie in mount Zoracte which he himselfe builded, but beinge disturbed by the frequẽt visitation of those of his frindes, retired himselfe to Mount Cassen, a place more remote, was there receaued with great ioie of Petrocias Abbott thereof, where he increased verie well in vertueand religion, and especially in humilitie. For beinge by the Abbott appointed to keepe sheepe (which office he more willinglie accepted, then the scepter when he was crowned) at a certaine tyme, when one of the sheepe was lame, he brought her vpon his owne shouldiers vnto the

the feild: he liued Anno 750. What shall I say of Trebellius kinge of the Bulgars, who through the blessed endeuours of Pope Nicholas the first, became a christian and bore such zeale to christian religion, that he expelled presentlie Photinus the heretique, and leauinge the kingdome to his sonne, became a mouncke. But vnderstandinge afterwardes that his said sonne caste off the yoke of Christ, and returned to his former impietie, he went out of the monasterie, & tooke his sonne prisoner, whome he seuerlie punished by putting out his eyes, perpetuall emprisonment, and depriuation of his kingdome, which he gaue to Albert his younger sonne, and instructinge him with sound councells and blessed admonitions of Christian obseruations, returned to his monasterie.

7. Another memorable example is of Iohn Brena kinge of Hierusalem, and Emperor of Constantinople, who in his feruent praiers saw saint Fraunces offering vnto him his habitt, and forthwith called his confessor and receaued the said habitt, in which he liued but fewe dayes: and though he came to the vieneyarde the 11. houre, yet he receaued neuerthelesse his wages. What kinge more famous for his great vertue and miracles, then kinge Henrie of Cyprus, who followed the same blessed course of life? In this blessed rancke wee may enroll Iohn,

kinge

kinge of Armenia, who resigninge his kingdome to Leo his nephew, which was soe large and soe great that he had vnder him 24. kinges, chose rather to be abiect and base in the house of God, then to commaunde in the tabernacles of sinners. But when the Turcks inuaded those kingdomes, and Leo beinge not able to resiste them, and seinge it was the quarrell of God, he girded himselfe with the sworde, leuied an armie, resisted the enemies of Christ, giuinge them a verie great ouerthrowe, but persecutinge the course of his victorious battell he was slaine, and made a blessed ende; What shall I say of the sonnes of Emperours and kinges, the 3. sonnes of Charles the great Emperor, as Vgon, Dagon and Pipine, two of them became religious of their owne accorde: the last was compelled to enter for that he aspired to the kingdome in his fathers life tyme, but when he tasted the sweetnesse of Christe his yoke, he imbraced the same willinglie, they liued Anno 83.

8. Vbian kinge of Ireland, had 3. sonnes, all were Mouncks and great Sainctes vid. Furseus, Follianus, and Vltanus, who leauinge their countrie, came into Fraunce in the time of Clodoneus kinge of that countrie, and builded the monasterie of Pontimacum, which euer since was verie famous. The emulation of the two sonnes of Brittaine shonld not be omitted, for whē

Iudaellus

Iudaellus who was next to succede in that kingdome, told his brother Iodocus of his purpose in takinge vpon him a religious obseruation, and that he should prepare himselfe for the gouernment thereof, he craued 8. dayes to deliberate vppon the matter, but when he entred in deepe discourse with himselfe, what a heauie and daungerous burden he should take vppon him, he preuented his brothers purpose, and fled into the monasterie, before he tooke any order to hinder his determination. The kinge of England called Richard, had two sonnes that were religious anno 862. the one was called Willebald, in Mount Casin, the other Winebad at Mardeburge in Saxonie. The kinge of Fraunce called Charles, had also two sonnes that were religious, Clotarius, and Charles the great, who professed the same institution anno 841. In whose register wee ought to enroll Frederique the sonne of Lodouicke anno 962. Henry the sonne of another Lodouicke Anno 1150. Lodouicke alsoe the sonne of Charles the second Kinge of Fraunce, and heire apparent of the crowne thereof: who beinge hostage in Spaine, became a Franciscan Frier. The like professsion alsoe Iames the sonne of the kinge of Maiorca embraced, which was the firit of the royall blood that euer entred that order, whose happie exãple Peter the sonne of the kinge of Arragon followed: who did not onlie proffit himselfe, but was alsoe by his deuoute sermons, a light to manny that walked in darcknes and in the shadowe of death.

9. If I should register all the kinges, Princes and Dukes which entred into religion, it should require an infinitt labour, although I ought not to omitt al, as Algorius Duke of Aquitane with his sonne Amandus, Anno 429. Also Anselmus Duke of Mantua anno 740. Dicladus & Arcigiadus, Duks of Suethlande anno 815. Vigestus of Spoleta 820. Willian Duke of Guyne, and Aquitane 411. another Williã also Duke of that place anno 912. who was soe humble that vppon a certaine time when the Abbott of Claima (in which Abby the said Duke serued God) bid him to bake some bread, he went most willingly to the hoat furnace, and hauinge not at that tyme wherwith to cleanse it, he did sweepe the hoate furnace with his habit, and receaued noe harme. Not inferior vnto him in this religious zeale, was another William Duke of Burgundie, who entred into saint Fruncis his order. Was there any mã found in the worlde these manny a hundreth yeares, more triumphant and victorious in warre, more prosperous and happie in peace, then Charles the fifte Emperor, who hauinge triumphed and ouercome all his mightie and potent enemies, chased and draue away the great Turcke with his armie of

mie of three hundred thowsand soldiors from the dreadfull siege of the cittie of Vienna, the capitall cittie of Austria, and from the destruction of Christendome, and supplantation of the catholique religion, tooke the rebellious and seditious princes of Germanie prisoners in the oxen fielde, hauinge but a handfull in respect of the great and mightie armie which he ouercame in in a sett battell, which they pitched by the instigation of that fatall and ominous Apostate Luther, beinge the onlie cause of all the miseries and callamities of the Christian world. He tooke alsо Frauncis the first by his captaine generall before Pauia in Lumbardie, who with 6000. soldiors came to besiege the said cittie, where all his army beinge ouerthrowen, was brought prisoner in his owne gallies to Madrill. He tamed alsoe all Affrique with his victorious and inuincible Armies, Wyone, Tuins, and Goleta, ouerthrewe Barbarosa beinge a Pyratt, and most infestuous to the Christians. Extinguished that raginge and furious flame of the Spanish rebellion, and all the citties and comons of the two kingdomes of Castile, the kingdome of Arragon & Valentia, all which reuolted from him, for that he placed in his owne absence, a Viceroye which was not natiue of their owne countrie, all the rebells, although he ouercame them, yet he pardoned them both in landes and goodes, he tooke manny citties and fortresses in Affrique, as Oran, Tanges Zeita, with many other places of great importance, and after atchieuing many other great victories, being wearie of the world, resigned his Empire vnto his brother Ferdinando, and his kingdomes and other states to his sonn Philipp the second, and retired himselfe to a monasterie of saint Hieromes order in Stremadura in Spaine, and ended the remainder of his daies there most happilie, by whose blessed examples many noble men were conuerted vnto God, by taking vppon them this religious vocation, as Charles de Borgia, Duke of Gandia, who enioyed great and honorable offices vnder the said Emperor, became a Iesuitt, and was generall of that blessed order of the societie of Iesus: and Anthony de Corduba the sonne of the Duke of Feria in Spaine, a neere cousin to the Duke of Gandia. Rodulphus of Aquauiua in Italie a Iesuitt, who beinge alsoe sent to the east Indies accordinge to the institution of that order, there with other fathers of his religion, suffered Martirdome by the Barbarians.

10. Amoungest these I may not omitt that worthie and blessed Duke Ioys of Fraunce, who first takinge vpon him the habitt and most austere profession of a poore Capuchine frier, was comaunded by the last

troubles

troubles and garboiles of that kingdome, to defend his countrie against the inuasion, and excursiōs of the hugonotts of Languedocke, which he perfourmed most worthily: but the warres being ended, he returned to his owne profession, and religion againe, who by his holie life, & incessant preaching, edified and conuerted many dissolute persons, perswaded them to despise the world, and the occasions of their wooe, and died three yeares past, whose happie memorie, will liue eternallie. I might alleadge many other worthie examples, but because they are as yet liuinge I will omitt them, for that wee are bid to praise men, but not before their death, and that accordinge to their merites. Thus in our holy religion, great personages haue humbled themselues to Christ his yoke, as it is prophesied by Esay; *Omnis mons & collis humiliabitur,* euerie mountaine and hilliocke shalbe humbled: which prophesie is perfourmed in great Monarques that submitted their scepter to the crosse of him that was crucified, and represented in their liues the liuely image of his bitter passion.

*Of Empresses, Queenes and Princes, who likewise forsooke the world to become religious.*

## CHAPTER VIII.

IN the first Rancke wee must place that worthie and blessed Empe-resse Theodora, who notwithstandinge shee was married vnto Theophilus the Emperor Anno 470. an heretique, yet remained still a firme Catholique, and he beinge dead, shee restored sacred images, and recalled backe againe holie people, that were exiled and banished for theire religion. Then sequestred herselfe from the incōberances of the gouernment of the Empire into a monasterie, where her mother Trurina had serued God for many yeares, whose blessed example the Empresse Augusta followed: and being importuned by the state of the Empire, came for a tyme out of the monasterie to appease some rebellion against her sonne, which was raised by his tutors, vnto whose custodie shee comitted him, which beinge appeased, shee returned to her monasterie againe: this was in the East anno 190.

2. In the Weast alsoe Ricarda, the wife of Carolus Crasus Emperor of the weast, did the like; who buildinge a monasterie in Alsa-

Alsatia, bestowed the residue of her life therein. Cunegundus Anno 1139. who being married to Henrie kinge of England, and afterwardes chosen Emperor, and being seperated from him for suspition of adulterie, contracted a better marriadge with Iesus Christ. Thrise happie was the other Cunegundus that was married to Henrie the first Emperor, who euer kept her virginitie, after whose death she spente the rest of her yeates in the Conuent of confugients: and is of the church registred amoungest the Sainctes. Agnes also the wife of the 3. Emperor, who beinge dead, shee resigned not only the Empire being at her disposition vntill her sonne should come to yeares, but also the Duchie of Bauaria, she beinge inheritrix thereof, and went to Rome Anno 1157. where she tooke vppon her a reguler profession; whose example Elizabeth the wife of Albert Emperor, and Archduke of Austria imitated: who beinge miserablie slaine, contemned the world, and liued religiouslie in a monasterie, builded by her selfe, all the daies of her life Anno 1290. whome her two daughters followed, the one was married to the king of Hungary, the other to the Earle of Ottigense, and also her two Neeces, the Queene of Poland, with her daughter.

3. Of Queenes also the number of them is not smale. The first Queene was Thesia Queene of Italie, the wife of Rachisines

aboue mentioned: for as her husband entred into a monasterie in Mount Casſine, ſo ſhe entred and went into another monasterie with her daughter Petruda. In Fraunce Radegundus beinge married to kinge Clotarius against her will, ſhee obtained licenſe of him to conſecrate her ſelfe to God in a monaſterie at Poiters, whoſe ſteeppes another Queene of Fraunce Adoera the wife of Chilper followed, with her daughter Childerada Anno 650. Batilda which was married to Clodoueus kinge of Frãce, being free from the yoke of weldocke by the death of her husbãd, went to Callice; where enrichinge the monaſterie that was there with ample and opulent poſſeſsions, ſhe enioyed the familiar preſẽce of a better ſpouſe. In Spaine wee haue examples of ſundrie Queenes which were to longe to relate, but I cannot omitt that worthie queene Nugnes, who firſt became religious herſelfe, and then her husband, Veremundus. Neither muſt queene Taraſia, paſſe vnmentioned, who being eſpouſed by her Brother Alphonſus kinge of Leon vnto Abdala kinge of Tolledo, could neũer be perſwaded to goe to bed with him, and the barborous kinge beinge taken away by an vgly diſeaſe, ſhe married herſelfe afterwardes to Chriſt in the monaſterie of ſaint Pelagius Anno 1005.

4. England hath not beene inferior to any

any of her conterminat kingdomes, in the feruent zeale that many Queenes had to this religious discipline. As Alfreda, which was fianced in marriage to the kinge of Northumberland, who beinge slaine before the matrimonie was consumated, together with her husbād Iuas, became religious. I cānot let passe that worthy example of Etheldrade, who being married to two kinges, kept her virgnitie vndefiled, and afterwardes became religious. What shall I say of her sister Seburga queene of Kente, and of Alfreda queene of Northumberland, who also became religious? I may not also ouerslipp with silence, Margarett the daughter of Bela kinge of Hungarie, who being consecrated to God by the vowe of her parētes, imbraced the blessed order of saint Dominique, and imploied her life in all religious exercise, especiallie in seruing the sicke and diseased persons, and refused the marriage of three kinges, of Polonia, Bohemia, and Cicilia, although the dispensatiō of the Pope in respect of her vowe, was laboured for.

5. Zanchia Queene of Hierusalem and Cicilia, after that her husband Robert was dead, entred the order of saint Frauncis at Naples, who earnestlie requested that none should call her queene. Agnes daughter to Oreth kinge of Bohemia, who was married vnto Frederique the second, neuer gaue any consent to matrimonie, and kept her selfe perpe-

perpetually continent vntill shee went into a monasterie, which her selfe builded at Prage. Chunegundus also the daughter of the king of Hungarie, who was married vnto that chast Bolestaus king of Polande, together with him, kept hirselfe a Virgin, and liued most religiouslie in a monasterie that shee her selfe hath builded. Ioane the daughter of the kinge of Hungarie, Isabella the kinge of Fraunce his daughter, and sister vnto S. Lewis, and Blanche daughter of Philipp kinge of France, all obserued the religious vow of virginitie and continence.

6. In our dayes God forgetteth not alsoe, to blesse his Curch with the like example of despisinge the worlde, and imbracinge the crosse of Iesus Christe, with his euangelicall counselles, yea in great personages, as in that most vertuous virgin Margarita de Austria, daughter of Maximilian the Emperor, and kinge Philipp the second of Spaine his sister, who professeth at this daie this blessed institution in S. Clara at Madrill in Spaine. Alsoe the two daughters of Charles ArchDuke of Austria and Stiria, and sisters vnto the Queenes of Spaine and Polande, and vnto the great Dutches of Florence, who discended from the greatest Potentates of the worlde, settinge at naught all the vaine promotions of the same, consecrated themselues to

serue

ſerue God in religious profeſsion.

7. But was it euer ſeene from the beginninge of the worlde, that any Kinge, Queene, Prince or noble man became a miniſter, or forſooke landes, or liuinge to imbrace perfection in proteſtante religion? was it euer ſeene that anny proteſtant followed the councell of Chriſt, to giue all that he had to the poore, to denie himſelfe, to take vpp his croſſe and to followe him? No trulie the contrarie is knowen, too well, for they neuer giue anny thinge to the poore, but take from them, all that the Catholique church purchaſed for them, who turne all ſacred thinges to prophane vſes, who robbe both God, the church & the poore of all their patrimonie; For they extorte from the poore inhabitantes 20. ſhillinges, ſome 30. ſome 40. both for marriadge and chriſtininge, and euerie one muſt pay ſo much; Yea euerie Goſſopp is compelled to paie the like, and this they take vpp from the Catholiques of Irelande, whoſe inhabitantes in all places are of that profeſsion, except the Engliſhe, ſoe that one Engliſh miniſter of that miſerable countrie, in a village called Iniſchortie in the countie of Wexford called Huſſe (an Engliſhman) tooke from one little hamlett neere that village, 14. crownes for marriage and chriſtninge in one fortnight; By which you may perceaue what he tooke in euerie other place

place of iurisdiction, he being in those partes the Bishopps officiall; By this cruel, and irreligious religion, manny of the poore inhabitantes of that countrie are disabled to keepe house, and are faine to begg, being not able to mantaine house through soe great an extortion, and yet this minister cannot vnderstand his parishoners, nor they him, excepting a verie fewe of the English that are resident, at Inischortie. Are there any laymen in the world more worldlie or more couetous to purchase landes for their childrenn, or are there any more greedie to hourde vpp wealth then they?

To conclude, it was neuer seene that anny man or wooman who imbraced protestancie, liued chast and continent, for by that profession none can be such, the meanes being taken awaye by which chastitie and continencie are to be obtayned, as fastinge, prayers, discipline, hair clothe, almesdeedes, contempt of his owne excellencie, and despising of the world.

*How greatlie religious people fructifie vnto God and to his Church: and that they are the best labourers which are therein.*

## CHAPTER IX.

1. S. Bernard saith, that they are appointed by God to pray for the bodie of the church, both for the quicke and for the dead; And as Nazianzen witnesseth, their praiers be the only diluge that washe awaie our sinnes, and purge the world; And as Eusebius affirmeth, they are cōsecrated vnto God for the whole stocke of mankinde. None knoweth what mischeefes and callamities they driue from the worlde, what singuler benefittes they obtaine of God, by whose praiers and workes of incomparable charitie, godes wrathe is appeased and made placable. Beside what blessed example giue they vnto the world? for had it not bene for them, the euangelicall vertues and counsells would haue bene quite extinguished, which they doe not only teach, but allso practize. For their modestie, humilitie, pietie, deuotion and contempt of all temporall honnors and allurementes, are forcible motiues, and infallible inducementes to all kinde of vertues, and therfore saint Iohn Chisostome calleth them, the lanternes and specta-

ſpectacles of the worlde, for of them the people doe learne how God is to be reuerenced, with what feare, loue and deuotion he is to be adored in the Sacramentes, with what reuerence and reſpect he is to be praied vnto, how patient wee ought to be in aduerſitie, how ſtout & inuincible wee ſhould behaue our ſelues in aduerſitie, how charible wee ought to ſhewe our ſelues to our neighbors, yea their whole liues is nothing els, then a continuall bearinge of Chriſtes croſſe, a ſecreat exhortation to all good examples of vertue and pietie, and a ſilent obiurgation and diſtaſtfullnes of all vice and wickdenes. And therfore S. Iohn Chriſoſtome, wiſhed the people to viſitte and frequent monaſteries & conuentes, for they are (ſaith he) without any allurementes and voide of all diſquietneſſeſſe and diſtractions, beſides (ſaid he) they are moſt ſecure and quiett hauens to fixe our ancker in. Moreouer, they oppoſe themſelues againſt all the enemies of the church, with whome they haue continuall and cruell skirmiſhes, and doe ſuſteine the heauie burden of their bloodie perſecutions, againſt whome they vphoulde and defende Chriſts religion in all places where the ſame is oppreſſed. And by their bleſſed labours, yea loſſe of life with violent effuſion of their blood, they plant & reſtore it againe in thoſe countries where it was ſupplanted.

*Chriſoſt. de deſpi. rerum. & hom. ad popul. 59.*

2. Omit-

2. Omittinge most of the examples which you may read in the Chronicles of their holie orders, I will here set downe some fewe only as a patterne and example of the rest. Remigius beinge a mouncke, conuerted kinge Clodoneus withall the Realme of Fraunce from Idolatrie vnto Christ Anno 530. Afterwardes he was made Archbishopp of Rehmes; S. Martin beinge a mouncke conuerted all Suethland from the Arrian heresie Anno 540. S. Augustine being sent by saint Gregorie into England conuerted that kingdome with their kinge Ethelbert anno 622. Lambertus the Mouncke conuerted Feslandria a prouince in Germanie. About that time Kilian an Irish mounck conuerted the Fraunckes in the managing of which buisinesse, he suffred martirdome. Wilfrid an English mouncke, and afterwardes Archbishopp of Yorck Anno 673. goinge from Rome, was by a tempest driuen into Holland, were he preached the ghospell of Christe and returned vnto the East Saxons, who beinge blinded with the darcknesse of infidelitie, were by him reduced vnto the faith of Iesus Christ: What should I say of all other nations, were not they all conuerted by the Apostles and religious people, was not Irelande conuerted by saint Patricke a reguler cannon of S. Augustins order Bishopp of Hippo? Thuringian, Frisland and Huss conuerted by Bonifacius

nifacius an English Mouncke, who afterwardes beinge Archbishopp of Moguntia, was martyred? The rest were to prolix to set downe; I referr yow to the Chronicles of holly orders, only I will content my selfe with the conuersion of America, and of the east & weast Indies, which was brought to passe by religious people.

3. The first that euer went thither for that purpose, were the fathers of S. Frauncis order, for when Christopher Columba, was suiter to Ferdinando kinge of Castile and Arragon, to send vnto him some shippes to discouer that land, and he making great difficultie to be at anny chardges in soe vncertaine an exploite, two Franciscan fathers intreated the kinge to further that proiect, and when the said Columba returned againe into Spaine, some of the Fathers of that order accompanied him in the iourny Anno 1303. Alittle afterwardes when other partes of the weast Indies were discouered by Vasta Gamaanno 1500.there went with him by the procurement and intreatie of Emanuell kinge of Portingall 8.fathers of that family, both learned and holie. Not longe afterwardes other fathers of saint Dominique & saint Augustines order followed them. Last of al, by the request of Iohn kinge of Portugal F.Francis Zauier of the societie of Iesus, went into the East Indies, by whose blessed industrie those spatious kingdomes, and

barbarous

barbarous nations; *Domino cooperante & sermonem confirmante sequentibus signis*. Our Lord concurringe withall, confirminge their words with signes that followed, were conuerted.

4. This religious institution, is at this daie to be seene in those countries of the east, yea amoungest the Barbarians themselues, which thorough Gods speciall assistance, was neuer extinguished in those places where it once began. For when the kinge of Portingalls fleete arriued at the gulfe of Arabia, an ould mounke the Father of 3000. mounckes, who saw the signe of the crosse in the vpper part of the mast of their shippes, presently thought them to be Christians, and made signes vnto them that they would speake with them; who when they spoke one with another, they did weepe for ioye, to see the Christians, and they deliuered a booke of praiers as a token, which was sent vnto the Pope by the handes of Michaell de Silua, theire ambassador for the kingdome of Portingall, which booke Lewis de Granada handled and saw, who relateth thus much as I haue sett downe. *Granad. Symb. fid. l. 4. c. 12.*

5. By this you may perceaue that protestantes are greater enemies to religion & Christian pietie, then all the Heathens, Barbarous nations and Turques, and all the reprobates in the world are, who doe permitt

religious persons and monasteries amoungest them, as the Arrabians, Turckes, and Iewes doe: yea many monasteries are permitted in Grecia, Constantinople, Hierusalem, Argell, and amoungest the Tartarians themselues. But when protestancie began first to start vp, it made hauocke of all religion, and like a most raginge swifte streame, destroied, ransaked, and spoiled all churches, monasteries, and sacred howses, cast downe Alters, and prophaned Sanctuaries, hanged Christes picture vppon the gallones, defloured sacred virgines, cast the blessed Eucharist vnto dogges, and imbreued their murtheringe handes, with the blood of innocent and religious persons, against whome they practized their vildest and bloodiest factes, & extended their greatest furie and rage: against whome alsoe they make newe, and neuer harde-of lawes and decrees, with most rigorous execution to punish them to death as traytors, and to execute all tormentes vpon them, as the vildest malefactors of the worlde.

6. Was there euer seene anny heathen contrie, cittie, towne or villadge conuerted vnto Christ by them? Was there any parte of the east or weast, restored vnto their former sanctitie and religion by them? Nay was there euer seene anny man sanctified in his life, or reformed in his manners by them? Manny countries of the north, haue bin subuer-

ſubuerted by them, manny floriſhinge prouinces and wealthie citties, ranſaked and brought to vtter deſolation, and turned into aſhes by them Such as were religiouſlie giuen, honeſtlie diſpoſed, temperatt in their diett, mortified in their members, humors, and paſsions, chaſt and continent in their bodies and mindes (when they were catholiques) as ſoone as once they came to be proteſtants, they lett the reines looſe to all irreligious miſdeamenor, intemperate behauior, and wanton diſſolution, and to all kinde of riotouſnes. Seing therefore that all Catholique religion, and religious diſcipline came from Chriſte, it muſt followe that Luthers doctrine and his ſectes came from the deuill: and as it impoſsible that two repugnant contraieties, can proceed from one principle, as extreame heate, and extreame colde cannot come from one ſubiect, ſo neither can Catholique religion, and Luthers opinion both flowe from one fountaine.

7. This will plainly appeare by what enſweth; For Luther himſelfe confeſſeth he had a longe diſputation with the diuill at midnight, who fierſly impugned catholique priesthoode, orders and priuate maſſe. In another place he affirmeth, that the diuill paſſed through his mouth, tom. 5. Gen. ep. ad elect. ſar. Replie of Kelliſon 91. When I am in company ſaith he, he hurteth me not. *Lib. de Miſſa. Ang. to. 6.* *Kellyſon ibid.*

when he findeth me alone, then he teacheth me manners. I haue (saith he) one or two diuills of the greatest sorte, which I take (saith he) to be doctors of diuinitie amoungest diuills. He confessed also, that he had eaten a bushell of salte with him. *Frequentius & proprius mihi condormit, quam mea Catherina*, and that he slept oftener and neerer vnto him then did his Catherine. Vnto Zuinglius also appeared a goblin or spiritt white or blacke, when he was intoxicated touchinge his opinion against Christs reale presence, and suggested vnto him the 12. of Exodus, *Phase, hoc est transitus Domini*, against the reale presence.

*Kellyson ibid.*

*Zuing. in subs. Euchar.*

8. Contrariwise, the catholique religion was founded in all countries, with many glorious miracles, and the preachers thereof, were most holie men, not detected with any notorious vice, yea were lanternes and lightes of all vertue and sanctitie: but the founders of the protestant religion and the pillers thereof, of all men were most abhominable in their liues and cõuersation, and neuer wrought miracles. The founders of catholique religion were moste charitable and humble: but the other most proude and cruell. The one were the Architects and plotters of all treasons, ouerthrowes, bloodie imbruments, and detestable tragedies, in all countries where they begunn: but it was neuer known nor read, that either S. Patricke that brought the Ca-

tholique religion to Irland, or Paladius that brought it for Scotland, or Damianus or S. Augustine that brought the same to England, or any other taught the same in any other countrie, did euer conspire in treason or murther, or deuised anny mischeefe against kinge, potentate, or countrie: or that euer anny man lost his life, landes, or goodes for not receauinge either themselues or their doctrine: or that euer any kinge was expelled out of his kingdome, for not receauinge the catholique religion into his countrie: or was forced to imbrace the same, as the founders of protestancie haue done. But it is wel knowen that Luther and Zuinglius were the first that euer preached the protestant religion, as it is proued in the Apologie of the protestant Church of England, and that they were the causes of all the mischeefe, warres and troubles, insurrection of subiectes against their princes, & ouerthrowinge and banishment of Princes by their owne subiects, out of all their kingdomes and states.

9. Lastlie it is knowen also, that our first founders and apostles came in simplicitie of spiritt, without troupes of horsemen, or bandes of soldiors, hauinge noe other standert but the crosse of Christ, nor noe other poulder, but the dust of their feete: but the protestant founders came with wilde-fire, gun-poulder, and cannon-shott, with their

cruell armies in all places, to bringe all to confusion an desolation that would not imbrace their sect; yea many holie martyres haue suffred death, for not forsakinge their old religiō, to accept these new deuised opinions of these sectaries, wherof I haue thought good to sett downe the names, wherby you may perceaue the constancie of Catholiques, and the cruelties of protestants. *Ex fructibus eorum cognoscetis eos.* For yow shall knowe them by their fruicte. I will first speake of Flanders, then of France, afterwardes of England, and last of all, of Irelande.

---

*The name of those that suffred death by the Gewses of Flanders, where the protestantes are soe called.*

## CHAPTER I.

1. THe Reuerend Father Nicholaus Picus guardian of a monasterie of S. Francis in Holland, together with ten of his brethren, Ierom Werdan viccar, Will. Hadne, Nicase Hez, Theodorique Emden, Anthony Hornarien, Anthony Werden, Godfrey Meruellan, Frauncis Rod of Bruxells, Peter Astun a lay brother, Cornell Wican a lay man, who after much torment and affliction, were

were ſent to the towne of Bill, where they were beaten with clubbes, hanged on the topp of the common ſtoare howſe of the towne in the night time, the 14. of Auguſt 1575. they cutt of their eares and their noſes, they ripped vp their bellies, and pulled out all the fatt they could gett, and ſold the ſame in all places of the prouince. They alſoe put to cruel death Leonard Veichle paſtor of Barcomia, Nicholas Poppell another paſtor of that place, Godfrey Dimens ſomtime rector of the vniuerſitie of Parris, but then Paſtor Gorcomienſis, Iohn Oſter, Wicanus, cannon regular of ſaint Auguſtines order, and ouerſeer of the Nunnes, Adrian Becan of the order of Premonſtrenſis, Iames Lacopins a monke of the ſame order, Iohannes Ons of the order of ſaint Dominique, Andrewe Walter Paſtor Hairnotenſis, beſides many other related by doctor Eſtius chauncelor of Douaie. In this cittie of Brill were put to cruell death 180. religious perſones at ſeuerall tymes. And the Crucifix which ſtood in the church of Gorcomend for the conſolation of the Chriſtians, they pulled downe and hanged the ſame vppon the gallowes: they ſnatched alſo the Euchariſt out of a Prieſts handes, & nailed it vnto a gibbet.

2. When the Prince of Orenge tooke the cittie of Ruremunde in Gerderlande, his ſoldiors, ruſhinge into the monaſterie of

the Carthusians, murthered three lay brethren vid. Albert Winda, Iohn Sittart, and Stewart Ruremund. And entringe into the church of that monasterie, they found the Prior thereof called Ioachinus, with the rest of the religious people prayinge vnto God, all which they murthered: in which cittie 29. priestes and religious persons were martired. When the Gewes had gotte by deceit Adernard in Flaunders, after spoilinge and robbinge all the churches and monasteries therof, they apprehended all the priests and religious persons, and brought them bound with the gentlemen of that cittie vnto the castle there, amoungest whom master Peter, licentiate of diuinitie and pastor of that cittie, a worshippfull aged man, was put to great tormentes, and at the last beinge tied hande and foote, was cast from the toppe of the tower headlonge into the riuer of Scaldis. After him allso they cast headlonge down into the riuer Paulus Couis, pastor of that cittie, Iohn Brackett Batcheler of diuinitie, Iames Deckerie, Iohn Opstall and Iohn Anuanne a noble man, al priests. They tooke allso that vertuous man, Iohn Machusius of saint Frauncis order, somtimes Bisshopp of Dauentrie, who beinge sore wounded of them, they left his poore carcasse like a dead carion vpō the streetes; other priests they tooke by the cittie of Ipris, and buried them quicke in the earth, with their face a-

boue

boue the grounde, which inſteed of a marck they ſhott at with bulletts.

3. When Delps, a cittie of Holland, was taken by the Prince of Aurenge, who ſeemed to ſhewe great fauor, vnto a moſt reuerend and learned man called, Cornellius Muſius confeſſor to the Nunnes of ſaint Agatha of that cittie, yet was he with vnuſuall and exquiſitt torments put to the cruelleſt death that could be inuented the 10. of December 1575. The ſame crueltie they ſhewed vppon Egelbert of Burges a Franciſcan friar in the cittie of Alcmaria, for they did ripp his belly, and cutt off his intralles with their kniues. With noe leſſe crueltie did they putt to death two Mouncks of the order of ſaint Hierome at Ganda a cittie in Holland, their names were Iohn Rixtell, and Adrian Textor, whome the Generall of the Gewſes cauſed to be ſtript of their cloathes, and with their ſwordes, forced them to runn vppon thicke hedges of quickſett, and to die thereon. The like crueltie he executed vppon William Gandan a Franciſcan Friar, Iames Gandan, Theodorick Gandan Cornelius Sconhewe, and Iaſper, cannone regular, Mr. Iohn Ierome natiue of Edome in Holland, who beinge taken with other Catholiques by Hornan, were brought vnto Scage in the north parte of that prouince, where after many horrible and abhominable interrogatorious, ſome of them died in that

in that miserable captiuitie; such as were left a liue, were bound hand and feete vpon their backes with their naked bellies vpwardes, and vppon euerie mans bellie, was set a panne, or caldron whelmed downwards, full of dormise and frogges in great quantitie: and vpon the said pannes or caldrons were put fiery coales, which burning heate of the fire when those frogges felt, and had noe other place to gett out, they turned all vppon the poore peoples Bellies, and did gnaw and teare there, vntill they made hoales through their backes, or at least some place to defend themselues from the rage of the fire.

4. Vrsula Tales a religious Nunne of the Begginage, after that her father (an ould man and magistrate of that place) with other catholiques were hanged by these rebells, she also was brought vnto a gibbett, and being asked whether shee would forgoe her faith and religion, and marrie with a soldior, shee most constantlie denied, and was cast into the riuer, and there was drowned. This religious Nunne, had a sister that was married, and because shee lamented the death of her father and kinsmen, her head was brocken by one of the soldiors, and that so sorelie, that the braines came foorth. Other & farr more detestable wickednesses were comitted by these tyrannicall reprobates, in other prouinces of Flanders, Holland,

land, Zeland, Brabant, Gelderland and Friſland, which you may read in the hiſtories of Flaunders: but this I ought not to omitt, that they were ſoe tormented with ſuch an inſatiable thirſt to ſhedd innocent blood that in their deteſtable conuenticle at the towne of ſaint Trudan in a vaulte vnder the grounde, they purpoſed and decreed to make a maſſacre of eccleſiaſticall perſons in all places of the 17. Prouinces in one night, which God preuented afterwardes: vnto whome all honnor and glorie, for his prouident mercie ſhewed therin. *Menſe Iulij 1566.*

5. And although the hugonottes of France, ſought diuers times to practiſe their tragicall plottes in that countrie, as in the times of Frauncis the firſt (in whoſe raigne they nayled a libell at the court gate of Parris, of their damnable doctrine printed in the yeare 1534. which being brought vnto his maieſtie, and peruſinge part of the contentes thereof he ſaid; Did I knowe my right hande to be infected with that venemous doctrine, I would preſentlie cut it off from my bodie) Henrie the ſecond, and Frauncis the ſecond, yet they could neuer performe their deſigmentes vntill the beginninge of Charles the 9. his raigne, who being but a childe of 12. yeares of age (and ſoe abuſinge his minoritie) they watched their time and oportunitie in the yeare of our Lord 1562. when euerie one that was wickedly diſpoſed

sed and irreligiouslie addicted, and as it were forsaken of God, began openly to shewe himselfe vpon the theater, wheron this wofull tragedie was plaied. For first they crowned their captaine generall Prince of Condie, kinge of Fraunce, and called him by the name of Lodouicke the 13. and the first Christian kinge of Fraunce. The cheefest rage of all their malice, was practized vpon those thinges which were most sacred and holy, as vpon the blessed Eucharisté, by treadinge the same vnder their feete, and castinge it vnto their dogges, and vsed that sacred and dreadfull hoast, together with the holy chrisme to cleanse their tayles withall, and called Christ vnder the veile of bread, *Iohn le Blanch*, White Iohn. The like outrage they extended vppon Churches, Monasteries, Alters, Chapples, Oratories, Images, Reliques, and Sepulchers, which they spoiled, ransacked destroied & burned. Vpon Priests Mounckes and religious persons which they put to the vildest and cruelest death that they could imagine: vppon sacred virgins and consecrated Nunnes, which they rauished and defloured: vppon challices and sanctified vessells and hallowed ornaments, which they prophaned and defiled.

6. Of 12. that shewed themselues the ringleaders vpon this bloodie theater, there were 9. of them Apostate Mounckes, which

Christ vomitted out of his sacred mouth: the captaine and leader of them all, was Beza, who sould his benefice for 700. crownes, and then cast forth his venime amongest the licentious courtiers, whome he perswaded with his doctrine (vid.) that it was noe offence before God to cōmit sacriledge, to spoile churches, to cogge, deceaue, lye, sweare and forsweare: whose doctrine herein being the religion of these newe sectaries, was most plausible and pleasinge to all miscreantes and malefactors, who abound-dantlie resorted vnto him, from all partes of Fraunce, and by which he determined to robb and spoile all the churches and monasteries of that kingdome in one night in the moneth of Ianuarie, and appointed people for that purpose in all places of the kingdom, which was first put in execution in the Prouince of Aquitaine, & had not the Duke of Guys come the sooner to Parris, they had not only surprised the churches & monasteries there, but also the cittie, court, & kinge; Thus frustrated of their expectation, they fled vnto Orlians, where before they were lett in by the Cittizens, they did solemnlie swere that they came thither by the comaundement of the kinge to keepe that cittie, and that they would offer violence to none, either in his person, conscience, or goodes, and that euerie one should haue the benefitt of the edict diuulged the last of

*Vide Sur.*

of Ianuarie (wherein it was decreede that the hugonotts should not spoile churches or monasteries) but they noe sooner entred the cittie, but they spoiled the churches and monasteries, burned Images, cast downe alters, yea cast downe the verie walls of the churches, and shewed more execrable wickednes towards all sacred thinges, then the verie Turckes, for they in takinge any cittie or towne from the Christians, doe only vse to cast downe the Images and Alters, and not destroy the churches also.

7. All the holy Reliques which those hugonotts could gett, they burned them; they burned the reliques of S. Damianus, religiouslie reserued in that place, as they also did S. Hillaries reliques at Poytiers. S. Ireneus at Lyons. S. Iustus and S. Bonauentur, and the reliques of S. Martyn. At towers they burned the image of Christ; in another place they trayled the same through the dirte. They spared the image of the diuill, & burned the Corpes of S. Frauncis the second, which was buried in the Chapple of the holly crosse, as they did burne the bones of Lodouick the 11. The churches which they broake not downe, they turned into stables and storehowses. Moreouer Beza comaunded all the Priests to be murthered, of whome receauing monny for their redeption, yet violated the faith and promise which he had formerly sworne, and broa-

ke

ke the oath and peace, which he had before vowed most religiouslie to obserue. Soe as it is manifest there were cruelly put to death, fiue thousand priests, of whom some were flayed aliue, others were rackte till they were dead. Aboue six hundreth monasteries razed to the verie earth, manny others were burned: they burned alsoe the holie auncient Bybles, which were kept in Fraunce for rare monuments, many citties were exhausted with continuall siege, their citizens were murthered, all the countrie was spoiled and ruinated, soe as these ciuill warres of the hugonotts, soe often renewed, did more consume and oppresse France with greater miseries and calamities, then all former warres it euer had abroade; For there was no trueth respected, or oath performed, if any garrison did yeld themselues vnto thẽ vpon hope of their oathes (which they neuer accomplished) to saue their liues, (as in steede of many examples, that of Petraforte alone will serue) neuerthelesse contrarie to the lawes of armes, to the number of two hunderth, were cast downe head longe from the toppe of a mightie high Rocke: all which perished with that headlong and violent fall. Such crueltie as this, more then Turkish, they exercised vppon euerie other place where they did carrie anny sway: but ecclesiasticall persons and religious people, of all others, felt the grea-

greateſt ſmarte, ſome whereof I will particularize in the next Chapter.

*Certaine cruell and bloodie factes comitted in Fraunce against the Catholicks, by thoſe that the vulgar ſorte doe cal Hugonottes, from the tyme that they ſtirred rebellion against the kinge, Anno 1562.*

## CHAPTER II.

1. WHen the cittie of Engoliſme in Fraunce was beſiedged of the hugonottes, it was yelded into their handes vpon condition, ratified with promiſes and oathes, that it ſhould be lawfull for the catholickes, aſwell eccleſiaſticall as others, to continue there without anny moleſtations or inquiſition. The heretiques neuertheleſſe, not reſpectinge the religious obſeruation of a ſolemne oath, entring the cittie, gathered together all the ſelected catholiques, and caſt them in to priſon, amoungeſt whome was Michaell Grellett of ſaint Francis order, and guardian of the monaſterie of ſaint Fraunc is in that cittie, who the next daie, after the cittie was yealded, was hanged vpon a tree by the cittie wall in preſence of Iaſpar Calligne then Admirall of Fraunce and generall of thoſe rebells, which death he ſuffred moſt conſtantlie and propheſied of the ſaid Admiralls

miralls ruyne, and who when he was cast from the rope, al that wicked crue cried out, *God prosper our Gospell.*

2. Iohn Virolea of that order, and reader to that monasterie, after that his preuie members were cutt off, was also murthered by them. Iohn Aurell also of that order, a man 80. yeares of age, his head beinge cutt with a twibill, was cast into a priuie. Peter Bonnen doctor of diuinitie, after eight mounthes imprisonnent was hanged at the wall of the cittie. In the house of one of the Cittizens of that cittie of Engolisme, they shutt vpp 30. catholiques which they cruelly put to death by diuers kindes of tormentes; They deuided them by couples, whom they soe chained and lincked together, that sufferinge noe food to be giuen vnto them, they were compelled to eate one another, and soe with extreame languor they perished with hunger. Some of them were diuided aud cut asũder in two partes by mighty ropes, which were thruste through their bodies: Some of them also were tied vnto postes, and fire put to their backes, by which they were tormented more by the torment of a prolix death, then by the agonie of a violent flame.

3. The hugonitt garrison that kept the cittie of Vnstorne, though they were diuers times courteouslie entertayned of a most noble woman called the ladie of Maren-

datt, yet they tooke her within her owne house and tyed her to hott glowinge gaddes of Iron, and leauinge her in that torment, they departed withall the spoile of the house with them. The chiefe Iudge of the cittie of Engolisme, after they had cut away his priuie members, was hanged at his owne house. They tooke a vertuous priest also called Lodouicke Fiard, of a village neere Engolisme, a verie vertuous man and of an exemplar life by the testimonie of all men, whome they compelled to hould his handes in a cauldron full of hoat scaulinge oyle, vntill the flesh was consumed and nothinge lefte but the bare bones, and cast the burninge oyle into his mouth, and soe shott him with bullets and killed him. They tooke alsoe another priest called Colinus Ginlebantius the vicare of S. Auzann, and when they had cutt off his priuie members, they cast him afterwardes into a cisterne full of burninge hoat oyle, where he ended his life. They killed alsoe two other priests, the one was of the parrish of Riniers, who after they had cut out his tounge, then they murthered him: the other master Iohn Bachelon, his foote beinge burned by a hoat burninge Iron, they strangled him.

4. Maister Simon Sicott viccar of saint Hillarie of Montierind, beinge a man of 60. yeares of age, and replenished withall vertues, was betrayed by a hugonot whome he

he ſuppoſed to be verie faithfull vnto him, and was brought captiue into Engoliſme, but his life and libertie was reſtored vnto him for a great ſome of monny, that his frindes did procure for his ranſome, yet departinge from the cittie he was purſued, & his tonge was cut off, and his eies were pulled out of his heade. Two other prieſts were hanged by one of their heeles, with the other heele free, and their heades downwardes: one of them was left in that miſerable torment and the other was kild outright. Another prieſt called maiſter Peter, of the parriſh of Reulinẽd was burried quicke. Maiſter Arnold Durande, and viccar of Fleacen was caſt in the riuer being of 80. yeares of age. A Franciſcan Friar of that age alſoe, was caſt headlonge from the walles of the cittie. Maiſter Octauianus Ronier viccar of S. Cybard, after ſundrie tormentes, was faſtened to a tree, and ſoe ſhott to death. Maiſter Frauncis Robaleon in the parriſh of Foncobrune viccar, was tyed vnto a yoke of Oxen that drewe a cart, and after manny ſtripes and terrible torments, gaue vpp the ghoaſt: ſo that in the dioceſſe of Engoliſme, in leſſe then in two yeares ſpace, 120. did there ſuffer martyrdome; prieſts, noblemen, gentlemen and others.

5. In the village called Floran, a little diſtant from S. Monehond, they tooke a prieſt, whoſe priuie members beinge cutt

off by the Surgean of Bethan, he bragged that he was the 17 prieſt that he had murthered after that manner, and was afterwardes ſcourged vnto death. In the cittie of Hande, in the dioceſſe of Carnutenſis, they cauſed a poore prieſt to ſay maſſe, only to ſcorne that bleſſed ſacrifice, which Chriſt inſtituted for the quicke and the dead, and at the eleuation, they ſnatched awaie the ſacred hoaſt which they ſtabbed with their daggers, and then murthered the poore prieſt. In a certaine Hamlett 7. miles diſtant from Orliás, called Patt, they tooke 25. catholiques who fled vnto the church, which they burned by puttinge fire to the doores thereof; they carried with them many prieſts bounde at their horſe tailes. After ſpoiling of the church of Clerins, they burned the reliques and bones of the kinge of Fraunce called Lodouick the 11. as alſo the bones of the kinge of Nauar, ſomtimes their owne generall.

6. Att ſaint Mucarie in Gaſconie, they cutt open the bellies of many prieſts, and made a deuiſe to draw out their bowells; in this cittie they buried many prieſts quick. In the cittie of Ancina, they tooke an ould prieſte, whoſe preuie members after they had cutt off, they roaſted them, and cauſed him to eat them. In the cittie of Vaſett in Gaſconie, when Frauncis Caſsius was Lewetenant vnder the king of Nauare, two ſouldiers of that garriſon, rauiſhed a widdowe,

dowe, and thē put gunponder into her priuie partes and gaue fire to the powlder, and soe her bellie burst & her bowells came foorth. The Lord of saint Columba, the gouernor Gohas and a great number of nobilitie being besiedged by the Earle Mount Gomerie, yelded themselues vnto him vpon certaine condicions, yet neuerthelesse they were kept in prison 9. mounthes, and paid their ransome: and being inuited to supper by the said Earle, of whome they suspected noe such guyle, he hauing promised them their libertie, yet he sent souldiers in their absence to their chambers, and as they returned from supper, were intertained with the bloodie edge of their swordes: and soe against faith and promise and after paying their rāsome, they were inhumanly murthered. In the cittie of Montbris, the Barron of Adrett caused many catholiques to be cast headlong from the topp of a high Turett, and caused also souldiers to attend their miserable fall, and to entertaine them with the pointes of their pikes.

7. Such was the impudencie and barbarousnes of a certaine hugonott, that he did weare a chaine about his necke of the eares of priests, & shewed the same to the chiefest captaines of the hugonittes. They did ripp the bellie of a certaine priest, and tooke out his bowells, in steede whereof they putt oates to serue their horse for a maunger. The

heretiques of the cittie of Neemes in Languedoc, did cast a great number of catholiques into a mightie deepe and large well of that cittie, and haue filled the same twise with mens bodies halfe dead. James Socius a wicked pirate, who obtaininge letters patentes of Ioan Alberte Queene of Nauare, which they call letters of mart, sayling towardes the Iles of Madera, and Canaria, mett with a shipp of Portingall, goinge towardes America, which he pursued and tooke. In which there were 40. of the fathers of the societie of Iesus, who were sent to the Prouince of Brazill to instruct them in Christian religion, but the wicked and cruell Tyrant, like a deuouring woolfe, seased vppon these poore religious people, whome he massacred and after dismembring of them, of some he cutt a legg, of othersome an arme, and soe he cast them all into the sea.

8. Lastly Anno 1567. in the Carthusian monasterie which they call Burfowtaine in the diocesse of Suesse 5. mounks of that blessed order were murthered by the heretiques that came to robb that monasterie, Iohn Motto, proctor thereof a most vertuous priest, Iohn Megnē priest, Iohn Aurill priest, Benedict Lenes lay brother, and Theobald priest. All these that I speake of neuer tooke weapons against them, but most patientlie endured martirdome at their handes: But

if I

if I should speake of soe manny as were put to most cruell death and were kild in al the Prouinces of Fraunce, citties, and townes thereof, and such that were betrayed by thē, I should make an infinitt volume, but I cannot omitt that worthie and inuincible. Prince Frauncis of Lorraine Duke of Gwise, whose murther was plotted by Beza and executed by Poltrott. These and the like examples ought to moue good christians to beware of these people.

9. Before the firie, and furious concupiscence of king Henry the 8. (who caused that vnfortunat deuorce betwixt him, and his vertuous Queene Katherine) there was no realme in Europe more opulent and more abundant in all things, then the kingdome of England: no kingdome more peaceable at home and more glorious and prosperous abroad: no king so victorious and triumphant ouer his enimies, as he: no courte so magnificent or so plawsible, being full of cheerfull shewes, and replenished with an vniuersall triumph, ioy and exaltation, the king liued in securitie without feare of forraine princes abroad, or treason or conspiracy of his subiectes at home: betwixt the one and the other there was interchangeable good offices, aswell of a princely bountifulnesse towardes the subiectes, as of a dutifull subiection towardes the prince: the king possessed the hearts of his sub-

iects,& they againe enioye the loue of their Prince. But when he violated and dissolued the indissoluble knott & bond of matrimonie, which no power in earth was able to
*Matt.19* disioyne (as our Sauiour saith) by this separation and diuorce, he separated himselfe also from Gods church: all thinges were subuerted and turned topsy turuie, all was filled which feares and suspitions at home, with warres and diuisions a broad, and with continuall frights and stranges allarmes of attempts and garboyles, aswell in the court, as in the countrie. The treasures were exhausted, the subiects impourished, religion suppressed, religious howses dissolued, the vertuous oppressed, the wicked aduanced and exalted, the nobilitie condemned and beheaded, and their goods confiscated, and all vertuous people, were fedd and sustained, *Pane lachrymarum & aquâ angustia*: with the bread of mourning and teares, and with the water of anguish and paine, so as whatsoeuer the prophett Hieremy spake of Hierusalem, may be applied to England after its apostacy; The
*Hier.c.1.* flourishing nation (saith he) is like a poore widdow, that wailes at night and her teares rune downe by her cheekes, her priests doe waile, her virgins do complaine, and she is euerie where oppressed, her nobilitie are suppressed, and many of her people ouerpressed with vnsufferable miseries and calamities.

lamities. *Facti sunt hostes eius in capite eius, & inimici eius locupletati sunt*. Her enimies are promoted into her highest promotions, and her aduersaries made riche by her spoyles. Know yee and behold, how distastfull it is to forsake God, and nott to haue his feare before your eyes. *A seculo confregisti iugum Domini*, thow hast bracken and cast off godes yoake euen from the beginninge, thy swoord deuoured the prophets, *quasi leo vastator generatio vestra*, a destroieng lion is your generation. And as King Henry the 8. himselfe said in this booke against Luther. *Eos qui pelluntur gremio matris Ecclesiæ, statim furijs corripi, atque agitari demonibus.* Such as are expulsed and thrust out of the bosome of our mother the Church, are foorthwith ouercharged with the furious and raginge flames of hellish spirits, and vanquished which diuills: which assertion I would to God, it had not bene verified of him that said it, nor sutable to the purpose wherunto the same is applied. But England to their great cost by experience knoweth this to be trew, howsoeuer otherwise they dissemble it.

10. But to retourne to him that applied the same against Luther, the stroake did rebound and reflect vppon his owne neck, for being excommunicated by Clemens 7. for putting away his married wife, and for marrieng Anne Bullen, *tradidit se* (as the Apostle *Anno Domini* 1533 *Regni eius* 24.

postle saith) *impudicitiæ, in operem immunditiæ* Ephes. 4. *omnis in auaritiam*, he yelded himselfe ouer to impudicitie, to the exercise of all vncleanesse, & couetuousnes: he caused himselfe to be decreed by perleamēt head of the church, made it high treason in him that would not sweare precisely in his conscience this to be trew, where many worthy personages, both ecclesiasticall and lay people for refusing this oath or otherwise resisting it, some were burned aliue, as father Foster of the order of saint Fruncis, Queene Cathrins confessor, other some were beheaded, as doctor Fisher Bishopp of Rochester, and Sr. Thomas Moore L. Chancler of England, and may others were hanged drawen and quartered. Yea he condemned the whole cleargie in a premunire, which afterwardes they redeemed with a submission & paimēt of a hundreth thowsand pounds, for that they acknowledged Cardinall Campeignes and Cardinall Wolsey as legats from Rome, notwitstanding that the king himselfe by his Ambassadors procured their coming. In the 24. yeeres of his raigne, also he prohibited all appeales in causes ecclesiasticall, reducing all spirituall authoritie of determining the same to the English Cleargie. He forbid all license or dispensations, and faculties from the church of Rome, and seemed to establish them in Thomas Cranmer Archbishopp of Canterburie, that he should grant

grant the ſame to the king againe the 26. of his raigne. Other his bloody factes and furious behauiour, yow may well perceaue by the Catalogue following

*A Catalogue of thoſe that ſuffred death, as well vnder king Henry, as Queene Elizabeth, & king Iames, from the yeare of our Lord 1535. & 27. of king Henryes raigne vnto the yeere 1618.*

IN the firſt rancke of theſe bleſſed martyrs, I ought not to forgett that bleſſed martyr S. Thomas of Canterburie, alias, Becker, who for defending the immunities of the Church, was murthered in king Henry the 2. his raigne, now againe was by king Henrie the 8. by act of parleament attainted of high treaſon, his aſhes and holy bones and reliques were burned, and of all churches dedicated to God in his honor, it was decreed by parleament that they ſhould not be named after him any more: to which purpoſe comiſsioners were appointed in all places of England and Ireland, and in the towne of Rathode in Meath, the church wherof is dedicated to God in S. Thomas his honor, the pariſhioners being commaunded to name their church after ſaint Peter, they anſwered, that the king may aſwell by parleament proclaime ſaint Peter

Peter a traitor as saint Thomas, and to preuent that, they nominated their church after the blessed Trinity.

## *Vnder King Henry the VIII.*

### Anno Christi 1535. Henrici 8. anno 27.

*Nic. Sād. lib. 1. de Schism. Ang. pag. 128. 129. 130.*

*IOhn Houghton Prior of the Carthusianus at London.*
*Augustine Webster Prior of the Carthusians at Exham.*
*Robert Laurence Prior of the Carthusians at Beuall.*
*Richard Reynolds Mounke of S. Brigitts order of Syon.*
*Iohn Hayle Priest, Vicar of Thistleworth.*
— *These were put to death at Tyburne the 29. of Aprill, for denying the Kings Supremacy.*

*Humfrey Mildemore*
*William Exmew*
*Sebastian Newdigate*
— *Charter house Monkes of London, suffered at Tyburne 18. Iune.*

*Iohn Rochester*
*Iames Warnet*
— *Carthusians, at Yorke 11. May.*

*Richard Bere*
*Thomas Greene*
*Iohn Dauis*
*Thomas Iohnson*
*William Greenwod*
*Thomas Scriuan*
*Robert Salt*
*Walter Persons*
*Thomas Reading*
— *Charter house Mounkes died in prison in Iune & Iuly.*

Wil-

William Horne Carterhouſe Monke 4. Aug. — Ric. Hal. in eius vita. Staples. de tribus Thom.

Iohn Fisher Card. of S. Vitalis, & Bishopp of Rocheſter, at Tower-Hill 22. Iune.

Syr Thomas More Knight, at the Tower-hill 6. Iuly.

## Anno Chriſti 1536. Henr. 8. 28.

Iohn Paſley Abbot of Whalley } at Lancaſter — Sand. ibi. l. 1. pag. 176. 177.
Iohn Caſtegate Monke } 10. March.

William Haddocke Monke, at Whaley 13. March.

N. N. Abbot of Sauley } at Lancaſter
N. Aſhe Monke of Geruaux } in March.

Robert Hobbes Abbot of Woborne, togeather with the Prior of the ſame Monaſterie and a Prieſt, ſuffered at Woborne in Bedfordshire, in March.

Doctor Maccarell with 4. other Prieſts, at Tyburne 29. March.

William Thruſt Abbot of Fontaines }
Adam Sodbury Abbot of Geruaux } at Tyburne
William Would Prior of Birlington } in Iune.
N. N. Abbot of Riuers }

## Anno 1537. Henr. 29.

Antony Brorby of the Order of S. Francis, ſtrangled with his owne girdle, at London 19. Iuly. — Sand. ibi. pag. 183. Boucher. de paſſ. Fratr. Franſc. pag. 8. 15. & 17.

Thomas Cort Franciſcan, famished to death in priſon 27. Iuly.

Thomas Belcham of the ſame Order, died in Newgate 3. Auguſt.

## Anno 1538. Henr. 30.

Iohn Foreſt Frier obſeruant, Confeſſour to queene Katherine, in Smithfield 23. May. — Boucher. ibid. & pag. 26.

Iohn Stone an Auguſtine friar, at Canterbury — Sand. ibid.

this

this yeare.

Two and thirty Religious men of the Order of S. Francis being cast into prison for denying the K. Supremacy, died there through cold, stech, and famine, in Aug. Sept. and October.

Sand. l. 1. pag. 973.

N. Croft Priest, N. Collins Priest, N. Holland Layman } at Tyburne.

## Anno 1539. Henr. 31.

Sand. pa. 181. 194. 197.

Adrian Fortescue, Thomas Dingley } Knights of S. Iohns of Ierusalem, at Towerhill 8. Iul.

Griffith Clarke Priest, N. Mayre Monke } At S. Thomas Wateringes 8.

Iohn Tauers Doctor of diuinity, Iohn Harris Priest } 30. Iulij.

Iohn Rugge, William Onion } Priests, at Reading, 14. Nouemb.

Hugh Faringdon Abbot of Rehding, at Rehding 22. Nouem.

Richard Whiting Abbot of Glastebury, Iohn Thorne, Roger Iames } Monks of Glastebury } at Glastend 22. Nouem.

Iohn Beck Abbot of Colchester, at Colchester 1. Decemb.

## Anno 1540. Henr. 32.

Sand. ibi. pag. 216. 217.

William Peterson, William Richardson } Priests, at Calais 10. April.

Thomas Abell, Edward Powell, Rich. Fetherstone } Priestes, in Smithfield 30. Iuly.

Lan-

William Horne Carterhouse Monke 4. Aug. Ric. Hal. in eius vita.

Iohn Fisher Card. of S. Vitalis, & Bishopp of Rochester, at Tower-Hill 22. Iune. Staples. de tribus Thom.

Syr Thomas More Knight, at the Tower-hill 6. Iuly.

## Anno Christi 1536. Henr. 8. 28.

Iohn Pasley Abbot of Whalley } at Lancaster 10. March. Sand. ibi. l. 1. pag. 176. 177.
Iohn Castegate Monke

William Haddocke Monke, at Whaley 13. March.

N. N. Abbot of Sauley } at Lancaster in March.
N. Asthe Monke of Geruaux

Robert Hobbes Abbot of Woborne, togeather with the Prior of the same Monasterie and a Priest, suffered at Woborne in Bedfordshire, in March.

Doctor Maccarell with 4. other Priests, at Tyburne 29. March.

William Thrust Abbot of Fontaines } at Tyburne in Iune.
Adam Sodbury Abbot of Geruaux
William Would Prior of Birlington
N. N. Abbot of Riuers

## Anno 1537. Henr. 29.

Antony Brorby of the Order of S. Francis, strangled with his owne girdle, at London 19. Iuly. Sand. ibi. pag. 183. Boucher. de pass. Fratr. Fransc. pag. 8. 15. & 17.

Thomas Cort Franciscan, famished to death in prison 27. Iuly.

Thomas Belcham of the same Order, died in Newgate 3. August.

## Anno 1538. Henr. 30.

Iohn Forest Frier obseruant, Confessour to queene Katherine, in Smithfield 23. May. Boucher. ibid. & pag. 26.

Iohn Stone an Augustine friar, at Canterbury Sand. ibid.

this

this yeare.

Two and thirty Religious men of the Order of S. Francis being cast into prison for denying the K. Supremacy, died there through cold, stech, and famine, in Aug. Sept. and October.

Sand. l. 1. pag. 973.

N. Croft Priest
N. Collins Priest } at Tyburne.
N. Holland Layman

## Anno 1539. Henr. 31.

Sand. pa. 181. 194. 197.

Adrian Fortescue } Knights of S. Iohns of Ierusalem, at Towerhill 8. Iul.
Thomas Dingley

Griffith Clarke Priest } At S. Thomas Wateringes 8.
N. Mayre Monke

Iohn Tauers Doctor of diuinity } 30. Iulij.
Iohn Harris Priest

Iohn Rugge } Priests, at Reading, 14. Nouemb.
William Onion

Hugh Faringdon Abbot of Rehding, at Rehding 22. Nouem.

Richard Whiting Abbot of Glastebury } at Glastend 22. Nouem.
Iohn Thorne } Monks of Glastebury
Roger Iames

Iohn Beck Abbot of Colchester, at Colchester 1. Decemb.

## Anno 1540. Henr. 32.

Sand. ibi. pag. 216. 217.

William Peterson } Priests, at Calais 10. April.
William Richardson

Thomas Abell } Priestes, in Smithfield 30. Iuly.
Edward Powell
Rich. Fetherstone

Lan-

grant the ſame to the king againe the 26. of his raigne. Other his bloody factes and furious behauiour, yow may well perceaue by the Catalogue following

*A Catalogue of thoſe that ſuffred death, as well vnder king Henry, as Queene Elizabeth, & king Iames, from the yeare of our Lord 1535. & 27. of king Henryes raigne vnto the yeere 1618.*

IN the firſt rancke of theſe bleſſed martyrs, I ought not to forgett that bleſſed martyr S. Thomas of Canterburie, alias, Becker, who for defending the immunities of the Church, was murthered in king Henry the 2. his raigne, now againe was by king Henrie the 8. by act of parleament attainted of high treaſon, his aſhes and holy bones and reliques were burned, and of all churches dedicated to God in his honor, it was decreed by parleament that they ſhould not be named after him any more: to which purpoſe comiſsioners were appointed in all places of England and Ireland, and in the towne of Rathode in Meath, the church wherof is dedicated to God in S. Thomas his honor, the pariſhioners being commaunded to name their church after ſaint Peter, they anſwered, that the king may aſwell by parleament proclaime ſaint

Peter

Peter a traitor as saint Thomas, and to preuent that, they nominated their church after the blessed Trinity.

## *Vnder King Henry the VIII.*

### Anno Christi 1535. Henrici 8. anno 27.

*Nic. Sãd. lib. 1. de Schism. Ang. pag. 128. 129. 130.*

| | |
|---|---|
| *IOhn Houghton Prior of the Carthusianus at London.*<br>*Augustine Webster Prior of the Carthusians at Exham.*<br>*Robert Laurence Prior of the Carthusians at Beuall.*<br>*Richard Reynolds Mounke of S. Brigitts order of Syon.*<br>*Iohn Hayle Priest, Vicar of Thistleworth.* | *These were put to death at Tyburne the 29. of Aprill, for denying the Kings Supremacy.* |
| *Humfrey Mildemore*<br>*William Exmew*<br>*Sebastian Newdigate* | *Charter house Monkes of London, suffered at Tyburne 18. Iune.* |
| *Iohn Rochester*<br>*Iames Warnet* | *Carthusians, at Yorke 11. May.* |
| *Richard Bere*<br>*Thomas Greene*<br>*Iohn Dauis*<br>*Thomas Iohnson*<br>*William Greenwod*<br>*Thomas Scriuan*<br>*Robert Salt*<br>*Walter Persons*<br>*Thomas Reading* | *Charter house Mounkes died in prison in Iune & Iuly.* |

Wil-

Laurēce Cocke Prior of Dancaster
Williame Horne Monke
Edmund Bromelie Priest
Giles Horne Gentleman
Clement Philpot Gentleman
Darby Genninges Layman
Robert Bird Layman
} At Tyburne 4. August.

Anno 1541. Henr. 33.

Dauid Genson Knight of the Rhodes 1. Iuly. Sand. pag. 180.

Anno 1543. Henr. 35.

German Gardener Priest
Iohn Larke Priest
Iohn Ireland Priest
Thomas Ashbey Layman
} at Tyburne 7. March. Sand. pag. 227.

Iohn Risby.
Thomas Rike.

## Vnder Queene Elizabeth.

Anno 1570. Elizabethæ 12.

Iohn Felton Gentleman, in S. Paules Churhyard 8. August. Nicol. Sander. l. 7. de visib. Monarc. pag. 734. & 736.

Anno 1571. Elizabeth 13.

Iohn Story Doctor of the Canon-law, at Tyburne 1. Iune.

Anno 1573. Elizabeth 15.

Thomas Woodhouse, Priest, at Tyburne 19. Iune. Concert. Eccles. Ang.

Anno

Anno 1577. Elizabeth. 19.

Concert. Eccles. Ang.

*Cuthbert Mayne the first Priest of the Seminaries, at Launston in Cornwall 29. Nou.*

Anno 1578. Elizab. 20.

Concert ibid.

*Iohn Nelson Priest, at Tyburne 3. February.*
*Thomas Sherwood Gentleman 7. Febr.*

Anno 1581. Elizab. 23.

Concert. Eccles. Ang. Sand. l. 3. de schism. Angl.

*Euerard Hanse Priest, at Tyburne 31. Iuly.*
*Edmund Campian Priest of the Societie of Iesus*
*Alexander Briant Priest of the same Society of Iesus*
*Raphe Sherwyn Priest*
} *at Tyburne 1. Dec.*

Anno 1582. Elizab. 24.

*Iohn Payne Priest, at Chelemsford in Essex 2. April.*

Concert. Eccles. Angl. & Sand. vbi supra.

*Thomas Ford Priest*
*Iohn Shert Priest*
*Robert Iohnson Priest*
} *at Tyburne 28. May.*

*Thomas Cottam Priest of the Society of Iesus*
*William Filby Priest*
*Luke Kirby Priest*
*Laurence Iohnson Priest*
} *at Tiburne 30. May.*

*William Lacy Priest*
*Richard Kirkman Priest*
} *at Yorke 22. August. 27.*

*Iames Tompson Priest, at yorke in Nouemb. 26.*

Anno 1583. Elizab. 25.

Concert. Eccles. Angl. & Sand. pa. 465. 466.

*William Hart Priest, at yorke 16. March.*
*Richard Tirkill Priest, at yorke 29. May.*
*Iohn Slade Layman, at Winchest 30. Octob.*
*Iohn Body Layman, at Andouer 2. Nouemb.*

Iames

*Iames Laburne Gentleman, at Lancaster.*

Anno 1584. Elizab. 26.

*William Carter Layman, at Tyburne 11. Ian.*

*George Haddocke Priest*
*Iohn Mundine Priest*
*Iames Fen Priest*
*Thomas Emersford Priest*
*Iohn Nutter Priest* } *at Tyburne 12. Feb.*

*Iames Bele Priest*
*Iohn Finch Layman* } *at Lancaster 20. April.*

*Richard White Layman, at Wrixam in Walles 8. Octob.*

*Iohn Finlye Priest, at yorke 8. August.*

*Concert. Eccles. Angl. pag. 127. 134 140. 143. 156. cum Sand. vbi supra.*

Anno 1585. Elizab. 27.

*Thomas Aufield Priest*
*Thomas Webley Layman* } *at Tyburne 6. Iuly.*

*Hugh Taylour Priest*
*Marmaduke Bowes Layman* } *at yorke 26. Nouemb.*

*N. Hamelton Priest, at yorke.*

*Concert. Eccles. Angl. pag. 203. Sand. pag. 485. 499.*

Anno 1586. Elizab. 28.

*Margret Cletherow pressed at yorke 25. March.*

*Edward Transam Priest*
*Nicol. Woodfine Priest* } *at Tyburne 21. January.*

*Richard Sergeant Priest*
*William Tompson Priest* } *at Tyburne 20. April.*

*Iohn Addams Priest*
*Iohn Low Priest*
*Robert Debdale Priest* } *at Tyburne 8. Octob.*

*Robert Anderton Priest*
*William Marsden* } *at Tyburne.*

*Francis Ingleby Priest, at yorke 3. Iune.*

*Concert. Eccles. Angl. pag. 204. 410. Sand. pa. 499.*

*Iohn Sandes Priest, at Glocester.*
*Iohn Finglow Priest.*
*Robert Bickerdicke Gentl. at yorke 23. Iuly.*
*Alexander Crow Priest, at yorke 30. Nouem.*
*Rich. Langly Gentleman, at yorke 1. Decem.*

Anno 1587. Elizab. 29.

*Concert. Eccles. Ang. pag. 207.*

*Mary Queene of Scotland, at Foderinghay-Castle 8. Febr.*
*Thomas Pilchard Priest, at Dorcester in March.*
*Stephen Rousam Priest, at Glocester.*
*Iohn Hamley Priest, at Chard.*
*Robert Sutton Priest, at Stafford.*
*Gabriell Thimbleby Priest.*
*George Douglas Priest, a Scotshman at yorcke 9. Sept.*

Anno 1588. Elizab. 30.

*Didacus de Yepes Episcop. Taracon. de persec. Angl. Hispanicè.*

*Edmund Sikes Priest, at yorke 23. March.*
*William Deane Priest* } *at Milēd-greene by London 28. Aug.*
*Henry VVebly Priest* }
*William Gunter Priest, at the Theater by London 28. August.*
*Robert Morton Priest* } *in Lincolnes Inne fields by London 28. Aug.*
*Hugh More Gentleman* }
*Thomas Acton alias Holford Priest, at Clarkenwell in London 28. Aug.*
*Richard Clarkeson Priest* }
*Thomas Felton laybrother of the order of the Minimes* } *at Hunslow 28. Aug.*
*Richard Liegh Priest* }
*Hugh Morgan Gent.* } *at Tyburne 30. Aug.*
*Edward Shelly Gent.* }
*Richard Flower Layman* }

Robert

Robert Martin Layman } at Tyburne 30. Aug.
Iohn Rocke Layman
Margaret Ward Gent.
Edward Iames Priest } at Cichester 1. Octob.
Raph Crochet Priest
Robert Wilcokes Priest
Edward Campian Priest } at Canterbury 1. Octob.
Christopher Buxton Priest
Robert Widmerpoole Layman
William Wigges Priest, at Kingston 1. Octob.
Iohn Robinson Priest, at Ipswich 1. Octob.
Iohn Weldon Priest, at Milend-greene by London 5. Octob.
William Hartley Priest } at Haliwell by London 5. Octob.
Richard Williams Priest
Robert Suttan Layman at Clarkenwell 5. Octo.
Edward Burden Priest, at yorke 29. Nou.
Iohn Hewit Priest.
Robert Ludlam Priest } at Darby.
Richard Sympson Priest
Nicolas Garlicke Priest
William Lampley Layman at Glocester.

## Anno 1589. Elizab. 31.

George Nicols Priest } at Oxford 5. Iuly.
Richard Yaxley Priest
Thomas Belson Gentleman
Iohn Annas Priest } at yorke 16. March.
Robert Dalby Priest
William Spenser Priest, at yorke 24. Sept.
Robert Hardestye Layman, at yorke 24. Sept.

Didacus de Yepes Episcop. de persec. Angl. Hispan.

Anno 1590. Elizabeth. 32.

*Christopher Bales Priest, in Fleetstreet in London 4. March.*

*Alexander Blake Layman in Grayes Inne lane in London 4. March.*

*Nicolas Horner Layman in Smithfield in London 4. March.*

*Miles Gerard Priest*<br>*Francis Dickinson Priest* } *at Rochester 30. Aprill.*

*Antony Middleton Priest at Clarkenwell in London 6. May.*

*Edward Iones Priest in Fleetstreet in London 6. May.*

Anno 1591. Elizab. 33.

*Edmund Geninges Priest*<br>*Swithin Welles Gent.* } *in Grayes Iune fields 10. Dec.*

*Eustach White Priest*<br>*Polidor Plasden Priest*<br>*Brian Lacy Gentleman*<br>*Iohn Mason Layman*<br>*Sydney Hodgson Layman* } *at Tyburne 10. Dec.*

*Andr. Philop. cont. Edic. Reginæ Angl. pag. 482.*

*Momfort Scot Priest*<br>*George Bisley Priest* } *in Fleestreet 2. Iuly.*

*William Dikinson Priest*<br>*Raph Milner Layman* } *at Winchester 7. Iuly.*

*Edmund Duke Priest*<br>*Richard Holiday Priest*<br>*Iohn Hogge Priest*<br>*Richard Hill Priest* } *at Durham.*

*William Pikes Layman at Dorcester.*

*Robert Thorpe Priest, at yorke 31. May.*

*Thomas Watkinson Layman, at yorke 31. May.*

Anno

Anno 1592. Elizab. 34.

*William Patteson Priest, at Tyburne 22. Ian.*

*Thomas Portmore Priest in S. Paules Churchyard in London 21. Febr.*

*Roger Ashton Gentleman, at Tyburne 23. Iune.*

Anno 1593. Elizab. 35.

*Iames Burden Layman, at Winchest. 25. Mar.* *Did yepes ibi. pag. 651.*

*Antony Page Priest, at yorke 30. April.*

*Ioseph Lampton Priest, at Newcastle 23. Iune.*

*William Dauis Priest, at Beumaris in Wales, in Septemb.*

*Edward Waterson Priest.*

Anno 1594. Elizab. 36.

*William Harington Priest, at Tyburne 18. Febr.* *Yepes vbi supr. pag. 633. 640. 641.*

*Iohn Cornelius Mohun Priest of the Society of Iesus*
*Thomas Bosgraue Gentleman*
*Patricke Samon Layman*
*Iohn Carey Layman*
} *at Dorcester 4. Iuly.*

*Iohn Ingram Priest, at Newcastle.*

*Iohn Boast Priest, at Doram 29. Iuly.*

*Iames Oldbaston Priest, at yorke 26. Nouemb.*

Anno 1595. Elizab 37.

*Robert Southwell Priest of the Societie of Iesus, at Tyburne 3. March.* *Did. yepes in hist. persecut. Angl. pag. 642.*

*Henry Walpole Priest of the Societie of Iesus*
*Alexander Raulins Priest*
} *at yorke 7. Apr.*

*William Freeman Priest.*

*Iohn Watkinson, alias Warcoppe Layman, at yorke.*

Anno 1596. Elizab. 38.

*George Errington Layman*
*William Knight Layman* } *at yorke 29. No.*
*William Gibson Layman*

Anno 1597. Elizab. 39.

*Yepes ubi supra. pag. 710. l. 5.*

*William Anlaby Priest, at yorke 4. Iuly.*
*Iohn Buckley, alias Iones Priest of the Order of S. Francis, at S. Thomas Waterings 12. Iuly.*
*Thomas Warcop. Henrie Abbot & Edward Fulthorpe Laymen, at yorke 4. Iuly.*

Anno 1598. Elizab 40.

*Christopher Robinson Priest, at Carlile.*

*Peter Snow Priest*
*Richard Horner Priest*
*Ralfe Grimston Layman* } *at yorke.*
*Iohn Britton Layman*

Anno 1599.

*Mathew Hayes Priest, at yorke.*

Anno 1600. Elizab, 42.

*Relatio 16 Mart. à Th. VV. edit.*

*Christopher Wharton Priest, at yorke 18. May.*
*Iohn Rigby Gentleman, at S. Thomas Wateringes 21. Iuly.*

*Robert Nutter Priest*
*Edward Thwinge Priest* } *at Lancaster in Iune.*

*Thomas Sprot Priest*
*Thomas Hunt Priest* } *at Lincolne in Iuly.*

*Thomas Palaser Priest*
*Iohn Norton Gentleman* } *at Durham in Iuly.*
*N. Talbot Gentleman*

Anno 1601. Elizab. 43

*Iohn Pibush Priest, at S. Thomas Wateringes 10. February.*

Roger

*Roger Filcocke Priest of the Society of Iesus*
*Marke Barkworth Priest of the Order of S. Benedict*
*Anne Heygham Gentlewoman widdow, to master Lyne.*
} *at Tybur. 27. Feb.*

*Relat. 16. Mart. pag. 93. & 94.*

*Robert Middleton Priest*
*Thrustan Hunt Priest*
} *at Lancaster.*

Anno 1602. Elizab. 44.

*Francis Page Priest of the Society of Iesus*
*Thomas Tichborne Priest*
*Robert Watkinson Priest*
*Iames Ducket Layman*
} *at Tyburne 29. Apr.*

*Mathew Harrison Priest*
*Antony Battie Layman*
} *at yorke in April.*

Anno 1603. Elizab. 45. & vltimo.

*William Richardson Priest, at Tyburne 27. February.*

## Vnder King Iames.

Anno 1614. Iacob. Reg. 2.

*Laurence Bayly Layman, as Lancaster in March.*

*Iohn Suker Priest*
*Robert Grissold Layman*
} *at Warwicke in August.*

Anno 1605. Iacobi 3.

*Thomas Wilborne Layman, at yorke 1. August.*
*Iohn Putchering Layman, at Rippon. 5. Septemb.*
*William Browne Layman, at Rippon.*

Anno 1606. Iacobi 4.

Edward Oldcorne Priest of the Society of Iesus
Raph Ashley Layman } at Worcester 7. Apr.

Henry Garnet priest, Superiour of the Society of Iesus in England, in S. Paules Churchyard 3. May.

Anno 1607. Iacob. 5.

Robert Drury priest, at Tyburne 26. January.

Anno 1608. Iacob. 6.

Mathew Flathers priest, at yorke 21. March.

George Geruis priest of the order of S. Benedict, at Tyburne 11. April.

Thomas Garnet priest of the Society of Iesus, at Tyburne 23. Iune.

Anno 1610.

George Napper priest, at Oxforde 10. of Nouember.

Cadwalladar priest in Wales.

N. Roberts priest of the order of S. Benedict, at Tyburne.

Thomas Somers priest, at Tyburne 10. of December.

Anno 1612.

N. Scot priest, of the order of S. Benedict, at Tyburne.

Richard Newport priest, together with him.

*A Compendium of the martyrs and confeßors of Ireland vnder Queene Elizabeth.*

## CHAPTER III.

1. WIlliam Walſh natiue of Donbuinein the dioceſſe of Meath firſt depriued of his buſhoprick and ſpoiled of all his goods, for not conforming himſelfe to the Queens iniunctious about the oath of her eccleſiiaſticall ſupremacie, and other lawes made againſt the holy Camons of the catholique church, was put into a deepe dungeon, wherin he was many yeeres afflicted with giues and fetters, vntill by the fauor of his keeper he made an eſcape and fled into Spaigne, and ſo ended the remainder of his bleſſed dayes at Alcala 1578.

2. Thomas Leorus Biſhopp of Kildare willingly reſigned his biſhoprick in king Edwards dayes, for that he could not with a ſafe conſcience poſſeſſe the ſame, and being to the great conſolation of his hart reſtored againe vnto the ſame in Queene Maries dayes, was again in Queene Elizabeths diſpoſſeſſed therof, and of all other his liuelyhood, well contented rather, *abiectus eſſe in domo Dei magis quam habitare in tabernaculis peccatorum*, he applied himſelfe being baniſhed to Munſter in Ireland, in teaching yong

yong children to reade their books and instructing them in the christiã doctrine: lightly he neuer came to any mans howse butt he exhorted therin, nor euer supped or dined, but in the later end therof he tooke occasion to edifie the people with one exhortation or another. Once being at the Earle of Desmounds howse at supper, a gentle woman beinge there, retourning home told to her friends as a great wounder, that Bishopp Leorus preached not at the later ende of his meat as he was accustomed: he neuer did forbeare to reproue and reprehend vice & wickednesse in any man whatsoeuer who was reproueable, and persisting still in all hollinesse and zeale of godes euerlasting trueth, vntill the last gaspe of his breath, he died of the age of 80. yeers at the Nasse in the prouince of Leinster in Ireland 1577.

3. Morris fitz Gibbon Archbishopp of Cashall, for the like cause was spoiled of all his goodes and suffred much laboure and trauaile, and at lenght fled out of the kingdome of Ireland and died in the porte of Portingall 1578. Edmond Taner Bishopp of Clone and Corcke doctor of diuinitie, who first being of the societie of Iesus, out of which through great sicknesse not without licence of his superiors and aduise of the phisitions was enforced to come foorth, and through the importunat sute of his frinds, was persuaded to take vppon him the digni-

dignitie, or rather the heauie bourden of a Biſhopp, eſpecially in dangerous ſeaſons of turbulent hereſies, by which he ſuffred great penury and want aſwell in priſon, as ont of it, he died about the yere of our Lord 1578.

4. Hugh Lacy Biſhopp of Limericke, did ſuffer great callamitie, aſwell vnder king Henry the 8. as king Edward his ſonne, in whoſe times he was thruſt from his place and function, and alſo compelled to fly the Realme for not yelding to the ſupremacie of the yong king in the ſpiritually regiment of the church: but being reſtored to his former dignitie in Queene Maries dayes by Cardinall Poole, his hollineſſe legat in England and Ireland, was in Queene Elizabeths time enforced to ſuffer the like reuolution, aſwell of his biſhippricke, as of all other things, and ſo to carrie the burden of Chriſts croſſe, he liued in woe, and ended the ſame in ioy, *Anno Domini 1577.*

5. Nicholas Skerret Archbiſhopp of Thomound a man of an innocent life, and moſt zealous in the profeſsion of the chriſtian faith, after ſuffering many difficulties and hard vſuadg in priſon, out of which he made an eſcape, fled into Portingall, and ended his holy life at Lisborne 1583.

6. Thomas O Hierly Biſhopp of Roſſe, a man of great fame for good life and bleſſed conuerſation, after long jmpriſonnent in the Tower of London, out of which he was enlar-

enlarged by the entreatie of Sr. Cormocke Ma-Teighe Lord of Munſtre, who then was at the Court in Englād, and after much affliction and tribulation liuing in woodes and montaines, ended his holy life *Anno* 1581.

7. Patricke Ohealy of the order of ſaint Frauncis Biſhopp of Maio, coming out of Spaine into Ireland, no ſooner landed, then by the ſherif and officers of that place, (which was at Dingell in the weaſt part of all Irland) but he was apprehended, together with a religious man of that order nobly deſcended, call Con Ornorcke, and were ſent to the Conteſſe of Deſmōd, who either to currie fauour which the ſtate of the kingdome, or for feare to be ill thought of if he had diſmiſſed them, or to be impeached of any imputation or ſuſpitiō of any conſpiracy with Sr. Iames fitz Morrice then on foote, reddy at that time to paſſe out of Gallicia in Spaine into Ireland with a ſupply of Spaniardes, did remitt them ouer to Limerick to be preſented before Mr. Iames Gould, then the Queens Attourney in the Prouince: as about that time allſo ſhee yelded her eldeſt ſonne to Sr. William Drury Lord Iuſtice of Ireland as an hoſtage that he ſhould reſt himſelfe ſecure without feare of the Earles loialtie & fidelitie to her maieſty for yelding her ſonn and heire apparent of Deſmond as a pleadg, and the holy Biſhopp as a priſoner: but as ſhee was carfull to continew the Earldome in her loynes, ſo the o-

ther was as warrie to preserue his owne reputation and credirt in his new promotion of Lord iustice, who was no les suspected to fauor the catholique religion (for he was in harte and will of that professіon) then the other was to further rebellion. *Sed quis vnquam tetigit Christum Domini & innocens fuit?* both the iustice and the contesse, were frustrated of their hope & deceaceaued of their expectation. *Maledictus qui confidit in homine*, and thincking to possesse the fauor of the world, they respected nott the fauor and iustice of God, whose wisdome surpasseth the prouidence of man. *timida & inepta prouidentia nostra.*

8. The Earle therfore of Desmond, within one month after the good Bishopp suffred, was proclaimed traitor, and most part of the Geraldines with their followers in a serious conflict betwixt themselues and the English (of whome Sr. Nicholas Malby was Cheeftaine) were ouerthrowen and putt to flight at the Abbay of Bertiff, in Irish called Eanighbegg, within 7. miles of Limericke weastward, and that most noble aũcient howse which was the only strenght and Bulwareke for the Crowne of England in dangerous seasons of that kingdome heertofore, is nowe altogether extinguished. And the Lord Iustice continewed no longer in his new dignitie then one month after the Bishopps execution, which was the

the ſpace of time that he challenged the Lorde Iuſtice to anſwer before the dreadfull throne of God for their innocent blood, I meane of him and his followe, and for their vniuſt iudgment, which was that they ſhould be executed by Marſhall law: wherfore they were deliuered to a band of ſoldiors, their handes being tide behind their backs, and their feete with roppes vppon garrans, of whome they were cruelly entertained al the way vntil they came to Kilmalocke, a towne diſtant 12. miles from Limericke, where they were hanged vppon trees; the fooliſh & cruell ſoldiors a whole ſenight after their death (for they were not permitted all that time to be buried) made butts of their carcaſes, to ſhutt and leuill att them with their bullets, calllng them by the name of papiſts, traitors, idolators. Immediatly after their execution, the ſaid L. iuſtice ſickned in the campe, and ended his life at Waterfoord, crieng out vpon thoſe bleſſed martirs, whome he had putt to death, but one moneth before.

9. Derby Ohurley Archbiſhopp of Caſhall, doctor of both lawes, and profeſſor of that facultie in the vniuerſitie of Rheames in Fraunce, vnder Cardinall Guiſe Archbiſhopp of the ſame, was taken in Ireland, and caſt into a darck Dungeon in the Caſtle of Dublin: and being ſore vexed with this vgly priſon and penſiue reſtrainct, was more

vexed

vexed and tormented by an vsuall and exquisitt torment of bootes full of boylling oile and talloe, into which he was cōpelled to putt his legges already wearied with heauie bolts, and to stād by a great fire, with which his flesh was consumed vnto the bare bones; all which he endured with great patience and constancy. And afterwardes, when by that torment he could not be wonne, nor by feare and alluring promisses of vncertaine and deceitfull promotion, could nott be inueigled, to relent or to faint in the profession of the catholique religion, or to embrace the protestant negatiue religion, was vpon fridaie morning in the dawning, strāgled with a wyth, in the moneth of May 1584. and so suffred a blessed martirdome, and enioieth a blessed crowne.

10. Redmond Ma-Goran primat of Ardmagh, was slaine in Conaght by Sr. Richard Bingham Anno 1598. Redmond Ogulloglior Bishopp of Derry, being almost 100. yeers of age, and 50. yeers a Bishopp, was with 3. priests about midnight, slaine in his owne howse neere Derry, by the garrison of Loghefoile, thorough the craft and drift of one Sr. Neyle Garrath Odonel, who afterwards falling into disgrace with the English, was impeached and arraigned for taking part with Odohirtyes conspiracy, and was comitted together with his sonne, prisoner in the tower of london anno 1600. Morihirtagh Obrien

Obrien Bishopp of Emly, being apprehended, was cast into the castle of Dublin where through penurie and straightnesse of his restraint, he died in the yeare 1586.

11. Peers Power Bishoppe of Fearnes, being taken and apprehended, was cast into the castle of Dublin, who either through the frailtie of the flesh, or through the extremity of his restraint, or els through the deceitfull promisses of temporall promotions, yelded to the supremacy of the Queene in the spirituall iurisdiction of the church: which being once granted, he destroied all articles of our catholique beleefe, and therfore he was sett at libertie. But being afterwardes sore amased and strocken with an inward sorrow for being so weake and so inconstant, in a point so highly importing the increase and honor of christian religion, and consequently our saluation, retourned like another Marcellinus vnto the place where he fell, and where he gaue so vild a scandall, deplored his fall, and greeuously lamented his errors: and so he was hardlier dealt with all, then euer before: but after long imprisonment and much affliction through godes prouidence, he made an escape and fled into Spaine (the common support and sanctuary of al distressed catholiques) where he died with great probation of a blessed and constant catholique Bishopp.

12. Richard Creogh, natiue of the cittie of

of Limericke in the prouince of Munster in Ireland, descended of welthie and honest parents, of an auncient familie in that cittie, who notwithstanding he imploied the prime of his youthfull dayes in the trade of marchandice, yet he profitted more in the spirituall exercise of deuotion and pietie then he did in the acquiring of riches and wordly designementes. And after some worldly losse, went beyond the seas, where he gaue himselfe to the studdy of vertue and learning, & made therin great and admirable encrease, and so became a priest, and not without expectation of such a one, as he liued and died afterwards. For his rare vertues he was made Archbishopp of Ardmagh and primat of all Ireland, and comming for his Country (where he perfourmed the office of a diligent pastor and a zealous prelate) was betraid by one of the country, and committed to close and ghastly prison in the Castle of Dublin. And after suffering much trouble in prison, was brought to his triall in the kings bench before Sr. Iohn Plunkett, then cheef iustice of that court, and being there endited and araigned of high treason and enforced to abide a Iury of gentlemen of the pale, he was found guiltles, but they for acquiting of him were all comitted to the said castle, and put to great fines. When they could get no way by law to make him away, or that his constancy could not be infringed, he was remitted ouer to the Tower of London, out of which he made an escape. But after arriuing in Ireland to helpe his flocke, the best he could, was againe apprehended, and sent ouer againe to the Tower, where he ended his life.

13. Cnohor O Duanna Bishopp of Downe Patricke and Connor, was apprehended the moneth of Iuly 1612. and committed to the Castle of Dublin, wherin he liued in continuall restrainct many yeers before, by the apprehension of one maister Smith secretary to Sr. Nicholas Bagnall, but being taken the 2. time, was hanged, drawen, and quartered, the first of Februarie 1612. One Patricke a vertuous priest suffred allso with him.

## *Of Priests.*

1. IOhn Traners doctor of diuinitie, being accused that he wrott against the supremacy of the king, was hanged drawen and quartered at Tiburne Anno 1535. which being at the place of executiō, he confessed, plainly, shewing the 3. fingers with which the wrott that matter: and his hand beinge strooken of and cast into the fire, euerie whitt was burned, but those 3. fingers could nott be burned, as Surius writeth.

2. Lawrence Moore (whom doctour Sāders in his letres 1580. to the Cardinall Com-

Commen of the warres of Ireland, called a holly prieſt ) being with the Spaniardes at the Forte called Dowy Nore, was betraied and deliuered ouer to the Lord Gray, then Lord deputie of Ireland (with two proper gentlemen, the one called Oliuer Plunket an Iriſh gentleman, the other called William Welſh an Engliſh gent.) by the Corronell of the Forte, called Sebaſtian de ſaint Ioſeph, for that they refuſed vppon any compoſition to yeld ouer the ſaid Forte, which they could well defend hauing no want of any thinge neither victuals, nor munutiõ, were comanded by the ſaid L. deputy to be brought to a ſmiths forge, and al their bones and Iointes to be beaten and cruſhed with a hammer, and this for the ſpace of a day, and night, the prieſts fingers being cutt off with a knife: but in that extreame paine they ſuffred, yett their liues were promiſed vnto them, if they would turne proteſtãtes. Al the Spaniards to the nũber of 900. except the ſaid Corronell and 10. more, were ſtript of their weapons, and were all ſlaine, and caſt ouer the cliffs into the ſea, for that Forte ſtood vppon a mightie rocke ouer the ſea, notwithſtanding the L. deputies word and faith vnto al them for their life, libertie, goods, and for ſafe conduct into Spaine. Of this euent the good prieſte told the ſaid Corronell, and the reſt of the Spaniards: this hapened vpon ſaint Martins eue 1580.

 3, Morris

3. Morris Kent natiue of Kilmalock, and bachelor of diuinitie, was apprehended and accused for hauing been Chaplaine to the Earle of Desmond. And for as much as a good and worshippfull Alderman, named Victor White, had of a pious zeale, and for the comfort of his owne soule, kept the said. Morris in his house, was for that cause appreheded & putt in prison for his guest: but the good priest to saue his hoast harmeles, appeared before the said L. president of his owne accord, who was hanged drawen and quartered. He was a holy and a vertuous man, of few wordes & very zealous: he suffred the 30. of Apprill 1585.

4. Edmond Odonel natiue of Limerick of the societie of Iesus, was apprehended for being suspected to carry letters from Rome to Sr. Iames fitz Morris, and therfore was hanged drawen and quartered at Corck by Sr. Iohn Perrot L. president of Munster, about the yeere of our Lord 1575. He was sent ouer as a fellow with father Goad an English Iesuit, who in company with F. Dauid Woulf priest of that society, were sent in a mission into that country by the procurement of primat Creogh to teach grammer about the beginning of Queene Elizabeths time.

5. Daniell Okeilan was apprehended at Yonghull by Sr. William Morgan and captaine Peers which then kept garrison in that

towne

towne. He was hanged with his legges vpwardes, and his head downewards: and then all the souldiors were comaunded to leuell at him with their bulletts; Comaundement was allso giuen that none should leuell at his harte, therby to encreale his paine by his lingering death: he was a priest of the order of S. Frauncis: this hapned the 28. of march 1580.

6. Daniell Hinnichan, Phillipp O See, Morris O scanlan of the order of S Frauncis, being old, impotent, and blind as other friers were, were all three slaine at the high alter of their monasterie called Lislaghtine 1580.

7. Teigh Odulan of the order of saint Frauncis, was apprehended at the monastery of Askettin and brought to Limericke, and there was hanged drawen and quartered. After his head was cutt of, he was heard to speake these woords. *Vias tuas demonstra mihi 1579.*

8. Richard French natiue of the countrie of Wexford a vertuous priest, after long imprisonment in the castle of Dublin and, in the castle of Wexford, ended his life 1581. Thomas Coursey viccar of Kensale, a most vertuous priest, was hanged by Marshall lawe, by Sr. Iohn Perrot L. president of Munster, for entreating Iames fitz Morris to restore the pray which he tooke from his parishioners of Beasale. 1577.

9. Glasuy O Boyll Abbot of Boyll of the diocesse of Elfyne in Connaght, and Ouen O Mulkeran Abbot of the monasterie of the holly Trinitie of that diocesse, were hanged and quartered by the L. Gray Anno 1580. Iohn Stephen priest, for that he said Masse to Feigh Ma-Hugh was hanged and quartered by the L. Burrowes 1597. Thady O Boyll guarden of the monasterie of Downigall, was slaine by the English in his owne monasterie. 6. Freers were slaine in the monasterie of Moynighan in Shaane O Neals warrs. Iohn O Onan, was hanged by Marshall lawe at Dublin 1618. Patricke O Dyry was hanged and quartered at Derry 1618. Brien O Carulan was hanged by Marshall law 1606.

10. Iohn O Calyhor, Brien O Trower moncks of the order of S. Bernard, were slaine in their owne monastery de Sācta Maria in Vlster. Felymy O Harra, a lay brother of the order of S. Fr. in his monasterie: so was Eneas Penny parish priest of Killagh, slaine at the alter in the parish church therof. Donoshew Ma Recdy priest was hanged at Colrahan. Cahall Ma-Goran, Rony O Donillan, Peter O Quillan, patricke O Kenna a Franciscan Freer, Georg Power viccar generall of the diocesse of Offory, Andrew Strich of Limericke, Brien O Murihirtagh viccar generall of the diocesse of Clonefart, Donoghow Omulony priest of Tho-

Thomond, Iohn Kelly of Louth, Sr Patrick of the Anally, Iohn Pillin P. of the order of saint Frauncis, Rory Ma-Henlea, Tirrelagh Ma-Inisky a lay man of the order of S. Francis, al these were catholique & died in the Castle of Dublin through hard vsadg and restrainct. Walter Fernan priest died in that castle through too much tortur of the racke. Iohn Walsh a vertuous priest died through famine and cold in the Castle of Weastchester. Two Welsh gentlemen, the one called Richard Waghan, the other Richard Downs, died through hard vsadg in in the Castle of Dublin.

11. Morris Vstace of Castle Martin in the diocesse of Kildare esquier, master of Arte and a Nouice of the societie of Iesus, being sent for by his father into Brugis in Flanders, came into Ireland (not without his superiours direction) to satisfie his Fathers will, who was apprehended hanged & quartered: who being so well descended, and religious withall, was much feared he wold work much amongest the people. In the meane time the L. viscont of Balinglas and L. Barron of Bilquillin was in open hostilitie, which agrauated the ielousie and suspition that he was accessary therunto.

12. For the like suspition these that followe were hanged drawen and quartered. Ma. Nicholas Nugent esquier cheef Iustice of the Common pleas Ma. Dauid Sutten

esquier together with his bother Mr. Iohn Sutton Gentleman. Mr. Thomas Vstace Gentleman, together with his sonne and heire, who said the letanies together with his father going vpp the ladder. Maister William Ougan of Ruth-Coffy esquier. Maister Robert Scurlock gentleman, maister Clench of the Scrine gentleman, maister Netherfild gentleman, maister Robert fitz Gerrad Bacheller of diuinitie, all these suffred for suspition of Baltinglas his warres 1581.

12. Mathew Lamport priest, a very godly and a deuout man, for that vppon a certaine night he entertained father Richford priest of the societie of Iesus, was hanged drawen and quartered. Robert Miller, Edward Cheeuers, Iohn O Lahy, for bringing ouer the said Richfoord with the L. of Baltinglas was hanged drawen and quartered Anno 1581. Peter Miller after hauing stustied in Spaine, for that he could nott haue his health, came into his countrie which is the county of Wexfoord, & being examined touching points of religion, and nott finding him conformable to the protestancie, many suspitions being laid to his charge, was hanged drawen and quartered Anno 1588. Christopher Roche natiue of Wexfoord, for that he could not enioy his health in Flanders where he was a student, passing by Bristoe to come for Ireland, was there adprehended, and was putt to the

the oath of the ſupremacy;which when he refuſed, he was carried vp to Lōdon where he was ſore whipt about the ſtreetes, and was putt into a moſt filthy priſon in gyues & fetters,and died there through extreamitie Anno 1590.

14. Iames Dudall of Drodart marchant,comming out of France was by contrarie windes driuen to the South coaſt of Englād,vnto whom the oath of the Queens ſupremacy was tendred: and for that he refuſed the ſame,he was ſent to Exceter Gayle, and there was hnaged d awen and quartered anno 1600. Patricke Hea of Wexfoord and honeſt man and zealous Catholique, being accuſedſed vnto the Lord Gray then deputie of the kingdome, that he did not only releeue Biſhoppes and prieſts in his houſe, but allſo tranſported them ouer into Spaine and France, was committed to the caſtle of Dublin, where through hard reſtraint he fell ſore ſicke; and by entreaty of his frinds was remitted to his houſe,where the died of the ſickneſſe he tooke in the priſon.

15. 20. Laymen, old, blind and impotent, retired themſelues vnto their pariſh church of Mohono (dedicated to S. Nicholas in the dioceſſe of Limericke) for a ſanctuary wherin they liued many dayes vntil ſuch time as the Engliſh Army paſsing by that way and finding them there, they ſett

fire on

fire in the church and burned them all anno Domini 1581. these poore old people, amoungest whome ther weare some old women, who could nott long haue liued although they had beene lett alone, for they were some of the age of 100 & of 80. yeers, very sicke and euen already languished for want of foode, which they could nott gett by reason the countrie was altogether spoiled and left wast by the soldiors, and the people of the countrie, fled into the montaines: yet nedes these people must add sorrowe vppon sorrowe, and crueltie vpon crueltie, to shew their rancore and the fruict of their ghospell. All these fornamed personnes, except the good and most vertuous Bishopp of Duanna with his chappleine, Brien of Carrulan, and Iohn O Onan, and Donoghowe Ma-Reddy, and Iohn Luneus priest who suffered vnder kinge Iames, all the rest suffred vnder Queene Elizabeth.

*Euerie*

*Euerie sect of heresies Challenging vnto themselues the trewe and Catholique Church, there is here set downe, the true notes and marcks, by which the same may be discerned.*

## CHAPTER I.

1. WEe must knowe, that the catholique church is as it were the sonne of the worlde, which doth cast foorthe her lightes, and shininge beames by certaine notes, by which shee may be discerned and knowen from the false religion of Pagans, Iewes, and heretiques. The first note is, the name Catholique, which as saint Augustine saith, if a pagan would aske of an heretique, where the catholique church is, he will not dare to shewe vnto him his owne familie. S. Cirill allso saith. *Si ieris in aliquam vrbem &c.* Yf you goe into anny cittie, you will not aske where is the church or howse of God, for then euerie heretique will say, he hath the howse and church of God, but yow will aske where is the catholique church, for that is the proper name of this holly church, the mother of all faithfull christians, which if yow aske after, noe heretique will shewe vnto yow his owne chur-

*Aug. lib. contra epistolam fundamenti cap. 4.*

*Cyrill. Catheches 18.*

churche.

2. The 2. note is Antiquitie, for that the true religion is more auncient then the falſe, and the catholique Romaine church, was before anny hereticall ſecte: for that all heretiques departed from the ſame, as S. Iohn ſaith. *Ex nobis prodierunt &c.* they went foorth from vs, as is ſett downe in the chapter of the firſt booke.

*Daniel. 9.* 3. The 3. note ie perpetuitie or duration,
*3. Note.* which neuer was nor euer ſhalbe interrup-
*Act. 2.* ted. *Regnum quod in æternum non diſsipabitur:*
*Timoth. 3.* a kingdome which ſhall neuer be ouerthro-
*Cypr. l. 4.* wen, nor euer be diſſolued, becauſe it is of
*Epiſt. 2.* God. Of heretiques, it is ſaid, they ſhall not preuaile further, and although as S. Ciprian ſaith, heretiques and ſciſmatiques in the beginning like a raginge and furious tempeſt, doe ſwallowe and conſume all thinges, yet they can not haue great encreaſe, for by their owne emulation they will faile. And S. Au-
*Pſal. 57.* guſtine (vppon the pſalme, *Ad nihilum deuenient*, they ſhalbe brought to nothinge, like a ſwifte ſtreame) ſaith. *Non vos terreant fratres &c.* Let not certaine violent ſtreames terrifie you, which for a time with violent irruptions doe thunder, for preſentlie they ſhall vaniſh, and ſhall not endure longe; many hereſies are dead although they ran ouer the banckes, yet now ſcarce is there any memorie of them.

4. Theodoretus doth write, that there were

were 76. sorte of heresies sprounge vpp vnto his time, and in his 3. booke of that worcke he saith, that all were extinguished sauing a fewe. S. Augustine doth recken 88. heresies of which he writing vppon the 57. psalme saith, that most of them were perished. Vnto Luthers time there were 200. sectes of heresies, and all of them are nowe extinguished, except a fewe Nestorians in the easte, and som other few Hussits in Bohemia. Was there euer any heresie in the world soe great, aswell for the multitude of Bishopps and doctors, Kinges, Princes and Emperors as that of the Arrians, as alsoe for the continuance of time remaining for the space of 200. yeares and vpward, and nowe what is become of it? Aboute 200. yeares agone the heresie of Albigens had more people to defend it in Fraunce, then the Caluinistes haue at this daie, as may be gathered by Paulus Emilius, and nowe there is noe memory thereof. The heresie of Luther, began in the yeare of our Lord 1525. Then Zuinglius gott vppe, and within two yeares after the Anabaptists disturbed Lutheranisme, and allured the moste parte of that secte, to imbrace theirs. After the Zuinglians, came Caluine, which besides fewe townes in Suiserlande, caused all the Zuinglians to followe and embrace his owne doctrine. Caluinistes themselues beinge dissolued into Libertines in Fraunce, into

*Theodoretus lib. de hæreticis fabulis.*

*Emilius li. 5. de rebus Gallor.*

into Puritantes in England, into Trinitaries in Pollande, into Samosettes in Transiluania. But the Catholique Church continued allwayes notwithstandinge all the world, (firste the Iewes, afterwardes the Pagans, and last of all heretiques) resisted and persecuted her, by whose persecution shee did euer florish and increase.

*4. Note.* 5. The 4. note is, the largnes and amplitude of the catholique church by the conuersion of the gentiles, for the catholique church ought not onlie to comprehend all times, but also all places, nations, and all kinde of people, and soe saint Vincentius Lyrinensis in his comentarie saith, that they be catholiques which houlde that doctrine which hath bene allwaies, in all places, and which was embraced of all: and soe the prophett said in the persõ of Christe. *Dabo tibi gentes &c.* I will giue nations vnto thee for thine inheritance, and the limittes of the earth for they possession: he shall rule from sea to sea. For the vnderstandinge of which marcke, wee must consider out of saint Augustine, and saint Beade, that the church was to be catholique, and not to exclude any time or any kinde of people, by which it is distinguished from the sinagoge, which was a perticular church and not Catholique, & was limited vnto a certaine tyme, that is to say, to the cominge of the Messias; as also vnto a certaine place which was

*In Psal. 2. Psal. 71. Aug. lib. de unitate Eccl. c. 6. Beda c. 6. Canticorum.*

was the temple of Hierusalem, out of which there could not be offered any sacrifice, and vnto a certaine familie which were the children of Iacob. Also wee must consider out of the same saint Augustine, that for the church to be catholique, it is not expedient, that it should be in all men of the world, but it is sufficient it should be made knowen in all Prouinces, and that it should fructifie in them, so that there be in all kingdomes some Catholiques, which shall be brought to passe before the second comminge of Christe: neither is it requisitt, that this be done at one tyme, for it is sufficient it be done successiuelie.

*Aug. Epi. 80. ad Hesichiu.*

*Matt. 24.*

6. It is likewise knowen, that the Catholique Romaine church hath gayned the whole world, for it did fructifie in euerie place thereof in the time of the Apostles, as saint Paule saith. In the time of S. Ireneus it was also spred throughout euerie knowen prouince. The same doe Tertulian, saint Cyprian, and Athanasius witnesse, that this churche was made knowen in their owne time in euerie place. Also saint Chrisostome, saint Aug. saint Hierom, Theodoretus, Leo the greate doe declare the same. In the time of saint Gregorie the great, the catholique Romaine church was imbraced in all the worlde. *Grego. epistola ad episcopos Orientis, Affricæ, Hispaniæ, Galliæ, Angliæ & Ciciliæ.* The same Beda doth declare in cap. 6. Cantic. and saint

*Coloss. 1. Iren li. 1. c. 3. Tertull. lib. cont. Iudeos c. 3. Cypr. li. de vnitate eccl. Atha. lib. de humanitate Christi. Chriso. & Hier. in c. Matt 24. Aug. epi. 80. ad Hesichium.*

Theod. li de legib. Leo magnus ser 1. de Sanctis Petro & Paulo. Prosper. lib. de ingratis.

saint Bernard dispútinge before Roger king of Cicilia, said that the easte and the weaste obeied the Bishopp of Rome at this verie daye. And saint Prosper saith. *Sedes Romana Petri &c.* Rome the seate of Peter, in respect of pastorall honnor, is become the head of the worlde, whatsoeuer it possesseth not by the sword, it houldeth by religion. The sectes of Mahomett, with the heresies of Nestorians and Ethiches, which as yet be in the easte, neuer came vnto the weaste; The secte of Luther or Caluine, neuer infected Asia, Affricke, Aegipte or Greece: noe countrie was euer conuerted by them, for they labour not to conuerte Ethnickes, but to corrupte and subuerte catholiques, and as Tertulian said of the heretiques in his time; *Cum hoc sit negotium illis, non Ethnicos conuertendi, sed nostros euertendi.* Their drifte is not to conuerte Ethnicks, but to peruert ours, for heresie is nothinge els then a manifeste corruption of the Catholique doctrine, and a reuolte or defection from the former religion of Christians.

Tertul. li. de praescriptionib.

7. The 5. note is the succesion of Bishoppes, in the Romaine church deriued from the Apostles, vnto our times, and soe all auncient doctors haue reckoned vp this succesion, as an irrefragable argument to shewe the true churche. Ireneus did recken the Romaine Bishoppes from saint Peter vnto Eleutherius, who was Pope in his time.

Irene. li. 3. cap. 3.

time. He said by this succession all heretiques were confounded. S. Ambrose did recken his Apostolique succession from saint Peter to saint Damasus, saint Cyprian from saint Peter to Cornelius, saint Bernard from saint Peter to Eugenius; saint August. from saint Peter vnto Anastasius who was Pope in his time, *& lib. contra epistolam fundamenti cap. 4. Tenet me in Ecclesia &c.* The successiõ of priestes from saint Peter the Apostle vnto whome Christe comended the feedinge of his sheepe vnto this present Bishop, holdes me in the church, the same alsoe doth saint Hierom proue. For wee must note, that such are true Bishopps in the churche, who descende from the Apostles, aswell by succession as by ordination: but the sectes of Lutherans and Caluinistes haue neither succession from any lawfull Bishopps or lawfull ordination, therfore they haue not succeeded in any Apostolique order or succession. And for this cause as saint Cyprian said, Nouatianus is not in the church, nor oughte to be called a Bishoppe, who despisinge apostolique tradition, succeded noe Bishoppe, and himselfe tooke that order vppon himselfe.

*Irene. li. 3. cap. 3. Tertul. de præscript. Aug. epi. 67. Optat. l. 2. cont. Parmen. cap. 4*

*Cyp. lib. 1. epist. 6. ad magnum.*

8. The 6. note is the vniuersall consent of the Catholique church in euerie point of doctrine of faith, as it is said in the Actes. *Multitudo credentium erat cor vnum, & anima vna*; and contrariwise the errors, alterations

*6. Note.*

and dissentions of these sectes in euerie article of their faith, as you may see in the
*Lib. 9. c. 1.* first Chapters and 9. booke: also in the 2.
*Lib. 2 c. 1.* booke cap. 1.

*7. Note.* 9. The 7. note is the, sanctitie of this Catholique doctrine, for the Catholique church is holie in her doctrine and profession, as the councell of Constantinople saith: which profession containes noe falshoode touchinge faith, nor any iniustice touchinge good manners: but these sectaries hould soe many absurdities against faith & good manners, as in the 1. li. Chapter 9. you may reade; But the Catholique church containes noe error, absurditie, or turpitude, nor doth it teach any thing against reason although it teacheth many things aboue reason: and therfore saint Augustine saith: *Nihil in Christianis ecclesiis turpe & flagitiosum:* there is nothinge in Christian churches, that is either filthie or obhominable, either whē godes precepts be insinuated, or miracles declared, or giftes praised, or benefitts asked.

*The 9. boock ca. 1*
*Aug. lib. 2 de ciuitate Dei.*

*8. Note.* 10. The 8. note is, the efficacie of the catholique doctrine in conuertinge the whole worlde vnto the standert of Christe, and that by poore weake and sillie persons without armour or munition, withoute feare of tormente or punishment; only by praiers, fastinge charitable woorks, miracles and all good examples of hollines of life. By these meanes

meanes all nations were conuerted to the catholique church; from impietie and all wickednes, vnto pietie and religion, from beastlie pleasures, vnto angelicall cõtinency, from the fleshe to the spirite, from beinge louers of the worlde, to despise, contemne and forsake the same, and to followe Christ their spouse. But these sectaries subuerted, many nations, not by sounde doctrine or good examples of life, but by terror and feare, theycaused many to forsake Christe and followe the worlde, I am sure these holie Saincts that conuerted the world, neuer drewe foorth any sworde, when they preached. I am sure when Sainct Vincent conuerted soe many, when saint Aug. conuerted Englande to the faith, beinge sent by saint Greg. or when saint Killian an Irishe saincte, conuerted the Francks beinge sent from Conon Pope, or when saint Patricke conuerted Ireland beinge sent by saint Celestine Pope, they neuer killed or murthered, burned or spoiled, nor made the subiectes to reuolte against their princes, or the princes to make tirannicall lawes against their subiects. But Caluine and Luther did sowe their pestilent heresie by burninge and spoilinge kingdomes, robbinge and ransakinge citties, killinge and murtheringe manny millions of people, castinge downe and razinge to the earth, manny churches and monasteries, rauishinge and deflouringe many Nunnes and Virgins and by bringinge euerie kingdome where the same was nourished, to a pittifull confusion.

*9. Note.* 11. The 9. note is, the hollines and sanctitie of life of such as founded our religion, for the holie Patriarches, Apostles, Doctors, Pastors and such as conuerted any countrie to the faith of Christ, were mirrours and spectacles of all sanctitie and religion as saint August. wittnesseth of the Mouncks of his tyme. *Isti sunt Episcopi & pastores docti, graues, sancti, &c.* these were learned Bishopps and graue, wise and holly pastors, most earnest defenders of the trueth, by whose planting, settinge, wateringe, and buildinge, the holy catholique church did increase, but the sectaries of these times, as in their doctrine they were most irreligious, soe in their liues and manners moste wicked and abhominable, as the protestant authors themselues doe auerre. The ministers of Tigur doe write, that Luther sought nothing but his owne priuate gaine, that he was insolent and stubborne, and Luther himselfe confessed that his pretence was not for the loue of God. In an other place he said, that such as followed this newe gospell, were farr woorse then when they were Papists, more couetous, and more giuen to reuenge. *Smudelinus in Coment. 4. super caput 21. lucæ*, said, Lutherans doe peruerte all thinges, that they turned fastinge into feastinge & surfetinge, prayers into

*Aug. lib. de morib. Eccl. c. 31 lib. 2. in Iulian.*

*In responsione ad libr. quem inscripserat Lutherus contra Zuing. disputatione habita lipsie contra Eck.*

*Luther. in postilla super euã. super euã. Dominic. Aduentus.*

into swearinge and blasphemies, adding that Christe is not soe much blasphemed of the verie Turcks. Erasmus also saith, that this gospell neuer reformed any vice in these newe gospellers, none that was an epicure, became sober by it, nor none that was cruell became meeke or gentle by it.

12. The like censure the ministers of Madeburge doe giue of them saying. When these people were Papistes, they were religiouslie addicted, they were giuen to much praiers, deuotion, and sanctifienge the saboath daie, they shewed great reuerence towardes churchmen, parents were carefull in the education of their childrenn, they were liberall and mercifull towardes the poore, and there was great obedience in the subiectes. The same Caluine wittnesseth, and in bis booke of scandalls he saith, when soe many thousandes doe pretend the gospell, fewe of them euer were refourmed of their wicked liues, and hauinge lett the raynes loose to all wickednes, they are not woorthy they should become Papists, Musculus doth confirme the same. Luther the first founder of this vnfortunate gospell said, that such as followed the same, were *odibile genus hominum.* A hatefull kind of people, and, althoughe they speake of the gospell, in their woorcks they are very diuills. Erasmus said that such as he knewe to be vertuous innocent, without deceite or craft,

*Madebur. Centuria 11. cap. 11 & Cen. 10.*

*Calu inst. lib. 4. cap. 10. scand. pag. 118.*

*Musc. in cap. de decalogo & de ministris verbis.*

*Luth. to. 5. Erasm. ad fratres inferiores Germanicæ.*

 when

when they were papists, becoming gospellers, were most wicked, craftie & deceitfull, and of viperous behauiour. If all these gospellers deliuered this censure of protestant religion (God almightie soe disposinge the enemies of trueth to declare the trueth) how much oughte Catholiques to confirme the same? for as all the heretiques that euer were at anny time, are by them in heresie: soe all the wickednes and vices of all the wicked & damnable people that euer were dispersed throughoute all the world at any tyme, are also by them and in them linked and vnited together. And Caluine himselfe declared the same, when he said, that these
*Calu. de scanda. pag.* 128 gospellers which had made shippwracke of their consciēce, haue also made shippwrack of their faith.

10. *Note.* 13. The 10. note or marcke is, the glory of miracles, miracles are verie necessarie, for
*Exodus* 4. the confirmation of anny newe faith, or for to make any extraordinarie mission allowable, for it is written in Exodus when Moises was sent from God vnto the people, he, said they will not beleue me, nor heare my aduice, and God did not answere him that whether they will or nill they should beleue him, but to the intent they should beleue him, he gaue him power to woorcke
*Matt.* 10. miracles, *vt credant quod apparuerit tibi Deus:* that they may beleeue that God appeared vnto thee. In the newe testament also it was said

ſaid vnto the Apoſtles, heale the ſicke, reuiue the dead, cleanſe the lepers, caſt foorth diuills; and in ſaint Iohn, Chriſte ſaid, if he had not wrought greater woorcks, then anny other, the Iewes had not ſinned in not beleeuinge in him. This is alſo declared in the laſt of ſaint Marcke, where our Lord is ſaid to confirme the preachinge of the Apoſtles by ſignes and tokens, that did follow. S. Auguſtine, yea Melancton himſelfe ſaid, that miracles were neceſſarie for the confirmation of the faith of any newe doctors, or newe doctrine, for trewe miracles canno be wrought but by the power of God, for miracles doe exceede the power and force of all creatures.

*Iohn. 15.*

*Hebr 2.*
*Aug. lib. 22. de ciuitate Dei cap 8.*
*Melancth. cap. 3. Matth.*

14. For this cauſe Luther ſought to delude the people by falſe miracles, for goinge about to diſpoſſeſſe a maide that was poſſeſſed of a deuill, he coulde not doe it, but was in danger to be ſlaine himſelfe of the deuill, as Staphilus ſaith, who was preſent at that that time. Alſo the ſaid Luther, as Iohn Cochleus writeth, went aboute to reſtore to life one that was drowned, but could not doe it; and beinge fruſtrated of his purpoſe, none coulde abide to be preſent through the filthie ſtinche that was in the place. Alſo Allanus Cope ſetteth downe the hiſtorie of one Mathewe in the borders of Hungarie, who beinge perſwaded by a certaine miniſter to faine himſelfe dead, and

*Staphilus abſoluta reſponſione.*
*Cochleus in actis Lutheri.*
*An 1523.*
*Copus l 6. dialogor.*

that as it were he should be raised vpp by him, in conclusion was found dead in deede. The like fiction Caluine vsed, who perswadinge one to faine himselfe dead, to the intent he might make the people beleeue, that he could worke a miracle vppon him, but when he thoughte to bringe his fiction to passe, the partie was found dead indeede.

*Hieron. Bolse. in vita Caluini c 13.*

5. But here protestants say, that S. Iohn Baptiste wrought noe miracles. Wherto I aunswere, that God wroughte wonderfull thinges aboue the capacitie of our naturall vnderstandinge, by which his missiō should not be suspected, the austeritie and sanctity of his behauiour and conuersation was a sufficient token that he was sent from God, but the Catholique church did florishe with miracles in all ages; First in the time of the Apostles; Secondarillie in the time of M. Aurelius by the Christian souldiors that were in his army, *vide Tertull.* Thirdlie wee haue the miracles, of Gregorie, Thaumaturgus as S. Basil setts downe *lib. de Spiritu Sancto cap. 29.* and saint Gregorie Nissenus in his life. Fourthlie wee haue the miracles of saint Anthonie, saint Hillarie, saint Martine, saint Nicholas, and others written by saint Athanasius, saint Hierom and Sulpitius: soe that in all ages of the church wee haue miracles, saint Bernard wrote manny miracles of saint Malachias, and this age we haue miracles of Francis Zauier prieste of the

*Tertul. in lib. ad Scapulum & in apolo. cap. 5. Euseb. l 5. hist. Oros. l. 7. hist.*

*Bernardus in vita eius.*

of the Societie of Ieſus, the Apoſtle of the eaſte Indies and of many others.

16. The 11. marke is, the perfection of life that Catholique religion doth teach, & the diſſolution and wanton behauiour that proteſtant religion tendes vnto. The trew Chriſtian religion ought to withdrawe and remooue our loue and affection from theſe vilde, baſe, and tranſitorie thinges, and to eleuate and lifte vppe our hartes mindes and thoughtes to the conſideration and contemplation of celeſtiall and heauenlie thinges, to abſtaine from the filthie exerciſe of wanton delightes and raginge concupiſcence, to ſett at naught all ſuche baites, as prouokes the fleſhe to rebell againſt the ſpiritt, to deſpiſe and contemne all worldlie honors, promotions and riches of this fraile life. Alſo it doth teache & perſwade, faſtinges, praiers, almeſdeeds, wearinge of heare cloath, auſteritie of life, and other afflictions of the corruptible and rebellious fleſh, by which the damnable allurements thereof ſhould be reſtrained, and extinguiſhed. Alſo it doth teach voluntarie pouertie, perpetuall chaſtitie, and perfecte obedience. But the doctrine of the proteſtant ſaies, that theſe exerciſes are but meere follies, and that they be but humane traditions, by which God is not pleaſed: that all abſtinence from fleſhe is but ſuperſtition, that vowes and votaries are but fained hollines, that it is impoſsible 11. *Note.*

to

to liue chaste or continente, that euerie one ought to haue a wife, and that it is as necessary for a man to haue a woman, as meate or drincke.

*Lutherus de vita coniugali.*

17. The true catholique religion teacheth, that good woorcks are necessarie for our saluation, the protestant saies that man deserues nothinge by any good woorcke he doth before God, and the more badd woorcks yow doe, the more yow are in godes fauour; soe as it makes the professors of this doctrine to runn headlounge to all kinde of mischeefe, takinge awaie all the meanes, by which he should be reclaimed, as the sacrament of pennance, contrition, and satisfaction, which they say were not instituted of Christe but fained of the people, with such like; soe allso they take away free will from man, affirming god to be the only cause of the sinnes that wee comitt. That none can keepe godes comaundemēts, and that wee are not bounde to keepe them. Allso the protestant religion takes from vs all feare of God or of hell, and soe giueth a scope to all mischeefe; That the comaundements pertaines not to the christians. That there is noe sinne but incredulitie: and that all are deceaued if they thincke to be saued by good woorcks, with many such vild and absurde doctrines, which make a man careles of his saluation, rechles of his behauior, and nothinge willinge to doe anny good, when

*Caluin. 2. instit. c. 7.*

when neither he that doth them is not recompensed or rewarded, or God offended or displeased by the saide doings. For as by the catholique religion Christ reformed the wicked inclination of man, gaue hoalsome precepts and councells to amend his desolute misdeamenor, instituted also Sacramēts to cure all diseases of our soules, and to purge our conscience from all filth of sinne, now by these carnall and wicked doctrine all ragged conuersation and discomposed misbehauiour is reuiued, and as Ouid saieth.

*In quorum subiere locum fraudesque dolique,* *Metamorphose.*
*Insidiæque & vis & amor sceleratus habendi.*
In place of simple dealinges and honestie,
Were brought into the world by heresie
Deceite, couetousnes, and leacherie.

18. The 12. note is, the perfecte rule that the Catholique church, and Catholiques haue, to direct them in their faith, for the church of Christe hath the holy ghoaste to instruct her in all trueth, and to guide her from all errors Iohn 14. 16. and wee Catholiques beleeuinge the church as wee are taughte in the Creede, when wee saye, I beleeue in the holy Catholique church, obeyinge her in all thinges as wee be comaunded by our Sauiour, wee cannot be deceaued by her, nor is it possible we can offend God in submittinge our selues to her doctrine, beinge comaunded by God to

*Io. 20. Luc. 10. Matt. 23. Matt. 19. Iacob. 4.*

*Matt. 18. 3 Reg. 4. Actor. 15*

to hearcken to her, and as Rebeca, vndertooke for Iacob to rid him of his fathers malediction, if he should followe her aduise: soe the Catholique church which Rebecca figured, shall deliuer vs from the enormitie of godes malediction, if wee shall obey her. But the protestants haue noe rule of their faith, for they doe not beleeue the churche neither the traditions and generall councells thereof, neither the auncient holye doctors of the same. The onlie rule they (as themselues saie) is the scripture. But this is noe certaine rule, for that wee are bounde to beleeue manny thinges which be
*Matt. 13.* not in the scripture, yea that which the
*Hebr. 13.* scripture doth teach the contrarie, as the obseruation of the saboath daye, and thinges strangled; Againe in many places the holy scripture doth wante explication of manny
*2. Petr. 3.* thinges, for saint Peter saith that the epistles of saint Paule are verie hard to be vnderstoode, which the vnlearned and vnstable depraue, as alsoe the reste of the scriptures to their owne perdition. Alsoe all heretiques doe alleadge the scriptures for them-
*Aug. li. 1. de Trin.* selues as saint Augustine sayes, for as saint
*Hier. aduersus Lucifer.* Hierom saith, the scripture doth not consiste in readinge, but in the sense and vnderstandinge thereof, and as for the vnderstandinge and sence of the same, there may be a thowsand controuersies: as for the trewe sense of these woordes. *Hoc est corpus meum*, this

this is my bodie, I am ſure Luther and Caluine are againſt one another touchinge the ſenſe and meaninge of thoſe woords. Therfore S. Auguſtine ſaith he would not beleeue the ghoſpell, had he not bene moued therunto by the auctoritie of the churche.

19. Soe as theſe proteſtants forſakinge the church, they haue noe rule of their faith, as may appeare by the deadly contention and debate which is daily betwixt them, as betwixt Lutherans, Caluiniſts, and Anabaptiſtes, for they charge on an other with hereſies, ſoe as each of theſe ſectes is diuided into manny ſectes, for there are 13. ſects of Lutherans differinge in opinions one from the other. Alſo amoungeſt the Caluiniſts, there are many, as the world can tell, for ſome of them would haue the kinge to be ſupreame head of the church: others doe repine againſt it, as the puritans doe. The Anabaptiſtes are diuided vnto 14. ſects, and eche of them haue ſeuerall and contrarie opinions touchinge the principall pointes of their faith; how can two lawiers pleadinge one againſt the other, and ech of them alleadginge lawe for himſelfe, determine the righte of the cauſe and the ſincere meaninge of the lawe, without there were ſome iudge vnto whome they ſhould, referr the controuerſie to be decided and debated? And becauſe theſe ſectaries will haue noe other iudge but the ſcripture, ech one allead-

alleadginge, and interpretinge the sense thereof accordinge to his priuate opinion, and corrupt affection, their controuersie can neuer be decided, nor their faith can neuer be setled or made certaine.

20. The 13. note is, the lawfull authoritie and mission of catholique pastors and preachers, whereof the Protestants are wholie destitute, no heretiqne being euer able to shew his next predecessor. For as the holie doctors affirme. There is no accesse to God, but by Iesus Christ. No accesse to Iesus Christ, but by the church. No accesse to the church, but by the Sacraments. No accesse to the Sacraments, but by a Priest. None can be a Priest, vnles he be ordained by a Bishopp. Neuer was there lawfull Bishopp ordained out of the catholique roman church. Wherfore (as saint Ierom said vnto his aduersarie) you are out of the communion of the church of Iesus Christ, because you haue not a priest of the order of the Mediator. This marke of the vocation and perpetuall succession of pastors in the church of Christ, hath euer ben most terrible vnto all heretiques: for euen as Baptisme, is the only doore to enter in to all other Sacraments, a Sacrament not reiterable, and whose character is indellible: euen so this Sacrament of holie Orders, and of entring into steward-ship, ouer the flock of Iesus Christ, was ordayned by our Sauiour, as neces-

necessarie, for distinguishing and discerning, such as be vsurpers, and robbers, from true and lawfull pastors, then the other of Baptisme, to knowe and discerne sheepe from Wolues, and Christs flock, from the troupes of infidels.

21. This argument doth so gaule and pinche the Protestants, that they are forced to fetch all the authoritie they haue for their vocation, only from the temporall prince, alledging the wordes of saint Paul, that all authoritie is from God: then saint Matth. that wee must giue vnto Cesar that which is Cesars: then saint Peter, that wee should be subiect to euerie humaine creature for godes sake: all which places aswell the puritantes as the Catholiques, doe interprete and vnderstand of temporall authoritie only for gouerning the common wealth, and not of spirituall direction and instruction of our soules in articles of our faith and saluation, for that all Princes and kinges were then, and 300. yeares after Christs passion, infidels and especially the Romaine Emperor of whome this was principally intended. Otherwise saint Peter and the Apostles who were put to death by them for their religion, were damned in not obeying and conforming themselues vnto those Princes in matters of faith and in the doctrine of saluation. The puritanes, which are called the reformed and seuere

Calui-

Caluinistes doe grounde themselues vpon the election of the people , and that the common and vulgar sorte should make, appointe, and elect cleargie or pastors to feede and gouerne them ; and alleadge the first and 6. chapter of the Actes of the Apostles, where it is said that it pleased the people to make choice of saint Mathias insteede of Iudas, and saint Stephen Philipp Procherus & 4. others to supplie the offices of Deacons, and afterwardes in the primitiue church wee finde that the people did choose , or nominate their Bishoppes . But to this puritanticall foundations, both the Catholiques and protestantes doe aunswere , that those elections, or nominations were permitted to the people , by the Apostles for their comfort , and that the parties so chosen , receaued authoritie and spiritual iurisdiction from the Apostles, and not from the people: as wee see this daie that in manny places , the people are permitted to make choice of their encombents , but are inuested and consecrated of the Bishoppes of euerie diocesse where the parishioners are permitted to haue this priuilege.

*Act. 1. & 6.*

*That*

*That there are many excellencies and effectes which should allure euerie one, to follow and imbrace the Catholique religion; And contrariwise, many enconueniences and blasphemies which the newe religion houldeth and teacheth. The first excellencie.*

## CHAPTER II.

1. THe first and cheefest excellency, is, to beleeue that God is the first trueth and first cause, from whome proceedeth all trueth, and by whom all causes haue their operation and their influence. The first goodnesse and sanctitie of whom all goodnesse and sanctitie doth depend; And as it is the proprietie of the sunne to giue light, of the fire to giue heate, of the water to make colde: so it is the nature, essence and proprietie of God with farr greater excellency, to do good and to communicat and impart the same vnto his creatures. And so saint Augustin saith. O God thow art perfect without deformitie, great without quantitie, good without qualitie, eternall without time, strong without infirmitie, trew without fāsshood, thow art present euerie where without ocupieng any place, and thow art inward and intimat to euery thing, being tyed or fastened to nothing.

2. Butt the new religion maketh God, crwell without mercy, in that he doth encomber his people with lawes and preceptes, which they cannott keep: wicked without goodneſſe, in that they make him the cauſe of all the euill and wickedneſſe which the wicked doe comitt, and for the which they are ſo ſeuerely puniſhed.

*The 2. excellencye, is the pure and holly doctrine which it profeſseth.*

## CHAPTER III.

1. SVch is the perfection of catholique doctrine, that it nether admitteth nor alloweth any thing againſt the light of reaſon, godes glory, or the good of our neghbors: it teatcheth the law, it comandeth vnder paine of damnation the perfourmance therof, and the morall precepts of the tenn commaundeth, which are certaine concluſions deriued from the ſame. But Luther ſaith, they pertaine nott to them, and all the ſchoole of proteſtantes do teach, that wee cannott keep or obſerue them: that God reſpecteth them nott, and that the good woorckes of a chriſtian do preiudice and derrogat from the merites of Chriſts paſsion. And ſo they take away all the meritorious woorckes of the iuſt, and all the force and induſtrie of mā propes

proper merites, and consequently al graces and inherent iustice of a sanctified soule by the extrinsicall and imputatiue iustice of Christ, and saith, that so they haue faith, God regardeth nott their woorkes: which is a wide gappe and dangerous gulfe to all wickednesse, dishonestie, loosnesse of life, and dissolute behauiour, & a quite defacing, dissanulling and abrogating, nott only of the law of nature, butt of all other lawes whatsoeuer, and therfore most pernitious and dangerous doctrine.

2. Besides these holy precepts, it perswadeth, though not commandeth, the Euangelicall counselles of our Sauiour, the cheefest wherof is perpetuall chastitie which is a celestiall vertue, by which a man forgoeth many encombrances of worldly cares, troubles and perturbations of minde, and affliction of his spirit, as saint Paule saith. *1. Cor.* The 2. counsell which our Sauiour gaue, was to a certaine yong man, sayeng vnto him if thou wilbe perfect, go and sell all that thow hast, giue the same to the poore and thou shalt haue treasure in heauen & follow me. By this counsell a christian doth eschew many tentations and snarres of the diuill, into which such as be rich do fall hedlong: and ar deliuered from troubles, vexations, and anxietis of minde, and of many contentious and litigious strifes and debates with his negboures, which for the most

part is incident to worldly people which
*Actio. 2.* blessed counsell was obserued of the chris-
tians at Hierusalem, at Alexandria in Ægipt, and at the lake Marian as Philo the Iew re-
*Matt. 5.* porteth. The 3. counsell is, to render good for euill, and to pray for our persecutors. The 4. counsell is, to giue almesse, and to pittie the poore, to be mercifull, to releeue the distressed: no vertue is so often inculcated as this, no vice so often discommended, or with greater punishmentes threatned, thẽ inhumanitie and crweltie. The 5. counsell is, to exercise our selues in continuall
*Matt. 25.* praiers, and so the Apostle wisheth vs al-
*1. Tim 2.*
*Luc. 18.* waise to pray: and our Sauiour also coun-
*Luc 11.* selleth the same by 3. examples. The first, of a carnall father in respect of his sonne, which yeldeth to his sonnes demande; The 2. of a frind that was vrged at the earnest inintreatie of another frind to rise out of his bedd at night, to giue vnto him what so earnestly he sought for; The 3. of an inflexible iudge that neuer yelded to any mans desire, yett at the earnest and importuuat suite of a poore woman, he was perswadeed to take comisseration of her.

3. The religion of protestantes not only barketh all the obseruations of the precepts of the lawe, but also forbiddeth and reiecteth all euangelicall counselles, sayeng that no man ought to accomplish them. As for virginitie, they say it is impossible. As for

for the poore they may starue for them, for any relefe or comfort they receaue of them. For they pull from them all that they haue. As for mercy, of all people none are so blouddy or so crwell, yea the very first preachers of this new religion as you may read. As for praiers, they cannot abide any order of time or deuotion for performing them: for they do nott only barcke, as another Vigilantius against euensongs, Masse and mattens, and against any obseruation of times, as att midnight, morning and euening, but allso against the English comon praier booke as you see.

*The 3. Excellencie, most diuine Sacraments, Which confer grace.*

## CHAPTER IV.

1. THe 3. Excellencie be the sacramentes. For although the written law lightneth our vnderstanding with many instructions and sownd doctrine, directing our vnderstanding to follow and embrace vertue and to discerne the good from the euill, yet it disposeth nor prepareth not our hartes with the loue of the one, nor our affection with the hatred of the other: it giueth light to the vnderstanding, but it healeth not the infirmitie and disease of our appetites. The lawe

teatcheth the way to heauen, but giueth no force to our weake soules to trauaile thither, which saint John auerreth. The law was giuen by Moyses, but grace and trueth was giuen by Christ, which is conferred by the sacramentes, and which are instrumentes to conuay the same vnto vs.

2. As there are many maladies, disseases and necessities: so there ar also many sacramentes which are as it were conduits that do deriue manny remedies and receipts to ech of them. And as the Humane body is first borne and so encreaseth, is fedd and receaueth diuers alterations, so there are many such varietie of alterations of the soule, which is borne and regenerated by water and the holy ghoast, which is baptisme and the grace and vertues which are giuen in baptisme are againe confirmed by the Sacrament of confirmation: which maketh the soule stoute and constant in the profession of his faith, which faith and grace hath neeede to be nourished, and augmented, which is don by the holie Sacrament of the Eucharist which is the body of Christ, which is the foode of our languished soule; which through many infirmities and diseases incident therunto, hath great need of a spirituall phisition to heale the same, by contrition confession and satisfaction. And for that after long and prolix sicknesse and disseases, there are many dregges of the old

*Ephe. 5. Mar. 16. in Clemen. ex summa trinitate & fidei Cath ca 1 Ezech. 36 Clemens epist. 4 Vrba ep. ad omnes fideles Melch ad epis. Hisp Ioh. 6. 1. Cor. 11. Iohn 2.*

old sicknesses stil left, for the healing and curing wherof the Sacrament of extreame vnction is ordained: as also that a christian in his cheefest agony of his spirituall extremitie should be releued and refreshed. *Ia. 5. conc. Flore.*

3. The other 2. Sacramentes are inioyned for the 2. states of people, the one for such as be married: the other for such as be ecclesiasticall and seruing in godes church. But the new religion hath no Sacrament, althoughe for some shew of litle deuotion they do not reiect the Sacramentes of Baptisme and Eucharist, yett they handle them without any deuotion or reuerence at all, as for Baptisme some or most of them doe holde, that it is not necessarie to our saluation, for they thincke that the childe is saued by the faith of his parents. As for the Eucharist, with they call the Lords supper, they make no more accompt of it then of anny common bread, whose effect is nothinge els ten to remember Christ his death, which may be don aswell by the one as by the other. *Matt. 19. Ephes. 5.*

*Tha 4. Excellencie is to fauor the good and to punish the wicked*

## CHAPTER V.

1. WHen the end of euery lawe is, to take away vice and wickednesse and the occasions therof, and to make mē sober, honest and vertuous, it is meete that the good should haue many priuiledges, fauors, and rewards, and the wicked should be punished, as we may read in Deutrono. wher god almightie threatneth death and destruction against the transgressors of his lawes and comandementes. The like also we may read in Ezech. But the new religion, taketh away both merits and rewards from the iust, and paine and punishmentes from the wicked: saying the more wicked you are, the neerer you are to Gods fauor and grace, as Luther affirmeth.

*Deut. 28. Ezech. 5. & 6.*

*The 5. Excellencie is the conuersion of all nations vnto Christe, and driuing Idolatrie out of the world.*

## CHAPTER VI.

THe more that princes persecuted christian religion, the more the same encreased, as Pliny the 2. being a Pagan

Pagan withnesseth. For when he saw such a multitude of christians to be put to death he wrott to the emperor Traian aduertizing him that there were thowsands of christians executed by exquisitt tormentes for no kind of offence but for being Christians, and the more they were tormented and afflicted, the more they encreased and florished, and the more the reuerence of the Idols decreased. But the new religion neuer conuerted the gentles from Idolatrie to Christian religion: whose only imployment and drift is to corrupt and confound the faithfull, and neuer to reforme themselues, charging the church with Idolatrie, as old heretiques haue done, Athanasius witnessing the same.

*The 6. Excellencie of the Catholique Religion is, that the same is proued and auerred by so many good witnesses, as sacred and learned doctors, blessed saincts, martyrs, and generall counsells.*

## CAPTER VII.

1. ARistotle saith, that a man is beleeued for three causes, and ought to be presupposed that he telles the trueth, 1. If he be wise. 2. If he be vertuous 3. If he be oure frind. For wee thincke that a wise man should not be deceaued, a good man should not

not lie, a frind ſhould not deceaue his frind. Such therfore as did beare witneſſe of our catholique religion, were wiſemen, eminent and exquiſitt in all ſciences and faculties, moſt holy and religious in their liues, as Dioniſius Areopagita diſciple to S. Paulę, ſaint Ignatius, Policarpus, Origines, ſaint Baſill the great, and his brother ſaint Gregorie Niſſenus, ſaint Iohn Chriſoſtom, Theodoretus, ſaint Nazianzenus, ſaint Gregorie, ſaint Aug. ſaint Hierom, ſaint Ambroſſe, ſaint Hillarius, ſaint Cyprian, Lactantius Firmianus, S. Vincentius Lirinenſis, Arnobius, ſaint Bernard, ſaint Bonauenture, Scotus, Alexander de Halles, with diuers others, for they had no cauſe but to tell the trueth. being honeſt & vertuous, & free from all inordinat affection, that ſhould otherwiſe reſtraine thē to declare the trueth therof: being people that were altogether addicted to the ſeruice of God, and moſt zealous of his glory and honor, which they preferred before all worldly deſignements and promotions.

2. Vnto theſe are annexed for confirmation of the trueth, all generall counſells of the world which were. 20. with the aprobation of Chriſts viccar generall in earth, together with all the bleſſed martyrs that euer were in all the perſecutions and tempeſtuous ſtormes, and agonies of the church, which ſhe ſuffred vnder 14. Kinge and Emperors

rors according to S. Aug. accompt. lib. 18. de ciuitate Dei. The first was of Nero, who was so infestuous to the Christians that he caused Rome to be sett on fire in diuers places, and laid the imputation of that infamie vppon them, wherby the Romanes should insult vppon them, and should destroy and massacre them euerie one, the Tirant himselfe commanding the same. The 2. was of Domitian, who caused S. Iohn the Euangelist to be cast into a Tunn of hoat burninge oyle, which caused also by his edict published, that all the bookes, of Christians should be burned. The 3. was of Traian in whose time. 3. holly Bishoppes suffred vid. Saint Clement the disciple of saint Peter, saint Ignatius disciple to saint Iohn the Euangelist, and saint Polycarpe. The 4. was of Antoninus Verus. The 5. of Seuerus. The 6. of Maximinus. The 7. of Decius who did put saint Laurence to death. The 8. of Valerian. The 9. of Aurelian. The 10. was the crwelest of Dioclesian of Maximinus. These persecutions were before Constantius the great, who was a Christian.

3. Vnto these saint August. added the persecution of Iulian the Apostata, which was most pernitious, for he depriued the Christians of offices and places in the common wealth, as also of all their goodes and studies of learning. Another was of Valens,

Valens: all these were Romane Emperors. Another was of Sapor king of Persia who caused his people to adore the sunne wherin 16000. thousand suffred: amoungest whome were many Bisshoppes, priests and many holly virgins dedicated to Christ. Before all these saint August. sets downe the first persecutiō of all, which was of Iudea vnder Herod, wherin the Apostle Saint Iames the greater suffred. Wee doe nott speake here of the persecutions of the Vandals in Affricke, or of other heretiques or infidels, but only of the Romane Emperors, whose persecution was nott only in one kingdome or prouince, but in all places, especially at Rome, at Alexandria, where S. Cathrin suffred, at Antioch, Nicomedia, Cesarea of Capadocia, & Cesarea of Palestin, in Ponto, in Helesponto, in Africa, in Ægipt, at Saragosa, at Parris where saint Denys of Areopagita with his followers were putt to death: at Syracusa where. S. Lucia: at Catanea where saint Agatha in Bithinia, in Achaia, at Smirna, at Thebes, and in all other places subiect to the Romans.

4. Were all these persecuting princes lawfull heads of Christes church, or some of them? If some, all should be, for the one ought to haue asmuch authoritie in that head-shipp as the other, if that stile or dignitie should rightly belong to the Imperiall

riall scepter, or should be annexed to the Royall authoritie, as a power or iurisdiction comprised aud comprehended within the maiestie of a regall dignitie, as some protestants do hold. Yf this be trew, all these blessed martyrs, wherof some of them were the blessed Apostles, as saint Peter and saint Paule who suffred vnder Nero, were damned as arrogant and dissobedient subiects, for not conforming themselues to their princes wills and humors in causes ecclesiasticall, and consequently none that was put to death by them, was a holy martyr but an obstinat and wilfull subiect, which is most foolish and absurd. If yow say that a king to be head of the church, ought to be a Christian, as some other English protestants do say. I aske of them, who was head of the church the space of the first 300. yeers after Christ, when all kings were infidels and persecutors thereof, as I haue declared? For either the church all that while was without a head, or els some other that was not a king must be a iudge and haue this authoritie and supreame iurisdiction of the king therin, and such ought to haue no les iurisdiction ouer the Christians in causes of their consciences and ecclesiasticall matters now, then at that time.

5. Nowe the Christians are no les nor no better, then they were in that golden age

*Epiph. heresi. Optat. lib. 2. contra Parmen. S. Aug. Epist. ad generosum quæ est 105. Hiero. & Prosper in continuatione chronici Eusebij.*

age of the primitiue church, and consequentlie the same ecclesiasticall iurisdiction ought to continew still in the church of Christ, which he builded, setled and founded vppon saint Peter and his successors, as vppon a firme Rocke, whose foundation shall neuer faile, against whome the gats of hell, with all the plottes and pollicies of Sathan, and the cunninge deuises and attempts of Matche-villian protestantes, shall not preuaile. And so in vaine they striue to build the same vppon any other fundation, then that which was alreddy laid downe by Christ himselfe (being the Corner and head stone of this foundation) vppon saint Peter, the Apostles, and prophetts and their successors for euer, I meane the Bishopps and priests, vnto whome he committed the authoritie and regiment ouer his flocke, to feed and defend them from the woulues, to saue them from the violent excursions of infidels and heretiques, vnto whome it is sad in the Actes of the Apostles. *Attendite vobis & vniuerso gregi in quo &c.* Loocke well to your selues, and to the vniuersall flocke, in which the holy ghost placed you Bishoppes and pastoures to gouerne and rule the church of God. And as this church is the mysticall body of Christ, and a spirituall Common wealth, so it should be gouerned and managed by spirituall parsons, and

*Act. 20. Matt. 10. Matt. vlt. Mar. vlt. Iohn 20. Iohn 21.*

and paſtours that ſhould haue ſpirituall orders, and conſequentlie ought to haue ſpirituall authoritie and iuriſdiction ouer her rebellious and obſtinat children, to chaſtice their rebellions diſobedience, to correct their offences, and to extend the rodd of diſcipline vppon them when they will nott obey her: otherwiſe it ſhould be a poore diſtreſſed common wealth, when none hath power or iuriſdiction therin to chaſtice the tranſgreſſor of her lawes, and ſo all her ſubiects may with libertie and impunitie keepe or breake them.

6. But no article or inunction of the proteſtant religion is of greater force amongeſt the proteſtants, ſpecially of England, then that the king is ſupreame head of the church, and that euery one whether he be a catholique or proteſtant, muſt not only encur the imputation of high treaſon, but alſo the pennalties and diſgrace of traitoures, that will not ſweare ſolemly and publickly, that he thinckes in his conſcience, this to be trew, which is nothing els then to enthrall and enforce a catholique, & perhapps ſome proteſtants, to a damnable and wilfull preiury againſt his owne conſcience that knoweth or atleaſt thincketh the contrary. Was not this new fundation and grownd of the Engliſh proteſtant church newly coyned the 26. yeer of king Henry 8. when the oath of ſupremacy was inuented, by the inſtigation

tion of his fatall and filthy pasſion of luſt and concupiſcence, and by the induſtry and ſuggeſtion of certaine cogging mates, as Thomas Cromwell, and Robert Barnes an apoſtat frier, the one beheaded, the other I meane the frier burned, rather of malice, then of any conſcience or honeſty, without which there can be no good religion; not warranted by ſcripture but deuiſed in the court, not by the beſt, but by the worſt, *quorum Deus venter eſt & quorum finis interitus, & gloria in confuſione &c.* not perſwaded by reaſon, but violentlie conſtrained, not ordained for the edification of the church, but for the deſtruction and confuſion of innocẽt chriſtiãs, not reſolued of by the ſchooles and learned diuines, but firſt determined by the king and enforced in the parleament: againſt the definition of all former parleaments, not only of England, but of all the world, againſt the decree of all the generall counſells therof: againſt all ſacred doctors; againſt common ſenſe, and honeſtie: againſt all lawes both ciuill and cannon, not only againſt catholiques, but againſt proteſtants in all other countries, yea againſt the puritans of England, againſt theſe conſtant confeſſors and bleſſed martyrs aboue recited, which acknowledged no ſuch ſupremacy in ſpirituall or eccleſiaſticall matters to any king or prince whatſoeuer that did putt them to death whoſe bleſſed blood

was

was patiently ſhed for the defence of Catholique religion: and laſtly againſt the practiſe of all former ages and antiquitie; For from Donaldus the firſt Chriſtian king of the Scots, according to ſaint Victor Anno 197. there were 84. Chriſtian kinges: from Ethelbert being made Chriſtian according to ſaint Aug. an. 600. vnto Edward the confeſſor 1006. there were 80. kings Chriſtian in Englād: after the cōqueſt ther were 20. vnto king Henry the 8. ſo as none were euer called head of the church before king Henry, after him Edward, Elizabeth, and king Iames. What ſhall I ſay of other holy and valiant martyrs, that ſuffred in theſe later perſecutions rayſed vpp by Luther and Caluins hereſie, and by the Princes that embraced the ſame? How many thouſandes ſuffred confiſcation of their goodes and landes, effuſion of their blood, confuſion of the world, deſolation and deſtruction of their wiues & children, woe and wreake and diſſolution of all things, ſuch a maſſe of miſerie and callamitie, wherin their miſerable and forlorne life was plunged withall, as no man can rehearſe without greefe, nor none can ſee without teares. How many thouſand did rott in vgly priſons, die in baniſhments, ſuffred patiently the creweleſt tormentes and yrckſomeſt death that could be imagined rather, then they would preferr the vaine fauor of man, before the fauor of God, antiquitie before noueltie, to forgoe, their auncient Catholique religion, to become of the new, to forgoe the firme Rocke of Christs church, to build their faith vpon them, that haue neither grownd or foundation of any supernaturall or theologicall faith at al, no certitude in their doctrine, no deuotion in their religion, no honestie in the profession therof, no vertue in their liues, no pietie in their schooles or synagoges, no charitie in their woorckes, no mortification in their members or passions, and consequentlie no conscience in their doings.

## *THE CONCLVSION.*

1. I Haue gentle reader exposed to thy vew, the Theater of catholique and protestant religion, where thou maist plainly behould, and see the of-spring, beginning, growndes, foundation, practise, mischeefe, and inconuenience of the one: and the ex-
*Lu. 13.* cellency of the other, by which thou maist
*Math. 13.* perceaue that the catholique religion ought to be compared to the wise husbandman, which did sow the good side in his grownd or farme: the protestant to resemble the enimie, which sowed the badd cockle and darnell; the one ought to be called positiue: the

the other negatiue: the one *ecclesia malignantium* : the other *militantium* : the one plantation of religion and deuotion: the other supplantation or rooting vp of the same.

2. The first subiect of corruptible and materiall things which the philosophers doe call; *Materia prima* which neuer holdeth her selfe setled or contented in any certaine course of any forme or composition, but is euermore mutable and changeable by a certaine naturall reuolution from one forme, and fashion to another (for that shee being disgusted with the one, euer more seeketh another) is not so vncertaine and vnconstant, as protestancy, which by a certaine fatall reuolution and babilonicall confusion groweth from one errour to another, from one mischeefe to another, from one sect to another, as appeareth by so many sectes forged and coined by this new religion within these 80. yeers, which are 240. in number, all in differrence and variance amongest themseluees, not in ceremonies or things indifferrent, but in the cheefest articles and substance of their religion, as many of themselues do auerre: the one detesting, condemning, and pronouncing their cursed sentence of Anathema against the other, as you may read aboue in the 2. booke cap. 1. The same may be con-

firmed by a certaine Prince of Germany, who being demaunded of what religion his bordering neighbours were, he answered he could describe of what religion they were the last yeere, but this yeere he could not well tell their religion, in respect of the mutabilitie and in constancy therof, see the preface, and cap 1.lib 2.

3. But the catholique religion is alwaies one and the selfe same, alwaise retaineth and holdeth the same continwance and vigour of trueth, not in diuersitie of sectes, but in simplicitie and vnitie of beleefe and profession, without duplicitie or disparitie, or contradiction of doctrine, or without absurditie or dishonestie in her maners and customes: because she hath the holy ghoast to assist and direct her in all trueth, and to protect and to defend her from all errors, misbeleefe, and infidelitie. For not only this new religion is changeable and variable in profession and doctrine, but also in condition, custome and behauiour, for alteration in faith and religion, procureth also a great alteration and inconstancy in mindes, and affections, in life and maners, as wee may knowe by such nations, who when they were catholiques, were mercifull, chast, sober, liberall & temperat: children were obedient to their parentes, and people faithfull of their promisse. But when they were tur-

turned proteſtantes, as they ſelues do affirme, they became moſt crwell, bloody, inſolent, lecherous, riotuous, couetuous, barbarous, luxurious, and intemperat.

4. For when proteſtancy laboreth to ſtoppe and intercept all the channells and fountaines of Gods grace, the enfluence of Chriſts paſsion, all the inſpiration of the holy ghoaſt from the ſoules of chriſtians, by which they ſhould be inwardly and formally iuſtified (to whome ought to be applied that which was ſpoken of the Iewes, that they reſiſted the holy ghoaſt) when it annulleth all the excellencies, vertues, operations, & effectes of the bleſſed Sacramentes, all the applications of the merites of Chriſtes paſsion & the vallour and vertue of his blood, which the eternall and euerlaſting father would haue to be religiouſly and deuoutly applied by religious meanes, and our owne proper endeuours to our owne ſanctificatiō: when it deſtroieth & reiecteth all the woorkes and merites of the iuſt, as proceeding and hauing their force, worth and valloure, from that bleſſed paſſion and death of Chriſt, and all the bleſſed rewardes correſpondent and proportionable vnto thoſe merites, by vertue of the foreſaid paſsion and blood, which they deny to be of that force to aboliſh and blot out our ſinnes, wickedneſſe and puniſhmentes

mentes due vnto the ſame, and ſo reiecting the force and vertue of Chriſts paſsion, and transferring and building the ſame vppon another fundation which they call imputatiue iuſtice of Chriſt, ſaying that Chriſt imputeth not vnto vs our offences, and as it were couers them, by that iuſtice by which he is iuſt himſelfe, nott by which he maketh vs iuſt: when vppon a kind of an arrogant faith and preſumptuous predeſtination, without any relation or referrence to his owne endeuoures, ſo as he beleue that Chriſt ſuffred for him, or that he is predeſtinated to be ſaued, he muſt be ſuch. When I ſay, proteſtancy is blinded and nuſled in this peruerſe doctrine, it being the only and cheefe article of their beleefe, which is againſt ſcripture, good life, comon reaſon, ſenſe, the definition of the catholique church, honeſtie of a chriſtian, and the pietie of a catholique yea againſt operation of grace or inſtinct of nature, it muſt run headlong vnto all deſperat blaſphemies and damnable miſcheefe, their vnbrideled concupiſcence and crwell diſpoſitions impelling them therunto. For when the tranſgreſsion of no lawe, or the attempt and conſummation of no acte, though neuer ſo exorbitant or ſo abhominable, is puniſhed; nor the good woorkes or merites or any execution, or exerciſe of vertue, or

mor-

mortification of any their pasſions is not regarded, for that (as they ſay) the merites of Chriſt his paſsion doe abrogat them, nay ſuch worckes or mortifications are iniurious to the ſame and doe (as they ſay) derogat from them. Wee muſt thincke them to be no otherwiſe then they are, taxed with the imputation of all thoſe cruell and vnchriſtian like Epithethes by their owne goſpellers, and when their religion is nothinge els then a path way to all diſſolute libertie and licentiouſneſſe, their liues and maners muſt be ſuch, for the corruption of the one, engendreth the diſſolution of the other.

5. Finallie this is the cauſe that wee ſee many lawes, decrees, and diſhoneſt plottes daylie deuiſed with their rigorous and cruell executions, nott againſt tranſgreſſors of godes lawes & the lawe of nature, but againſt honeſt and vertuous people; ſo as the reputation of an honeſt, conſcionable, and well diſpoſed perſon, cannot be without the imputation of a dangerous traitour, whoſe life, goodes and landes muſt waite and lye open as a pray and bootie for euerie miſcreant, who as he exceedeth others in villanie and wickedneſſe, muſt excell them alſo in promotion and authoritie, *cuius maledictione os plenum eſt & amaritudine & dolo, ſub lingua eius labor & dolor*, whoſe Pſal. 9.

tonge

tonge is full of malediction, bitternesse and
Idem deceit, so as the decay and downefall of
the good, must be the raising vpp and ad-
Psal. 9. uancement of the badde. *Exurge Domine non confortetur homo: iudicentur gentes in conspectu tuo. Constitue Domine legislatorem super eos, vt sciant gentes quoniam homines sunt.* Arise Lord, let not man be strengthned, let the Gentiles be iudged in thy sight. Appoint Lord, a law-giuer ouer them, that the Gentiles may know that they be men.

FINIS.